NEW PERSPECTIVES ON

Microsoft® Word 2013

INTRODUCTORY

NEW PERSPECTIVES ON

Microsoft® Word 2013

INTRODUCTORY

S. Scott Zimmerman
Brigham Young University

Beverly B. Zimmerman
Brigham Young University

Ann Shaffer
Katherine T. Pinard

CENGAGE
Learning®

Australia • Brazil • Japan • Korea • Mexico • Singapore • Spain • United Kingdom • United States

New Perspectives on Microsoft Word 2013, Introductory

Director of Development: Marah Bellegarde

Executive Editor: Donna Gridley

Associate Acquisitions Editor: Amanda Lyons

Product Development Manager: Leigh Hefferon

Senior Product Manager: Kathy Finnegan

Product Manager: Julia Leroux-Lindsey

Developmental Editor: Mary Pat Shaffer

Editorial Assistant: Melissa Stehler

Brand Manager: Elinor Gregory

Market Development Managers: Kristie Clark, Gretchen Swann

Senior Content Project Manager: Jennifer Goguen McGrail

Composition: GEX Publishing Services

Art Director: GEX Publishing Services

Text Designer: Althea Chen

Cover Art: © Sorin Popa/Shutterstock

Copyeditor: Michael Beckett

Proofreader: Lisa Weidenfeld

Indexer: Alexandra Nickerson

Library of Congress Control Number: 2013941752

ISBN-13: 978-1-285-09114-3

ISBN-10: 1-285-09114-0

Cengage Learning
200 First Stamford Place, 4th Floor
Stamford, CT 06902
USA

Cengage Learning is a leading provider of customized learning solutions with office locations around the globe, including Singapore, the United Kingdom, Australia, Mexico, Brazil, and Japan. Locate your local office at:
www.cengage.com/global

Cengage Learning products are represented in Canada by Nelson Education, Ltd.

For your course and learning solutions, visit **www.cengage.com**

Purchase any of our products at your local college store or at our preferred online store **www.cengagebrain.com**

ProSkills Icons © 2014 Cengage Learning.

Printed in the United States of America
2 3 4 5 6 7 19 18 17 16 15 14 13

Preface

The New Perspectives Series' critical-thinking, problem-solving approach is the ideal way to prepare students to transcend point-and-click skills and take advantage of all that Microsoft Office 2013 has to offer.

In developing the New Perspectives Series, our goal was to create books that give students the software concepts and practical skills they need to succeed beyond the classroom. We've updated our proven case-based pedagogy with more practical content to make learning skills more meaningful to students.

With the New Perspectives Series, students understand *why* they are learning *what* they are learning, and are fully prepared to apply their skills to real-life situations.

About This Book

"This comprehensive and well-written text provides students with a thorough understanding of Word, using real-world, relevant examples. This text works well in both a face-to-face and online environment."
—Diane Kosharek
Madison Area
Technical College

This book provides thorough coverage of Microsoft Word 2013, and includes the following:

- Detailed, hands-on instruction of Microsoft Word 2013, including creating, editing, and formatting documents; creating MLA-style research papers; working with tables; using advanced page layout techniques; working with graphics; performing a mail merge; and collaborating with others
- Expanded coverage of inline and floating objects and text boxes, with more figures illustrating completed documents in the Case Problems
- Exploration of features new to Word 2013, including Read Mode, the DESIGN tab, saving a Word document as a PDF, and opening a PDF in Word

New for this edition!

- Each tutorial has been updated with new case scenarios throughout, which provide a rich and realistic context for students to apply the concepts and skills presented.
- A new Troubleshoot type of Case Problem, in which certain steps of the exercise require students to identify and correct errors—which are intentionally placed in the files students work with—promotes problem solving and critical thinking.
- The new "Managing Your Files" tutorial at the beginning of the book provides students with a solid foundation in organizing their files and folders.

System Requirements

This book assumes a typical installation of Microsoft Word 2013 and Microsoft Windows 8 Professional. (You can also complete the material in this text using another version of Windows 8 or using Windows 7. You may see only minor differences in how some windows look.) The browser used for any steps that require a browser is Internet Explorer 10.

www.cengage.com/series/newperspectives

The New Perspectives Approach

Context

Each tutorial begins with a problem presented in a "real-world" case that is meaningful to students. The case sets the scene to help students understand what they will do in the tutorial.

Hands-on Approach

Each tutorial is divided into manageable sessions that combine reading and hands-on, step-by-step work. Colorful screenshots help guide students through the steps. **Trouble?** tips anticipate common mistakes or problems to help students stay on track and continue with the tutorial.

VISUAL OVERVIEW

Visual Overviews

Each session begins with a Visual Overview, a two-page spread that includes colorful, enlarged screenshots with numerous callouts and key term definitions, giving students a comprehensive preview of the topics covered in the session, as well as a handy study guide.

PROSKILLS

ProSkills Boxes and Exercises

ProSkills boxes provide guidance for how to use the software in real-world, professional situations, and related ProSkills exercises integrate the technology skills students learn with one or more of the following soft skills: decision making, problem solving, teamwork, verbal communication, and written communication.

KEY STEP

Key Steps

Important steps are highlighted in yellow with attached margin notes to help students pay close attention to completing the steps correctly and avoid time-consuming rework.

INSIGHT

InSight Boxes

InSight boxes offer expert advice and best practices to help students achieve a deeper understanding of the concepts behind the software features and skills.

TIP

Margin Tips

Margin Tips provide helpful hints and shortcuts for more efficient use of the software. The Tips appear in the margin at key points throughout each tutorial, giving students extra information when and where they need it.

REVIEW

APPLY

Assessment

Retention is a key component to learning. At the end of each session, a series of Quick Check questions helps students test their understanding of the material before moving on. Engaging end-of-tutorial Review Assignments and Case Problems have always been a hallmark feature of the New Perspectives Series. Colorful bars and headings identify the type of exercise, making it easy to understand both the goal and level of challenge a particular assignment holds.

REFERENCE

TASK REFERENCE

GLOSSARY/INDEX

Reference

Within each tutorial, Reference boxes appear before a set of steps to provide a succinct summary and preview of how to perform a task. In addition, a complete Task Reference at the back of the book provides quick access to information on how to carry out common tasks. Finally, each book includes a combination Glossary/Index to promote easy reference of material.

www.cengage.com/series/newperspectives

Our Complete System of Instruction

Coverage To Meet Your Needs

Whether you're looking for just a small amount of coverage or enough to fill a semester-long class, we can provide you with a textbook that meets your needs.

- Brief books typically cover the essential skills in just 2 to 4 tutorials.
- Introductory books build and expand on those skills and contain an average of 5 to 8 tutorials.
- Comprehensive books are great for a full-semester class, and contain 9 to 12+ tutorials.

So if the book you're holding does not provide the right amount of coverage for you, there's probably another offering available. Go to our Web site or contact your Cengage Learning sales representative to find out what else we offer.

CourseCasts – Learning on the Go. Always available…always relevant.

Want to keep up with the latest technology trends relevant to you? Visit http://coursecasts.course.com to find a library of weekly updated podcasts, CourseCasts, and download them to your mp3 player.

Ken Baldauf, host of CourseCasts, is a faculty member of the Florida State University Computer Science Department where he is responsible for teaching technology classes to thousands of FSU students each year. Ken is an expert in the latest technology trends; he gathers and sorts through the most pertinent news and information for CourseCasts so your students can spend their time enjoying technology, rather than trying to figure it out. Open or close your lecture with a discussion based on the latest CourseCast.

Visit us at http://coursecasts.course.com to learn on the go!

Instructor Resources

We offer more than just a book. We have all the tools you need to enhance your lectures, check students' work, and generate exams in a new, easier-to-use and completely revised package. This book's Instructor's Manual, ExamView testbank, PowerPoint presentations, data files, solution files, figure files, and a sample syllabus are all available on a single CD-ROM or for downloading at http://www.cengage.com.

SAM: Skills Assessment Manager

Get your students workplace-ready with SAM, the premier proficiency-based assessment and training solution for Microsoft Office! SAM's active, hands-on environment helps students master computer skills and concepts that are essential to academic and career success.

Skill-based assessments, interactive trainings, business-centric projects, and comprehensive remediation engage students in mastering the latest Microsoft Office programs on their own, allowing instructors to spend class time teaching. SAM's efficient course setup and robust grading features provide faculty with consistency across sections. Fully interactive MindTap Readers integrate market-leading Cengage Learning content with SAM, creating a comprehensive online student learning environment.

Acknowledgments

We owe a tremendous thank you to our reviewers, all seasoned educators, who educated us about the needs of their students so that we could shape the tutorials in this book accordingly. We are extremely grateful for all their suggestions and insights: John Bojonny, Brown Mackie College; Diane Kosharek, Madison Area Technical College; Kerrie Specker, Rio Salado College; and Bradley West, Sinclair Community College.

Mary Pat Shaffer, our Developmental Editor, is the best there is. She made writing (and rewriting, and rewriting) this book a pleasure. A special thank you to Kathy Finnegan, the hardest working Product Manager in the publishing business. For all their help and support, we are grateful to the whole New Perspectives team, including Donna Gridley, Executive Editor; Amanda Lyons, Associate Acquisitions Editor; Julia Leroux-Lindsey, Product Manager; and Melissa Stehler, Editorial Assistant. Thanks to Jennifer Goguen McGrail, Senior Content Project Manager, who oversaw the million details involved in transforming the manuscript into the final book, all the while making it look easy. As always, we relied on the ace Manuscript Quality Assurance (MQA) testers at Cengage Learning, who provided detailed comments on every tutorial at several stages in the process. Many thanks to Chris Scriver, MQA Project Leader, and to our excellent MQA testers: John Freitas, Serge Palladino, Susan Pedicini, and Danielle Shaw.

– Scott Zimmerman
– Beverly Zimmerman
– Ann Shaffer
– Katherine T. Pinard

BRIEF CONTENTS

TABLE OF CONTENTS

Tutorial 2 Navigating and Formatting a Document

Editing an Academic Document According to MLA Style

Tutorial 3 Creating Tables and a Multipage Report

Writing a Recommendation

OBJECTIVES

- Explore the differences between Windows 7 and Windows 8
- Plan the organization of files and folders
- Use File Explorer to view and manage libraries, folders, and files
- Open and save files
- Create folders
- Copy and move files and folders
- Compress and extract files

Managing Your Files

Organizing Files and Folders with Windows 8

Case | *Savvy Traveler*

After spending a summer traveling in Italy, Matt Marino started Savvy Traveler, a travel company that organizes small tours in Europe. To market his company, Matt created flyers, brochures, webpages, and other materials that describe the tours he offers. Matt uses the Savvy Traveler office computer to locate and store photos, illustrations, and text documents he can include in his marketing materials. He recently hired you to help manage the office. To keep Matt connected to the office while traveling, he just purchased a new laptop computer running Windows 8. He is familiar with Windows 7, so he needs an overview explaining how Windows 8 is different. Matt asks you to train him on using Windows 8 to organize his files and folders. Although he has only a few files, he knows it's a good idea to set up a logical organization now so he can find his work later as he stores more files and folders on the computer.

In this tutorial, you'll explore the differences between Windows 7 and Windows 8, especially those related to file management tools. You'll also work with Matt to devise a plan for managing his files. You'll learn how Windows 8 organizes files and folders, and then create files and folders yourself and organize them on Matt's computer. You'll also use techniques to display the information you need in folder windows, and explore options for working with compressed files.

STARTING DATA FILES

FM → Tutorial	Review	Case1	Case2
Artists.rtf	Banner.png	Fall Classes.rtf	Budget1.xlsx
Chianti.jpg	Colosseum.jpg	Instructors.txt	Budget2.xlsx
Florence.jpg	Lectures.xlsx	Kings Canyon.jpg	Report1.xlsx
List.rtf	Rome.jpg	Mojave.jpg	Report2.xlsx
Logo.png	Rome.rtf	Redwoods.jpg	Report3.xlsx
Market.jpg	Schedule.rtf	Spring Classes.rtf	Report4.xlsx
Marketing.txt	Tours.rtf	Summer Classes.rtf	Tips1.rtf
Tour Rates.rtf		Winter Classes.rtf	Tips1 – Copy.rtf
Tuscany.rtf		Workshops.rtf	Tips2.rtf
		Yosemite.jpg	Tips2 – Copy.rtf

Visual Overview:

You use the Change your view button to change the size of the icons in the window.

In Windows 7, you use **Windows Explorer** to navigate the contents of your computer.

Use the arrow buttons in the Address bar to navigate to other locations on your computer.

The **file path** is a notation that indicates a file's location on your computer.

Use the Search box to search for files in the current folder.

The Windows Explorer **toolbar** provides buttons for completing tasks.

Windows Explorer includes a **navigation pane**, which displays icons and links to resources and locations on your computer.

By default, Windows Explorer includes the **Details pane** at the bottom of the window, which displays the properties of the selected object.

Windows provides **libraries** so you can organize files by category—documents, music, pictures, and video.

A thumbnail image previews the file contents for certain types of files.

The zipped folder icon indicates a **compressed folder**, which stores files so they take up less disk space.

Windows 7

Comparing Windows 7 & Windows 8

The **View tab** on the ribbon contains options for specifying how the information displays in File Explorer.

Windows provides **libraries** so you can organize files by category—documents, music, pictures, and videos.

The **Quick Access toolbar** contains buttons for viewing properties and creating a folder.

Use the arrow buttons in the Address bar to navigate to other locations on your computer.

The **file path** in the Address bar shows a file's location on your computer.

In Windows 8, you use **File Explorer** to navigate the contents of your computer.

File Explorer includes a ribbon with tools organized on tabs for working with files and folders.

A thumbnail image previews the file contents for certain types of files.

A **filename** is the name you give to a file when you save it to identify the file's contents.

A **file icon** indicates the file type.

Clicking the Computer icon in the navigation pane shows the drives on your computer.

Data Files for this tutorial are stored on a removable disk on this computer.

You can use the Large icons view button on the status bar or in the Layout group on the View tab to switch to Large icons view.

File Explorer includes a **navigation pane**, which displays icons and links to resources and locations on your computer.

Windows 8

Exploring the Differences Between Windows 7 and Windows 8

Windows 8, the most recent version of the Microsoft operating system, is significantly different from Windows 7, the previous version. The major difference is that Windows 8 is designed for touchscreen computers such as tablets and laptops with touch-activated displays, though it runs on computers with more traditional pointing devices such as a mouse or a trackpad. This design change affects many of the fundamental Windows features you use to work on a computer. Figure 1 compares how to perform typical tasks in Windows 7 and Windows 8.

Figure 1 Comparing Windows 7 and Windows 8

Task	Windows 7 Method	Windows 8 Method
Start applications (sometimes called apps)	**Start menu** Open the Start menu by clicking the Start button.	**Start screen** The Start screen appears when you start Windows.
Access applications, documents, settings, and other resources	**Start menu** Use the Start menu, All Programs list, and Search box.	**Charms bar** The Charms bar appears when you point to the upper-right or lower-right corner of the screen, and displays buttons, called charms, for interacting with Windows 8 and accessing applications.
Select objects and commands	**Icons** Icons are small and detailed, designed for interaction with mechanical pointing devices.	**Icons and tiles** Icons and tiles are large and simplified, designed for interaction with your fingertips.
Open and work in applications	**Desktop** Applications all use a single desktop interface featuring windows and dialog boxes.	**Windows 8 and desktop** Applications use one of two interfaces: the Windows 8 interface (featuring tiles and a full-screen layout) or the desktop.
Display content out of view	**Vertical scrolling** Applications allow more vertical scrolling than horizontal scrolling.	**Horizontal scrolling** The Start screen and applications allow more horizontal scrolling than vertical scrolling to take advantage of wide-screen monitors.
Store files	**Physical storage devices** Windows primarily provides access to disks physically connected to the computer.	**Cloud storage locations** A Microsoft user account provides access to information stored online.
Enter text	**Physical keyboard** Type on the keyboard attached to the computer.	**On-screen keyboard** If your computer does not have a physical keyboard, type using the on-screen keyboard.

© 2014 Cengage Learning

Although Windows 7 introduced a few gestures for touchscreen users, Windows 8 expands the use of gestures and interactions. In Windows 8, you can use touch gestures to do nearly everything you can do with a pointing device. Figure 2 lists common Windows 8 interactions and their touch and mouse equivalents.

| Figure 2 | Windows 8 touch and mouse interactions |

Interaction	Touch Gesture	Mouse Action
Display a ScreenTip, text that identifies the name or purpose of the button	Touch and hold (or press) an object such as a button.	Point to an object such as a button.
Display an Apps bar, which displays options related to the current task and access to the Apps screen	Swipe from the top or bottom of the screen toward the center.	Right-click the bottom edge of the screen.
Display the Charms bar	Swipe from the right edge of the screen toward the center.	Point to the upper-right or lower-right corner of the screen.
Display thumbnails of open apps (the Switch List)	Swipe from the left edge of the screen toward the center.	Point to the upper-left corner of the screen, and then drag the pointer down.
Drag an object	Press and then drag.	Click, hold, and then drag.
Scroll the Start screen	Swipe from the right edge of the screen to the left.	Click the scroll arrows, or drag the scroll bar.
Select an object or perform an action such as starting an app	Tap the object.	Click the object.
Zoom	Pinch two fingers to zoom out or move the fingers apart to zoom in.	Click the Zoom button.

© 2014 Cengage Learning

Despite the substantial differences between how you interact with Windows 7 and Windows 8, the steps you follow to perform work in either operating system are the same. In a typical computer session, you start an application and open a **file**, often referred to as a document, which is a collection of data that has a name and is stored on a computer. You view, add, or change the file contents, and then save and close the file. You can complete all of these steps using Windows 7 or Windows 8. Because most of your work involves files, you need to understand how to save and organize files so you can easily find and open them when necessary.

Organizing Files and Folders

Knowing how to save, locate, and organize computer files makes you more productive when you are working with a computer. After you create a file, you can open it, edit its contents, print the file, and save it again—usually using the same application you used to create the file. You organize files by storing them in folders. A **folder** is a container for files. You need to organize files and folders so that you can find them easily and work efficiently.

A file cabinet is a common metaphor for computer file organization. As shown in Figure 3, a computer is like a file cabinet that has two or more drawers—each drawer is a storage device, or **disk**. Each disk contains folders that hold files. To make it easy to retrieve files, you arrange them logically into folders. For example, one folder might contain financial data, another might contain your creative work, and another could contain information you're gathering for an upcoming vacation.

Figure 3	Computer as a file cabinet

disks contain folders

folders contain files

each drawer is a storage device, or disk

© 2014 Cengage Learning

A computer can store folders and files on different types of disks, ranging from removable media—such as **USB drives** (also called USB flash drives) and digital video discs (DVDs)—to **hard disks**, or fixed disks, which are permanently housed in a computer. Hard disks are the most popular type of computer storage because they provide an economical way to store many gigabytes of data. (A **gigabyte**, or **GB**, is about 1 billion bytes, with each byte roughly equivalent to a character of data.)

To have your computer access a removable disk, you must insert the disk into a **drive**, which is a device that can retrieve and sometimes record data on a disk. A computer's hard disk is already contained in a drive inside the computer, so you don't need to insert it each time you use the computer.

A computer distinguishes one drive from another by assigning each a drive letter. The hard disk is assigned to drive C. The remaining drives can have any other letters, but are usually assigned in the order that the drives were installed on the computer—so your USB drive might be drive D or drive F.

Understanding How to Organize Files and Folders

Windows stores thousands of files in many folders on the hard disk of your computer. These are system files that Windows needs to display the Start screen and desktop, use drives, and perform other operating system tasks. To keep the system stable and to find files quickly, Windows organizes the folders and files in a hierarchy, or **file system**. At the top of the hierarchy, Windows stores folders and important files that it needs when you turn on the computer. This location is called the **root directory** and is usually drive C (the hard disk). As Figure 4 shows, the root directory contains all the other folders and files on the computer. The figure also shows that folders can contain other folders. An effectively organized computer contains a few folders in the root directory, and those folders contain other folders, also called **subfolders**.

| Figure 4 | Organizing folders and files on a hard disk |

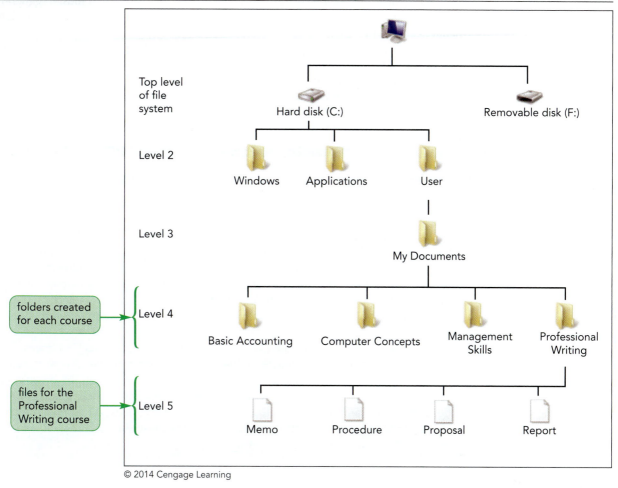

© 2014 Cengage Learning

The root directory is the top level of the hard disk and is for system files and folders only. You should not store your own work in the root directory because your files could interfere with Windows or an application. (If you are working in a computer lab, you might not be allowed to access the root directory.)

Do not delete or move any files or folders from the root directory of the hard disk; doing so could disrupt the system so that you can't start or run the computer. In fact, you should not reorganize or change any folder that contains installed software because Windows 8 expects to find the files for specific applications within certain folders. In Figure 4, folders containing software are stored at Level 2 of the file system. If you reorganize or change these folders, Windows 8 can't locate and start the applications stored in those folders. Likewise, you should not make changes to the folder (usually named Windows) that contains the Windows 8 operating system.

Level 2 of the file system also includes a folder for your user account, such as the User folder. This folder contains all of your system settings, preferences, and other user account information. It also contains subfolders, such as the My Documents folder, for your personal files. The folders in Level 3 of the file system are designed to contain subfolders for your personal files. You can create as many subfolders at Level 4 of the file system as you need to store other folders and files and keep them organized.

Figure 4 shows how you could organize your files on a hard disk if you were taking a full semester of business classes. To duplicate this organization, you would open the main folder for your documents, such as My Documents, create four folders—one each for the Basic Accounting, Computer Concepts, Management Skills, and Professional Writing courses—and then store the writing assignments you complete in the Professional Writing folder.

If you store your files on removable media, such as a USB drive, you can use a simpler organization because you do not have to account for system files. In general, the larger the storage medium, the more levels of folders you should use because large media can store more files and, therefore, need better organization. For example, if you were organizing your files on a 12 GB USB drive, you could create folders in the top level of the USB drive for each general category of documents you store—one each for Courses, Creative, Financials, and Vacation. The Courses folder could then include one folder for each course (Basic Accounting, Computer Concepts, Management Skills, and Professional Writing), and each of those folders could contain the appropriate files.

PROSKILLS

Decision Making: Determining Where to Store Files

When you create and save files on your computer's hard disk, you should store them in subfolders. The top level of the hard disk is off-limits for your files because they could interfere with system files. If you are working on your own computer, store your files within the My Documents folder in the Documents library, which is where many applications save your files by default. When you use a computer on the job, your employer might assign a main folder to you for storing your work. In either case, if you simply store all your files in one folder, you will soon have trouble finding the files you want. Instead, you should create subfolders within a main folder to separate files in a way that makes sense for you.

Even if you store most of your files on removable media, such as USB drives, you still need to organize those files into folders and subfolders. Before you start creating folders, whether on a hard disk or removable disk, you need to plan the organization you will use. Following your plan increases your efficiency because you don't have to pause and decide which folder to use when you save your files. A file organization plan also makes you more productive in your computer work—the next time you need a particular file, you'll know where to find it.

Exploring Files and Folders

As shown in the Visual Overview, you use File Explorer in Windows 8 to explore the files and folders on your computer. File Explorer displays the contents of your computer by using icons to represent drives, folders, and files. When you open File Explorer, it shows the contents of the Windows built-in libraries by default. Windows provides these libraries so you can organize files by category—documents, music, pictures, and video. A library can display these categories of files together, no matter where the files are actually stored. For example, you might keep some music files in a folder named Albums on your hard disk. You might also keep music files in a Songs folder on a USB drive. Although the Albums and Songs folders are physically stored in different locations, you can set up the Music library to display both folders in the same File Explorer window. You can then search and arrange the files as a single collection to quickly find the music you want to open and play. In this way, you use libraries to organize your files into categories so you can easily locate and work with files.

The File Explorer window is divided into two sections, called panes. The left pane is the navigation pane, which contains icons and links to locations on your computer. The right pane displays the contents of the location selected in the navigation pane. If the navigation pane showed all the contents on your computer at once, it could be a very long list. Instead, you open drives and folders only when you want to see what they contain. For example, to display the hierarchy of the folders and other locations on your computer, you select the Computer icon in the navigation pane, and then select the icon for a drive, such as Local Disk (C:) or Removable Disk (F:). You can then open and explore folders on that drive.

If a folder contains undisplayed subfolders, an expand icon appears to the left of the folder icon. (The same is true for drives.) To view the folders contained in an object, you click the expand icon. A collapse icon then appears next to the folder icon; click the collapse icon to hide the folder's subfolders. To view the files contained in a folder, you click the folder icon, and the files appear in the right pane. See Figure 5.

Figure 5 Viewing files in File Explorer

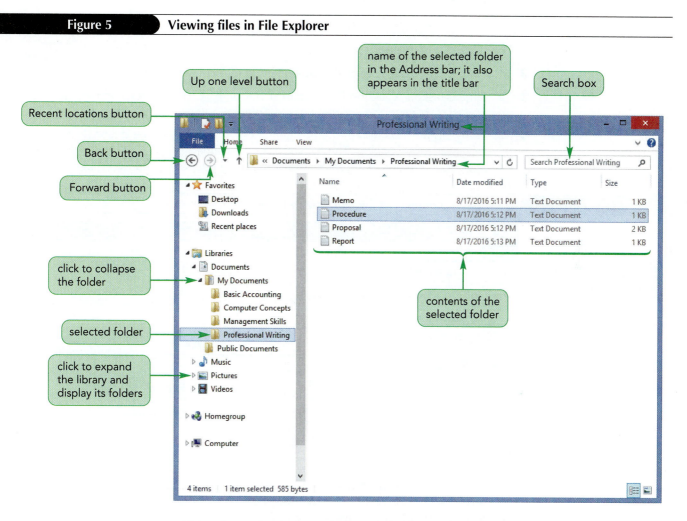

Using the navigation pane helps you explore your computer and orients you to your current location. As you move, copy, delete, and perform other tasks with the files and folders in the right pane of File Explorer, you can refer to the navigation pane to see how your changes affect the overall organization of the selected location.

In addition to using the navigation pane, you can explore your computer in File Explorer using the following navigation techniques:

- Opening drives and folders in the right pane—To view the contents of a drive or folder, double-click the drive or folder icon in the right pane of File Explorer.
- Using the Address bar—You can use the Address bar to navigate to a different folder. The Address bar displays the file path for your current folder. (Recall that a file path shows the location of a folder or file.) Click a folder name such as My Documents in the Address bar to navigate to that folder, or click an arrow button to navigate to a different location in the folder's hierarchy.
- Clicking the Back, Forward, Recent locations, and Up to buttons—Use the Back, Forward, and Recent locations buttons to navigate to other folders you have already opened. Use the Up to button to navigate up to the folder containing the current folder.
- Using the Search box—To find a file or folder stored in the current folder or its subfolders, type a word or phrase in the Search box. The search begins as soon as you

start typing. Windows finds files based on text in the filename, text within the file, and other properties of the file.

You'll practice using some of these navigation techniques later in the tutorial. Right now, you'll show Matt how to open File Explorer. Your computer should be turned on and displaying the Start screen.

To open File Explorer:

▶ **1.** On the Start screen, click the **Desktop** tile to display the desktop.

▶ **2.** On the taskbar, click the **File Explorer** button 📁. The File Explorer window opens, displaying the contents of the default libraries.

▶ **3.** In the Libraries section of the navigation pane, click the **expand** icon ▷ next to the Documents icon. The folders in the Documents library appear in the navigation pane; see Figure 6. The contents of your computer will differ.

| Figure 6 | Viewing the contents of the Documents library |

Trouble? If your window displays icons in a size or arrangement different from the one shown in the figure, you can still explore files and folders. The same is true for all the figures in this tutorial.

▶ **4.** In the navigation pane, click the **My Documents** folder to display its contents in the right pane.

TIP

When you are working in the navigation pane, you only need to click a folder to open it; you do not need to double-click it.

As Figure 6 shows, the File Explorer window includes a ribbon, which is collapsed by default so it displays only tab names, such as File, Home, Share, and View. The Visual Overview shows the expanded ribbon, which displays the options for the selected tab. You'll work with the ribbon and learn how to expand it later in the tutorial.

Navigating to Your Data Files

To navigate to the files you want, it helps to know the file path because the file path tells you exactly where the file is stored in the hierarchy of drives and folders on your computer. For example, Matt has a file named "Logo," which contains an image of the company's logo. If Matt stored the Logo file in a folder named "Marketing" and saved that folder in a folder named "Savvy Traveler" on drive F (a USB drive) on his computer, the Address bar would show the following file path for the Logo file:

Computer ▸ Removable Disk (F:) ▸ Savvy Traveler ▸ Marketing ▸ Logo.png

This path has five parts, with each part separated by an arrow button:

- Computer—The main container for the file, such as "Computer" or "Network"
- Removable Disk (F:)—The drive name, including the drive letter followed by a colon, which indicates a drive rather than a folder
- Savvy Traveler—The top-level folder on drive F
- Marketing—A subfolder in the Savvy Traveler folder
- Logo.png—The name of the file

Although File Explorer uses arrow buttons to separate locations in a file path, printed documents use backslashes (\). For example, if you read an instruction to open the Logo file in the Savvy Traveler\Marketing folder on your USB drive, you know you must navigate to the USB drive attached to your computer, open the Savvy Traveler folder, and then open the Marketing folder to find the Logo file.

File Explorer displays the file path in the Address bar so you can keep track of your current location as you navigate between drives and folders. You can use File Explorer to navigate to the Data Files you need for this tutorial. Before you perform the following steps, you should know where you stored your Data Files, such as on a USB drive. The following steps assume that drive is Removable Disk (F:), a USB drive. If necessary, substitute the appropriate drive on your system when you perform the steps.

To navigate to your Data Files:

1. Make sure your computer can access your Data Files for this tutorial. For example, if you are using a USB drive, insert the drive into the USB port.

 Trouble? If you don't have the starting Data Files, you need to get them before you can proceed. Your instructor will either give you the Data Files or ask you to obtain them from a specified location (such as a network drive). If you have any questions about the Data Files, see your instructor or technical support person for assistance.

2. In the navigation pane of File Explorer, click the **expand** icon ▷ next to the Computer icon to display the drives on your computer, if necessary.

3. Click the **expand** icon ▷ next to the drive containing your Data Files, such as Removable Disk (F:). A list of the folders on that drive appears below the drive name.

4. If the list of folders does not include the FM folder, continue clicking the **expand** icon ▷ to navigate to the folder that contains the FM folder.

5. Click the **expand** icon ▷ next to the FM folder to expand the folder, and then click the **FM** folder so that its contents appear in the navigation pane and in the right pane of the folder window. The FM folder contains the Case1, Case2, Review, and Tutorial folders, as shown in Figure 7. The other folders on your computer might vary.

Figure 7 Navigating to the FM folder

- file path displayed in the Address bar
- contents of the FM folder; your Date modified information might differ
- selected FM folder is expanded in the navigation pane
- the name of the selected folder appears in the File Explorer title bar
- your Data Files might be stored on a different drive
- Tutorial folder

6. In the navigation pane, click the **Tutorial** folder. The files it contains appear in the right pane.

You can change the appearance of the File Explorer window to suit your preferences. You'll do so next so you can see more details about folders and files.

Changing the View

TIP

The default view for any folder in the Pictures library is Large icons view, which provides a thumbnail image of the file contents.

File Explorer provides eight ways to view the contents of a folder: Extra large icons, Large icons, Medium icons, Small icons, List, Details, Tiles, and Content. For example, the files in the Tutorial folder are currently displayed in Details view, which is the default view for all folders except those stored in the Pictures library. Details view displays a small icon to identify each file's type and lists file details in columns, such as the date the file was last modified, the file type, and the size of the file. Although only Details view lists the file details, you can see these details in any other view by pointing to a file to display a ScreenTip.

To change the view of File Explorer to any of the eight views, you use the View tab on the ribbon. To switch to Details view or Large icons view, you can use the view buttons on the status bar.

REFERENCE

Changing the View in File Explorer

- Click a view button on the status bar.

or

- Click the View tab on the ribbon.
- In the Layout group, click the view option; or click the More button, if necessary, and then click a view option.

You'll show Matt how to change the view of the Tutorial folder in the File Explorer window.

To change the view of the Tutorial folder in File Explorer:

1. On the ribbon, click the **View** tab.

2. In the Layout group, click **Medium icons**. The files appear in Medium icons view in File Explorer. See Figure 8.

Figure 8 Files in the Tutorial folder in Medium icons view

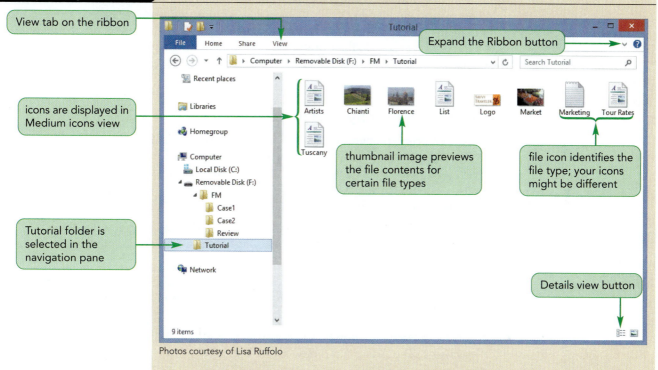

Photos courtesy of Lisa Ruffolo

Because the icons used to identify types of files depend on the applications installed on your computer, the file icons that appear in your window might be different.

TIP

When you change the view, it only changes the view for the currently selected folder.

3. On the status bar, click the **Large icons view** button. The window shows the files with large icons and no file details.

When you clicked the View tab in the previous steps, the ribbon expanded so you could select an option and then collapsed after you clicked the Medium icons option. You can keep the ribbon expanded in the File Explorer window so you can easily access all of its options. You'll show Matt how to expand the ribbon and then use the View tab to switch to Details view.

To expand the ribbon in File Explorer:

1. Click the **Expand the Ribbon** button to expand the ribbon. The Expand the Ribbon button changes to the Minimize the Ribbon button, which you could click if you wanted to collapse the ribbon.

2. On the View tab, in the Layout group, click **Details**. The window shows the files with small icons and lists the file details.

No matter which view you use, you can sort the file list by the name of the files or another detail, such as size, type, or date. When you **sort** files, you list them in ascending order (A to Z, 0 to 9, or earliest to latest date) or descending order (Z to A, 9 to 0, or latest to earliest date) by a file detail. If you're viewing music files, you can sort by details such as contributing artists or album title; and if you're viewing picture files, you can sort by details such as date taken or size. Sorting can help you find a particular file in a long file listing. For example, suppose you want to work on a document that you know you edited on June 4, 2016, but you can't remember the name of the file. You can sort the file list by date modified to find the file you want.

When you are working in Details view in File Explorer, you sort by clicking a column heading that appears at the top of the file list. In other views, you use the View tab on the ribbon to sort. In the Current view group, click the Sort by button, and then click a file detail.

TIP

To sort by a file detail that does not appear as a column heading, right-click any column heading and then select a file detail.

To sort the file list by date modified:

1. At the top of the file list, click the **Date modified** column heading button. The down arrow that appears above the label of the Date modified button indicates that the files are sorted in descending (newest to oldest) order by the date the file was modified. At the top of the list is the List file, which was modified on June 18, 2016.

 Trouble? If your folder window does not contain a Date modified column, right-click any column heading, click Date modified on the shortcut menu, and then repeat Step 1.

2. Click the **Date modified** column heading button again. The up arrow on the Date modified button indicates that the sort order is reversed, with the files listed in ascending (oldest to newest) order.

3. Click the **Name** column heading button to sort the files in alphabetical order by name. The Artists file is now listed first.

Now that Matt is comfortable working in File Explorer, you're ready to show him how to manage his files and folders.

Managing Files and Folders

As discussed earlier, you manage your personal files and folders by storing them according to a logical organization so that they are easy to find later. You can organize files as you create, edit, and save them, or you can do so later by creating folders, if necessary, and then moving and copying files into the folders.

To create a file-organization plan for Matt's files, you can review Figure 8 and look for files that logically belong together. In the Tutorial folder, Chianti, Florence, Logo, and Market are all graphics files that Matt uses for marketing and sales. He created the Artists and Tuscany files to describe Italian tours. The Marketing and Tour Rates files relate to business finances. Matt thinks the List file contains a task list for completing a project, but he isn't sure of its contents. He does recall creating the file using WordPad.

If the List file does contain a project task list, you can organize the files by creating four folders—one for graphics, one for tours, another for the financial files, and a fourth folder for projects. When you create a folder, you give it a name, preferably one that

describes its contents. A folder name can have up to 255 characters, and any character is allowed, except / \ : * ? " < > and |. Considering these conventions, you could create four folders to contain Matt's files, as follows:

- Marketing Graphics folder—Chianti, Florence, Logo, and Market files
- Tours folder—Artists and Tuscany files
- Financial folder—Marketing and Tour Rates files
- Projects folder—List file

Before you start creating folders according to this plan, you need to verify the contents of the List file. You can do so by opening the file.

Opening a File

TIP

To select the default application for opening a file, right-click the file in File Explorer, point to Open with, and then click Choose default application. Click an application in the list that opens, and then click OK.

You can open a file from a running application or from File Explorer. To open a file in a running application, you select the application's Open command to access the Open dialog box, which you use to navigate to the file you want, select the file, and then open it. In the Open dialog box, you use the same tools that are available in File Explorer to navigate to the file you want to open. If the application you want to use is not running, you can open a file by double-clicking it in the right pane of File Explorer. The file usually opens in the application that you used to create or edit it.

Occasionally, File Explorer will open the file in an application other than the one you want to use to work with the file. For example, double-clicking a digital picture file usually opens the picture in a picture viewer application. If you want to edit the picture, you must open the file in a graphics editing application. When you need to specify an application to open a file, you can right-click the file, point to Open with on the shortcut menu, and then click the name of the application that you want to use.

Matt says that he might want to edit the List file to add another task. You'll show him how to use File Explorer to open the file in WordPad, which he used to create the file, and then edit it.

To open and edit the List file:

1. In the right pane of File Explorer, right-click the **List** file, and then point to **Open with** on the shortcut menu to display a list of applications that can open the file. See Figure 9.

 Trouble? If a list does not appear when you point to Open with on the shortcut menu, click Open with to display a window asking how you want to open this file.

Figure 9 **Shortcut menu for opening a file**

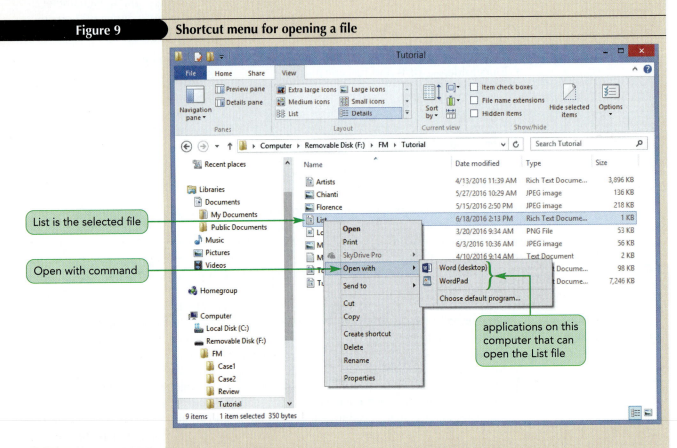

List is the selected file

Open with command

applications on this computer that can open the List file

TIP

In File Explorer, you can also double-click a file to open it in the default application for that file type.

2. Click **WordPad** to open the List file in WordPad. The file contains a task list for the marketing project, which includes three items.

 Trouble? If you had to click Open with instead of pointing to it, in the window that asks how you want to open this file, click Keep using WordPad.

3. Press the **Ctrl+End** keys to move the insertion point to the end of the document, press the **Enter** key if necessary to start a new line, and then type **4. Review the Tours in Italy webpage.**

Now that you've added text to the List file, you need to save it to preserve the changes you made.

Saving a File

As you are creating or editing a file, you should save it frequently so you don't lose your work. When you save a file, you need to decide what name to use for the file and where to store it. Most applications provide a default location for saving a file, which makes it easy to find the file again later. However, you can select a different location depending on where you want to store the file.

Besides a storage location, every file must have a filename, which provides important information about the file, including its contents and purpose. A filename such as Italian Tours.docx has the following three parts:

- Main part of the filename—When you save a file, you need to provide only the main part of the filename, such as "Italian Tours."
- Dot—The dot (.) separates the main part of the filename from the extension.
- Extension—The **extension** includes the three or four characters that follow the dot in the filename and identify the file's type.

Similar to folder names, the main part of a filename can have up to 255 characters. This gives you plenty of room to name your file accurately enough so that you'll recognize the contents of the file just by looking at the filename. You can use spaces and certain punctuation symbols in your filenames. However, filenames cannot contain the symbols / \ : * ? " < > or | because these characters have special meanings in Windows 8.

Windows and other software add the dot and the extension to a filename, though File Explorer does not display them by default. Instead, File Explorer shows the file icon associated with the extension or a thumbnail for some types of files, such as graphics. For example, in a file named Italian Tours.docx, the docx extension identifies the file as one created in Microsoft Word, a word-processing application. File Explorer displays this file using a Microsoft Word icon and the main part of its filename. For a file named Italian Tours.png, the png extension identifies the file as one created in a graphics application such as Paint. In Details view or List view, File Explorer displays this file using a Paint icon and the main part of its filename. In other views, File Explorer does not use an icon, but displays the file contents in a thumbnail. File Explorer treats the Italian Tours.docx and Italian Tours.png files differently because their extensions distinguish them as different types of files, even though the main parts of their filenames are identical.

When you save a new file, you use the Save As dialog box to provide a filename and select a location for the file. You can create a folder for the new file at the same time you save the file. When you edit a file you saved previously, you can use the application's Save command to save your changes to the file, keeping the same name and location. If you want to save the edited file with a different name or in a different location, however, you need to use the Save As dialog box to specify the new name or location.

As with the Open dialog box, you specify the file location in the Save As dialog box using the same navigation techniques and tools that are available in File Explorer. You might need to click the Browse Folders button to expand the Save As dialog box so it displays these tools. In addition, the Save As dialog box always includes a File name box where you specify a filename.

INSIGHT

Saving Files on SkyDrive

Some Windows 8 applications, such as Microsoft Office, include SkyDrive as a location for saving and opening files. **SkyDrive** is a Microsoft service that provides up to 7 GB of online storage space for your files at no charge. You can purchase additional space if you need it. For example, if you create a document in Microsoft Word, your SkyDrive appears as a location for saving the document. (Your SkyDrive appears with your username, such as Matt's SkyDrive.) If you have a Microsoft account, you can select a folder on your SkyDrive to save the document online. (If you don't have a Microsoft account, you can sign up for one by visiting the SkyDrive website.) Because the file is stored online, it takes up no storage space on your computer and is available from any computer with an Internet connection. You access the document by opening it in Word or by visiting the SkyDrive website, and then signing in to your Microsoft account. To share the document with other people, you can send them a link to the document via email. They can use the link to access the document even if they do not have a Microsoft account.

One reason that Matt had trouble remembering the contents of the List file is that "List" is not a descriptive name. A better name for this file is Task List. You will save this document in the Tutorial subfolder of the FM folder provided with your Data Files. You will also use the Save As dialog box to specify a new name for the file as you save it.

To save the List file with a new name:

1. On the ribbon in the WordPad window, click the **File** tab to display commands for working with files.

2. Click **Save as** to open the Save As dialog box, as shown in Figure 10. The Tutorial folder is selected as the storage location for this file because you opened the file from this folder.

| Figure 10 | Saving a file using the Save As dialog box |

use the navigation pane or the Address bar to navigate to a different location for saving the file

the Save As dialog box displays the original location of the file as the default storage location

type the name for the file in the File name box

clicking the Hide Folders button collapses the dialog box

Save as type box

Trouble? If the navigation pane does not appear in the Save As dialog box, click the Browse Folders button. The Browse Folders button toggles to become the Hide Folders button.

3. With the current filename selected in the File name box, type **Task List**. The Save as type box shows that WordPad will save this file as a Rich Text Format (RTF) file, which is the default file type for WordPad files.

Trouble? If the current filename is not selected in the File name box, drag to select the text in the File name box and then type Task List.

4. Click the **Save** button. The Save As dialog box closes, WordPad saves the Task List file in the Tutorial folder, and the new filename appears in the WordPad title bar.

5. On the title bar, click the **Close** button to close WordPad.

Now you're ready to start creating the folders you need to organize Matt's files.

Creating Folders

You originally proposed creating four new folders for Matt's files: Marketing Graphics, Tours, Financial, and Projects. Matt asks you to create these folders now. After that, you'll move his files to the appropriate folders. You create folders in File Explorer using one of three methods: using the New folder button in the New group on the Home tab; using the New folder button on the Quick Access Toolbar; or right-clicking to display a shortcut menu that includes the New command.

INSIGHT

Guidelines for Creating Folders

Consider the following guidelines as you create folders:

- Keep folder names short yet descriptive of the folder's contents. Long folder names can be more difficult to display in their entirety in folder windows, so use names that are short but clear. Choose names that will be meaningful later, such as project names or course numbers.
- Create subfolders to organize files. If a file list in File Explorer is so long that you must scroll the window, you should probably organize those files into subfolders.
- Develop standards for naming folders. Use a consistent naming scheme that is clear to you, such as one that uses a project name as the name of the main folder, and includes step numbers in each subfolder name (for example, 1-Outline, 2-First Draft, 3-Final Draft, and so on).

In the following steps, you will create the four folders for Matt in your Tutorial folder. Because it is easier to work with files using large file icons, you'll switch to Large icons view first.

To create the folders:

1. On the status bar in the File Explorer window, click the **Large icons view** button 🖼 to switch to Large icons view.

2. Click the **Home** tab to display the Home tab on the ribbon.

3. In the New group, click the **New folder** button. A folder icon with the label "New folder" appears in the right pane of the File Explorer window. See Figure 11.

| Figure 11 | Creating a new folder in the Tutorial folder |

Quick Access Toolbar

type to replace the selected text with a different folder name

new folder; its location on your screen might differ

Photos courtesy of Lisa Ruffolo

Trouble? If the "New folder" name is not selected, right-click the new folder, click Rename on the shortcut menu, and then continue with Step 4.

Windows uses "New folder" as a placeholder, and selects the text so that you can replace it immediately by typing a new name. You do not need to press the Backspace or Delete key to delete the text.

4. Type **Marketing Graphics** as the folder name, and then press the **Enter** key. The new folder is named Marketing Graphics and is the selected item in the right pane. To create a second folder, you can use a shortcut menu.

5. In the right pane, right-click a blank area, point to **New** on the shortcut menu, and then click **Folder**. A folder icon appears in the right pane with the "New folder" text selected.

6. Type **Tours** as the name of the new folder, and then press the **Enter** key. To create the third folder, you can use the Quick Access Toolbar.

7. On the Quick Access Toolbar, click the **New folder** button 📁, type **Financial**, and then press the **Enter** key to create and name the folder.

8. Create a new folder in the Tutorial folder named **Projects**.

After creating four folders, you're ready to organize Matt's files by moving them into the appropriate folders.

Moving and Copying Files and Folders

You can either move or copy a file from its current location to a new location. **Moving** a file removes it from its current location and places it in a new location that you specify. **Copying** a file places a duplicate version of the file in a new location that you specify, while leaving the original file intact in its current location. You can also move and copy folders. When you do, you move or copy all the files contained in the folder. (You'll practice copying folders in a Case Problem at the end of this tutorial.)

In File Explorer, you can move and copy files by using the Move to or Copy to buttons in the Organize group on the Home tab; using the Copy and Cut commands on a file's shortcut menu; or using keyboard shortcuts. When you copy or move files using these methods, you are using the **Clipboard**, a temporary storage area for files and information that you copy or move from one location to place in another.

You can also move files by dragging the files in the File Explorer window. You will now organize Matt's files by moving them to the appropriate folders you have created. You'll start by moving the Marketing file to the Financial folder by dragging the file.

To move the Marketing file by dragging it:

1. In File Explorer, point to the **Marketing** file in the right pane, and then press and hold the mouse button.

2. While still pressing the mouse button, drag the **Marketing** file to the **Financial** folder. See Figure 12.

Figure 12	Dragging a file to move it to a folder

Marketing file is selected

Marketing Graphics

Financial folder

Move to Financial ScreenTip

TIP

If you drag a file or folder to a location on a different drive, the file is copied, not moved, to preserve the file in its original location.

3. When the Move to Financial ScreenTip appears, release the mouse button. The Marketing file is removed from the main Tutorial folder and stored in the Financial subfolder.

 Trouble? If you released the mouse button before the Move to Financial ScreenTip appeared, press the Ctrl+Z keys to undo the move, and then repeat Steps 1–3.

 Trouble? If you moved the Market file instead of the Marketing file, press the Ctrl+Z keys to undo the move, and then repeat Steps 1–3.

4. In the right pane, double-click the **Financial** folder to verify that it contains the Marketing file.

Trouble? If the Marketing file does not appear in the Financial folder, you probably moved it to a different folder. Press the Ctrl+Z keys to undo the move, and then repeat Steps 1–3.

▶ **5.** Click the **Back** button ⊖ on the Address bar to return to the Tutorial folder.

You'll move the remaining files into the folders using the Clipboard.

To move files using the Clipboard:

▶ **1.** Right-click the **Artists** file, and then click **Cut** on the shortcut menu. Although the file icon still appears selected in the right pane of File Explorer, Windows removes the Artists file from the Tutorial folder and stores it on the Clipboard.

▶ **2.** In the right pane, right-click the **Tours** folder, and then click **Paste** on the shortcut menu. Windows pastes the Artists file from the Clipboard to the Tours folder. The Artists file icon no longer appears in the File Explorer window, which is currently displaying the contents of the Tutorial folder.

▶ **3.** In the navigation pane, click the **expand** icon ▷ next to the Tutorial folder, if necessary, to display its contents, and then click the **Tours** folder to view its contents in the right pane. The Tours folder now contains the Artists file. See Figure 13.

Figure 13 **Artists file in its new location**

Artists file is now stored in the Tours folder

selected folder

Next, you'll use the Clipboard again to move the Tuscany file from the Tutorial folder to the Tours folder. But this time, you'll access the Clipboard using the ribbon.

▶ **4.** On the Address bar, point to the **Up to** button ⬆ to display its ScreenTip (Up to "Tutorial"), click the **Up to** button ⬆ to return to the Tutorial folder, and then click the **Tuscany** file to select it.

▶ **5.** On the Home tab, in the Clipboard group, click the **Cut** button to remove the Tuscany file from the Tutorial folder and temporarily store it on the Clipboard.

▶ **6.** In the Address bar, click the **arrow** button ▶ to the right of "Tutorial" to display a list of subfolders in the Tutorial folder, and then click **Tours** to display the contents of the Tours folder in File Explorer.

▶ **7.** In the Clipboard group, click the **Paste** button to paste the Tuscany file in the Tours folder. The Tours folder now contains the Artists and Tuscany files.

Finally, you'll move the Task List file from the Tutorial folder to the Projects folder using the Move to button in the Organize group on the Home tab. This button and the Copy to button are ideal when you want to move or copy files without leaving the current folder. When you select a file and then click the Move to or Copy to button, a list of locations appears, including all of the Windows libraries and one or more folders you open frequently. You can click a location in the list to move the selected file to that library or folder. You can also select the Choose location option to open the Move Items or Copy Items dialog box, and then select a location for the file, which you'll do in the following steps.

To move the Task List file using the Move to button:

▶ **1.** In the Address bar, click **Tutorial** to return to the Tutorial folder, and then click the **Task List** file to select it.

▶ **2.** On the Home tab, in the Organize group, click the **Move to** button to display a list of locations to which you can move the selected file. The Projects folder is not included on this list because you haven't opened it yet.

▶ **3.** Click **Choose location** to open the Move Items dialog box. See Figure 14.

| Figure 14 | Move Items dialog box |

locations on your computer; yours might differ

▶ **4.** If necessary, scroll the list of locations, and then click the **expand** icon ▷ next to the drive containing your Data Files, such as Removable Disk (F:).

▶ **5.** Navigate to the FM ▶ Tutorial folder, and then click the **Projects** folder to select it.

▶ **6.** Click the **Move** button to close the dialog box and move the Task List file to the Projects folder.

▶ **7.** Open the Projects folder to confirm that it contains the Task List file.

One way to save steps when moving or copying multiple files or folders is to select all the files and folders you want to move or copy, and then work with them as a group. You can use several techniques to select multiple files or folders at the same time, which are described in Figure 15.

Figure 15	Selecting multiple files or folders

Items to Select in the Right Pane of File Explorer	Method
Files or folders listed together	Click the first item, press and hold the Shift key, click the last item, and then release the Shift key.
	or
	Drag the pointer to create a selection box around all the items you want to include.
Files or folders not listed together	Press and hold the Ctrl key, click each item you want to select, and then release the Ctrl key.
All files and folders	On the Home tab, in the Select group, click the Select all button.

Items to Deselect in the Right Pane of File Explorer	Method
Single file or folder in a selected group	Press and hold the Ctrl key, click each item you want to remove from the selection, and then release the Ctrl key.
All selected files and folders	Click a blank area of the File Explorer window.

© 2014 Cengage Learning

Next, you'll copy the four graphics files from the Tutorial folder to the Marketing Graphics folder using the Clipboard. To do this efficiently, you will select multiple files at once.

To copy multiple files at once using the Clipboard:

▶ **1.** Display the contents of the Tutorial folder in File Explorer.

▶ **2.** Click the **Chianti** file, press and hold the **Shift** key, click the **Market** file, and then release the **Shift** key.

▶ **3.** Press and hold the **Ctrl** key, click the **List** file to deselect it, and then release the **Ctrl** key. Four files—Chianti, Florence, Logo, and Market—are selected in the Tutorial folder window.

▶ **4.** Right-click a selected file, and then click **Copy** on the shortcut menu. Windows copies the selected files to the Clipboard.

▶ **5.** Right-click the **Marketing Graphics** folder, and then click **Paste** on the shortcut menu.

▶ **6.** Open the **Marketing Graphics** folder to verify it contains the four files you copied, and then return to the Tutorial folder.

7. Right-click the **Tour Rates** file, and then click **Copy** on the shortcut menu.

8. In the right pane, double-click the **Financial** folder to open it, right-click a blank area of the right pane, and then click **Paste** on the shortcut menu.

INSIGHT

Duplicating Your Folder Organization

If you work on two computers, such as one computer at an office or school and another computer at home, you can duplicate the folders you use on both computers to simplify the process of transferring files from one computer to another. For example, if you have four folders in your My Documents folder on your work computer, create these same four folders on a USB drive and in the My Documents folder of your home computer. If you change a file on the hard disk of your home computer, you can copy the most recent version of the file to the corresponding folder on your USB drive so the file is available when you are at work. You also then have a **backup**, or duplicate copy, of important files. Having a backup of your files is invaluable if your computer has a fatal error.

All the files that originally appeared in the Tutorial folder are now stored in appropriate subfolders. You can streamline the organization of the Tutorial folder by deleting the duplicate files you no longer need.

Deleting Files and Folders

TIP

In most cases, a file deleted from a USB drive does not go into the Recycle Bin. Instead, it is deleted when Windows 8 removes its icon, and the file cannot be recovered.

You should periodically delete files and folders you no longer need so that your main folders and disks don't get cluttered. In File Explorer, you delete a file or folder by deleting its icon. When you delete a file from a hard disk, Windows 8 removes the file from the folder but stores the file contents in the Recycle Bin. The Recycle Bin is an area on your hard disk that holds deleted files until you remove them permanently. When you delete a folder from the hard disk, the folder and all of its files are stored in the Recycle Bin. If you change your mind and want to retrieve a deleted file or folder, you can double-click the Recycle Bin on the desktop, right-click the file or folder you want to retrieve, and then click Restore. However, after you empty the Recycle Bin, you can no longer recover the files it contained.

Because you copied the Chianti, Florence, Logo, Market, and Tour Rates files to the subfolders in the Tutorial folder, you can safely delete the original files. You can also delete the List file because you no longer need it. You can delete a file or folder using various methods, including using a shortcut menu or selecting one or more files and then pressing the Delete key.

To delete files in the Tutorial folder:

1. Display the Tutorial folder in the File Explorer window.

2. In the right pane, click **Chianti**, press and hold the **Shift** key, click **Tour Rates**, and then release the **Shift** key. All files in the Tutorial folder are now selected. None of the subfolders should be selected.

3. Right-click the selected files, and then click **Delete** on the shortcut menu. A message box appears, asking if you're sure you want to permanently delete these files.

4. Click the **Yes** button to confirm that you want to delete the files.

Make sure you have copied the selected files to the Marketing Graphics and Financial folders before completing this step.

Renaming Files

After creating and naming a file or folder, you might realize that a different name would be more meaningful or descriptive. You can easily rename a file or folder by using the Rename command on the file's shortcut menu.

Now that you've organized Matt's files into folders, he reviews your work and notes that the Artists file was originally created to store text specifically about Florentine painters and sculptors. You can rename that file to give it a more descriptive filename.

To rename the Artists file:

1. In the right pane of the File Explorer window, double-click the **Tours** folder to display its contents.

2. Right-click the **Artists** file, and then click **Rename** on the shortcut menu. The filename is highlighted and a box appears around it.

3. Type **Florentine Artists**, and then press the **Enter** key. The file now appears with the new name.

 Trouble? If you make a mistake while typing and you haven't pressed the Enter key yet, press the Backspace key until you delete the mistake and then complete Step 3. If you've already pressed the Enter key, repeat Steps 2 and 3 to rename the file again.

 Trouble? If your computer is set to display filename extensions, a message might appear asking if you are sure you want to change the filename extension. Click the No button, and then repeat Steps 2 and 3.

Working with Compressed Files

You compress a file or a folder of files so it occupies less space on the disk. It can be useful to compress files before transferring them from one location to another, such as from your hard disk to a removable disk or vice versa, or from one computer to another via email. You can then transfer the files more quickly. Also, if you or your email contacts can send and receive files only up to a certain size, compressing large files might make them small enough to send and receive. Compare two folders—a folder named Photos that contains files totaling about 8.6 MB, and a compressed folder containing the same files but requiring only 6.5 MB of disk space. In this case, the compressed files use about 25 percent less disk space than the uncompressed files.

You can compress one or more files in File Explorer using the Zip button, which is located in the Send group on the Share tab of the ribbon. Windows stores the compressed files in a special type of folder called an **archive**, or a compressed folder. File Explorer uses an icon of a folder with a zipper to represent a compressed folder. To compress additional files or folders, you drag them into the compressed folder. You can open a file directly from a compressed folder, although you cannot modify the file. To edit and save a compressed file, you must extract it first. When you **extract** a file, you create an uncompressed copy of the file in a folder you specify. The original file remains in the compressed folder.

Matt suggests that you compress the files and folders in the Tutorial folder so that you can more quickly transfer them to another location.

To compress the folders and files in the Tutorial folder:

TIP

Another way to compress files is to select the files, right-click the selection, point to Send to on the shortcut menu, and then click Compressed (zipped) folder.

1. In File Explorer, navigate to the Tutorial folder, and then select all the folders in the Tutorial folder.

2. Click the **Share** tab on the ribbon.

3. In the Send group, click the **Zip** button. After a few moments, a new compressed folder appears in the Tutorial window with the filename selected. By default, File Explorer uses the name of the first selected item as the name of the compressed folder. You'll replace the name with a more descriptive one.

4. Type **Savvy Traveler**, and then press the **Enter** key to rename the compressed folder. See Figure 16.

Figure 16 Compressing files and folders

5. Double-click the **Savvy Traveler** compressed folder to open it, open the **Tours** folder, and then note the size of the compressed Tuscany file, which is 1,815 KB.

6. Navigate back to the Tutorial folder.

You can move and copy the files and folders from an opened compressed folder to other locations, although you cannot rename the files. More often, you extract all of the files from the compressed folder to a new location that you specify, preserving the files in their original folders as appropriate.

To extract the compressed files:

1. Click the **Savvy Traveler** compressed folder to select it, and then click the **Compressed Folder Tools Extract** tab on the ribbon.

2. In the Extract all group, click the **Extract all** button. The Extract Compressed (Zipped) Folders Wizard starts and opens the Select a Destination and Extract Files dialog box.

3. Press the **End** key to deselect the path in the box and move the insertion point to the end of the path, press the **Backspace** key as many times as necessary to delete the Savvy Traveler text, and then type **Backups**. The final three parts of the path in the box should be \FM\Tutorial\Backups. See Figure 17.

| Figure 17 | Extracting files from a compressed folder |

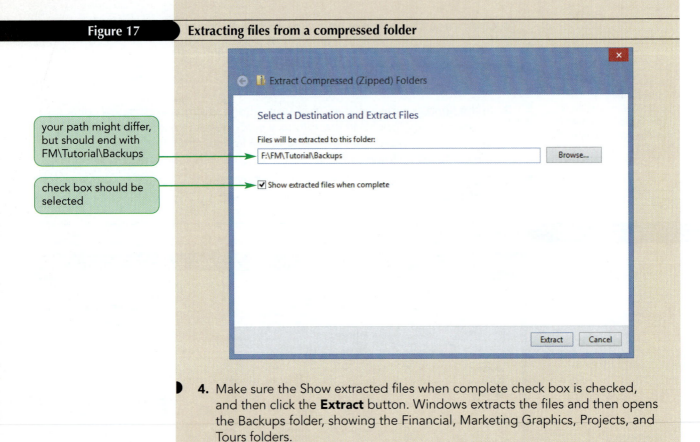

your path might differ, but should end with FM\Tutorial\Backups

check box should be selected

4. Make sure the Show extracted files when complete check box is checked, and then click the **Extract** button. Windows extracts the files and then opens the Backups folder, showing the Financial, Marketing Graphics, Projects, and Tours folders.

5. Open each folder to make sure it contains the files you worked with in this tutorial. When you open the Tours folder, note the uncompressed size of the Tuscany file, which is about four times as large as its compressed version.

6. Close all open windows.

In this tutorial, you examined the purpose of organizing files and folders, and you planned and created an organization for a set of related files and folders. You also explored your computer using File Explorer and learned how to navigate to your Data Files using the navigation pane. You used File Explorer to manage files and folders by opening and saving files; creating folders; and selecting, moving, and copying files. You also renamed and deleted files according to your organization plan. Finally, you compressed and extracted files.

Quick Check

1. You organize files by storing them in _____.
2. What is the purpose of the Address bar in File Explorer?
3. A filename _____ identifies the file's type and indicates the application that created the file.
4. Explain how to use File Explorer to navigate to a file in the following location: E: ► Courses ► Computer Basics ► Operating Systems.txt.
5. One way to move files and folders is to use the _____, a temporary storage area for files and information that you copied or moved from one place and plan to use somewhere else.
6. What happens if you click the first file in a folder window, press the Shift key, click the last file, and then release the Shift key?
7. When you delete a file from a hard disk, Windows removes the file from the folder but stores the file contents in the _____.
8. Describe how to compress a file or folder.
9. What are the benefits of compressing files and folders?

Review Assignments

Data Files needed for the Review Assignments: Banner.png, Colosseum.jpg, Lectures.xlsx, Rome.jpg, Rome.rtf, Schedule.rtf, Tours.rtf

Matt has saved a few files from his old computer to a removable disk. He gives you these files in a single, unorganized folder, and asks you to organize them logically into subfolders. To do this, you will need to devise a plan for managing the files, and then create the subfolders you need. Next, you will rename, copy, move, and delete files, and then perform other management tasks to make it easy for Matt to work with these files and folders. Complete the following steps:

1. Use File Explorer to navigate to and open the FM ▸ Review folder provided with your Data Files. Examine the seven files in this folder and consider the best way to organize the files.
2. Open the **Rome** text file in WordPad, and then add the following tip to the end of the document: **Dine on the Italian schedule, with the main meal in the middle of the day.**
3. Save the document as **Rome Dining Tips** in the Review folder. Close the WordPad window.
4. In the Review folder, create three folders: **Business**, **Destinations**, and **Supplements**.
5. To organize the files into the correct folders, complete the following steps:
 - Move the Banner and Schedule files from the Review folder to the Business folder.
 - Move the Colosseum and Rome JPEG image files and the Rome Dining Tips and Tours text files to the Destinations folder.
 - Copy the Lectures file to the Supplements folder.
6. Copy the Tours file in the Destinations folder to the Business folder.
7. Rename the Schedule file in the Business folder as **2016 Schedule**. Rename the Lectures file in the Supplements folder as **On-site Lectures**.
8. Delete the Lectures file and the Rome text file from the Review folder.
9. Create a compressed (zipped) folder in the Review folder named **Rome** that contains all the files and folders in the Review folder.
10. Extract the contents of the Rome compressed folder to a new folder named **Rome Backups** in the Review folder. (*Hint:* The file path will end with \FM\Review\Rome Backups.)
11. Close the File Explorer window.

Case Problem 1

APPLY

See the Starting Data Files section at the beginning of this tutorial for the list of Data Files needed for this Case Problem.

Bay Shore Arts Center Casey Sullivan started the Bay Shore Arts Center in Monterey, California, to provide workshops and courses on art and photography. Attracting students from the San Francisco and San José areas, Casey's business has grown and she now holds classes five days a week. She recently started a course on fine art landscape photography, which has quickly become her most popular offering. Casey hired you to help her design new classes and manage other parts of her growing business, including maintaining electronic business files and communications. Your first task is to organize the files on her new Windows 8 computer. Complete the following steps:

1. Open File Explorer. In the FM ▶ Case1 folder provided with your Data Files, create three folders: **Classes**, **Landscapes**, and **Management**.
2. Move the Fall Classes, Spring Classes, Summer Classes, and Winter Classes files from the Case1 folder to the Classes folder.
3. Rename the four files in the Classes folder by deleting the word "Classes" from each filename.
4. Move the four JPEG image files from the Case1 folder to the Landscapes folder.
5. Copy the remaining two files to the Management folder.
6. Copy the Workshops file to the Classes folder.
7. Delete the Instructors and Workshops files from the Case1 folder.
8. Make a copy of the Landscapes folder in the Case1 folder. The name of the duplicate folder appears as Landscapes – Copy. Rename the Landscapes – Copy folder as **California Photos**.
9. Copy the Workshops file from the Classes folder to the California Photos folder. Rename this file **California Workshops**.
10. Compress the graphics files in the California Photos folder in a new compressed folder named **Photos**.
11. Move the compressed Photos folder to the Case1 folder.
12. Close File Explorer.

Case Problem 2

See the Starting Data Files section at the beginning of this tutorial for the list of Data Files needed for this Case Problem.

Charlotte Area Business Incubator Antoine Jackson is the director of the Charlotte Area Business Incubator, a service run by the University of North Carolina in Charlotte to consult with new and struggling small businesses. You work as an intern at the business incubator and spend part of your time organizing client files. Since Antoine started using Windows 8, he has been having trouble finding files on his computer. He sometimes creates duplicates of files and then doesn't know which copy is the most current. Complete the following steps:

1. Navigate to the FM ▶ Case2 folder provided with your Data Files, and then examine the files in this folder. Based on the filenames and file types, begin to create an organization plan for the files.

⚙ **Troubleshoot** 2. Open the Tips1 and the Tips1 – Copy files and consider the problem these files could cause. Close the files and then fix the problem, renaming one or more files as necessary to reflect the contents.

⚙ **Troubleshoot** 3. Open the Tips2 and the Tips2 – Copy files and compare their contents. Change the filenames to clarify the purpose and contents of the files.

4. Complete the organization plan for Antoine's files. In the FM ▶ Case2 folder, create the subfolders you need according to your plan.

5. Move the files in the Case2 folder to the subfolders you created. When you finish, the Case2 folder should contain at least two subfolders containing files.

6. Rename the spreadsheet files in each subfolder according to the following descriptions.
 - Budget1: **Website budget**
 - Budget2: **Marketing budget**
 - Report1: **Travel expense report**
 - Report2: **Project expense report**
 - Report3: **Balance sheet**
 - Report4: **Event budget**

⚙ **Troubleshoot** 7. Make sure all files have descriptive names that accurately reflect their contents.

⚙ **Troubleshoot** 8. Based on the work you did in Steps 6 and 7, move files as necessary to improve the file organization.

9. Close File Explorer.

WORD

Creating and Editing a Document

Writing a Business Letter and Formatting a Flyer

OBJECTIVES

Session 1.1
- Create and save a document
- Enter text and correct errors as you type
- Use AutoComplete and AutoCorrect
- Select text and move the insertion point
- Undo and redo actions
- Adjust paragraph spacing, line spacing, and margins
- Preview and print a document
- Create an envelope

Session 1.2
- Open an existing document
- Use the Spelling and Grammar task panes
- Change page orientation, font, font color, and font size
- Apply text effects and align text
- Copy formatting with the Format Painter
- Insert a paragraph border and shading
- Delete, insert, and edit a photo
- Use Word Help

Case | *Sandy Hill Portrait Studio*

Sandy Hill Portrait Studio in Baltimore, Maryland, specializes in wedding photography and family portraits. It also offers weekend and evening classes for new and experienced photographers. The sales manager, Tim Bartolutti, has asked you to create a cover letter to accompany a set of prints that he needs to send to a client, and an envelope for sending a class schedule to another client. He also wants your help creating a flyer announcing a class that focuses on photographing pets.

You will create the letter and flyer using **Microsoft Office Word 2013** (or simply **Word**), a word-processing program. You'll start by opening Word and saving a new document. Then you'll type the text of the cover letter and print it. In the process of entering the text, you'll learn several ways to correct typing errors and how to adjust paragraph and line spacing. When you create the envelope, you'll learn how to save it as part of a document for later use. As you work on the flyer, you will learn how to open an existing document, change the way text is laid out on the page, format text, and insert and resize a photo. Finally, you'll learn how to use Word's Help system.

STARTING DATA FILES

Word1 → Tutorial

Pet.docx
Poodle.jpg

Review

Flower.docx
Mixed Flowers.jpg

Case1

(none)

Case2

Church.jpg
Walking.docx

Case3

Mushroom.docx
Mycology.docx

Case4

(none)

Session 1.1 Visual Overview:

The **Quick Access Toolbar** is a collection of buttons that provides one-click access to commonly used commands, such as Save, Undo, and Repeat.

Each **tab** includes commands related to particular activities or tasks. The HOME tab includes options for formatting and editing text.

The **title bar** displays the name of the open file and the program.

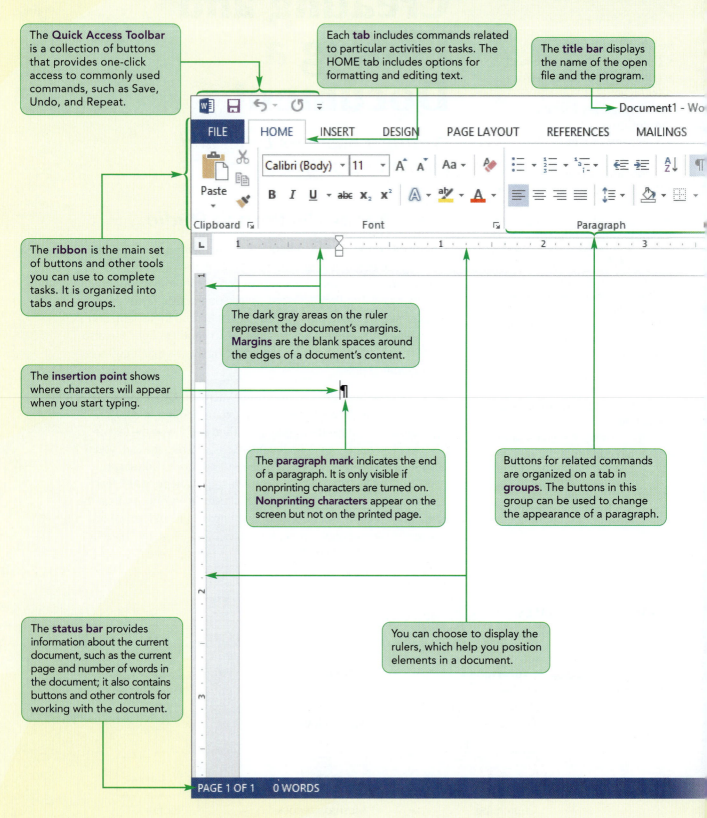

The **ribbon** is the main set of buttons and other tools you can use to complete tasks. It is organized into tabs and groups.

The dark gray areas on the ruler represent the document's margins. **Margins** are the blank spaces around the edges of a document's content.

The **insertion point** shows where characters will appear when you start typing.

The **paragraph mark** indicates the end of a paragraph. It is only visible if nonprinting characters are turned on. **Nonprinting characters** appear on the screen but not on the printed page.

Buttons for related commands are organized on a tab in **groups**. The buttons in this group can be used to change the appearance of a paragraph.

The **status bar** provides information about the current document, such as the current page and number of words in the document; it also contains buttons and other controls for working with the document.

You can choose to display the rulers, which help you position elements in a document.

The Word Window

The Show/Hide button is selected, meaning that nonprinting characters are displayed in the document.

You can click the Ribbon Display Options button to display a menu with options for how the ribbon looks. If the ribbon is hidden, click Show Tabs and Commands in this menu to redisplay it.

You use the Minimize button to reduce the Word window to an icon in the taskbar. You can click the icon later to display the Word window again.

You use the Restore Down button to reduce the Word window to a smaller size; the Restore Down button is then replaced with the Maximize button, which you can click to restore the Word window to its full size.

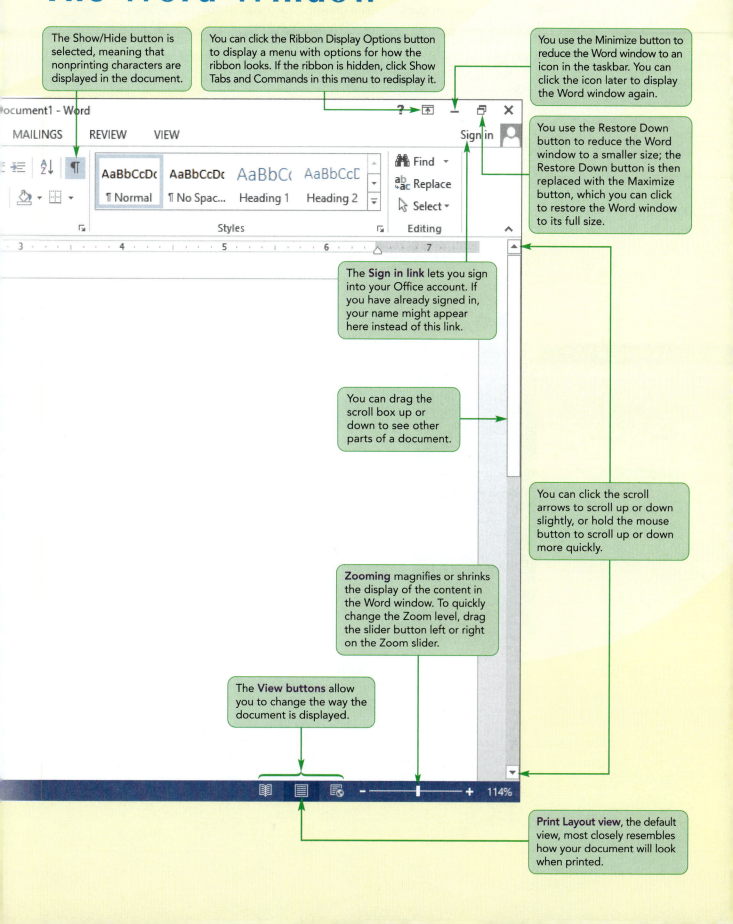

The **Sign in link** lets you sign into your Office account. If you have already signed in, your name might appear here instead of this link.

You can drag the scroll box up or down to see other parts of a document.

You can click the scroll arrows to scroll up or down slightly, or hold the mouse button to scroll up or down more quickly.

Zooming magnifies or shrinks the display of the content in the Word window. To quickly change the Zoom level, drag the slider button left or right on the Zoom slider.

The **View buttons** allow you to change the way the document is displayed.

Print Layout view, the default view, most closely resembles how your document will look when printed.

Starting Word

With Word, you can quickly create polished, professional documents. You can type a document, adjust margins and spacing, create columns and tables, add graphics, and then easily make revisions and corrections. In this session, you will create one of the most common types of documents—a block style business letter.

To begin creating the letter, you first need to start Word and then set up the Word window.

To start Microsoft Word:

1. Display the Windows Start screen, if necessary.

 Using Windows 7? To complete Step 1, click the Start button on the taskbar.

2. Click the **Word 2013** tile.

 Word starts and displays the Recent screen in Backstage view, with template options for new documents on the right. A list of recently opened documents might appear on the left. **Backstage view** provides access to various screens with commands that allow you to manage files and Word options. See Figure 1-1.

Figure 1-1	Recent screen in Backstage view

a list of recently opened documents might appear here

click to open a new, blank document

your list of available templates may differ

Trouble? If you don't see Word 2013 on the Windows Start screen, type Word 2013 to display the Apps screen with the Word 2013 tile highlighted, and then click the tile. If you still can't find Word 2013, ask your instructor or technical support person for help.

Using Windows 7? To complete Step 2, point to All Programs on the Start menu, click Microsoft Office 2013, and then click Word 2013.

3. Click **Blank document**. The Word window opens, with the ribbon displayed.

Trouble? If you don't see the ribbon, click the Ribbon Display Options button 🔼, as shown in the Session 1.1 Visual Overview, and then click Show Tabs and Commands.

Don't be concerned if your Word window doesn't match the Session 1.1 Visual Overview exactly. You'll have a chance to adjust its appearance shortly.

Working in Touch Mode

You can interact with the Word screen using a mouse, or, if you have a touch screen, you can work in Touch Mode, using a finger instead of the mouse pointer. In **Touch Mode**, extra space around the buttons on the ribbon allows your finger to tap the specific button you need. The figures in this text show the screen with Mouse Mode on, but it's helpful to learn how to switch back and forth between Touch Mode and Mouse Mode.

Note: The following steps assume that you are using a mouse. If you are instead using a touch device, please read these steps but don't complete them so that you remain working in Touch Mode.

To switch between Touch and Mouse Mode:

1. On the Quick Access Toolbar, click the **Customize Quick Access Toolbar** button 🔽 to open the menu. The Touch/Mouse Mode command near the bottom of the menu does not have a checkmark next to it, indicating that it is currently not selected.

 Trouble? If the Touch/Mouse Mode command has a checkmark next to it, press the Esc key to close the menu, and then skip to Step 3.

2. On the menu, click **Touch/Mouse Mode**. The menu closes, and the Touch/Mouse Mode button 👆 appears on the Quick Access Toolbar.

3. On the Quick Access Toolbar, click the **Touch/Mouse Mode** button 👆. A menu opens with two options—Mouse and Touch. The icon next to Mouse is shaded blue to indicate it is selected.

 Trouble? If the icon next to Touch is shaded blue, press the Esc key to close the menu and skip to Step 5.

4. On the menu, click **Touch**. The menu closes, and the ribbon increases in height so that there is more space around each button on the ribbon. See Figure 1-2.

Figure 1-2 **Word window in Touch Mode**

expanded ribbon, with buttons farther apart than in Mouse Mode

Touch/Mouse Mode button

Customize Quick Access Toolbar button

insertion point

Trouble? If you are working with a touch screen and want to use Touch Mode, skip Steps 5 and 6.

▶ **5.** On the Quick Access Toolbar, click the **Touch/Mouse Mode** button 👆, and then click **Mouse**. The ribbon changes back to its Mouse Mode appearance, as shown in the Session 1-1 Visual Overview.

▶ **6.** On the Quick Access Toolbar, click the **Customize Quick Access Toolbar** button ⤓, and then click **Touch/Mouse Mode** to deselect it. The Touch/Mouse Mode button is removed from the Quick Access Toolbar.

Setting Up the Word Window

Before you start using Word, you should make sure you can locate and identify the different elements of the Word window, as shown in the Session 1.1 Visual Overview. In the following steps, you'll make sure your screen matches the Visual Overview.

To set up your Word window to match the figures in this book:

▶ **1.** If the Word window does not fill the entire screen, click the **Maximize** button ▢ in the upper-right corner of the Word window.

The insertion point on your computer should be positioned about an inch from the top of the document, as shown in Figure 1-2, with the top margin visible.

Trouble? If the insertion point appears at the top of the document, with no white space above it, position the mouse pointer between the top of the document and the horizontal ruler, until it changes to ⇕, double-click, and then scroll up to top of the document.

▶ **2.** On the ribbon, click the **VIEW** tab. The ribbon changes to display options for changing the appearance of the Word window.

▶ **3.** In the Show group, click the **Ruler** check box to insert a checkmark, if necessary. If the rulers were not displayed, they are displayed now.

Next, you'll change the Zoom level to a setting that ensures that your Word window will match the figures in this book. To increase or decrease the screen's magnification, you could drag the slider button on the Zoom slider in the lower-right corner of the Word window. But to choose a specific Zoom level, it's easier to use the Zoom dialog box.

TIP

Changing the Zoom level affects only the way the document is displayed on the screen; it does not affect the document itself.

▶ **4.** In the Zoom group, click the **Zoom** button to open the Zoom dialog box. Double-click the **Percent** box to select the current zoom percentage, type **120**, and then click the **OK** button to close the Zoom dialog box.

▶ **5.** On the status bar, click the **Print Layout** button 🗐 to select it, if necessary. As shown in the Session 1.1 Visual Overview, the Print Layout button is the middle of the three View buttons located on the right side of the status bar. The Print Layout button in the Views group on the View tab is also now selected.

Before typing a document, you should make sure nonprinting characters are displayed. Nonprinting characters provide a visual representation of details you might otherwise miss. For example, the (¶) character marks the end of a paragraph, and the (•) character marks the space between words.

To verify that nonprinting characters are displayed:

 1. On the ribbon, click the **HOME** tab.

 2. In the blank Word document, look for the paragraph mark (¶) in the first line of the document, just to the right of the blinking insertion point.

 Trouble? If you don't see the paragraph mark, click the Show/Hide ¶ button ¶ in the Paragraph group.

 In the Paragraph group, the Show/Hide ¶ button should be highlighted in blue, indicating that it is selected, and the paragraph mark (¶) should appear in the first line of the document, just to the right of the insertion point.

Saving a Document

Before you begin working on a document, you should save it with a new name. When you use the Save button on the Quick Access Toolbar to save a document for the first time, Word displays the Save As screen in Backstage view. In the Save As screen, you can select the location where you want to store your document. After that, when you click the Save button, Word saves your document to the same location you specified earlier, and with the same name.

To save the document:

 1. On the Quick Access Toolbar, click the **Save** button 🖫. Word switches to the Save As screen in Backstage view, as shown in Figure 1-3.

Figure 1-3	Save As screen in Backstage view

navigation bar

click to return to the document window

Save As selected in the navigation bar

click to open the Save As dialog box

you might see additional folders here; if you want to save a document in a folder that is listed here, click the folder to open the Save As dialog box with that folder selected

Because a document is now open, more commands are available in Backstage view than when you started Word. The **navigation bar** on the left contains commands for working with the open document and for changing settings that control how Word works.

▶ **2.** Click **Computer**, if necessary, and then click the **Browse** button. The Save As dialog box opens.

Trouble? If your instructor wants you to save your files to your SkyDrive account, click SkyDrive, log in to your account, if necessary, and then click the Browse button.

▶ **3.** Navigate to the location specified by your instructor. The default filename, "Doc1," appears in the File name box. You will change that to something more descriptive. See Figure 1-4.

Figure 1-4 | **Save As dialog box**

▶ **4.** Click the File name box, and then type **Robbins Letter**. The text you type replaces the selected text in the File name box.

▶ **5.** Click the **Save** button. The file is saved, the dialog box and Backstage view close, and the document window appears again, with the new filename in the title bar.

Now that you have saved the document, you can begin typing the letter. Tim has asked you to type a block style letter to accompany a set of family portraits that will be sent to Sonia Robbins, a regular client. Figure 1-5 shows the block style letter you will create in this tutorial.

| Figure 1-5 | Completed block style letter |

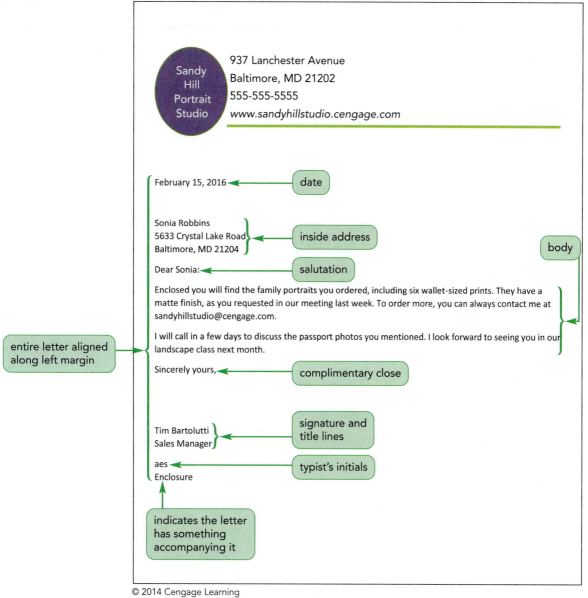

937 Lanchester Avenue
Baltimore, MD 21202
555-555-5555
www.sandyhillstudio.cengage.com

Sandy Hill Portrait Studio

February 15, 2016 ← **date**

Sonia Robbins
5633 Crystal Lake Road ← **inside address**
Baltimore, MD 21204

Dear Sonia: ← **salutation**

Enclosed you will find the family portraits you ordered, including six wallet-sized prints. They have a matte finish, as you requested in our meeting last week. To order more, you can always contact me at sandyhillstudio@cengage.com.

I will call in a few days to discuss the passport photos you mentioned. I look forward to seeing you in our landscape class next month.

Sincerely yours, ← **complimentary close**

Tim Bartolutti
Sales Manager ← **signature and title lines**

aes ← **typist's initials**
Enclosure

entire letter aligned along left margin

body

indicates the letter has something accompanying it

© 2014 Cengage Learning

PROSKILLS

Written Communication: Creating a Business Letter

Several styles are considered acceptable for business letters. The main differences among the styles have to do with how parts of the letter are indented from the left margin. In the block style, which you will use in this tutorial, each line of text starts at the left margin. In other words, nothing is indented. Another style is to indent the first line of each paragraph. The choice of style is largely a matter of personal preference, or it can be determined by the standards used in a particular business or organization. To further enhance your skills in writing business correspondence, you should consult an authoritative book on business writing that provides guidelines for creating a variety of business documents, such as *Business Communication: Process & Product,* by Mary Ellen Guffey.

Entering Text

The letters you type in a Word document appear at the current location of the blinking insertion point.

Inserting a Date with AutoComplete

The first item in a block style business letter is the date. Tim plans to send the letter to Sonia on February 15, so you need to insert that date into the document. To do so, you can take advantage of **AutoComplete**, a Word feature that automatically inserts dates and other regularly used items for you. In this case, you can type the first few characters of the month and let Word insert the rest.

To insert the date:

1. Type **Febr** (the first four letters of February). A ScreenTip appears above the letters, as shown in Figure 1-6, suggesting "February" as the complete word.

Figure 1-6 AutoComplete suggestion

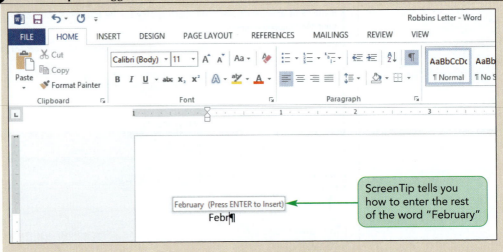

ScreenTip tells you how to enter the rest of the word "February"

A **ScreenTip** is a box with descriptive text about an object or button you are pointing to.

If you wanted to type something other than "February," you could continue typing to complete the word. You want to accept the AutoComplete suggestion.

2. Press the **Enter** key. The rest of the word "February" is inserted in the document. Note that AutoComplete works for long month names like February but not shorter ones like May, because "Ma" could be the beginning of many words besides "May."

3. Press the **spacebar,** type **15, 2016** and then press the **Enter** key twice, leaving a blank paragraph between the date and the line where you will begin typing the inside address, which contains the recipient's name and address. Notice the nonprinting character (•) after the word "February" and before the number "15," which indicates a space. Word inserts this nonprinting character every time you press the spacebar.

Trouble? If February happens to be the current month, you will see a second AutoComplete suggestion displaying the current date after you press the spacebar. To ignore that AutoComplete suggestion, continue typing the rest of the date as instructed in Step 3.

Continuing to Type the Block Style Letter

In a block style business letter, the inside address appears below the date, with one blank paragraph in between. Some style guides recommend including even more space between the date and the inside address. But in the short letter you are typing, more space would make the document look out of balance.

To insert the inside address:

1. Type the following information, pressing the **Enter** key after each item:

 Sonia Robbins

 5633 Crystal Lake Road

 Baltimore, MD 21204

 Remember to press the Enter key after you type the zip code. Your screen should look like Figure 1-7. Don't be concerned if the lines of the inside address seem too far apart. You'll use the default spacing for now, and then adjust it after you finish typing the letter.

Figure 1-7 Letter with inside address

blank paragraph between the date and the inside address

insertion point

Trouble? If you make a mistake while typing, press the Backspace key to delete the incorrect character, and then type the correct character.

Now you can move on to the salutation and the body of the letter. As you type the body of the letter, notice that Word automatically moves the insertion point to a new line when the current line is full.

To type the salutation and the body of the letter:

1. Type **Dear Sonia:** and then press the **Enter** key to start a new paragraph for the body of the letter.

2. Type the following sentence, including the period: **Enclosed you will find the family portraits you ordered, including six wallet-sized prints.**

3. Press the **spacebar**. Note that you should only include one space between sentences.

4. Type the following sentence, including the period: **They have a matte finish, as you requested in our conversation last week.**

5. On the Quick Access Toolbar, click the **Save** button 🖫. Word saves the document as Robbins Letter to the same location you specified earlier.

TIP

The obsolete practice of pressing the spacebar twice at the end of a sentence dates back to the age of typewriters, when the extra space made it easier to see where one sentence ended and another began.

The next sentence you need to type includes Tim's email address.

Typing a Hyperlink

When you type an email address and then press the spacebar or the Enter key, Word converts it to a hyperlink, with blue font and an underline. A **hyperlink** is text or a graphic you can click to jump to another file or to somewhere else in the same file. The two most common types of hyperlinks are: 1) an email hyperlink, which you can click to open an email message to the recipient specified by the hyperlink; and 2) a web hyperlink, which opens a webpage in a browser. Hyperlinks are useful in documents that you plan to distribute via email. In printed documents, where blue font and underlines can be distracting, you'll usually want to convert a hyperlink back to regular text.

To add a sentence containing an email address:

1. Press the **spacebar**, and then type the following sentence, including the period: **To order more, you can always contact me at sandyhillstudio@cengage.com.**

2. Press the **Enter** key. Word converts the email address to a hyperlink, with blue font and an underline.

3. Position the mouse pointer over the hyperlink. A ScreenTip appears, indicating that you could press and hold the Ctrl key and then click the link to follow it—that is, to open an email message addressed to Sandy Hill Portrait Studio.

4. With the mouse pointer positioned over the hyperlink, right-click—that is, press the right mouse button. A shortcut menu opens with commands related to working with hyperlinks.

 You can right-click many items in the Word window to display a **shortcut menu** with commands related to the item you right-clicked. The **Mini toolbar** also appears when you right-click or select text, giving you easy access to the buttons and settings most often used when formatting text. See Figure 1-8.

Figure 1-8 **Shortcut menu**

5. Click **Remove Hyperlink** in the shortcut menu. The shortcut menu and the Mini toolbar are no longer visible. The email address is now formatted in black, like the rest of the document text.

6. On the Quick Access Toolbar, click the **Save** button.

Using the Undo and Redo Buttons

To undo (or reverse) the last thing you did in a document, click the Undo button on the Quick Access Toolbar. To restore your original change, click the Redo button, which reverses the action of the Undo button (or redoes the undo). To undo more than your last action, you can continue to click the Undo button, or you can click the Undo button arrow on the Quick Access Toolbar to open a list of your most recent actions. When you click an action in the list, Word undoes every action in the list up to and including the action you clicked.

Tim asks you to change the word "conversation" to "meeting" in the second-to-last sentence you typed. You'll make the change now. If Tim decides he doesn't like it after all, you can always undo it. To delete a character, space, or blank paragraph to the right of the insertion point, you use the Delete key; or to delete an entire word, you can use the Ctrl+Delete key combination. To delete a character, space, or blank paragraph to the left of the insertion point, you use the Backspace key; or to delete an entire word, you can use the Ctrl+Backspace key combination.

To change the word "conversation":

1. Press the ↑ key once and then press the → key as necessary to move the insertion point to the left of the "c" in the word "conversation."

▶ **2.** Press and hold the **Ctrl** key, and then press the **Delete** key to delete the word "conversation."

▶ **3.** Type **meeting** as a replacement, and then press the **spacebar**.

 After reviewing the sentence, Tim decides he prefers the original wording, so you'll undo the change.

▶ **4.** On the Quick Access Toolbar, click the **Undo** button ↺. The word "meeting" is removed from the sentence.

▶ **5.** Click the **Undo** button ↺ again to restore the word "conversation."

 Tim decides that he does want to use "meeting" after all. Instead of retyping it, you'll redo the undo.

▶ **6.** On the Quick Access Toolbar, click the **Redo** button ↻ twice. The word "meeting" replaces "conversation" in the document, so that the phrase reads "…in our meeting last week."

 You can also press the Ctrl+Z keys to execute the Undo command, and press the Ctrl+Y keys to execute the Redo command.

▶ **7.** Press and hold the **Ctrl** key, and then press the **End** key to move the insertion point to the blank paragraph at the end of the document.

▶ **8.** On the Quick Access Toolbar, click the **Save** button 🖫. Word saves your letter with the same name and to the same location you specified earlier.

In the previous steps, you used the arrow keys and a key combination to move the insertion point to specific locations in the document. For your reference, Figure 1-9 summarizes the most common keystrokes for moving the insertion point in a document.

Figure 1-9 ▶ **Keystrokes for moving the insertion point**

To Move the Insertion Point	Press
Left or right one character at a time	← or →
Up or down one line at a time	↑ or ↓
Left or right one word at a time	Ctrl+← or Ctrl+→
Up or down one paragraph at a time	Ctrl+↑ or Ctrl+↓
To the beginning or to the end of the current line	Home or End
To the beginning or to the end of the document	Ctrl+Home or Ctrl+End
To the previous screen or to the next screen	Page Up or Page Down
To the top or to the bottom of the document window	Alt+Ctrl+Page Up or Alt+Ctrl+Page Down

© 2014 Cengage Learning

Correcting Errors as You Type

As you have seen, you can use the Backspace or Delete keys to remove an error, and then you can type a correction. In many cases, however, Word's AutoCorrect feature will do the work for you. Among other things, **AutoCorrect** automatically corrects common typing errors, such as typing "adn" instead of "and." For example, you might have noticed AutoCorrect at work if you forgot to capitalize the first letter in a sentence as you typed the letter. After you type this kind of error, AutoCorrect automatically corrects it when you press the spacebar, the Tab key, or the Enter key.

Word draws your attention to other potential errors by marking them with wavy underlines. If you type a word that doesn't match the correct spelling in Word's dictionary, or if a word is not in the dictionary at all, a wavy red line appears beneath it. A wavy red underline also appears if you mistakenly type the same word twice in a row. Misused words (for example, "your" instead of "you're") are underlined with a wavy blue line. Likewise, punctuation errors, problems with possessives and plurals, and grammatical errors are marked with a wavy blue underline.

You'll see how this works as you continue typing the letter and make some intentional typing errors.

To learn more about correcting errors as you type:

1. Type the following sentence, including the errors shown here: **i will call in a few few days to disuss teh pasport photos you mentioned.**

As you type, AutoCorrect changes the lowercase "i" at the beginning of the sentence to uppercase. It also changes "teh" to "the" and "pasport" to "passport." The spelling error "disuss" and the second "few" are marked with wavy red underlines. You will correct these errors after you finish typing the rest of the paragraph.

2. Press the **spacebar**, and then type the following sentence, including the extra period and the other errors: **I look forward too seeing you in our landscape class next month..** The word "too" is underlined with a wavy blue line, indicating a misused word. The sentence also contains a punctuation error, but Word won't identify it until you start a new sentence or press the Enter key to begin a new paragraph.

3. Press the **Enter** key to begin a new paragraph. As shown in Figure 1-10, the two periods at the end of the sentence are now underlined in blue.

Figure 1-10	Errors marked in the document

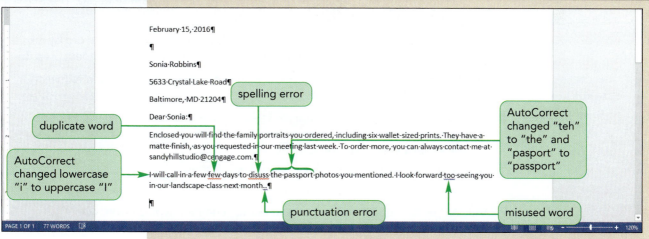

To correct an error marked with a wavy underline, you can right-click the error, and then click a replacement in the shortcut menu. If you don't see the correct word in the shortcut menu, click anywhere in the document to close the menu, and then type the correction yourself. You can also bypass the shortcut menu entirely, and simply delete the error and type a correction.

To correct the spelling and grammar errors:

▶ **1.** Right-click **disuss** to display the shortcut menu shown in Figure 1-11.

Figure 1-11 **Shortcut menu with suggested spellings**

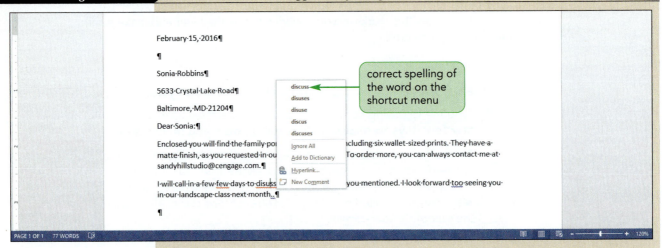

Trouble? If you see a shortcut menu other than the one shown in Figure 1-11, you didn't right-click exactly on the word "disuss." Press the Esc key to close the menu, and then repeat Step 1.

▶ **2.** On the shortcut menu, click **discuss**. The correct word is inserted into the sentence, and the shortcut menu closes. You could use a shortcut menu to remove the second instance of "few," but in the next step you'll try a different method—selecting the word and deleting it.

▶ **3.** Double-click anywhere in the underlined word **few**. The word and the space following it are highlighted in gray, indicating that they are selected. The Mini toolbar is also visible, but you can ignore it.

Trouble? If the entire paragraph is selected, you triple-clicked the word by mistake. Click anywhere in the document to deselect it, and then repeat Step 3.

▶ **4.** Press the **Delete** key. The second instance of "few" and the space following it are deleted from the sentence.

▶ **5.** Use the shortcut menu to replace the underlined word "too" with "to," and then click to the right of the second period after "month" and press the **Backspace** key to delete it.

▶ **6.** On the Quick Access Toolbar, click the **Save** button 💾.

TIP

To deselect highlighted text, click anywhere in the document.

You can see how quick and easy it is to correct common typing errors with AutoCorrect and the wavy red and blue underlines, especially in a short document that you are typing yourself. If you are working on a longer document or a document typed by someone else, you'll also want to have Word check the entire document for errors. You'll learn how to do this in Session 1.2.

Next, you'll finish typing the letter.

To finish typing the letter:

1. Press the **Ctrl+End** keys. The insertion point moves to the end of the document.

2. Type **Sincerely yours,** (including the comma).

3. Press the **Enter** key three times to leave space for the signature.

4. Type **Tim Bartolutti** and then press the **Enter** key. Because Tim's last name is not in Word's dictionary, a wavy red line appears below it. You can ignore this for now.

5. Type your first, middle, and last initials in lowercase, and then press the **Enter** key. AutoCorrect wrongly assumes your first initial is the first letter of a new sentence, and changes it to uppercase.

6. On the Quick Access Toolbar, click the **Undo** button. Word reverses the change, replacing the uppercase initial with a lowercase one.

7. Type **Enclosure**. At this point, your screen should look similar to Figure 1-12. Notice that as you continue to add lines to the letter, the top part of the letter scrolls off the screen. For example, in Figure 1-12, you can no longer see the date.

TIP

You only need to include your initials in a letter if you are typing it for someone else.

Figure 1-12 **Robbins Letter**

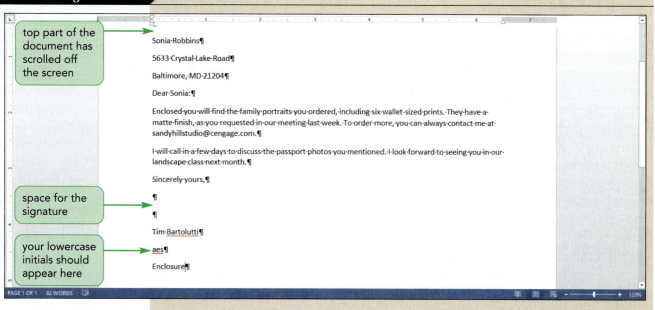

- top part of the document has scrolled off the screen
- space for the signature
- your lowercase initials should appear here

Sonia·Robbins¶

5633·Crystal·Lake·Road¶

Baltimore,·MD·21204¶

Dear·Sonia:¶

Enclosed·you·will·find·the·family·portraits·you·ordered,·including·six·wallet-sized·prints.·They·have·a·matte·finish,·as·you·requested·in·our·meeting·last·week.·To·order·more,·you·can·always·contact·me·at·sandyhillstudio@cengage.com.¶

I·will·call·in·a·few·days·to·discuss·the·passport·photos·you·mentioned.·I·look·forward·to·seeing·you·in·our·landscape·class·next·month.¶

Sincerely·yours,¶

¶

¶

Tim·Bartolutti¶

aes¶

Enclosure¶

PAGE 1 OF 1 82 WORDS

8. Save the document.

Now that you have finished typing the letter, you need to proofread it.

Proofreading a Document

After you finish typing a document, you need to proofread it carefully from start to finish. Part of proofreading a document in Word is removing all wavy underlines, either by correcting the text or by telling Word to ignore the underlined text because it isn't really an error. For example, Tim's last name is marked as an error, when in fact it is spelled correctly. You need to tell Word to ignore "Bartolutti" wherever it occurs in the letter. You need to do the same for your initials.

To proofread and correct the remaining marked errors in the letter:

1. Right-click **Bartolutti**. A shortcut menu opens.

2. On the shortcut menu, click **Ignore All** to indicate that Word should ignore the word "Bartolutti" each time it occurs in this document. (The Ignore All option can be particularly helpful in a longer document.) The wavy red underline disappears from below Tim's last name. If your initials do not form a word, a red wavy underline appears beneath them; otherwise, a blue wavy underline appears there.

3. If you see a wavy red underline below your initials, right-click your initials. On the shortcut menu, click **Ignore All** to remove the red wavy underline. If you didn't see a wavy blue underline below your initials before, you should see one now.

4. Right-click your initials again. On the shortcut menu, click **Ignore Once** to remove the blue underline.

5. Read the entire letter to proofread it for typing errors. Correct any errors using the techniques you have just learned.

6. Save the document.

The text of the letter is finished. Now you need to think about how it looks—that is, you need to think about the document's **formatting**. First, you need to adjust the spacing in the inside address.

Adjusting Paragraph and Line Spacing

When typing a letter, you might need to adjust two types of spacing—paragraph spacing and line spacing. **Paragraph spacing** is the space that appears directly above and below a paragraph. In Word, any text that ends with a paragraph mark symbol (¶) is a paragraph. So, a **paragraph** can be a group of words that is many lines long, a single word, or even a blank line, in which case you see a paragraph mark alone on a single line. Paragraph spacing is measured in points; a **point** is 1/72 of an inch. The default setting for paragraph spacing in Word is 0 points before each paragraph and 8 points after each paragraph. When laying out a complicated document, resist the temptation to simply press the Enter key to insert extra space between paragraphs. Changing the paragraph spacing gives you much more control over the final result.

Line spacing is the space between lines of text within a paragraph. Word offers a number of preset line spacing options. The 1.0 setting, which is often called **single-spacing**, allows the least amount of space between lines. All other line spacing options are measured as multiples of 1.0 spacing. For example, 2.0 spacing (sometimes called **double-spacing**) allows for twice the space of single-spacing. The default line spacing setting is 1.08, which allows a little more space between lines than 1.0 spacing.

Now consider the line and paragraph spacing in the Robbins letter. The three lines of the inside address are too far apart. That's because each line of the inside address is actually a separate paragraph. Word inserted the default 8 points of paragraph spacing after each of these separate paragraphs. See Figure 1-13.

Figure 1-13 **Line and paragraph spacing in the letter to Sonia Robbins**

line spacing separates lines of text within a paragraph

Sonia·Robbins¶

5633·Crystal·Lake·Road¶

Baltimore,·MD·21204¶

paragraph spacing makes the lines of the inside address too far apart

Dear·Sonia:¶

Enclosed·you·will·find·the·family·portraits·you·ordered,·including·six·wallet-sized·prints.·They·have·a·matte·finish,·as·you·requested·in·our·meeting·last·week.·To·order·more,·you·can·always·contact·me·at·sandyhillstudio@cengage.com.¶

I·will·call·in·a·few·days·to·discuss·the·passport·photos·you·mentioned.·I·look·forward·to·seeing·you·in·our·landscape·class·next·month.¶

Sincerely·yours,¶

¶

¶

paragraph spacing separates one paragraph from another

Tim·Bartolutti¶

aes¶

Enclosure¶

PAGE 1 OF 1 82 WORDS 120%

To follow the conventions of a block style business letter, the three paragraphs that make up the inside address should have the same spacing as the lines of text within a single paragraph—that is, they need to be closer together. You can accomplish this by removing the 8 points of paragraph spacing after the first two paragraphs in the inside address. To conform to the block style business letter format, you also need to close up the spacing between your initials and the word "Enclosure" at the end of the letter.

To adjust paragraph and line spacing in Word, you use the Line and Paragraph Spacing button in the Paragraph group on the HOME tab. Clicking this button displays a menu of preset line spacing options (1.0, 1.15, 2.0, and so on). The menu also includes two paragraph spacing options, which allow you to add 12 points before a paragraph or remove the default 8 points of space after a paragraph.

Next you'll adjust the paragraph spacing in the inside address and after your initials. In the process, you'll also learn some techniques for selecting text in a document.

To adjust the paragraph spacing in the inside address and after your initials:

1. Move the pointer to the white space just to the left of "Sonia Robbins" until it changes to a right-facing arrow.

2. Click the mouse button. The entire name, including the paragraph symbol after it, is selected.

3. Press and hold the mouse button, drag the pointer down to select the next paragraph of the inside address as well, and then release the mouse button.

 The name and street address are selected as well as the paragraph marks at the end of each paragraph. You did not select the paragraph containing the city, state, and zip code because you do not need to change its paragraph spacing. See Figure 1-14.

TIP

The white space in the left margin is sometimes referred to as the selection bar because you click it to select text.

Figure 1-14 Inside address selected

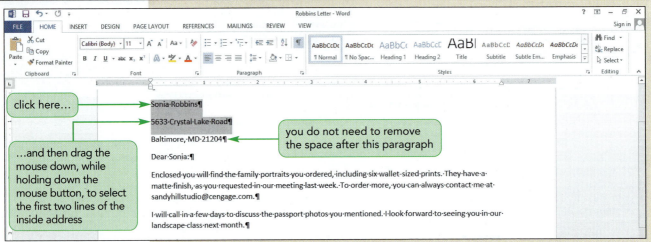

4. Make sure the HOME tab is selected on the ribbon.

5. In the Paragraph group on the HOME tab, click the **Line and Paragraph Spacing** button. A menu of line spacing options appears, with two paragraph spacing options at the bottom. See Figure 1-15. At the moment, you are only interested in the paragraph spacing options. Your goal is to remove the default 8 points of space after the first two paragraphs in the inside address.

Figure 1-15 Line and paragraph spacing options

6. Click **Remove Space After Paragraph**. The menu closes, and the paragraphs are now closer together.

7. Double-click your initials to select them and the paragraph symbol after them.

8. In the Paragraph group, click the **Line and Paragraph Spacing** button, click **Remove Space After Paragraph**, and then click anywhere in the document to deselect your initials.

Another way to compress lines of text is to press the Shift+Enter keys at the end of a line. This inserts a **manual line break**, also called a **soft return**, which moves the insertion point to a new line without starting a new paragraph. You will use this technique now as you add Tim's title below his name in the signature line.

To use a manual line break to move the insertion point to a new line without starting a new paragraph:

▶ **1.** Click to the right of the "i" in "Bartolutti."

▶ **2.** Press the **Shift+Enter** keys. Word inserts a small arrow symbol ↵ , indicating a manual line break, and the insertion point moves to the line below Tim's name.

▶ **3.** Type **Sales Manager**. Tim's title now appears directly below his name with no intervening paragraph spacing, just like the lines of the inside address.

▶ **4.** Save the document.

INSIGHT

Understanding Spacing Between Paragraphs

When discussing the correct format for letters, many business style guides talk about single-spacing and double-spacing between paragraphs. In these style guides, to single-space between paragraphs means to press the Enter key once after each paragraph. Likewise, to double-space between paragraphs means to press the Enter key twice after each paragraph. With the default paragraph spacing in Word 2013, however, you only need to press the Enter key once after a paragraph. The space Word adds after a paragraph is not quite the equivalent of double-spacing, but it is enough to make it easy to see where one paragraph ends and another begins. Keep this in mind if you're accustomed to pressing the Enter key twice; otherwise, you could end up with more space than you want between paragraphs.

As you corrected line and paragraph spacing in the previous set of steps, you used the mouse to select text. Word provides multiple ways to select, or highlight, text as you work. Figure 1-16 summarizes these methods and explains when to use them most effectively.

Figure 1-16	Methods for selecting text

To Select	Mouse	Keyboard	Mouse and Keyboard
A word	Double-click the word	Move the insertion point to the beginning of the word, press and hold Ctrl+Shift, and then press →	
A line	Click in the white space to the left of the line	Move the insertion point to the beginning of the line, press and hold Shift, and then press ↓	
A sentence	Click at the beginning of the sentence, then drag the pointer until the sentence is selected		Press and hold Ctrl, then click any location within the sentence
Multiple lines	Click and drag in the white space to the left of the lines	Move the insertion point to the beginning of the first line, press and hold Shift, and then press ↓ until all the lines are selected	
A paragraph	Double-click in the white space to the left of the paragraph, or triple-click at any location within the paragraph	Move the insertion point to the beginning of the paragraph, press and hold Ctrl+Shift, and then press ↓	
Multiple paragraphs	Click in the white space to the left of the first paragraph you want to select, and then drag to select the remaining paragraphs	Move the insertion point to the beginning of the first paragraph, press and hold Ctrl+Shift, and then press ↓ until all the paragraphs are selected	
An entire document	Triple-click in the white space to the left of the document text	Press Ctrl+A	Press and hold Ctrl, and click in the white space to the left of the document text
A block of text	Click at the beginning of the block, then drag the pointer until the entire block is selected		Click at the beginning of the block, press and hold Shift, and then click at the end of the block
Nonadjacent blocks of text			Press and hold Ctrl, then drag the mouse pointer to select multiple blocks of nonadjacent text

© 2014 Cengage Learning

Adjusting the Margins

Another important aspect of document formatting is the amount of margin space between the document text and the edge of the page. You can check the document's margins by changing the Zoom level to display the entire page.

To change the Zoom level to display the entire page:

▶ **1.** On the ribbon, click the **VIEW** tab.

▶ **2.** In the Zoom group, click the **One Page** button. The entire document is now visible in the Word window. See Figure 1-17.

| Figure 1-17 | Document zoomed to show entire page |

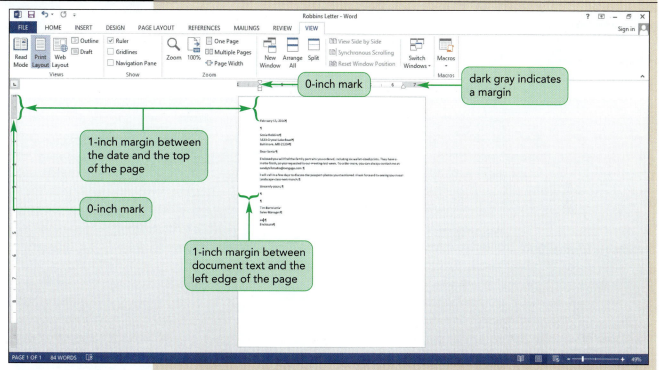

On the rulers, the margins appear dark gray. By default, Word documents include 1-inch margins on all sides of the document. By looking at the vertical ruler, you can see that the date in the letter, the first line in the document, is located 1 inch from the top of the page. Likewise, the horizontal ruler indicates the document text begins 1 inch from the left edge of the page.

Reading the measurements on the rulers can be tricky at first. On the horizontal ruler, the 0-inch mark is like the origin on a number line. You measure from the 0-inch mark to the left or to the right. On the vertical ruler, you measure up or down from the 0-inch mark.

Tim plans to print the letter on Sandy Hill Portrait Studio letterhead, which includes a graphic and the company's address. To allow more blank space for the letterhead, and to move the text down so it doesn't look so crowded at the top of the page, you need to increase the top margin. The settings for changing the page margins are located on the PAGE LAYOUT tab on the ribbon.

To change the page margins:

▶ **1.** On the ribbon, click the **PAGE LAYOUT** tab. The PAGE LAYOUT tab displays options for adjusting the layout of your document.

2. In the Page Setup group, click the **Margins** button. The Margins gallery opens, as shown in Figure 1-18.

Figure 1-18 Margins gallery

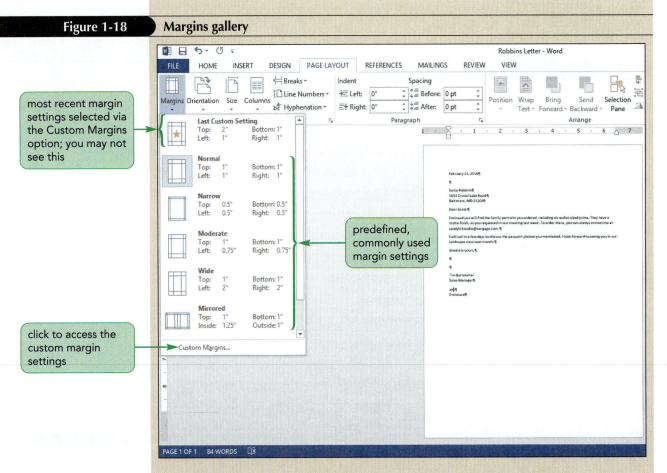

most recent margin settings selected via the Custom Margins option; you may not see this

predefined, commonly used margin settings

click to access the custom margin settings

In the Margins gallery, you can choose from a number of predefined margin options, or you can click the Custom Margins command to select your own settings. After you create custom margin settings, the most recent set appears as an option at the top of the menu. For the Robbins letter, you will create custom margins.

3. Click **Custom Margins**. The Page Setup dialog box opens with the Margins tab displayed. The default margin settings are displayed in the boxes at the top of the Margins tab. The top margin of 1" is already selected, ready for you to type a new margin setting.

4. In the Top box in the Margins section, type **2.5**. You do not need to type an inch mark ("). See Figure 1-19.

Figure 1-19 **Creating custom margins in the Page Setup dialog box**

enter a Top margin of 2.5

allows you to make this new margin setting the default for all new Word documents

▶ **5.** Click the **OK** button. The text of the letter is now lower on the page. The page looks less crowded, with room for the company's letterhead.

▶ **6.** Change the Zoom level back to **120%**, and then save the document.

For most documents, the Word default of 1-inch margins is fine. In some professional settings, however, you might need to use a particular custom margin setting for all your documents. In that case, define the custom margins using the Margins tab in the Page Setup dialog box, and then click the Set As Default button to make your settings the default for all new documents. Keep in mind that most printers can't print to the edge of the page; if you select custom margins that are too narrow for your printer's specifications, Word alerts you to change your margin settings.

Previewing and Printing a Document

To make sure the document is ready to print, and to avoid wasting paper and time, you should first review it in Backstage view to make sure it will look right when printed. Like the One Page zoom setting you used earlier, the Print option in Backstage view displays a full-page preview of the document, allowing you to see how it will fit on the printed page. However, you cannot actually edit this preview. It simply provides one last opportunity to look at the document before printing.

To preview the document:

▶ **1.** Proofread the document one last time and correct any remaining errors.

▶ **2.** Click the **FILE** tab to display Backstage view.

▶ **3.** In the navigation bar, click **Print**.

The Print screen displays a full-page version of your document, showing how the letter will fit on the printed page. The Print settings to the left of the preview allow you to control a variety of print options. For example, you can change the number of copies from the default setting of "1." The 1 Page Per Sheet button opens a menu where you can choose to print multiple pages on a single sheet of paper, or to scale the printed page to a particular paper size. You can also use the navigation controls at the bottom of the screen to display other pages in a document. See Figure 1-20.

| Figure 1-20 | Print settings in Backstage view |

click to close Backstage view and return to the document

click when you are ready to print

in a multipage document, click to display subsequent pages

click to open a menu where you can choose to print multiple pages on a single sheet of paper, or to scale the printed page to a particular paper size

specify the number of copies here

preview of the page when printed

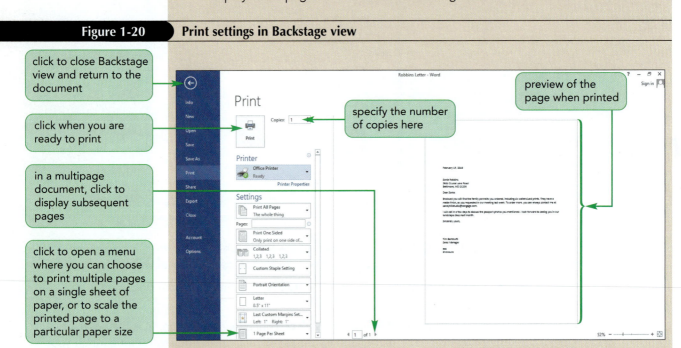

4. Review your document and make sure its overall layout matches that of the document in Figure 1-20. If you notice a problem with paragraph breaks or spacing, click the **Back** button ⊛ at the top of the navigation bar to return to the document, make any necessary changes, and then start again at Step 2.

At this point, you can print the document or you can leave Backstage view and return to the document in Print Layout view. In the following steps, you should only print the document if your instructor asks you to. If you will be printing the document, make sure your printer is turned on and contains paper.

To leave Backstage view or to print the document:

1. Click the **Back** button ⊛ at the top of the navigation bar to leave Backstage view and return to the document in Print Layout view, or click the **Print** button. Backstage view closes, and the letter prints if you clicked the Print button.

2. Click the **FILE** tab, and then click **Close** in the navigation bar to close the document without closing Word.

Next, Tim asks you to create an envelope he can use to send a class schedule to another client.

Creating an Envelope

Before you can create the envelope, you need to open a new, blank document. To create a new document, you can start with a blank document—as you did with the letter to Sonia Robbins—or you can start with one that already contains formatting and generic text commonly used in a variety of professional documents, such as a fax cover sheet or a memo. These preformatted files are called **templates**. You could use a template to create a formatted envelope, but first you'll learn how to create one on your own in a new, blank document. You'll have a chance to try out a template in the Case Problems at the end of this tutorial.

To create a new document for the envelope:

▶ **1.** Click the **FILE** tab, and then click **New** in the navigation bar. The New screen is similar to the one you saw when you first started Word, with a blank document in the upper-left corner, along with a variety of templates. See Figure 1-21.

Figure 1-21	New options in Backstage view

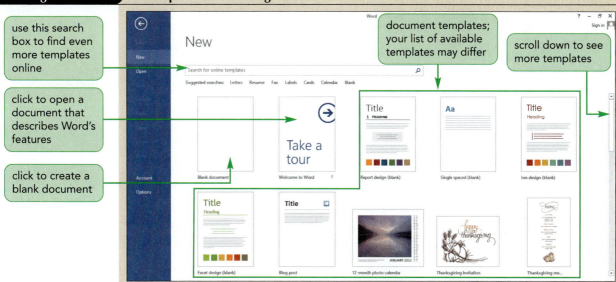

use this search box to find even more templates online

click to open a document that describes Word's features

click to create a blank document

document templates; your list of available templates may differ

scroll down to see more templates

▶ **2.** Click **Blank document**. A new document named Document2 opens in the document window, with the HOME tab selected on the ribbon.

▶ **3.** If necessary, change the Zoom level to **120%**, and display nonprinting characters and the rulers.

▶ **4.** Save the new document as **Keating Envelope** in the location specified by your instructor.

To create the envelope:

1. On the ribbon, click the **MAILINGS** tab. The ribbon changes to display the various Mailings options.

2. In the Create group, click the **Envelopes** button. The Envelopes and Labels dialog box opens, with the Envelopes tab displayed. The insertion point appears in the Delivery address box, ready for you to type the recipient's address. Depending on how your computer is set up, and whether you are working on your own computer or a school computer, you might see an address in the Return address box.

3. In the Delivery address box, type the following address, pressing the Enter key to start each new line:

 Lakeisha Keating

 2245 Farley Lane

 Baltimore, MD 21206

 Because Tim will be using the studio's printed envelopes, you don't need to print a return address on this envelope.

4. Click the **Omit** check box to insert a checkmark, if necessary.

 At this point, if you had a printer stocked with envelopes, you could click the Print button to print the envelope. To save an envelope for printing later, you need to add it to the document. Your Envelopes and Labels dialog box should match the one in Figure 1-22.

Figure 1-22 **Envelopes and Labels dialog box**

5. Click the **Add to Document** button. The dialog box closes, and you return to the document window. The envelope is inserted at the top of your document, with 1.0 line spacing. The double line with the words "Section Break (Next Page)" is related to how the envelope is formatted, and will not be visible when you print the envelope. The envelope will print in the standard business envelope format.

6. Save the document. Tim will print the envelope later, so you can close the document now.

7. Click the **FILE** tab and then click **Close** in the navigation bar. The document closes, but Word remains open.

INSIGHT

Creating Documents with Templates

Microsoft offers predesigned templates for all kinds of documents, including calendars, reports, and thank you cards. You can use the scroll bar on the right of the New screen (shown earlier in Figure 1-21) to scroll down to see more templates, or you can use the Search for online templates box in the New screen to search among hundreds of other options available at Office.com. When you open a template, you actually open a new document containing the formatting and text stored in the template, leaving the original template untouched. A typical template includes placeholder text that you replace with your own information.

Templates allow you to create stylish, professional-looking documents quickly and easily. To use them effectively, however, you need to be knowledgeable about Word and its many options for manipulating text, graphics, and page layouts. Otherwise, the complicated formatting of some Word templates can be more frustrating than helpful. As you become a more experienced Word user, you'll learn how to create your own templates.

You're finished creating the cover letter and the envelope. In the next session, you will modify a flyer that announces an upcoming class by formatting the text and adding a photo.

REVIEW

Session 1.1 Quick Check

1. In a block style letter, does each line of text start at the left or right margin?
2. What do you call the recipient's address, which appears below the date in a block style letter?
3. Explain how to use a hyperlink in a Word document to open a new email message.
4. Explain how to display nonprinting characters.
5. Define the term "paragraph spacing."
6. How does Word indicate a potential spelling error?

Session 1.2 Visual Overview:

Alignment buttons control the text's **alignment**—that is, the way it lines up between the left and right margins. Here, the Center button is selected because the text containing the insertion point is center-aligned.

You can click the Clear All Formatting button to restore selected text to the default font, font size, and color.

Clicking the Format Painter button displays the Format Painter pointer, which you can use to copy formatting from the selected text to other text in the document.

The Font group on the HOME tab includes the Font box and the Font size box for setting the text's font and the font size, respectively. A **font** is a set of characters that uses the same typeface.

You click the Shading button arrow to apply a colored background to a selected paragraph.

This document has a landscape orientation, meaning it is wider than it is tall.

You can insert a photo or another type of picture in a document by using the **Pictures button** located on the INSERT tab of the ribbon. After you insert a photo or another picture, you can format it with a style that adds a border or a shadow, or changes its shape.

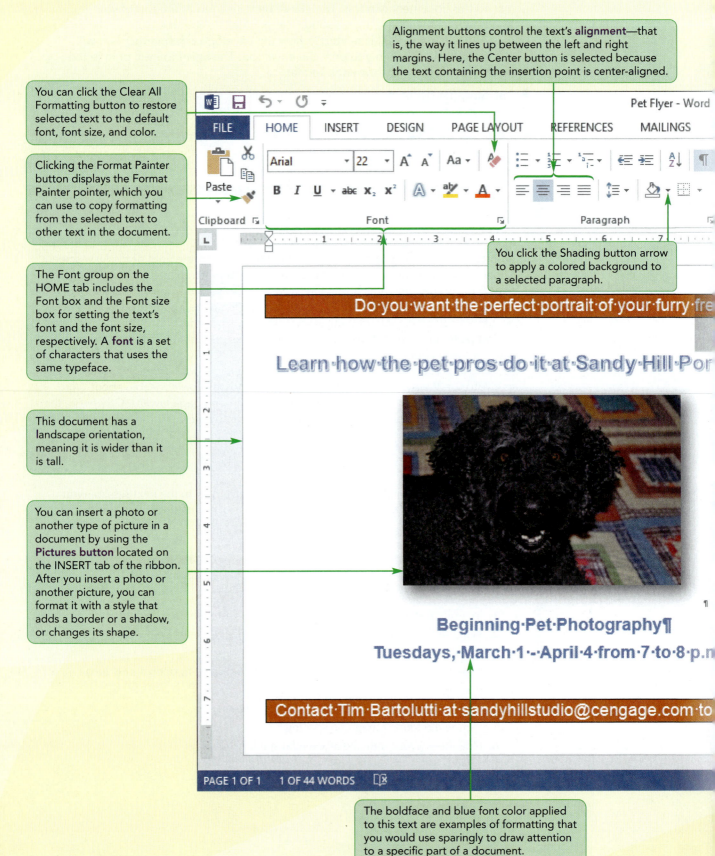

The boldface and blue font color applied to this text are examples of formatting that you would use sparingly to draw attention to a specific part of a document.

Courtesy of Ann Shaffer

Formatting a Document

The black border and dark orange shading around this paragraph are examples of **paragraph formatting** because they affect the entire paragraph.

The Microsoft Word Help button opens the **Word Help** window, where you can find information about Word commands and features, as well as instructions for using them.

You use the Borders button arrow to apply an outline to the selected paragraph. The image on the Borders button reflects the most recently used Border option.

The blue font color and white outline used for this paragraph are examples of **text effects**, special visual enhancements such as outlines, shading, shadows, and reflections, that you add to the text's font.

The misspelled word is highlighted in the document. A suggested correction is highlighted in the Spelling task pane.

A **task pane** is a window that helps you navigate through a complex task or feature. This one, the **Spelling task pane**, opens when you click the Spelling & Grammar button in the Proofing group on the HOME tab. You can use it to correct spelling errors. Similarly, you can use the **Grammar task pane** to correct grammar errors.

The white font color used on this text is an example of **character formatting** because it affects individual characters.

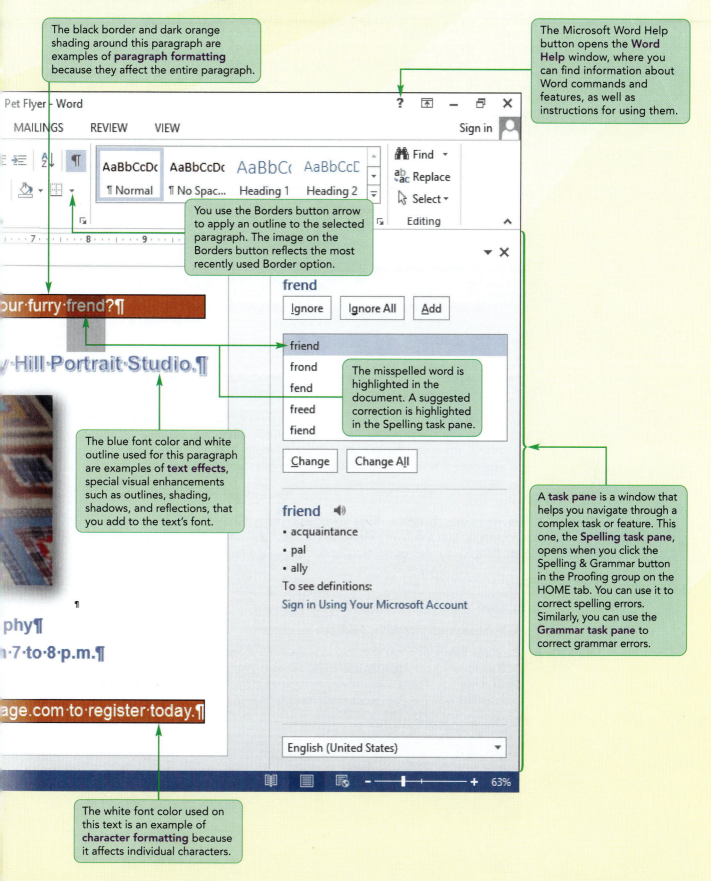

Opening an Existing Document

In this session, you'll complete a flyer announcing a pet photography class. Tim has already typed the text of the flyer, inserted a photo into it, and saved it as a Word document. He would like you to check the document for spelling and grammar errors, format the flyer to make it eye-catching and easy to read, and then replace the current photo with a new one. You'll start by opening the document.

To open the flyer document:

▶ 1. On the ribbon, click the **FILE** tab to open Backstage view, and then verify that **Open** is selected in the navigation bar. On the left side of the Open screen is a list of places you can go to locate other documents, and on the right is a list of recently opened documents.

 Trouble? If you closed Word at the end of the previous session, start Word now, click Open Other Documents at the bottom of the navigation bar in Backstage view, and then begin with Step 2.

▶ 2. Click **Computer**, and then click the **Browse** button. The Open dialog box opens.

 Trouble? If your instructor asked you to store your files to your SkyDrive account, click SkyDrive, log in to your account, if necessary, and then click the Browse button.

▶ 3. Navigate to the Word1 ▸ Tutorial folder included with your Data Files, click **Pet**, and then click the **Open** button. The document opens with the insertion point blinking in the first line of the document.

 Trouble? If you don't have the starting Data Files, you need to get them before you can proceed. Your instructor will either give you the Data Files or ask you to obtain them from a specified location (such as a network drive). If you have any questions about the Data Files, see your instructor or technical support person for assistance.

Before making changes to Tim's document, you will save it with a new name. Saving the document with a different filename creates a copy of the file and leaves the original file unchanged in case you want to work through the tutorial again.

To save the document with a new name:

▶ 1. On the ribbon, click the **FILE** tab.

▶ 2. In the navigation bar in Backstage view, click **Save As**. Save the document as **Pet Flyer** in the location specified by your instructor. Backstage view closes, and the document window appears again with the new filename in the title bar. The original Pet document closes, remaining unchanged.

PROSKILLS

Decision Making: Creating Effective Documents

Before you create a new document or revise an existing document, take a moment to think about your audience. Ask yourself these questions:

- Who is your audience?
- What do they know?
- What do they need to know?
- How can the document you are creating change your audience's behavior or opinions?

Every decision you make about your document should be based on your answers to these questions. To take a simple example, if you are creating a flyer to announce an upcoming seminar on college financial aid, your audience would be students and their parents. They probably all know what the term "financial aid" means, so you don't need to explain that in your flyer. Instead, you can focus on telling them what they need to know—the date, time, and location of the seminar. The behavior you want to affect, in this case, is whether or not your audience will show up for the seminar. By making the flyer professional looking and easy to read, you increase the chance that they will.

You might find it more challenging to answer these questions about your audience when creating more complicated documents, such as corporate reports. But the focus remains the same—connecting with the audience. As you are deciding what information to include in your document, remember that the goal of a professional document is to convey the information as effectively as possible to your target audience.

Before revising a document for someone else, it's a good idea to familiarize yourself with its overall structure.

To review the document:

1. Verify that the document is displayed in Print Layout view and that nonprinting characters are displayed. For now, you can ignore the wavy underlines that appear in the document.

2. Change the Zoom level to **120%**, if necessary.

 At this point, the document is very simple. By the time you are finished, it will look like the document shown in the Session 1.2 Visual Overview, with the spelling and grammar errors corrected. Figure 1-23 summarizes the tasks you will perform.

| Figure 1-23 | Formatting changes requested by Tim |

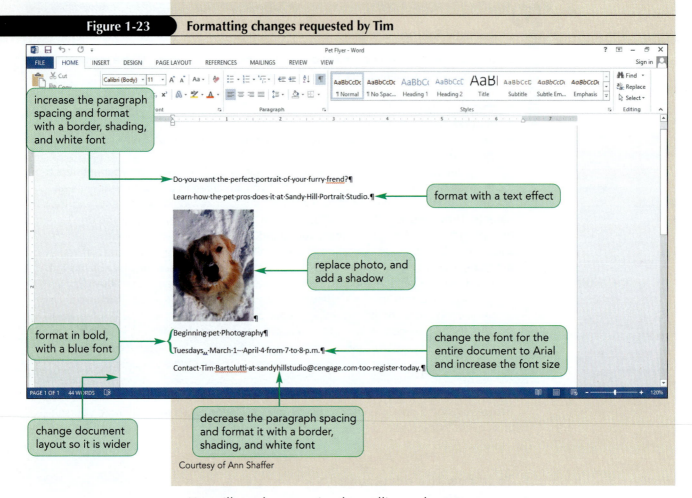

increase the paragraph spacing and format with a border, shading, and white font

Do·you·want·the·perfect·portrait·of·your·furry·frend?¶

Learn·how·the·pet·pros·does·it·at·Sandy·Hill·Portrait·Studio.¶

format with a text effect

replace photo, and add a shadow

format in bold, with a blue font

Beginning·pet·Photography¶

Tuesdays,·March·1–April·4·from·7·to·8·p.m.¶

Contact·Tim·Bartolutti·at·sandyhillstudio@cengage.com·too·register·today.¶

change the font for the entire document to Arial and increase the font size

change document layout so it is wider

decrease the paragraph spacing and format it with a border, shading, and white font

Courtesy of Ann Shaffer

You will start by correcting the spelling and grammar errors.

Using the Spelling and Grammar Task Panes

As you learned in Tutorial 1, Word marks possible spelling and grammatical errors with wavy underlines as you type so you can quickly go back and correct those errors. A more thorough way of checking the spelling in a document is to use the Spelling and Grammar task panes to check a document word by word for a variety of errors. You can customize the spelling and grammar settings to add or ignore certain types of errors.

Tim asks you to use the Spelling and Grammar task panes to check the flyer for mistakes. Before you do, you'll configure the grammar settings to look for subject/verb agreement, in addition to other types of errors.

To customize the grammar settings:

1. On the ribbon, click the **FILE** tab, and then click **Options** in the navigation bar. The Word Options dialog box opens. You can use this dialog box to change a variety of settings related to how Word looks and works.

2. In the left pane, click **Proofing**, and then, in the "When correcting spelling and grammar in Word" section, click the **Settings** button. The Grammar Settings dialog box opens.

3. If necessary, scroll down in the Grammar Settings dialog box to display all the check boxes under "Grammar," and then click the **Subject-verb agreement** check box to insert a checkmark. See Figure 1-24.

Figure 1-24	Grammar Settings dialog box

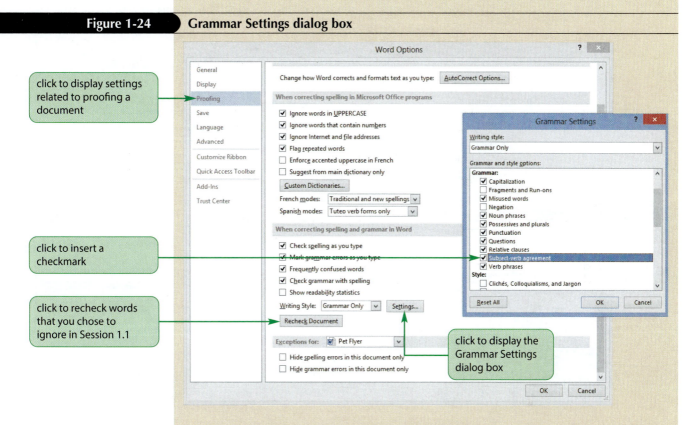

4. Click the **OK** button to close the Grammar Settings dialog box and return to the Word Options dialog box.

To ensure that Word checks the entire Pet Flyer document, and doesn't skip any words that you chose to ignore when you checked the Robbins Letter in Session 1.1, you can click the Recheck Document button.

5. Click the **Recheck Document** button, and then click **Yes** in the warning dialog box.

6. In the Word Options dialog box, click the **OK** button to close the dialog box.

You return to the Pet Flyer document, where three errors are now marked with wavy blue underlines. The two new errors are related to subject-verb agreement. You should also see two words marked with wavy red underlines, including Tim's last name in the final paragraph.

Now you are ready to check the document's spelling and grammar. All errors marked with red underlines are considered spelling errors, while all errors marked with blue underlines are considered grammatical errors.

To check the Pet Flyer document for spelling and grammatical errors:

1. Press the **Ctrl+Home** keys, if necessary, to move the insertion point to the beginning of the document, to the left of the "D" in "Do." By placing the insertion point at the beginning of the document, you ensure that Word will check the entire document from start to finish without having to go back and check an earlier part.

2. On the ribbon, click the **REVIEW** tab. The ribbon changes to display reviewing options.

3. In the Proofing group, click the **Spelling & Grammar** button.

 The Spelling task pane opens on the right side of the Word window, with the word "frend" listed as a possible spelling error. The same word is highlighted in gray in the document. In the task pane's list of possible corrections, the correctly spelled word "friend" is highlighted in light blue. See Figure 1-25.

Figure 1-25	Spelling task pane

Courtesy of Ann Shaffer

4. In the task pane, click the **Change** button. The misspelled word "frend" is replaced with "friend."

 Next, Word highlights the entire second sentence, indicating another possible error. The Spelling task pane changes to the Grammar task pane, and the information at the bottom of the task pane explains that the error is related to subject-verb agreement.

5. Verify that "pros do" is selected in the Grammar task pane, and then click the **Change** button. The second to last paragraph of text is now highlighted in the document. The explanation at the bottom of the task pane indicates that the error is related to punctuation.

6. Verify that the comma is selected in the Grammar task pane, and then click the **Change** button.

 Tim's last name is now highlighted in the document, and the Grammar task pane changes to the Spelling task pane. Although the Spelling task pane doesn't recognize "Bartolutti" as a word, it is spelled correctly, so you can ignore it.

7. Click the **Ignore** button in the Spelling task pane.

The last paragraph in the document is highlighted, and the Grammar task pane indicates a possible subject-verb agreement problem related to the word "register." However, the real problem is the word "too," just before "register." It should be replaced with "to." You can fix this problem by typing directly in the document.

8. In the document, click to the right of the word "too," delete the second letter "o," and then click the **Resume** button in the task pane. The task pane closes and a dialog box opens indicating that the spelling and grammar check is complete.

9. Click the **OK** button to close the dialog box.

Finally, you'll restore the grammar settings to their original configuration.

10. Click the **FILE** tab, and then click **Options**.

11. In the Word Options dialog box, click **Proofing**, and then click the **Settings** button.

12. Scroll down, and then click the **Subject-verb agreement** check box to remove the checkmark.

13. Click the **OK** button to close the Grammar Settings dialog box, and then click the **OK** button to close the Word Options dialog box.

PROSKILLS

Written Communication: Proofreading Your Document

Although the Spelling and Grammar task panes are useful tools, they won't always catch every error in a document, and they sometimes flag "errors" that are actually correct. This means there is no substitute for careful proofreading. Always take the time to read through your document to check for errors the Spelling and Grammar task panes might have missed. Keep in mind that the Spelling and Grammar task panes cannot pinpoint inaccurate phrases or poorly chosen words. You'll have to find those yourself. To produce a professional document, you must read it carefully several times. It's a good idea to ask one or two other people to read your documents as well; they might catch something you missed.

You still need to proofread the Pet Flyer document. You'll do that next.

To proofread the Pet Flyer document:

1. Review the document text for any remaining errors. In the third paragraph of text, change the lowercase "p" in "pet" to an uppercase "P."

2. In the last line of text, replace "Tim Bartolutti" with your first and last name, and then save the document. Including your name in the document will make it easier for you to find your copy later if you print it on a shared printer.

Now you're ready to begin formatting the document. You will start by turning the page so it is wider than it is tall. In other words, you will change the document's **orientation**.

Changing Page Orientation

Portrait orientation, with the page taller than it is wide, is the default page orientation for Word documents because it is the orientation most commonly used for letters, reports, and other formal documents. However, Tim wants you to format the pet flyer in **landscape orientation**—that is, with the page turned so it is wider than it is tall to better accommodate the photo. You can accomplish this task by using the Orientation button located on the PAGE LAYOUT tab on the ribbon. After you change the page orientation, you will select narrower margins so you can maximize the amount of color on the page.

To change the page orientation:

▶ 1. Change the document zoom setting to **One Page** so that you can see the entire document.

▶ 2. On the ribbon, click the **PAGE LAYOUT** tab. The ribbon changes to display options for formatting the overall layout of text and images in the document.

▶ 3. In the Page Setup group, click the **Orientation** button, and then click **Landscape** on the menu. The document changes to landscape orientation.

▶ 4. In the Page Setup group, click the **Margins** button, and then click the **Narrow** option on the menu. The margins shrink from 1 inch to .5 inch on all four sides. See Figure 1-26.

Figure 1-26 ▶ **Document in landscape orientation with narrow margins**

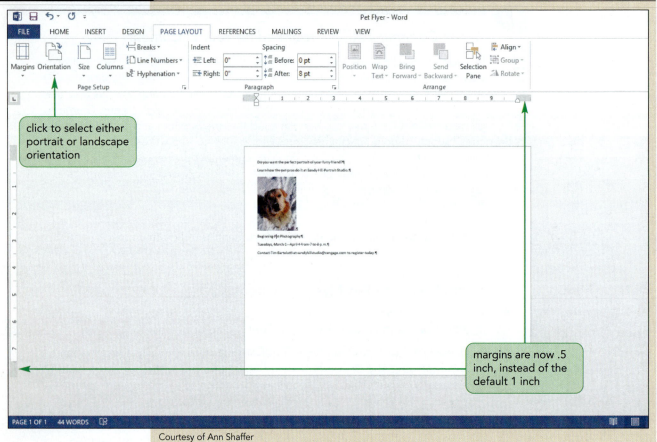

click to select either portrait or landscape orientation

margins are now .5 inch, instead of the default 1 inch

Courtesy of Ann Shaffer

Changing the Font and Font Size

Tim typed the document in the default font size, 11 point, and the default font, Calibri, but he would like to switch to the Arial font instead. Also, he wants to increase the size of all five paragraphs of the document text. To apply these changes, you start by selecting the text you want to format. Then you select the options you want in the Font group on the HOME tab.

To change the font and font size:

1. On the ribbon, click the HOME tab.

2. Change the document Zoom level to **120%**.

3. To verify that the insertion point is located at the beginning of the document, press the **Ctrl+HOME** keys.

4. Press and hold the **Shift** key, and then click to the right of the second paragraph marker, at the end of the second paragraph of text. The first two paragraphs of text are selected, as shown in Figure 1-27.

Figure 1-27 Selected text, with default font displayed in Font box

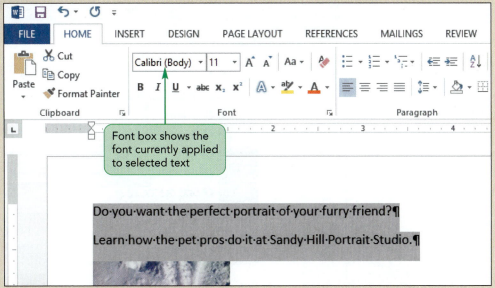

Courtesy of Ann Shaffer

The Font box in the Font group displays the name of the font applied to the selected text, which in this case is Calibri. The word "Body" next to the font name indicates that the Calibri font is intended for formatting body text. **Body text** is ordinary text, as opposed to titles or headings.

5. In the Font group on the HOME tab, click the **Font** arrow. A list of available fonts appears, with Calibri Light and Calibri at the top of the list. Calibri is highlighted in blue, indicating that this font is currently applied to the selected text. The word "Headings" next to the font name "Calibri Light" indicates that Calibri Light is intended for formatting headings.

Below Calibri Light and Calibri, you might see a list of fonts that have been used recently on your computer, followed by a complete alphabetical list of all available fonts. (You won't see the list of recently used fonts if you just installed Word.) You need to scroll the list to see all the available fonts. Each name in the list is formatted with the relevant font. For example, the name "Arial" appears in the Arial font. See Figure 1-28.

Figure 1-28	**Font list**

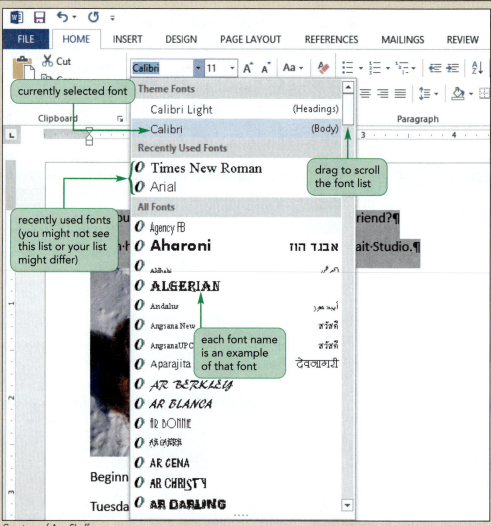

Courtesy of Ann Shaffer

6. Without clicking, move the pointer over a dramatic-looking font in the font list, such as Algerian or Arial Black, and then move the pointer over another font.

The selected text in the document changes to show a Live Preview of the font the pointer is resting on. **Live Preview** shows the results that would occur in your document if you clicked the option you are pointing to.

7. When you are finished reviewing the Font list, click **Arial**. The Font menu closes, and the selected text is formatted in Arial.

Next, you will make the text more eye-catching by increasing the font size. The Font Size box currently displays the number "11," indicating that the selected text is formatted in 11-point font.

8. Verify that the two paragraphs are still selected, and then click the **Font Size** arrow in the Font group to display a menu of font sizes. As with the Font menu, you can move the pointer over options in the Font Size menu to see a Live Preview of that option.

9. On the Font Size menu, click **22**. The selected text increases significantly in size and the Font Size menu closes.

10. Select the three paragraphs of text below the photo, format them in the Arial font, and then increase the paragraphs' font size to 22 points.

11. Click a blank area of the document to deselect the text, and then save the document.

Tim examines the flyer and decides he would like to apply more character formatting, which affects the appearance of individual characters, in the middle three paragraphs. After that, you can turn your attention to paragraph formatting, which affects the appearance of the entire paragraph.

Applying Text Effects, Font Colors, and Font Styles

To really make text stand out, you can use text effects. You access these options by clicking the Text Effects button in the Font group on the HOME tab. Keep in mind that text effects can be very dramatic. For formal, professional documents, you probably only need to use **bold** or *italic* to make a word or paragraph stand out.

Tim suggests applying text effects to the second paragraph.

To apply text effects to the second paragraph:

1. Scroll up, if necessary, to display the beginning of the document, and then click in the selection bar to the left of the second paragraph. The entire second paragraph is selected.

2. In the Font group on the HOME tab, click the **Text Effects and Typography** button [A ▾].

 A gallery of text effects appears. Options that allow you to fine-tune a particular text effect, perhaps by changing the color or adding an even more pronounced shadow, are listed below the gallery. A gallery is a menu or grid that shows a visual representation of the options available when you click a button.

3. In the middle of the bottom row of the gallery, place the pointer over the blue letter "A." This displays a ScreenTip with the text effect's full name, which is "Fill - Blue, Accent 1, Outline - Background 1, Hard Shadow - Accent 1." A Live Preview of the effect appears in the document. See Figure 1-29.

Figure 1-29 **Live Preview of a text effect**

Courtesy of Ann Shaffer

4. In the bottom row of the gallery, click the blue letter "A." The text effect is applied to the selected paragraph and the Text Effects gallery closes. The second paragraph is formatted in blue, as shown in the Session 1.2 Visual Overview. The Bold button in the Font group is now highlighted because bold formatting is part of this text effect.

Next, to make the text stand out a bit more, you'll increase the font size. This time, instead of using the Font Size button, you'll use a different method.

5. In the Font group, click the **Increase Font Size** button A˄. The font size increases from 22 points to 24 points.

6. Click the **Increase Font Size** button A˄ again. The font size increases to 26 points. If you need to decrease the font size of selected text, you can use the Decrease Font Size button.

Tim asks you to emphasize the third and fourth paragraphs by adding bold and a blue font color.

To apply a font color and bold:

1. Select the third and fourth paragraphs of text, which contain the class name as well as the dates and times.

2. In the Font group on the Home tab, click the **Font Color button arrow** A ˅. A gallery of font colors appears. Black is the default font color and appears at the top of the Font Color gallery, with the word "Automatic" next to it.

The options in the Theme Colors section of the menu are complementary colors that work well when used together in a document. The options in the Standard Colors section are more limited. For more advanced color options, you could use the More Colors or Gradient options. Tim prefers a simple blue.

Trouble? If the class name turned red, you clicked the Font Color button A instead of the arrow next to it. On the Quick Access Toolbar, click the Undo button ↶, and then repeat Step 2.

3. In the Theme Colors section, place the mouse pointer over the square that's second from the right in the top row. A ScreenTip with the color's name, "Blue, Accent 5," appears. A Live Preview of the color appears in the document, where the text you selected in Step 1 now appears formatted in blue. See Figure 1-30.

Figure 1-30	Font Color gallery showing a Live Preview

Courtesy of Ann Shaffer

4. Click the **Blue, Accent 5** square. The Font color gallery closes, and the selected text is formatted in blue. On the Font Color button, the bar below the letter "A" is now blue, indicating that if you select text and click the Font Color button, the text will automatically change to blue.

5. In the Font group, click the **Bold** button **B**. The selected text is now formatted in bold, with thicker, darker lettering.

TIP

You can use other buttons in the Font group on the HOME tab to apply other character attributes, such as underline, italic, or superscript.

Next, you will complete some paragraph formatting, starting with paragraph alignment.

Aligning Text

Alignment refers to how text and graphics line up between the page margins. By default, Word aligns text along the left margin, with the text along the right margin **ragged**, or uneven. This is called **left alignment**. With **right alignment**, the text is aligned along the right margin and is ragged along the left margin. With **center alignment**, text is centered between the left and right margins and is ragged along both the left and right margins. With **justified alignment**, full lines of text are spaced between both the left and the right margins, and no text is ragged. Text in newspaper columns is often justified. See Figure 1-31.

Figure 1-31	Varieties of text alignment

left alignment

The term "alignment" refers to the way a paragraph lines up between the margins. The term "alignment" refers to the way a paragraph lines up between the margins.

right alignment

The term "alignment" refers to the way a paragraph lines up between the margins. The term "alignment" refers to the way a paragraph lines up between the margins.

center alignment

The term "alignment" refers to the way a paragraph lines up between the margins.

justified alignment

The term "alignment" refers to the way a paragraph lines up between the margins. The term "alignment" refers to the way a paragraph lines up between the margins.

© 2014 Cengage Learning

The Paragraph group on the HOME tab includes a button for each of the four major types of alignment described in Figure 1-31: the Align Left button, the Center button, the Align Right button, and the Justify button. To align a single paragraph, click anywhere in that paragraph, and then click the appropriate alignment button. To align multiple paragraphs, select the paragraphs first, and then click an alignment button.

You need to center all the text in the flyer now. You can center the photo at the same time.

To center-align the text:

Use the Ctrl+A keys to select the entire document, instead of dragging the mouse pointer. It's easy to miss part of the document when you drag the mouse pointer.

1. Press the **Ctrl+A** keys to select the entire document, and make sure the HOME tab is still selected.

2. In the Paragraph group, click the **Center** button ☰, and then click a blank area of the document to deselect the selected paragraphs. The text and photo are now centered on the page, similar to the centered text shown earlier in the Session 1.2 Visual Overview.

3. Save the document.

Adding a Paragraph Border and Shading

A **paragraph border** is an outline that appears around one or more paragraphs in a document. You can choose to apply only a partial border—for example, a bottom border that appears as an underline under the last line of text in the paragraph—or an entire box around a paragraph. You can select different colors and line weights for the border as well, making it more prominent or less prominent as needed. You apply paragraph borders using the Borders button in the Paragraph group on the HOME tab. **Shading** is background color that you can apply to one or more paragraphs and can be used in conjunction with a border for a more defined effect. You apply shading using the Shading button in the Paragraph group on the HOME tab.

Now you will apply a border and shading to the first paragraph, as shown earlier in the Session 1.2 Visual Overview. Then you will use the Format Painter to copy this formatting to the last paragraph in the document.

To add shading and a paragraph border:

1. Select the first paragraph. Be sure to select the paragraph mark at the end of the paragraph.

2. On the HOME tab, in the Paragraph group, click the **Borders button arrow**. A gallery of border options appears, as shown in Figure 1-32. To apply a complete outline around the selected text, you use the Outside Borders option.

Figure 1-32 **Border gallery**

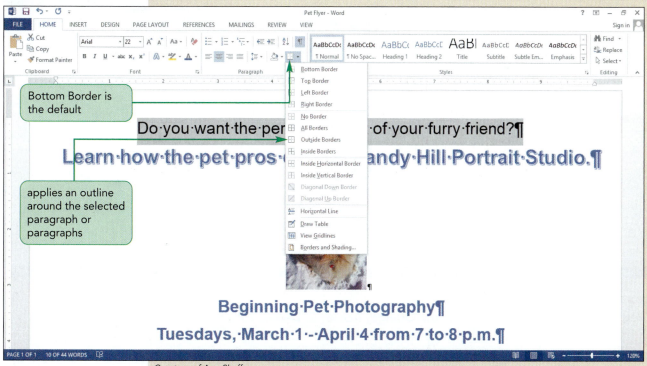

Courtesy of Ann Shaffer

Trouble? If the gallery does not open, and instead the paragraph becomes underlined with a single underline, you clicked the Borders button instead of the arrow next to it. On the Quick Access Toolbar, click the Undo button, and then repeat Step 2.

3. In the Border gallery, click **Outside Borders**. The menu closes and a black border appears around the selected paragraph, spanning the width of the page. In the Paragraph group, the Borders button changes to show the Outside Borders option.

 Trouble? If the border around the first paragraph doesn't extend all the way to the left and right margins, and instead only encloses the text, you didn't select the paragraph mark as directed in Step 1. Click the Undo button 🔄 repeatedly to remove the border, and begin again with Step 1.

4. In the Paragraph group, click the **Shading button arrow** 🎨▾. A gallery of shading options opens, divided into Theme Colors and Standard Colors. You will use a shade of orange in the sixth column from the left.

5. In the second row from the bottom in the Theme Colors section, move the pointer over the square in the sixth column from the left to display a ScreenTip that reads "Orange, Accent 2, Darker 25%." A Live Preview of the color appears in the document. See Figure 1-33.

Figure 1-33	**Shading gallery with a Live Preview displayed**

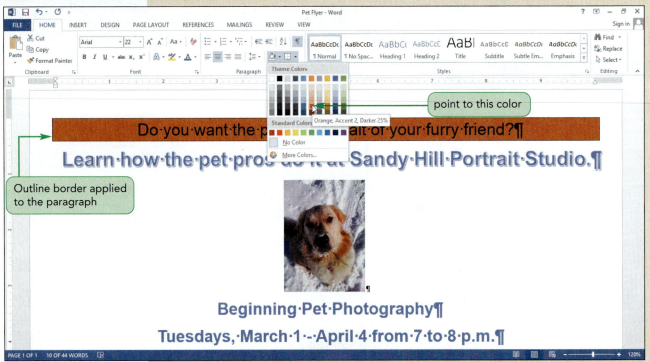

Courtesy of Ann Shaffer

6. Click the **Orange, Accent 2, Darker 25%** square to apply the shading to the selected text.

 On a dark background like the one you just applied, a white font creates a striking effect. Tim asks you to change the font color for this paragraph to white.

7. Make sure the HOME tab is still selected.

8. In the Font group, click the **Font Color button arrow** 🅰▾ to open the Font Color gallery, and then click the **white** square in the top row of the Theme Colors. The Font Color gallery closes and the paragraph is now formatted with white font.

9. Click a blank area of the document to deselect the text, review the change, and then save the document. See Figure 1-34.

Figure 1-34 **Paragraph formatted with dark orange shading, a black border, and white font**

To add balance to the flyer, Tim suggests formatting the last paragraph in the document with the same shading, border, and font color as the first paragraph. You'll do that next.

Copying Formatting with the Format Painter

You could select the last paragraph and then apply the border, shading, and font color one step at a time. But it's easier to copy all the formatting from the first paragraph to the last paragraph using the Format Painter button in the Clipboard group on the HOME tab.

REFERENCE

Using the Format Painter

- Select the text whose formatting you want to copy.
- On the HOME tab, in the Clipboard group, click the Format Painter button; or to copy formatting to multiple sections of nonadjacent text, double-click the Format Painter button.
- The mouse pointer changes to the Format Painter pointer, the I-beam pointer with a paintbrush.
- Click the words you want to format, or drag to select and format entire paragraphs.
- When you are finished formatting the text, click the Format Painter button again to turn off the Format Painter.

You'll use the Format Painter now.

To use the Format Painter:

1. Change the document Zoom level to **One Page** so you can easily see both the first and last paragraphs.

2. Select the first paragraph, which is formatted with the dark orange shading, the border, and the white font color.

3. On the ribbon, click the HOME tab.

4. In the Clipboard group, click the **Format Painter** button to activate, or turn on, the Format Painter.

5. Move the pointer over the document. The pointer changes to the Format Painter pointer 🖌I when you move the mouse pointer near an item that can be formatted. See Figure 1-35.

Figure 1-35 **Format Painter**

Format Painter is turned on

Format Painter copies the formatting of the selected paragraph

paintbrush pointer

Courtesy of Ann Shaffer

TIP

To turn off the Format Painter without using it, press the Esc key.

6. Click and drag the Format Painter pointer to select the last paragraph in the document. The paragraph is now formatted with dark orange shading, a black border, and white font. The mouse pointer returns to its original I-beam shape.

 Trouble? If the text in the newly formatted paragraph wrapped to a second line, replace your full name with your first name, or, if necessary, use only your initials so the paragraph is only one line long.

7. Click anywhere in the document to deselect the text, review the change, and then save the document.

You're almost finished working on the document's paragraph formatting. Your last step is to increase the paragraph spacing below the first paragraph and above the last paragraph. This will give the shaded text even more weight on the page. To complete this task, you will use the settings on the PAGE LAYOUT tab, which offer more options than the Line and Paragraph Spacing button on the HOME tab.

To increase the paragraph spacing below the first paragraph and above the last paragraph:

1. Click anywhere in the first paragraph, and then click the **PAGE LAYOUT** tab. On this tab, the Paragraph group contains settings that control paragraph spacing. Currently, the paragraph spacing for the first paragraph is set to the default 0 points before the paragraph and 8 points after.

2. In the Paragraph group, click the **After** box to select the current setting, type **42**, and then press the **Enter** key. The added space causes the second paragraph to move down 42 points.

3. Click anywhere in the last paragraph.

4. On the PAGE LAYOUT tab, in the Paragraph group, click the **Before** box to select the current setting, type **42**, and then press the **Enter** key. The added space causes the last paragraph to move down 42 points.

INSIGHT

Formatting Professional Documents

In more formal documents, use color and special effects sparingly. The goal of letters, reports, and many other types of documents is to convey important information, not to dazzle the reader with fancy fonts and colors. Such elements only serve to distract the reader from your main point. In formal documents, it's a good idea to limit the number of colors to two and to stick with left alignment for text. In a document like the flyer you're currently working on, you have a little more leeway because the goal of the document is to attract attention. However, you still want it to look professional.

Finally, Tim wants you to replace the photo of the golden retriever with one that will look better in the document's new landscape orientation. You'll replace the photo, and then you'll resize it so the flyer fills the entire page.

Working with Pictures

A **picture** is a photo or another type of image that you insert into a document. To work with a picture, you first need to select it. Once a picture is selected, a contextual tab—the PICTURE TOOLS FORMAT tab—appears on the ribbon, with options for editing the picture and adding effects such as a border, a shadow, a reflection, or a new shape. A **contextual tab** appears on the ribbon only when an object is selected. It contains commands related to the selected object so you can manipulate, edit, and format the selected object. You can also use the mouse to resize or move a selected picture. To insert a new picture, you use the Pictures button in the Illustrations group on the INSERT tab.

To delete the current photo and insert a new one:

▶ **1.** Click the photo to select it.

The squares, called **handles**, around the edge of the photo indicate the photo is selected. The Layout Options button, to the right of the photo, gives you access to options that control how the document text flows around the photo. You don't need to worry about these options now. Finally, note that the PICTURE TOOLS FORMAT tab appeared on the ribbon when you selected the photo. See Figure 1-36.

Figure 1-36 **Selected photo**

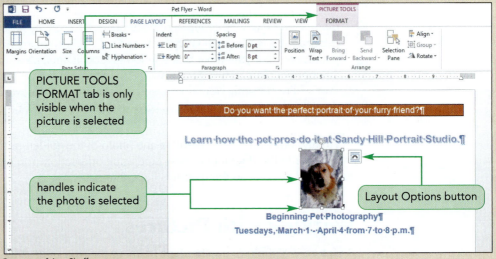

Courtesy of Ann Shaffer

> **2.** Press the **Delete** key. The photo is deleted from the document. The insertion point blinks next to the paragraph symbol. You will insert the new photo in that paragraph.

> **3.** On the ribbon, click the **INSERT** tab. The ribbon changes to display the Insert options.

> **4.** In the Illustrations group, click the **Pictures** button. The Insert Picture dialog box opens.

> **5.** Navigate to the Word1 ▸ Tutorial folder included with your Data Files, and then click **Poodle** to select the file. The name of the selected file appears in the File name box.

> **6.** Click the **Insert** button to close the Insert Picture dialog box and insert the photo. An image of a black poodle appears in the document, below the text. The photo is selected, as indicated by the handles that appear on its border.

Now you need to enlarge the photo to fit the available space on the page. You could do so by clicking one of the picture's corner handles, holding down the mouse button, and then dragging the handle to resize the picture. But using the Shape Height and Shape Width boxes on the PICTURE TOOLS FORMAT tab gives you more precise results.

To resize the photo:

> **1.** Make sure the PICTURE TOOLS FORMAT tab is still selected on the ribbon.

> **2.** In the Size group on the far right edge of the ribbon, locate the Shape Height box, which tells you that the height of the selected picture is currently 2.46". The Shape Width box tells you that the width of the picture is 3.69". As you'll see in the next step, when you change one of these measurements, the other changes accordingly, keeping the overall shape of the picture the same. See Figure 1-37.

| Figure 1-37 | Shape Height and Shape Width boxes |

Courtesy of Ann Shaffer

▶ **3.** Click the **up arrow** in the Shape Height box in the Size group. The photo increases in size slightly. The measurement in the Shape Height box increases to 2.5" and the measurement in the Shape Width box increases to 3.75".

▶ **4.** Click the **up arrow** in the Shape Height box repeatedly until the picture is 3.3" tall and 4.95" wide.

Finally, to make the photo more noticeable, you can add a **picture style**, which is a collection of formatting options, such as a frame, a rounded shape, and a shadow. You can apply a picture style to a selected picture by clicking the style you want in the Picture Styles gallery on the PICTURE TOOLS FORMAT tab. In the following steps, you'll start by displaying the gallery.

To add a style to the photo:

▶ **1.** Make sure the PICTURE TOOLS FORMAT tab is still selected on the ribbon.

▶ **2.** In the Picture Styles group, click the **More** button to the right of the Picture Styles gallery to open the gallery and display more picture styles. Some of the picture styles simply add a border, while others change the picture's shape. Other styles combine these options with effects such as a shadow or a reflection.

▶ **3.** Place the mouse pointer over various styles to observe the Live Previews in the document, and then place the mouse pointer over the Drop Shadow Rectangle style, which is the middle style in the top row. See Figure 1-38.

Figure 1-38 Previewing a picture style

place the mouse pointer over this style

Live Preview of the picture style

Courtesy of Ann Shaffer

TIP

To return a picture to its original appearance, click the Reset Picture button in the Adjust group on the PICTURE TOOLS FORMAT tab.

4. In the gallery, click the **Drop Shadow Rectangle** style to apply it to the photo and close the gallery. The photo is formatted with a shadow on the bottom and right sides, as shown earlier in the Session 1.2 Visual Overview.

5. Click anywhere outside the photo to deselect it, and then, save the document.

6. Click the **FILE** tab, and then click **Close** in the navigation bar to close the document without closing Word.

INSIGHT

Working with Inline Pictures

By default, when you insert a picture in a document, it is treated as an inline object, which means its position changes in the document as you add or delete text. Also, because it is an inline object, you can align the picture just as you would align text, using the alignment buttons in the Paragraph group on the HOME tab. Essentially, you can treat an inline picture as just another paragraph.

When you become a more advanced Word user, you'll learn how to wrap text around a picture so that the text flows around the picture—with the picture maintaining its position on the page no matter how much text you add to or delete from the document. The alignment buttons don't work on pictures that have text wrapped around them. Instead, you can drag the picture to the desired position on the page.

The flyer is complete and ready for Tim to print later. Because Tim is considering creating a promotional brochure that would include numerous photographs, he asks you to look up information about other ways to format a picture. You can do that using Word's Help system.

Getting Help

To get the most out of Help, your computer must be connected to the Internet so it can access the reference information stored at Office.com.

To look up information in Help:

TIP

You can also open the Word Help window by pressing the F1 key.

1. Verify that your computer is connected to the Internet, and then, on the title bar, click the **Microsoft Word Help** button ⁇. The Word Help window opens, with its Home page displayed. You might see the topics shown in Figure 1-39, or you might see other topics. You can click the various options in the Word Help window to browse among topics, or you can use the Search online help box to look up information on a particular topic.

Figure 1-39 Word Help window

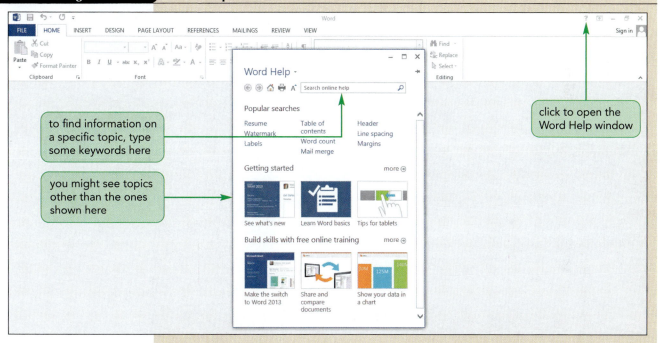

to find information on a specific topic, type some keywords here

you might see topics other than the ones shown here

click to open the Word Help window

2. Click in the **Search online help** box, type **format picture**, and then press the **Enter** key. The Word Help window displays a list of articles related to inserting pictures in a document.

3. Click the first topic listed, and then read the article to see if it contains any information about formatting pictures that might be useful to Tim. Note that to print information about a topic, you can click the Print button near the top of the Word Help window.

4. When are you finished reading the article, click the **Back** button ⬅ near the top of the Word Help window to return to the previous list of topics.

5. Click the **Home** button 🏠 to return to the Home page.

6. Click the **Close** button ❌ in the upper-right corner to close the Word Help window.

Word Help is a great way to learn more about Word's many features. Articles on basic skills provide step-by-step guides for completing tasks, while more elaborate, online tutorials walk you through more complicated tasks. Be sure to take some time on your own to explore Word Help so you can find the information you want when you need it.

REVIEW

Session 1.2 Quick Check

1. Explain how to open the Spelling and Grammar task panes.
2. What is the default page orientation for Word documents?
3. What is the default font size?
4. Explain how to use the Format Painter button.
5. What button do you use to insert a photo in a document?
6. Explain how to open the Help window.

SAM Projects

Put your skills into practice with SAM Projects! SAM Projects for this tutorial can be found online. If you have a SAM account, go to www.cengage.com/sam2013 to download the most recent Project Instructions and Start Files.

Review Assignments

Data Files needed for the Review Assignments: Flower.docx, Mixed Flowers.jpg

Tim asks you to write a cover letter to accompany a wedding photography contract. After that, he wants you to create an envelope for the letter, and to format a flyer announcing a class about photographing flowers. Change the Zoom level as necessary while you are working. Complete the following steps:

1. Open a new, blank document and then save the document as **Sommer Letter** in the location specified by your instructor.
2. Type the date **February 16, 2016** using AutoComplete for "February."
3. Press the Enter key twice, and then type the following inside address, using the default paragraph spacing and pressing the Enter key once after each line:

 Kiley Sommer
 2355 Greenwillow Drive
 Baltimore, MD 21204

4. Type **Dear Ms. Sommer:** as the salutation, press the Enter key, and then type the following as the body of the letter:

 Enclosed you will find the contract summarizing our plans for your wedding. Please return your signed copy to me by next Monday, along with the down payment specified in the contract.

 As you'll see, the second page of the contract lists the specific shots we've already agreed on. For more ideas about possible group shots, please see our website at www.sandyhillstudio. cengage.com. Of course, the photographer will be taking candid shots throughout the day.

5. Press the Enter key, type **Sincerely yours,** as the complimentary closing, press the Enter key three times, type **Tim Bartolutti** as the signature line, insert a manual line break, and type **Sales Manager** as his title.
6. Press the Enter key, type your initials, insert a manual line break, and then use the Undo button to make your initials all lowercase, if necessary.
7. Type **Enclosure** and save the document.
8. Scroll to the beginning of the document and proofread your work. Remove any wavy underlines by using a shortcut menu or by typing a correction yourself. Remove the hyperlink formatting from the web address.
9. Remove the paragraph spacing from the first two lines of the inside address.
10. Change the top margin to 2.75 inches. Leave the other margins at their default settings.
11. Save your changes to the letter, preview it, print it if your instructor asks you to, and then close it.
12. Create a new, blank document, and then create an envelope. Use Kiley Sommer's address (from Step 3) as the delivery address. Use your school's name and address for the return address. Add the envelope to the document. If you are asked if you want to save the return address as the new return address, click No.

13. Save the document as **Sommer Envelope** in the location specified by your instructor, and then close the document.

14. Open the file **Flower**, located in the Word1 ▶ Review folder included with your Data Files, and then check your screen to make sure your settings match those in the tutorial.

15. Save the document as **Flower Flyer** in the location specified by your instructor.

16. Configure the grammar settings to check for subject-verb agreement errors, and then use the Spelling and Grammar task panes to correct any errors marked with wavy underlines. When you are finished, return the grammar settings to their original configuration.

17. Proofread the document and correct any other errors. Be sure to change "gardens" to "garden's" in the first paragraph.

18. Change the page orientation to Landscape and the margins to Narrow.

19. Format the document text in 22-point Times New Roman font.

20. Center the text and the photo.

21. Format the first paragraph with an outside border, and then add green shading, using the Green, Accent 6, Darker 25% color in the Theme Colors section of the Shading gallery. Format the paragraph text in white.

22. Format the last paragraph in the document using the same formatting you applied to the first paragraph.

23. Increase the paragraph spacing after the first paragraph to 42 points. Increase the paragraph spacing before the last paragraph in the document to 42 points.

24. Format the second paragraph with the Fill - Orange, Accent 2, Outline - Accent 2 text effect. Increase the paragraph's font size to 26 points.

25. Format the third and fourth paragraphs (containing the class name, date, and time) in green, using the Green, Accent 6, Darker 50% font color, and then add bold and italic.

26. Delete the photo and replace it with the **Mixed Flowers.jpg** photo, located in the Word1 ▶ Review folder included with your Data Files.

27. Resize the new photo so that it is 3.8" tall, and then add the Soft Edge Rectangle style in the Pictures Styles gallery.

28. Save your changes to the flyer, preview it, and then close it.

29. Start Word Help and look up the topic "work with pictures." Read the article, return to the Help home page, and then close Help.

Case Problem 1

APPLY

There are no Data Files needed for this Case Problem.

Prairie Public Health Consultants You are a program administrator at Prairie Public Health Consultants. Over the past few months, you have collected handwritten surveys from high school students about their exercise habits. Now you need to send the surveys to the researcher in charge of compiling the data. Create a cover letter to accompany the surveys by completing the following steps. Because your office is currently out of letterhead, you'll start the letter by typing a return address. As you type the letter, remember to include the appropriate number of blank paragraphs between the various parts of the letter. Complete the following steps:

1. Open a new, blank document, and then save the document as **Prairie Letter** in the location specified by your instructor. If necessary, change the Zoom level to 120%.

2. Type the following return address, using the default paragraph spacing, and replacing [Your Name] with your first and last names:

[Your Name]

Prairie Public Health Consultants

6833 Erickson Lane

Des Moines, IA 50301

3. Type **November 7, 2016** as the date, leaving a blank paragraph between the last line of the return address and the date.

4. Type the following inside address, using the default paragraph spacing and leaving the appropriate number of blank paragraphs after the date:

Dr. Anna Witinski

4643 University Circle

Ames, IA 50010

5. Type **Dear Dr. Witinski:** as the salutation.

6. To begin the body of the letter, type the following paragraph:

Enclosed please find the surveys I have collected so far. I hope to have another 200 for you in a week, but I thought you would like to get started on these now. After you've had a chance to review the surveys, please call or email me with your answers to these questions:

7. Add the following questions as separate paragraphs, using the default paragraph spacing:

Do you need help tabulating the survey responses?

Should we consider expanding the survey to additional schools?

Should we rephrase any of the survey questions?

8. Insert a new paragraph before the second question, and then add the following as the new second question in the list:

Have you hired a student to help you with your analysis?

9. Insert a new paragraph after the last question, and then type the complimentary closing **Sincerely,** (including the comma).

10. Leave the appropriate amount of space for your signature, type your full name, insert a manual line break, and then type **Program Administrator**.

11. Type **Enclosure** in the appropriate place.

12. Use the Spelling and Grammar task panes to correct any errors. Instruct the Spelling task pane to ignore the recipient's name.

13. Italicize the four paragraphs containing the questions.

14. Remove the paragraph spacing from the first three lines of the return address. Do the same for the first two paragraphs of the inside address.

15. Center the four paragraphs containing the return address, format them in 16-point font, and then add the Fill - Black, Text 1, Shadow text effect.

16. Save the document, preview it, and then close it.

17. Create a new, blank document, and create an envelope. Use Dr. Witinski's address (from Step 4) as the delivery address. Use the return address shown in Step 2. Add the envelope to the document. If you are asked if you want to save the return address as the new return address, click No.

18. Save the document as **Witinski Envelope** in the location specified by your instructor, and then close the document.

CREATE

Case Problem 2

Data Files needed for this Case Problem: Church.jpg, Walking.docx

Walking Tours of Old San Juan You work as the guest services coordinator at Hotel Azul, a luxury resort hotel in San Juan, Puerto Rico. You need to create a flyer promoting a daily walking tour of Old San Juan, the historic Colonial section of Puerto Rico's capital city. Complete the following steps:

1. Open the file **Walking** located in the Word1 ▸ Case2 folder included with your Data Files, and then save the document as **Walking Tour Flyer** in the location specified by your instructor.

2. In the document, replace "Student Name" with your first and last names.

3. Use the Spelling and Grammar task panes to correct any errors, including problems with subject-verb agreement. Instruct the Spelling task pane to ignore the Spanish church names, as well as your name if Word marks it with a wavy underline.

4. Change the page margins to Narrow.

5. Complete the flyer as shown in Figure 1-40. Use the file **Church.jpg** located in the Word1 ▸ Case2 folder included with your Data Files. Use the default line spacing and paragraph spacing unless otherwise specified in Figure 1-40.

Figure 1-40 **Formatted Walking Tour flyer**

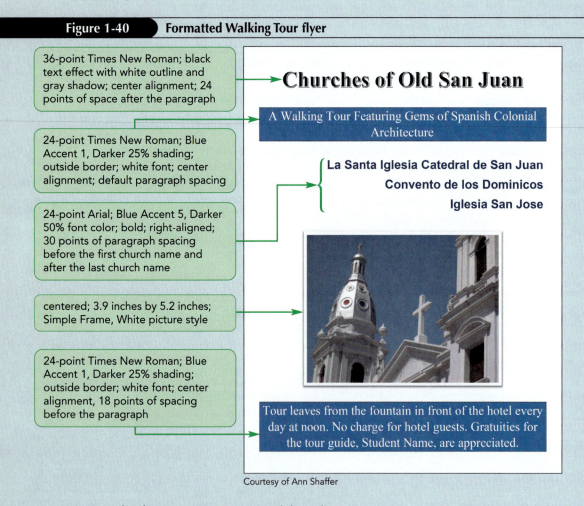

36-point Times New Roman; black text effect with white outline and gray shadow; center alignment; 24 points of space after the paragraph

24-point Times New Roman; Blue Accent 1, Darker 25% shading; outside border; white font; center alignment; default paragraph spacing

24-point Arial; Blue Accent 5, Darker 50% font color; bold; right-aligned; 30 points of paragraph spacing before the first church name and after the last church name

centered; 3.9 inches by 5.2 inches; Simple Frame, White picture style

24-point Times New Roman; Blue Accent 1, Darker 25% shading; outside border; white font; center alignment, 18 points of spacing before the paragraph

Churches of Old San Juan

A Walking Tour Featuring Gems of Spanish Colonial Architecture

La Santa Iglesia Catedral de San Juan

Convento de los Dominicos

Iglesia San Jose

Tour leaves from the fountain in front of the hotel every day at noon. No charge for hotel guests. Gratuities for the tour guide, Student Name, are appreciated.

Courtesy of Ann Shaffer

6. Save the document, preview it, and then close it.

TROUBLESHOOT

Case Problem 3

Data Files needed for this Case Problem: Mushroom.docx, Mycology.docx

Green Valley Arborists You work as the office manager for Green Valley Arborists, a tree care service in Billings, Montana. One of the company's arborists noticed a bright orange fungus growing on a tree stump in a client's backyard. She has started writing a letter to a mycologist at the local community college to ask if he can identify the fungus. The letter is almost finished, but the arborist needs help correcting errors and formatting the text to match the block style. The photo itself is stored in a separate document. The arborist mistakenly applied a picture style to the photo that is inappropriate for professional correspondence. She asks you to remove the picture style and then format the page. Complete the following steps:

1. Open the file **Mycology** located in the Word1 ▶ Case3 folder included with your Data Files, and then save the document as **Mycology Letter** in the location specified by your instructor.
2. Use the Spelling and Grammar task panes to correct any errors, including subject-verb errors. When you are finished, return the Grammar settings to their original configuration.

⚙ **Troubleshoot** 3. Make any necessary changes to ensure that the letter matches the formatting of a block style business letter, including the appropriate paragraph spacing. Keep in mind that the letter will include an enclosure. Include your initials where appropriate.

⚙ **Troubleshoot** 4. The letterhead for Green Valley Arborists requires a top margin of 2.5 inches. Determine if the layout of the letter will work with the letterhead, make any necessary changes, and then save the letter.

5. Save the document and preview it.
6. With the letter still open, create an envelope. Use the delivery address taken from the letter, but edit the delivery address. Click the Omit check box to deselect it (if necessary), and then, for the return address, type your school's name and address. Add the envelope to the document. If you are asked if you want to save the return address as the new default return address, answer No.
7. Save the document, preview it, and then close it.
8. Open the file **Mushroom** located in the Word1 ▶ Case3 folder included with your Data Files, and then save the document as **Mushroom Photo** in the location specified by your instructor.

⚙ **Troubleshoot** 9. Reset the picture to its original appearance, before the arborist mistakenly added the style with the reflection.

⚙ **Troubleshoot** 10. Modify the page layout and adjust the size of the photo so the photo fills as much of the page as possible without overlapping the page margins.

11. Save the document, preview it, and then close it.

Case Problem 4

There are no Data Files needed for this Case Problem.

Hapsburg Interior Design As a design assistant at Hapsburg Interior Design, you are responsible for distributing manufacturer samples throughout the office so the firm's designers can stay up to date on newly available paint colors, wallpaper patterns, and fabrics. Along with each sample, you need to include an explanatory memo. Complete the following steps:

✚ **Explore** 1. Open a new document—but instead of selecting the Blank document option, search for a memo template online. In the list of search results, click the Memo (Simple design) template, and then click the Create button. A memo template opens in the Word window. Above the memo template is the Document Properties panel, where you could enter information about the document that might be useful later. You don't need the panel for this project, so you can ignore it, as well as any entries in the text boxes in the panel.

2. Save the document as **Samples Memo** in the location specified by your instructor. If you see a dialog box indicating that the document will be upgraded to the newest file format, click the OK button. Note that of the hundreds of templates available online, only a small portion have been created in the most recent version of Word, so you will often see this dialog box when working with templates.

✚ **Explore** 3. In the document, click the text "[Company name]." The placeholder text appears in a box with gray highlighting. The box containing the highlighted text (with the small rectangle attached) is called a document control. You can enter text in a document control just as you enter text in a dialog box. Type **Hapsburg Interior Design**, and then press the Tab key. The "[Recipient names]" placeholder text now appears in a document control next to the word "To." (*Hint*: As you work on the memo in the following steps, keep in mind that if you accidentally double-click the word "memo" at the top of the document, you will access the header portion of the document, which normally closed to editing. In that case, press the Esc key to return to the main document.)

4. Type **All Designers** and then press the Tab key twice. A document control is now visible to the right of the word "From." Depending on how your computer is set up, you might see your name or another name here, or the document control might be empty. Delete the name, if necessary, and then type your first and last names.

✚ **Explore** 5. Continue using the Tab key to edit the remaining document controls as indicated below. If you press the Tab key too many times and accidentally skip a document control, you can click the document control to select it.

 • In the CC: document control, delete the placeholder text.
 • In the Date document control, click the down arrow, and then click the current date in the calendar.
 • In the Re: document control, type **Rowley Fabrics**.
 • In the Comments document control, type **Here are the latest offerings from Rowley Fabrics. After you have reviewed the collection, please write your initials at the bottom of this memo and pass the collection on to another designer. If you are the last of the group to review the samples, please return them to my desk. Thank you.**

6. Use the Spelling and Grammar task panes to correct any underlined errors, and then proofread the document to look for any additional errors.

7. Save the document, preview it, and then close it.

Navigating and Formatting a Document

Editing an Academic Document According to MLA Style

OBJECTIVES

Session 2.1
- Read, reply to, delete, and add comments
- Create bulleted and numbered lists
- Move text using drag and drop
- Cut and paste text
- Copy and paste text
- Navigate through a document using the Navigation pane
- Find and replace text
- Format text with styles
- Apply a theme to a document

Session 2.2
- Review the MLA style for research papers
- Indent paragraphs
- Insert and modify page numbers
- Create citations
- Create and update a bibliography
- Modify a source

Case | *Rivas-Garcia College*

Kaya Cho, a student at Rivas-Garcia College, works part-time in the college's Media Studies department. She has written a handout describing the requirements for a Media Studies major, and asks you to help her finish it. The text of the handout needs some reorganization and other editing. It also needs formatting so the finished document looks professional and is easy to read.

Kaya is also taking a Media Studies class this semester, and is writing a research paper on the history of newspapers. To complete the paper, she needs to follow a set of very specific formatting and style guidelines for academic documents.

Kaya has asked you to help her edit these two very different documents. In Session 2.1, you will review and respond to some comments in the handout, and then revise and format that document. In Session 2.2, you will review the MLA style for research papers, and then format Kaya's research paper to match the MLA specifications.

STARTING DATA FILES

Word2 → **Tutorial**
Media.docx
Newspaper.docx

Review
Broadcast.docx
Situation.docx

Case1
Yoga.docx

Case2
Hamlet.docx

Case3
Capital.docx
Sarah.docx

Case4
Movie.docx

Session 2.1 Visual Overview:

Use the Bullets button to create a bulleted list from selected paragraphs.

Use the Numbering button to create a numbered list from selected paragraphs.

Click the **Search for more things button** to access advanced search tools, or to select something to search for besides text.

The **Navigation pane** allows you to search for text in the document, with the results highlighted in yellow in the document.

You can type the text you want to search for here.

This text is formatted with the Heading 1 style for the Office theme.

The **bullet** before each of these paragraphs identifies the four paragraphs as items in a list.

This document has two pages.

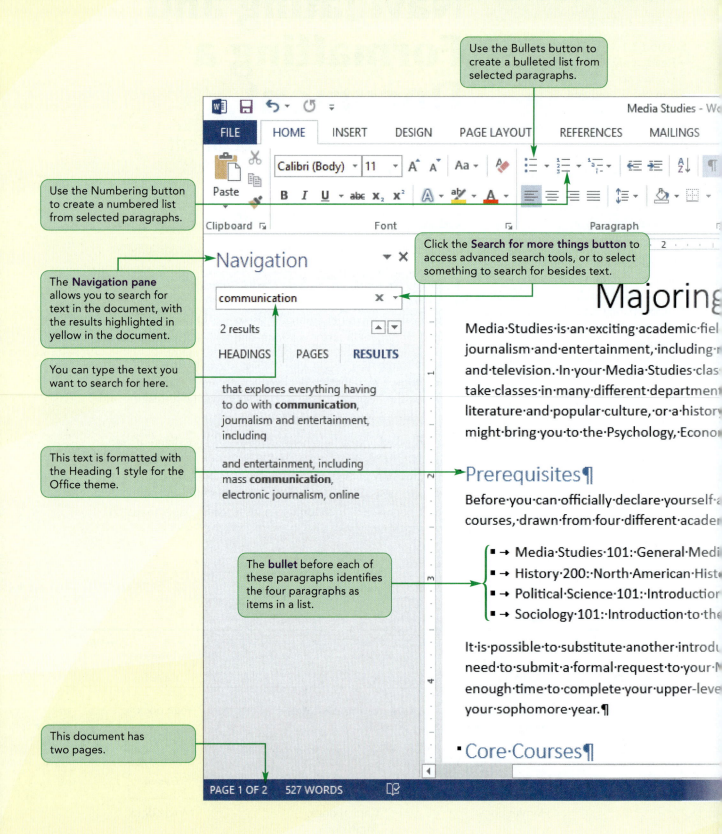

Working with Lists and Styles

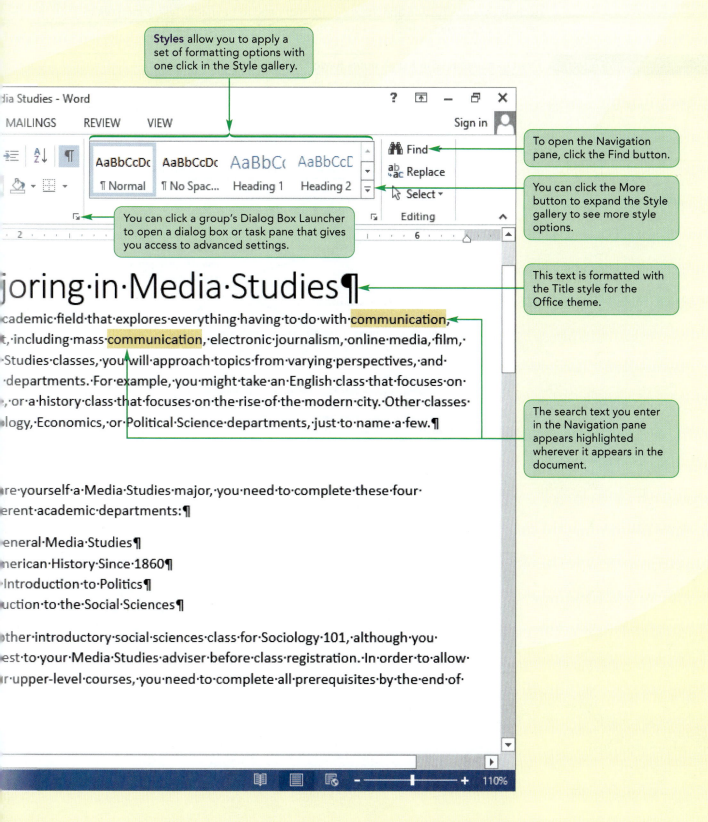

Styles allow you to apply a set of formatting options with one click in the Style gallery.

To open the Navigation pane, click the Find button.

You can click the More button to expand the Style gallery to see more style options.

You can click a group's Dialog Box Launcher to open a dialog box or task pane that gives you access to advanced settings.

This text is formatted with the Title style for the Office theme.

The search text you enter in the Navigation pane appears highlighted wherever it appears in the document.

Reviewing the Document

Before revising a document for someone else, it's a good idea to familiarize yourself with its overall structure and the revisions that need to be made. Take a moment to review Kaya's notes, which are shown in Figure 2-1.

Figure 2-1 Draft of handout with Kaya's notes (page 1)

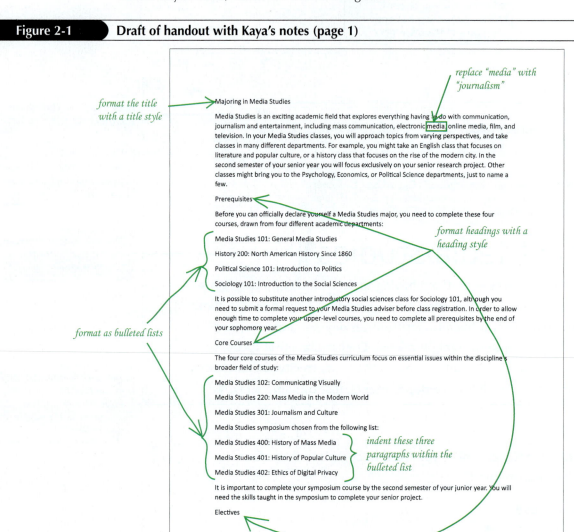

© 2014 Cengage Learning

Figure 2-1 Draft of handout with Kaya's notes (page 2)

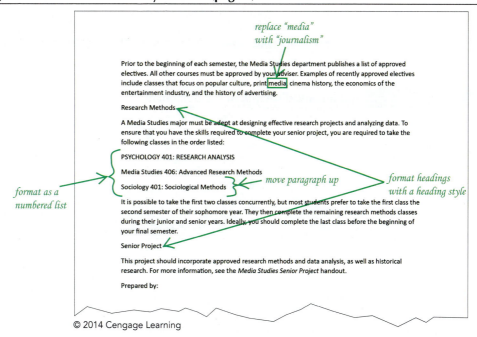

© 2014 Cengage Learning

Kaya also included additional guidance in some comments she added to the document file. A **comment** is like an electronic sticky note attached to a word, phrase, or paragraph in a document. Comments appear in the margin, along with the name of the person who added them. Within a single document, you can add new comments, reply to existing comments, and delete comments.

You will open the document now, save it with a new name, and then review Kaya's comments in Word.

To open and rename the document:

1. Open the document named **Media** located in the Word2 ▸ Tutorial folder included with your Data Files.

2. Save the document as **Media Studies** in the location specified by your instructor.

3. Verify that the document is displayed in Print Layout view, that the zoom is set to **120%**, and that the rulers and nonprinting characters are displayed.

4. On the ribbon, click the **REVIEW** tab to display the tools used for working with comments. Comments can be displayed in several different ways, so your first step is to make sure the comments in the Media Studies document are displayed to match the figures in this book—using Simple Markup view.

5. In the Tracking group, click the **Display for Review** arrow, and then click **Simple Markup** to select it, if necessary. At this point, you might see comment icons to the right of the document text, or you might see the full text of each comment.

6. In the Comments group, click the **Show Comments** button several times to practice displaying and hiding the comments, and then, when you are finished, make sure the Show Comments button is selected so the full text of each comment is displayed.

7. At the bottom of the Word window, drag the horizontal scroll bar all the way to the right so you can read the full text of each comment. See Figure 2-2. Note that the comments on your screen might be a different color than the ones shown in the figure.

Figure 2-2 **Comments displayed in the document**

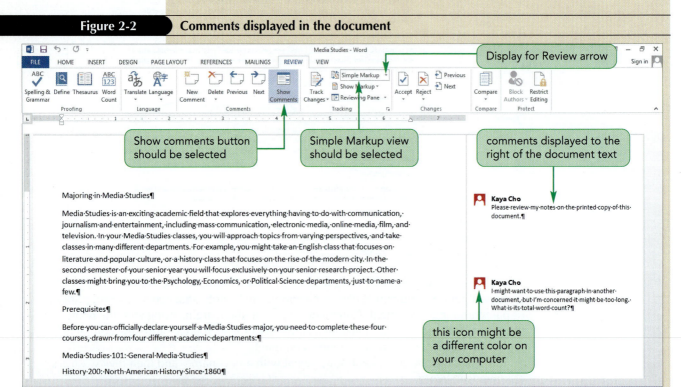

Note that when working on a small monitor, it can be helpful to switch the document Zoom level to Page Width, in which case Word automatically reduces the width of the document to accommodate the comments on the right.

8. Read the document, including the comments. The handout includes the title "Majoring in Media Studies" at the top, as well as headings (such as "Prerequisites" and "Core Courses") that divide the document into parts. Right now the headings are hard to spot because they don't look different from the surrounding text. Kaya used the default font size, 11-point, and the default font, Calibri (Body), for all the text in the document. Note, too, that the document includes some short paragraphs that would work better as bulleted or numbered lists.

9. Scroll down until you can see the first line on page 2, which begins "Prior to the beginning of each semester...." and then click anywhere in that sentence. The message "PAGE 2 OF 2" in the status bar, in the lower-left corner of the Word window, tells you that the insertion point is currently located on page 2 of the two-page document. The shaded space between the first and second pages of the document indicates a page break. To hide the top and bottom margins in a document, as well as the space between pages, you can double-click the shaded space between any two pages.

10. Position the mouse pointer over the shaded space between page 1 and page 2 until the pointer changes to ⇤⇥, and then double-click. The shaded space disappears. Instead, the two pages are now separated by a gray, horizontal line.

Trouble? If the HEADER & FOOTER TOOLS DESIGN tab appears on the ribbon, you double-clicked the top or bottom of one of the pages, instead of in the space between them. Click the Close Header and Footer button on the DESIGN tab, and then repeat Step 10.

▶ **11.** Use the ✥ pointer to double-click the gray horizontal line between pages 1 and 2. The shaded space between the two pages is redisplayed.

Working with Comments

Now that you are familiar with the Media Studies document, you can review and respond to Kaya's comments. The Comment group on the REVIEW tab includes helpful tools for working with comments.

Working with Comments

- On the ribbon, click the REVIEW tab.
- To display comments in an easy-to-read view, in the Tracking group, click the Display for Review button, and then click Simple Markup.
- To see the text of each comment in Simple Markup view, click the Show Comments button in the Comments group.
- To move the insertion point to the next or previous comment in the document, click the Next button or the Previous button in the Comments group.
- To delete a comment, click anywhere in the comment, and then click the Delete button in the Comments group.
- To delete all the comments in a document, click the Delete button arrow in the Comments group, and then click Delete All Comments in Document.
- To add a new comment, select the document text you want to comment on, click the New Comment button in the Comments group, and then type the comment text.
- To reply to a comment, click the Reply button to the right of the comment, and then type your reply.
- To indicate that a comment or an individual reply to a comment is no longer a concern, right-click the comment or reply, and then click Mark Comment Done in the shortcut menu. To mark a comment and all of the replies attached to it as done, right-click the original comment and then click Mark Comment Done.

To review and respond to the comments in the document:

▶ **1.** Press the **Ctrl+Home** keys to move the insertion point to the beginning of the document.

▶ **2.** On the REVIEW tab, in the Comments group, click the **Next** button. The first comment now has an outline, indicating that it is selected. See Figure 2-3.

In the document, the word "Majoring" is highlighted. A line connects the comment to the word "Majoring," indicating that the comment is attached to that word. Because Kaya created the comment, her name appears at the beginning of the comment, followed by the date on which she created it. The insertion point blinks at the beginning of the comment, and is ready for you to edit the comment if you want.

Figure 2-3	Comment attached to document text

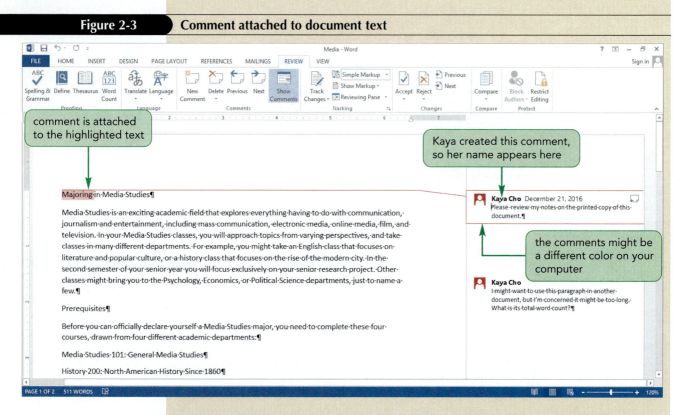

3. Read the comment, and then in the Comments group, click the **Next** button to select the next comment. According to this comment, Kaya wants to know the total word count of the paragraph the comment is attached to. You can get this information by selecting the entire paragraph and locating the word count in the status bar.

4. Triple-click anywhere in the second paragraph of the document (which begins "Media studies is an exciting academic field…") to select the paragraph. In the status bar, the message "110 of 511" tells you that 110 of the document's 511 words are currently selected. So the answer to Kaya's question is 110.

5. Point to the second comment to select it again, click the **Reply** button ⤶, and then type **110**. Your reply appears below Kaya's original comment.

Trouble? If you do not see the Reply button in the comment box, drag the horizontal scroll bar at the bottom of the Word window to the right until you can see it.

The name that appears in your reply comment is taken from the User name box in the General tab of the Word Options dialog box. If your name is the username for your computer, your name appears attached to the comment. If you are working on a shared computer at school, or on a computer owned by someone else, another name will appear in the comment.

You can quickly open the General tab of the Word Options dialog box by clicking the Dialog Box Launcher in the Tracking group on the REVIEW tab, and then clicking Change User Name. From there, you can change the username and the initials associated with your copy of Word. However, there is no need to change these settings for this tutorial, and you should never change them on a shared computer at school unless specifically instructed to do so by your instructor.

6. In the Comments group, click the **Next** button to move the insertion point to the next comment, which asks you to insert your name after "Prepared by:" at the end of the document.

7. Click after the colon in "Prepared by:", press the **spacebar**, and then type your first and last name. To indicate that you have complied with Kaya's request by adding your name, you could right-click the comment, and then click Mark Comment Done. However, in this case, you'll simply delete the comment. Kaya also asks you to delete the first comment in the document.

8. Click anywhere in the final comment, and then in the Comments group, click the **Delete** button.

9. In the Comments group, click the **Previous** button three times to select the comment at the beginning of the document, and then click the **Delete** button to delete the comment.

As you reviewed the document, you might have noticed that, on page 2, one of the class names in the Research Methods section appears in all uppercase letters. This is probably just a typing mistake. You can correct it, and then add a comment that points out the change to Kaya.

To correct the mistake and add a comment:

1. Scroll down to page 2, and then select the fourth paragraph on the page, which contains the text "PSYCHOLOGY 401: RESEARCH ANALYSIS."

2. On the ribbon, click the **HOME** tab.

3. In the Font group, click the **Change Case** button Aa ▾, and then click **Capitalize Each Word**. The text changes to read "Psychology 401: Research Analysis."

4. Verify that the paragraph is still selected, and then click the **REVIEW** tab on the ribbon.

5. In the Comments group, click the **New Comment** button. A new comment appears, with the insertion point ready for you to begin typing.

6. In the new comment, type **I assumed you didn't want this all uppercase, so I changed it.** and then save the document.

You can now hide the text of the comments because you are finished working with them.

7. In the Comments group, click the **Show Comments** button. You now see a comment icon in the document margin rather than on the right side of the Word screen. A comment icon alerts you to the presence of a comment without taking up all the space required to display the comment text. You can click a comment icon to read a particular comment without displaying the text of all the comments.

8. Click the comment icon 💬. The comment icon is highlighted, and the full comment is displayed, as shown in Figure 2-4.

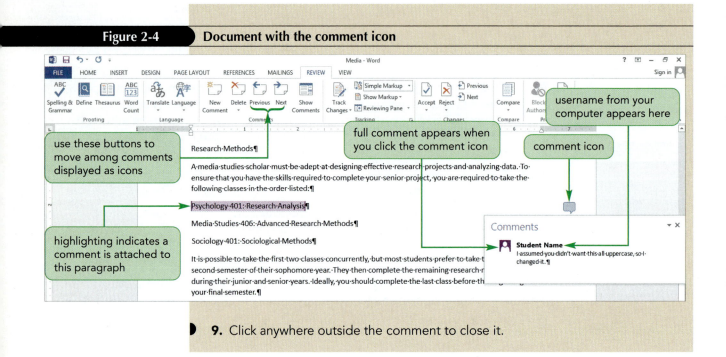

Figure 2-4 Document with the comment icon

9. Click anywhere outside the comment to close it.

Creating Bulleted and Numbered Lists

A **bulleted list** is a group of related paragraphs with a black circle or other character to the left of each paragraph. For a group of related paragraphs that have a particular order (such as steps in a procedure), you can use consecutive numbers instead of bullets to create a **numbered list**. If you insert a new paragraph, delete a paragraph, or reorder the paragraphs in a numbered list, Word adjusts the numbers to make sure they remain consecutive.

PROSKILLS

Written Communication: Organizing Information in Lists

Bulleted and numbered lists are both great ways to draw the reader's attention to information. But it's important to know how to use them. Use numbers when your list contains items that are arranged by priority in a specific order. For example, in a document reviewing the procedure for performing CPR, it makes sense to use numbers for the sequential steps. Use bullets when the items in the list are of equal importance, or when they can be accomplished in any order. For example, in a resume, you could use bullets for a list of professional certifications.

To add bullets to a series of paragraphs, you use the Bullets button in the Paragraph group on the HOME tab. To create a numbered list, you use the Numbering button in the Paragraph group instead. Both the Bullets button and the Numbering button have arrows you can click to open a gallery of bullet or numbering styles.

Kaya asks you to format the list of prerequisites on page 1 as a bulleted list. She also asks you to format the list of core courses on page 1 as a separate bulleted list. Finally, you need to format the list of research methods classes on page 2 as a numbered list.

To apply bullets to paragraphs:

1. Scroll up until you see the paragraphs containing the list of prerequisites, which begins with "Media Studies 101: General Media Studies," and then select this paragraph and the three that follow it.

2. On the ribbon, click the **HOME** tab.

3. In the Paragraph group, click the **Bullets** button ⊞. Black circles appear as bullets before each item in the list. Also, the bulleted list is indented and the paragraph spacing between the items is reduced.

 After reviewing the default, round bullet in the document, Kaya decides she would prefer square bullets.

4. In the Paragraph group, click the **Bullets button arrow** ⊞ ▾. A gallery of bullet styles opens. See Figure 2-5.

Figure 2-5 Bullets gallery

The Recently Used Bullets section appears at the top of the gallery of bullet styles; it displays the bullet styles that have been used since you started Word, which, in this case, is just the round black bullet style that was applied by default when you clicked the Bullets button. The **Bullet Library**, which offers a variety of bullet styles, is shown below the Recently Used Bullets. To create your own bullets from a picture file or from a set of predesigned symbols including diamonds, hearts, or Greek letters, click Define New Bullet, and then click the Symbol button or the Picture button in the Define New Bullet dialog box.

5. Move the mouse pointer over the bullet styles in the Bullet Library to see a Live Preview of the bullet styles in the document. Kaya prefers the black square style.

6. In the Bullet Library, click the **black square**. The round bullets are replaced with square bullets.

Next, you need to format the list of core courses on page 1 with square bullets. When you first start Word, the Bullets button applies the default, round bullets you saw earlier. But after you select a new bullet style, the Bullets button applies the last bullet style you used. So, to add square bullets to the decorating styles list, you just have to select the list and click the Bullets button.

To add bullets to the list of core courses:

1. Scroll down in the document and select the paragraphs listing the core courses, starting with "Media Studies 102: Communicating Visually" and ending with "Media Studies 402: Ethics of Digital Privacy."

2. In the Paragraph group, click the **Bullets** button ⊟. The list is now formatted with square black bullets.

The list is finished except for one issue. A Media Studies major only needs to take one of the last three classes in the list, but that's not clear because of the way the list is currently formatted. To clarify this information, you can use the Increase Indent button in the Paragraph group to indent the last three bullets. When you do this, Word inserts a different style bullet to make the indented paragraphs visually subordinate to the bulleted paragraphs above.

To indent the last three bullets:

1. In the list of core courses, select the last three paragraphs.

TIP

To remove the indent from selected text, click the Decrease Indent button in the Paragraph group.

2. In the Paragraph group, click the **Increase Indent** button ⊞. The three paragraphs move to the right, and the black square bullets are replaced with open circle bullets.

Next, you will format the list of research methods classes on page 2. Kaya wants you to format this information as a numbered list because the classes must be taken in a specific order.

To apply numbers to the list of research methods classes:

1. Scroll down to page 2 until you see the "Psychology 401: Research Analysis" paragraph. You added a comment to this paragraph earlier, but that will have no effect on the process of creating the numbered list.

2. Select the three paragraphs containing the list of research methods classes, starting with "Psychology 401: Research Analysis" and ending with "Sociology 401: Sociological Methods."

3. In the Paragraph group, click the **Numbering** button ⊟. Consecutive numbers appear in front of each item in the list. See Figure 2-6.

Figure 2-6 Numbered list

click to apply the default or most recently used numbering style

click the arrow to display a gallery of numbering styles

default numbering style is applied to selected paragraphs

A·Media·Studies·major·must·be·adept·at·designing·effective·research·projects·and·analyzing·data.·To·ensure·that·you·have·the·skills·required·to·complete·your·senior·project,·you·are·required·to·take·the·following·classes·in·the·order·listed:¶

1.→ Psychology·401:·Research·Analysis¶
2.→ Media·Studies·406:·Advanced·Research·Methods¶
3.→ Sociology·401:·Sociological·Methods¶

It·is·possible·to·take·the·first·two·classes·concurrently,·but·most·students·prefer·to·take·the·first·class·the·

▶ **4.** Click anywhere in the document to deselect the numbered list, and then save the document.

TIP

The Numbering button is a toggle button, which means you can click it to add or remove numbering from selected text.

As with the Bullets button arrow, you can click the Numbering button arrow and then select from a library of numbering styles. You can also indent paragraphs in a numbered list to create an outline, in which case the indented paragraphs will be preceded by lowercase letters instead of numbers. To apply a different list style to the outline (for example, with Roman numerals and uppercase letters), select the list, click the Multilevel List button in the Paragraph group, and then click a multilevel list style.

Moving Text in a Document

One of the most useful features of a word-processing program is the ability to move text easily. For example, Kaya wants to reorder the information in the numbered list. You could do this by deleting a paragraph and then retyping it at a new location. However, it's easier to select and then move the text. Word provides several ways to move text—drag and drop, cut and paste, and copy and paste.

Dragging and Dropping Text

To move text with **drag and drop**, you select the text you want to move, press and hold the mouse button while you drag the selected text to a new location, and then release the mouse button.

In the numbered list you just created, Kaya wants you to move the paragraph that reads "Sociology 401 Sociological Methods" up so it is the first item in the list.

To move text using drag and drop:

▶ **1.** Select the third paragraph in the numbered list, "Sociology 401: Sociological Methods," being sure to include the paragraph marker at the end. The number 3 remains unselected because it's not actually part of the paragraph text.

▶ **2.** Position the pointer over the selected text. The pointer changes to a left-facing arrow ⭦.

3. Press and hold the mouse button until the drag-and-drop pointer appears. A dark black insertion point appears within the selected text.

4. Without releasing the mouse button, drag the pointer to the beginning of the list until the insertion point is positioned to the left of the "P" in "Psychology 401: Research Analysis." Use the insertion point, rather than the mouse pointer, to guide the text to its new location. See Figure 2-7.

 Trouble? If the numbers in the numbered list appear highlighted in gray, you moved the mouse pointer too close to the numbers. Ignore the highlighting and position the insertion point just to the left of the "P" in "Psychology 401: Research Analysis."

| Figure 2-7 | Moving text with the drag-and-drop pointer |

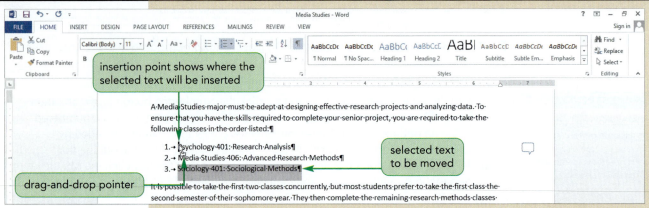

5. Release the mouse button, and then click a blank area of the document to deselect the text. The text "Sociology 401: Sociological Methods" is now the first item in the list, and the remaining paragraphs have been renumbered as paragraphs 2 and 3. See Figure 2-8.

| Figure 2-8 | Text in new location |

The Paste Options button appears near the newly inserted text, providing access to more advanced options related to pasting text. You don't need to use the Paste Options button right now; it will disappear when you start performing another task.

Trouble? If the selected text moves to the wrong location, click the Undo button 🔄 on the Quick Access Toolbar, and then repeat Steps 2 through 5.

▶ **6.** Save the document.

Dragging and dropping works well when you are moving text a short distance. When you are moving text from one page to another, it's easier to cut, copy, and paste text using the Clipboard.

Cutting or Copying and Pasting Text Using the Clipboard

The **Office Clipboard** is a temporary storage area on your computer that holds objects such as text or graphics until you need them. To **cut** means to remove text or another item from a document and place it on the Clipboard. Once you've cut something, you can paste it somewhere else. To **copy** means to copy a selected item to the Clipboard, leaving the item in its original location. To **paste** means to insert a copy of whatever is on the Clipboard into the document, at the insertion point. When you paste an item from the Clipboard into a document, the item remains on the Clipboard so you can paste it again somewhere else if you want. The buttons for cutting, copying, and pasting are located in the Clipboard group on the HOME tab.

By default, Word pastes text in a new location in a document with the same formatting it had in its old location. To select other ways to paste text, you can use the Paste Options button, which appears next to newly pasted text, or the Paste button arrow in the Clipboard group. Both buttons display a menu of paste options. Two particularly useful paste options are Merge Formatting, which combines the formatting of the copied text with the formatting of the text in the new location, and Keep Text Only, which inserts the text using the formatting of the surrounding text in the new location.

When you need to keep track of multiple pieces of cut or copied text, it's helpful to open the **Clipboard task pane**, which displays the contents of the Clipboard. You open the Clipboard task pane by clicking the Dialog Box Launcher in the Clipboard group on the HOME tab. When the Clipboard task pane is displayed, the Clipboard can store up to 24 text items. When the Clipboard task pane is *not* displayed, the Clipboard can hold only the most recently copied item.

Kaya would like to move the second-to-last sentence under the heading "Majoring in Media Studies" on page 1. You'll use cut and paste to move this sentence to a new location.

To move text using cut and paste:

▶ **1.** Make sure the HOME tab is selected on the ribbon.

▶ **2.** Scroll up until you can see the second paragraph in the document, just below the heading "Majoring in Media Studies."

▶ **3.** Press and hold the **Ctrl** key, and then click anywhere in the sentence near the end of the second paragraph, which begins "In the second semester of your senior year...." The entire sentence and the space following it are selected.

TIP

You can also press the Ctrl+X keys to cut selected text. Press the Ctrl+V keys to paste the most recently copied item.

4. In the Clipboard group, click the **Cut** button. The selected text is removed from the document and copied to the Clipboard.

5. Scroll down to page 2, and then click at the beginning of the second-to-last paragraph in the document, just to the left of the "T" in "This project should…."

6. In the Clipboard group, click the **Paste** button. The sentence and the space following it are displayed in the new location. The Paste Options button appears near the newly inserted sentence.

 Trouble? If a menu opens below the Paste button, you clicked the Paste button arrow instead of the Paste button. Press the Esc key to close the menu, and then repeat Step 6, taking care not to click the arrow below the Paste button.

7. Save the document.

Kaya explains that she'll be using some text from the Media Studies document as the basis for another department handout. She asks you to copy that information and paste it into a new document. You can do this using the Clipboard task pane.

To copy text to paste into a new document:

1. In the Clipboard group, click the **Dialog Box Launcher**. The Clipboard task pane opens on the left side of the document window, as shown in Figure 2-9.

Figure 2-9	**Clipboard task pane**

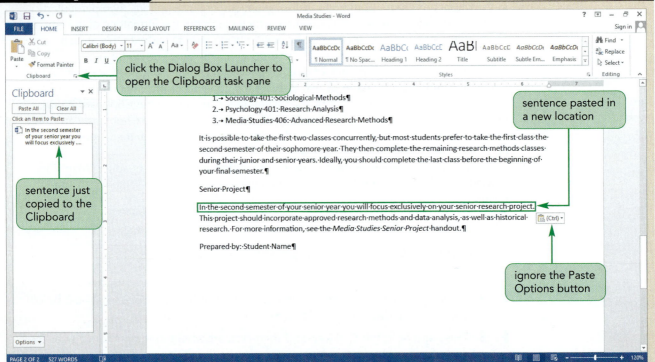

Notice the Clipboard contains the sentence you copied in the last set of steps, although you can only see the first part of the sentence. You'll copy the last two sentences in the current paragraph for use in Kaya's other document.

2. Select the text **This project should incorporate approved research methods and data analysis, as well as historical research. For more information, see the *Media Studies Senior Project* handout.** Do not select the paragraph mark.

TIP

You can also copy selected text by pressing the Ctrl+C keys.

3. In the Clipboard group, click the **Copy** button. The first few words of the text appear at the top of the Clipboard task pane, but in fact the entire two sentences are now stored on the Clipboard.

4. Click anywhere in the document to deselect the text, scroll up, if necessary, and then locate the first sentence on page 2.

5. Press and hold the **Ctrl** key, and then click anywhere in the first sentence on page 2, which begins "A Media Studies major must be adept…." The sentence and the space following it are selected.

6. In the Clipboard group, click the **Copy** button. The first part of the sentence appears at the top of the Clipboard task pane, as shown in Figure 2-10.

Figure 2-10	Items in the Clipboard task pane

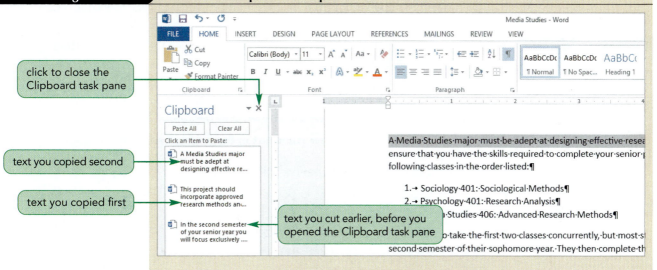

click to close the Clipboard task pane

text you copied second

text you copied first

text you cut earlier, before you opened the Clipboard task pane

Now you can use the Clipboard task pane to insert the copied text into a new document.

To insert the copied text into a new document:

1. Open a new, blank document. If necessary, open the Clipboard task pane.

2. In the Clipboard task pane, click the second item in the list of copied items, which begins "This project should incorporate…." The text is inserted in the document and the "*Media Studies Senior Project*" title retains its italic formatting.

Kaya doesn't want to keep the italic formatting in the newly pasted text. You can remove this formatting by using the Paste Options button, which is visible just below the pasted text.

3. Click the **Paste Options** button (Ctrl)▾ in the document. The Paste Options menu opens, as shown in Figure 2-11.

Figure 2-11 **Paste Options menu**

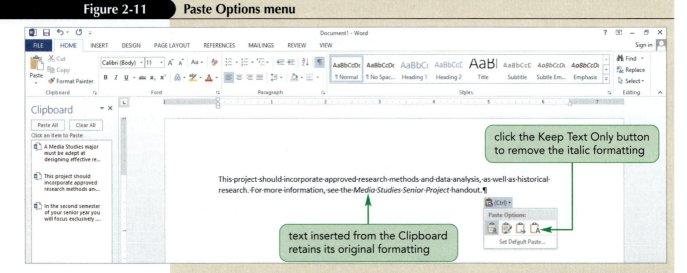

click the Keep Text Only button to remove the italic formatting

This·project·should·incorporate·approved·research·methods·and·data·analysis,·as·well·as·historical· research.·For·more·information,·see·the·*Media·Studies·Senior·Project*·handout.¶

text inserted from the Clipboard retains its original formatting

To paste the text without the italic formatting, you can click the Keep Text Only button.

4. Click the **Keep Text Only** button. Word removes the italic formatting from "Media Studies Senior Project."

TIP

To select a paste option before pasting an item, click the Paste button arrow in the Clipboard group, and then click the paste option you want.

5. Press the **Enter** key to start a new paragraph, and then click the first item in the Clipboard task pane, which begins "A Media Studies major must be adept...." The text is inserted as the second paragraph in the document.

6. Save the document as **New Handout** in the location specified by your instructor, and then close it. You return to the Media Studies document, where the Clipboard task pane is still open.

7. In the Clipboard task pane, click the **Clear All** button. The copied items are removed from the Clipboard.

8. In the Clipboard task pane, click the **Close** button. The Clipboard task pane closes.

9. Click anywhere in the document to deselect the paragraph, and then save the document.

Using the Navigation Pane

The Navigation pane simplifies the process of moving through a document page by page. You can also use the Navigation pane to locate a particular word or phrase. You start by typing the text you're searching for—the **search text**—in the Search box at the top of the Navigation pane. As shown in the Session 2.1 Visual Overview, Word highlights every instance of the search text in the document. At the same time, a list of the **search results** appears in the Navigation pane. You can click a search result to go immediately to that location in the document.

To become familiar with the Navigation pane, you'll use it to navigate through the Media Studies document page by page. You'll start by moving the insertion point to the beginning of the document.

To navigate through the document page by page:

1. Press the **Ctrl+Home** keys to move the insertion point to the beginning of the document, making sure the HOME tab is still selected on the ribbon.

2. In the Editing group, click the **Find** button. The Navigation pane opens on the left side of the Word window.

 In the Search document box at the top, you can type the text you want to find. The three links below the Search document box—HEADINGS, PAGES, and RESULTS—allow you to navigate through the document in different ways. As you become a more experienced Word user, you'll learn how to use the HEADINGS link; for now, you'll ignore it. To move quickly among the pages of a document, you can use the PAGES link.

3. In the Navigation pane, click the **PAGES** link. The Navigation pane displays thumbnail icons of the document's two pages, as shown in Figure 2-12. You can click a page in the Navigation pane to display that page in the document window.

Figure 2-12	Document pages displayed in the Navigation pane

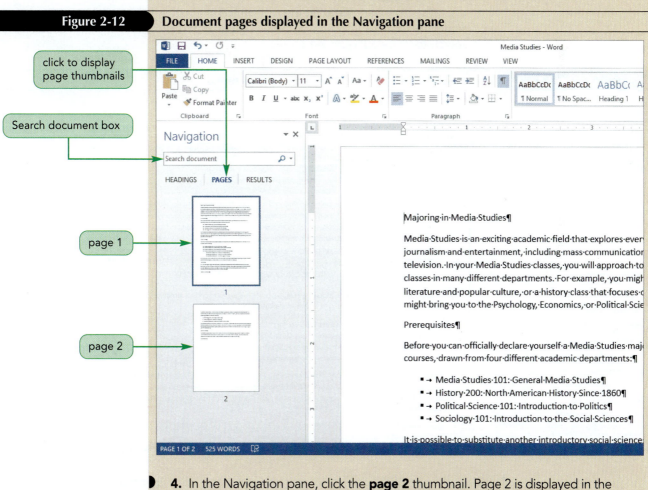

4. In the Navigation pane, click the **page 2** thumbnail. Page 2 is displayed in the document window, with the insertion point blinking at the beginning of the page.

5. In the Navigation pane, click the **page 1** thumbnail to move the insertion point back to the beginning of the document.

Kaya thinks she might have mistakenly used the word "media" when she actually meant to use "journalism" in certain parts of the document. She asks you to use the Navigation pane to find all instances of "media."

To search for the word "media" in the document:

1. In the Navigation pane, click the **RESULTS** link, click the **Search document** box, and then type **media**. You do not have to press the Enter key.

 Every instance of the word "media" is highlighted in yellow in the document. The yellow highlight is only temporary; it will disappear as soon as you begin to perform any other task in the document. A full list of the 24 search results is displayed in the Navigation pane. Some of the search results contain the word "Media" (with an uppercase "M") while others contain the word "media" (with a lowercase "m"). To narrow the search results, you need to tell Word to match the case of the search text.

2. In the Navigation pane, click the **Search for more things** button . This displays a two-part menu. In the bottom part, you can select other items to search for, such as graphics or tables. The top part provides more advanced search tools. See Figure 2-13.

| Figure 2-13 | Navigation pane with Search for more things menu |

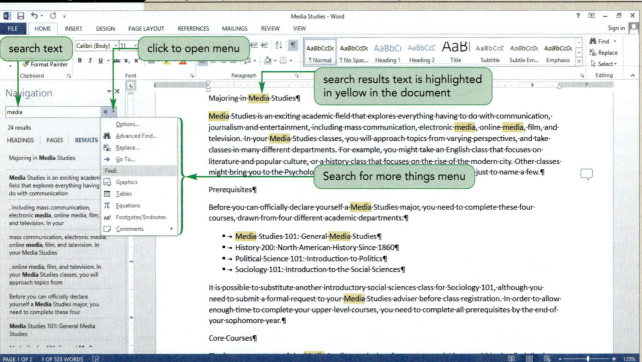

3. At the top of the Search for more things menu, click **Options** to open the Find Options dialog box.

The check boxes in this dialog box allow you to fine-tune your search. For example, to ensure that Word finds the search text only when it appears as a separate word, and not when it appears as part of another word, you could select the Find whole words only check box. Right now, you are only concerned with making sure the search results have the same case as the search text.

4. Click the **Match case** check box to select it, and then click the **OK** button to close the Find Options dialog box. Now you can search the document again.

5. Press the **Ctrl+Home** keys to move the insertion point to the beginning of the document, click the **Search document** box in the Navigation pane, and then type **media**. This time, there are only three search results in the Navigation pane, and they all start with a lowercase "m."

 To move among the search results, you can use the up and down arrows in the Navigation pane.

6. In the Navigation pane, click the **down arrow** button ⏷. Word selects the first instance of "media" in the Navigation pane, as indicated by a blue outline. Also, in the document, the first instance has a gray selection highlight over the yellow highlight. See Figure 2-14.

Figure 2-14 **Navigation pane with the first search result selected**

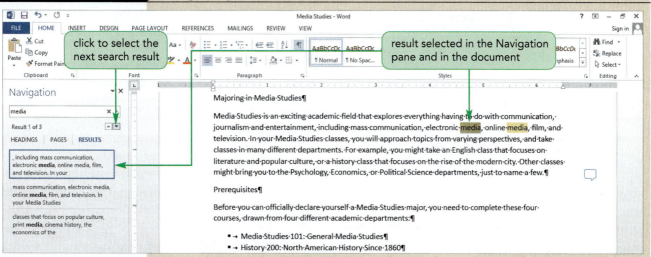

Trouble? If the second instance of "media" is selected in the Navigation pane, then you pressed the Enter key after typing "media" in Step 5. Click the up arrow button ⏶ to select the first instance.

7. In the Navigation pane, click the **down arrow** button ⏷. Word selects the second instance of "media" in the document and in the Navigation pane.

8. Click the **down arrow** button ⏷ again to select the third search result, in the paragraph after "Electives," and then click the **up arrow** button ⏶ to select the second search result again.

 You can also select a search result in the document by clicking a search result in the Navigation pane.

9. In the Navigation pane, click the third search result, which begins "classes that focus on popular culture...." The third search result is selected in the document and in the Navigation pane.

After reviewing the search results, Kaya decides she would like to replace two of the three instances of "media" with the word "journalism." You can do that by using the Find and Replace dialog box.

Finding and Replacing Text

To open the Find and Replace dialog box from the Navigation pane, click the Find more things button, and then click Replace. This opens the **Find and Replace dialog box**, with the Replace tab displayed by default. The Replace tab provides options for finding a specific word or phrase in the document and replacing it with another word or phrase. To use the Replace tab, type the search text in the Find what box, and then type the text you want to substitute in the Replace with box. You can also click the More button on the Replace tab to display the Search Options section, which includes the same options you saw earlier in the Find Options dialog box, including the Find whole words only check box and the Match case check box.

After you have typed the search text and selected any search options, you can click the Find Next button to select the first occurrence of the search text; you can then decide whether or not to substitute the search text with the replacement text.

REFERENCE

Finding and Replacing Text

- Press the Ctrl+Home keys to move the insertion point to the beginning of the document.
- In the Editing group on the HOME tab, click the Replace button; or, in the Navigation pane, click the Search for more things button, and then click Replace.
- In the Find and Replace dialog box, click the More button, if necessary, to expand the dialog box and display the Search Options section of the Replace tab.
- In the Find what box, type the search text.
- In the Replace with box, type the replacement text.
- Select the appropriate check boxes in the Search Options section of the dialog box to narrow your search.
- Click the Find Next button.
- Click the Replace button to substitute the found text with the replacement text and find the next occurrence.
- Click the Replace All button to substitute all occurrences of the found text with the replacement text without reviewing each occurrence. Use this option only if you are absolutely certain that the results will be what you expect.

You'll use the Find and Replace dialog box now to replace two instances of "media" with "journalism."

To replace two instances of "media" with "journalism":

1. Press the **Ctrl+Home** keys to move the insertion point to the beginning of the document.

2. In the Navigation pane, click the **Search for more things** button ▼ to open the menu, and then click **Replace**. The Find and Replace dialog box opens with the Replace tab on top.

 The search text you entered earlier in the Navigation pane, "media," appears in the Find what box. If you hadn't already conducted a search, you would need to type your search text now. Because you selected the Match case check box earlier in the Find Options dialog box, "Match Case" appears below the Find what box.

3. In the lower-left corner of the dialog box, click the **More** button to display the search options. Because you selected the Match case check box earlier in the Find Options dialog box, it is selected here.

 Trouble? If you see the Less button instead of the More button, the search options are already displayed.

4. Click the **Replace with** box, and then type **journalism**.

5. Click the **Find Next** button. Word highlights the first instance of "media" in the document. See Figure 2-15.

Figure 2-15 **Find and Replace dialog box**

6. Click the **Replace** button. Word replaces "media" with "journalism," so the text reads "electronic journalism." Then, Word selects the next instance of "media," which happens to be in the same sentence. Kaya does not want to replace this instance, so you can find the next one.

7. Click the **Find Next** button. Word selects the last instance of "media," located in the sentence just before the "Research Methods" heading.

▶ **8.** Click the **Replace** button. Word makes the substitution, so the text reads "print journalism," and then displays a message box telling you that Word has finished searching the document.

▶ **9.** Click the **OK** button to close the message box, and then in the Find and Replace dialog box, click the **Close** button.

You are finished with the Navigation pane, so you can close it. But first you need to restore the search options to their original settings. It's a good practice to restore the original search settings so that future searches are not affected by any settings that might not apply.

To restore the search options to their original settings:

▶ **1.** In the Navigation pane, open the Find Options dialog box, deselect the Match case check box, and then click the **OK** button to close the Find Options dialog box.

▶ **2.** Click the **Close** button ☒ in the upper-right corner of the Navigation pane.

▶ **3.** Save the document.

INSIGHT

Searching for Formatting

You can search for formatting just as you can search for text. For example, you might want to check a document to look for text formatted in bold and the Arial font. To search for formatting from within the Navigation pane, click the Search for more things button to display the menu, and then click Advanced Find. The Find and Replace dialog box opens with the Find tab displayed. Click the More button, if necessary, to display the Search Options section of the Find tab. Click the Format button at the bottom of the Search Options section, click the category of formatting you want to look for (such as Font or Paragraph), and then select the formatting you want to find.

You can look for formatting that occurs only on specific text, or you can look for formatting that occurs anywhere in a document. If you're looking for text formatted in a certain way (such as all instances of "Media Studies" that are bold), enter the text in the Find what box and then specify the formatting you're looking for. To find formatting on any text in a document, leave the Find what box empty, and then specify the formatting. Use the Find Next button to move through the document, from one instance of the specified formatting to another.

You can follow the same basic steps on the Replace tab to replace one type of formatting with another. First, click the Find what box and select the desired formatting. Then click the Replace with box and select the desired formatting. If you want, type search text and replacement text in the appropriate boxes. Then proceed as with any Find and Replace operation.

Now that the text in the Media Studies document is final, you will turn your attention to styles and themes, which affect the look of the entire document.

Working with Styles

A style is a set of formatting options that you can apply by clicking an icon in the Style gallery on the HOME tab. Each style is designed for a particular use. For example, the Title style is intended for formatting the title at the beginning of a document.

All the text you type into a document has a style applied to it. By default, text is formatted in the Normal style, which applies 11-point Calibri font, left alignment, 1.08 line spacing, and a small amount of extra space between paragraphs. In other words, the Normal style applies the default formatting you learned about when you first began typing a Word document.

Note that some styles apply **paragraph-level formatting**—that is, they are set up to format an entire paragraph, including the paragraph and line spacing. The Normal, Heading, and Title styles all apply paragraph-level formatting. Other styles apply **character-level formatting**—that is, they are set up to format only individual characters or words (for example, emphasizing a phrase by adding italic formatting and changing the font color).

One row of the Style gallery is always visible on the HOME tab. To display the entire Style gallery, click the More button in the Styles group. After you begin applying styles in a document, the visible row of the Style gallery changes to show the most recently used styles.

You are ready to use the Style gallery to format the document title.

To display the entire Style gallery and then format the document title with a style:

▶ 1. Press the **Ctrl+Home** keys to move the insertion point to the beginning of the document, if necessary.

▶ 2. Make sure the HOME tab is still selected and locate the More button in the Styles group, as shown earlier in the Session 2.1 Visual Overview.

▶ 3. In the Styles group, click the **More** button. The Style gallery opens, displaying a total of 16 styles arranged in two rows, as shown in Figure 2-16. If your screen is set at a lower resolution than the screenshots in this book, the Style gallery on your screen might contain more than two rows.

| Figure 2-16 | Displaying the Style gallery |

You don't actually need any of the styles in the bottom row now, so you can close the Style gallery.

▶ 4. Press the **Esc** key to close the Style gallery.

5. Click anywhere in the first paragraph, "Majoring in Media Studies," and then point to (but don't click) the **Title** style, which is the fifth style from the left in the top row of the gallery. The ScreenTip "Title" is displayed, and a Live Preview of the style appears in the paragraph containing the insertion point, as shown in Figure 2-17. The Title style changes the font to 28-point Calibri Light.

Figure 2-17 ▸ **Title style in the Style gallery**

6. Click the **Title** style. The style is applied to the paragraph. To finish the title, you need to center it.

7. In the Paragraph group, click the **Center** button ▤. The title is centered in the document.

Next, you will format the document headings using the heading styles, which have different levels. The highest level, Heading 1, is used for the major headings in a document, and it applies the most noticeable formatting with a larger font than the other heading styles. (In heading styles, the highest, or most important, level has the lowest number.) The Heading 2 style is used for headings that are subordinate to the highest level headings; it applies slightly less dramatic formatting than the Heading 1 style.

The Media Studies handout only has one level of headings, so you will only apply the Heading 1 style.

To format text with the Heading 1 style:

1. Click anywhere in the "Prerequisites" paragraph.

2. On the HOME tab, in the Style gallery, click the **Heading 1** style. The paragraph is now formatted in blue, 16-point Calibri Light. The Heading 1 style also inserts some paragraph space above the heading.

TIP

On most computers, you can press the F4 key to repeat your most recent action.

3. Scroll down, click anywhere in the "Core Courses" paragraph, and then click the **Heading 1** style in the Style gallery.

4. Repeat Step 3 to apply the Heading 1 style to the "Electives" paragraph, the "Research Methods" paragraph and the "Senior Project" paragraph. When you are finished, scroll up to the beginning of the document to review the new formatting. See Figure 2-18.

Figure 2-18 **Document with Title and Heading 1 styles**

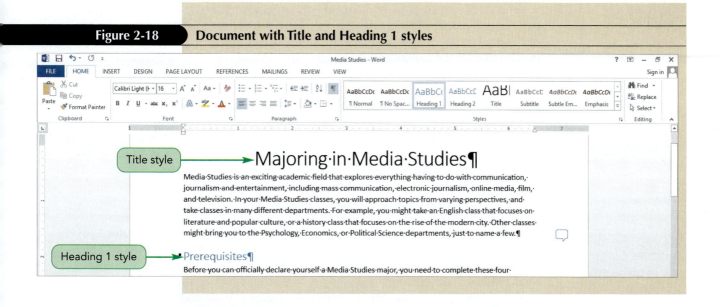

Understanding the Benefits of Heading Styles

By default, the Style gallery offers 16 styles, each designed for a specific purpose. As you gain more experience with Word, you will learn how to use a wider array of styles. You'll also learn how to create your own styles. Styles allow you to change a document's formatting in an instant. But the benefits of heading styles go far beyond attractive formatting. Heading styles allow you to reorganize a document or generate a table of contents with a click of the mouse. Also, the heading styles are set up to keep a heading and the body text that follows it together, so a heading is never separated from its body text by a page break. Each Word document includes nine levels of heading styles, although only the Heading 1 and Heading 2 styles are available by default in the Style gallery. Whenever you use the lowest heading style in the Style gallery, the next-lowest level is added to the Style gallery. For example, after you use the Heading 2 style, the Heading 3 style appears in the Styles group in the Style gallery.

After you format a document with a variety of styles, you can alter the look of the document by changing the document's theme.

Working with Themes

A **theme** is a coordinated collection of fonts, colors, and other visual effects designed to give a document a cohesive, polished look. A variety of themes are installed with Word, with more available online at <u>Office.com</u>. When you open a new blank document in Word, the Office theme is applied by default. To change a document's theme, you click the Themes button, which is located in the Document Formatting group on the DESIGN tab, and then click the theme you want. Pointing to the Themes button displays a ScreenTip that tells you what theme is currently applied to the document.

When applying color to a document, you usually have the option of selecting a color from a palette of colors designed to match the current theme, or from a palette of standard colors. For instance, recall that the colors in the Font Color gallery are divided into Theme Colors and Standard Colors. When you select a Standard Color, such as Dark Red, that color remains the same no matter which theme you apply to the document. But when you click one of the Theme Colors, you are essentially telling Word to use the color located in that particular spot on the Theme Colors palette. Then, if you change the document's theme later, Word substitutes a color from the same location on the Theme Colors palette. This ensures that all the colors in a document are drawn from a group of colors coordinated to look good together. So as a rule, if you are going to use multiple colors in a document (perhaps for paragraph shading and font color), it's a good idea to stick with the Theme Colors.

A similar substitution takes place with fonts when you change the theme. However, to understand how this works, you need to understand the difference between headings and body text. Kaya's document includes the headings "Prerequisites," "Core Courses," "Electives," "Research Methods," and "Senior Project"—all of which you have formatted with the Heading1 style. The title of the document, "Majoring in Media Studies," is now formatted with the Title style, which is also a type of heading style. Everything else in the Media Studies document is body text.

To ensure that your documents have a harmonious look, each theme assigns a font for headings and a font for body text. Typically, in a given theme, the same font is used for both headings and body text, but not always. In the Office theme, for instance, they are slightly different; the heading font is Calibri Light, and the body font is Calibri. These two fonts appear at the top of the Font list as "Calibri Light (Headings)" and "Calibri (Body)" when you click the Font box arrow in the Font group on the HOME tab. When you begin typing text in a new document with the Office theme, the text is formatted as body text with the Calibri font by default.

When applying a font to selected text, you can choose one of the two theme fonts at the top of the Font list, or you can choose one of the other fonts in the Font list. If you choose one of the other fonts and then change the document theme, that font remains the same. But if you use one of the theme fonts and then change the document theme, Word substitutes the appropriate font from the new theme. When you paste text into a document that has a different theme, Word applies the theme fonts and colors of the new document. To retain the original formatting, use the Keep Source Formatting option in the Paste Options menu.

Figure 2-19 compares elements of the default Office theme with the Integral theme. The Integral theme was chosen for this example because, like the Office theme, its heading and body fonts are different.

Figure 2-19	Comparing the Office theme to the Integral theme

© 2014 Cengage Learning

Each document theme is designed to convey a specific look and feel. The Office theme is designed to be appropriate for standard business documents. Other themes are designed to give documents a flashier look. Because Kaya has not yet selected a new theme, the Office theme is currently applied to the Media Studies document. However, she thinks the Facet theme might be more appropriate for the Media Studies document. She asks you to apply it now.

To change the document's theme:

1. If necessary, press the **Ctrl+Home** keys to move the insertion point to the beginning of the document. With the title and first heading visible, you will more easily see what happens when you change the document's theme.

2. On the ribbon, click the **DESIGN** tab.

3. In the Document Formatting group, point to the **Themes** button. A ScreenTip appears containing the text "Current: Office Theme" as well as general information about themes.

4. In the Document Formatting group, click the **Themes** button. The Themes gallery opens. See Figure 2-20.

Figure 2-20 **Themes gallery displayed**

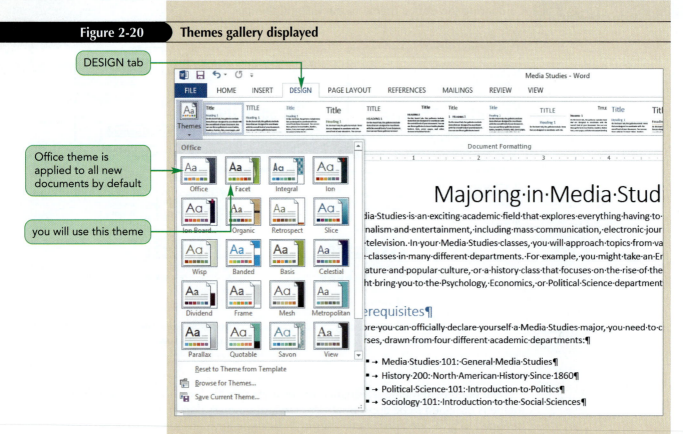

DESIGN tab

Office theme is applied to all new documents by default

you will use this theme

5. Move the mouse pointer (without clicking it) over the various themes in the gallery to see a Live Preview of each theme in the document. The heading and body fonts as well as the heading colors change to reflect the fonts associated with the various themes.

6. In the Themes gallery, click the **Facet** theme. The text in the Media Studies document changes to the body and heading fonts of the Facet theme, with the headings formatted in green. To see exactly what the Facet theme fonts are, you can point to the Fonts button in the Document Formatting group.

7. In the Document Formatting group, point to the **Fonts** button. A ScreenTip appears, listing the currently selected theme (Facet), the heading font (Trebuchet MS), and the body font (Trebuchet MS). See Figure 2-21.

Figure 2-21 **Fonts for the Facet theme**

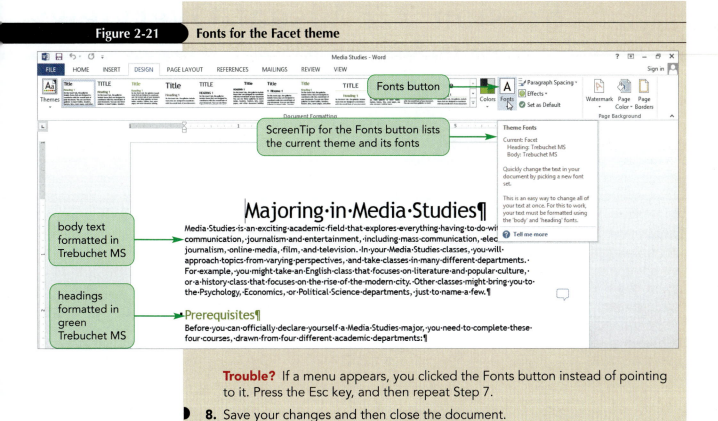

Trouble? If a menu appears, you clicked the Fonts button instead of pointing to it. Press the Esc key, and then repeat Step 7.

▶ **8.** Save your changes and then close the document.

Kaya's Media Studies document is ready to be handed in to her supervisor. The use of styles, bulleted and numbered lists, and a new theme gives the document a professional look appropriate for use in a department handout.

REVIEW

Session 2.1 Quick Check

1. Explain how to display comments to the right of the document text in Simple Markup view.
2. What term refers to the process of using the mouse to drag text to a new location?
3. How can you ensure that the Navigation pane will find "ZIP code" instead of "zip code"?
4. What is a style?
5. What style is applied to all text in a new document by default?
6. Explain the relationship between a document's theme and styles.

Session 2.2 Visual Overview:

Use an easy-to-read font, such as the default Calibri, set to 12 point.

An MLA-style research paper does not require a separate title page; instead, type your name, your instructor's name, the course number, and the date in the upper-left corner of the first page.

An MLA-style research paper requires 1-inch margins.

Center the title. Do not add any other special formatting unless your title includes the title of another work, in which case you should italicize the title of the other work.

Indent the first line of each paragraph, except for the headings.

Include only one space between the end of a sentence and the beginning of the next.

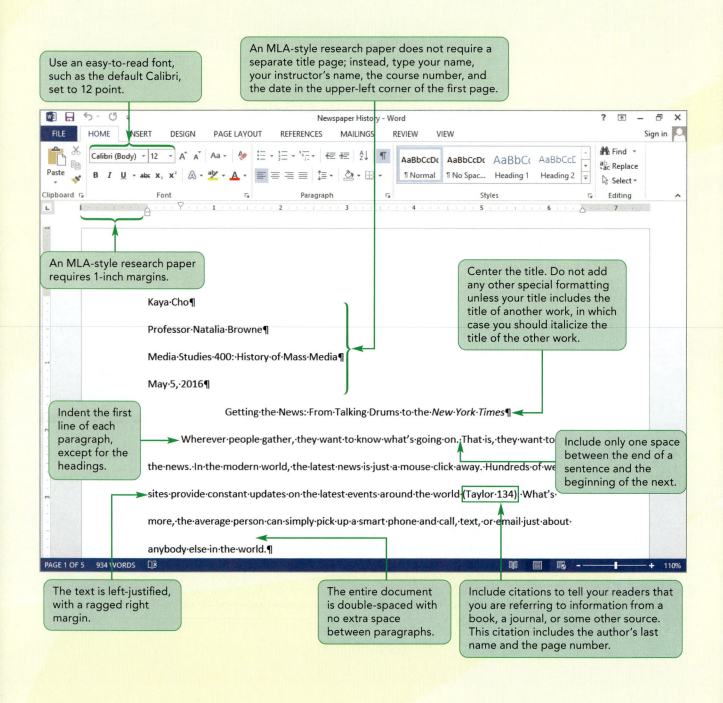

The text is left-justified, with a ragged right margin.

The entire document is double-spaced with no extra space between paragraphs.

Include citations to tell your readers that you are referring to information from a book, a journal, or some other source. This citation includes the author's last name and the page number.

MLA Formatting Guidelines

The REFERENCES tab includes options that help you create a research paper.

In the Style box, specify the style of research paper you are creating. For college research papers, the MLA style is commonly used.

After you create all the citations, click the Bibliography button to create a list of all the sources mentioned in your citations. This list is known as a **bibliography** or, in the MLA style, a **works cited list**.

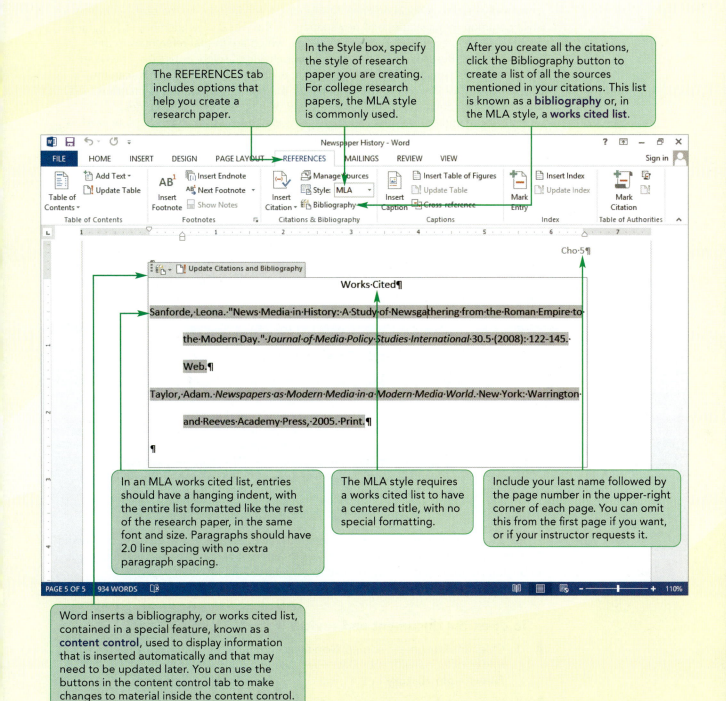

In an MLA works cited list, entries should have a hanging indent, with the entire list formatted like the rest of the research paper, in the same font and size. Paragraphs should have 2.0 line spacing with no extra paragraph spacing.

The MLA style requires a works cited list to have a centered title, with no special formatting.

Include your last name followed by the page number in the upper-right corner of each page. You can omit this from the first page if you want, or if your instructor requests it.

Word inserts a bibliography, or works cited list, contained in a special feature, known as a **content control**, used to display information that is inserted automatically and that may need to be updated later. You can use the buttons in the content control tab to make changes to material inside the content control.

Reviewing the MLA Style

A **style guide** is a set of rules that describe the preferred format and style for a certain type of writing. People in different fields use different style guides, with each style guide designed to suit the needs of a specific discipline. For example, journalists commonly use the *Associated Press Stylebook*, which focuses on the concise writing style common in magazines and newspapers. In the world of academics, style guides emphasize the proper way to create **citations**, which are formal references to the work of others. Researchers in the social and behavioral sciences use the **American Psychological Association (APA) style**, which is designed to help readers scan an article quickly for key points and emphasizes the date of publication in citations. Other scientific and technical fields have their own specialized style guides.

In the humanities, the **Modern Language Association (MLA) style** is widely used. This is the style Kaya has used for her research paper. She followed the guidelines specified in the *MLA Handbook for Writers of Research Papers*, published by the Modern Language Association of America. These guidelines focus on specifications for formatting a research document and citing the sources used in research conducted for a paper. The major formatting features of an MLA-style research paper are illustrated in the Session 2.2 Visual Overview. Compared to style guides for technical fields, the MLA style is very flexible, making it easy to include citations without disrupting the natural flow of the writing. MLA-style citations of other writers' works take the form of a brief parenthetical entry, with a complete reference to each item included in the alphabetized bibliography, also known as the works cited list, at the end of the research paper.

INSIGHT

Formatting an MLA-Style Research Paper

The MLA guidelines were developed, in part, to simplify the process of transforming a manuscript into a journal article or a chapter of a book. The style calls for minimal formatting; the simpler the formatting in a manuscript, the easier it is to turn the text into a published document. The MLA guidelines were also designed to ensure consistency in documents, so that all research papers look alike. Therefore, you should apply no special formatting to the text in an MLA-style research paper. Headings should be formatted like the other text in the document, with no bold or heading styles.

Kaya has started writing a research paper on the history of newspapers for her Media Studies class. You'll open the draft of Kaya's research paper and determine what needs to be done to make it meet the MLA style guidelines for a research paper.

To open the document and review it for MLA style:

1. Open the document named **Newspaper** located in the Word2 ▶ Tutorial folder included with your Data Files, and then save the document as **Newspaper History** in the location specified by your instructor.

2. Verify that the document is displayed in Print Layout view, and that the rulers and nonprinting characters are displayed. Make sure the Zoom level is set to **120%**.

3. Review the document to familiarize yourself with its structure. First, notice the parts of the document that already match the MLA style. Kaya included a block of information in the upper-left corner of the first page, giving her name, her instructor's name, the course name, and the date. The title at the top of the first page also meets the MLA guidelines in that it is centered and does not have any special formatting except for "*New York Times*," which is italicized because it is the name of a newspaper. The headings ("Early News Media," "Merchant Newsletters," "Modern American Newspapers," and "Looking to the Future") have no special formatting; but unlike the title, they are left-aligned. Finally, the body text is left-aligned with a ragged right margin, and the entire document is formatted in the same font, Calibri, which is easy to read.

What needs to be changed in order to make Kaya's paper consistent with the MLA style? Currently, the entire document is formatted using the default settings, which are the Normal style for the Office theme. To transform the document into an MLA-style research paper, you need to complete the checklist shown in Figure 2-22.

Figure 2-22 Checklist for formatting a default Word document to match the MLA style

✓ Double-space the entire document.

✓ Remove paragraph spacing from the entire document.

✓ Increase the font size for the entire document to 12 points.

✓ Indent the first line of each body paragraph .5 inch from the left margin.

✓ Add the page number (preceded by your last name) in the upper-right corner of each page. If you prefer, you can omit this from the first page.

© 2014 Cengage Learning

You'll take care of the first three items in the checklist now.

To begin applying MLA formatting to the document:

1. Press the **Ctrl+A** keys to select the entire document.

2. Make sure the HOME tab is selected on the ribbon.

3. In the Paragraph group, click the **Line and Paragraph Spacing** button ⬍≡▾, and then click **2.0**.

4. Click the **Line and Spacing** button ⬍≡▾ again, and then click **Remove Space After Paragraph**. The entire document is now double-spaced, with no paragraph spacing, and the entire document is still selected.

5. In the Font group, click the **Font Size** arrow, and then click **12**. The entire document is formatted in 12-point font.

6. Click anywhere in the document to deselect the text.

7. In the first paragraph of the document, replace Kaya's name with your first and last name, and then save the document.

Now you need to indent the first line of each body paragraph.

Indenting a Paragraph

Word offers a number of options for indenting a paragraph. You can move an entire paragraph to the right, or you can create specialized indents, such as a **hanging indent**, where all lines except the first line of the paragraph are indented from the left margin. As you saw in the Session 2.2 Visual Overview, all the body paragraphs (that is, all the paragraphs except the information in the upper-left corner of the first page, the title, and the headings) have a first-line indent in MLA research papers. Figure 2-23 shows some examples of other common paragraph indents.

Figure 2-23 Common paragraph indents

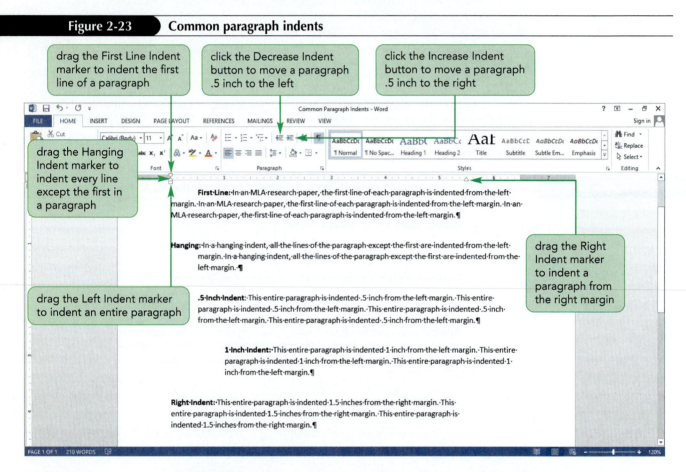

To quickly indent an entire paragraph .5 inch from the left, position the insertion point in the paragraph you want to indent and then click the Increase Indent button in the Paragraph group on the HOME tab. You can continue to indent the paragraph in increments of .5 inch by repeatedly clicking the Increase Indent button. To move an indented paragraph back to the left .5 inch, click the Decrease Indent button.

To create first line, hanging, or right indents, you can use the indent markers on the ruler. First, click in the paragraph you want to indent, or select multiple paragraphs. Then drag the appropriate indent marker to the left or right on the horizontal ruler. The indent markers are small and can be hard to see. As shown in Figure 2-23, the **First Line Indent marker** looks like the top half of an hourglass; the **Hanging Indent marker** looks like the bottom half. The rectangle below the Hanging Indent marker is the **Left Indent marker**. The **Right Indent Marker** looks just like the Hanging Indent marker except that it is located on the far-right side of the horizontal ruler.

Note that when you indent an entire paragraph using the Increase Indent button, the three indent markers, shown stacked on top of one another in Figure 2-23, move as a unit along with the paragraphs you are indenting.

In Kaya's paper, you will indent the first lines of the body paragraphs .5 inch from the left margin, as specified by the MLA style.

To indent the first line of each paragraph:

1. On the first page of the document, just below the title, click anywhere in the first main paragraph, which begins "Wherever people gather...."

2. On the horizontal ruler, position the mouse pointer over the First Line Indent marker . When you see the ScreenTip that reads "First Line Indent," you know the mouse is positioned correctly.

3. Press and hold the mouse button as you drag the **First Line Indent** marker to the right, to the .5-inch mark on the horizontal ruler. As you drag, a vertical guide line appears over the document, and the first line of the paragraph moves right. See Figure 2-24.

Figure 2-24	**Dragging the First Line Indent marker**

First Line Indent marker

.5-inch mark

as you drag the indent marker, a guide line appears and the first line of the paragraph moves right

4. When the First Line Indent marker is positioned at the .5-inch mark on the ruler, release the mouse button. The first line of the paragraph containing the insertion point indents .5 inch and the vertical guide line disappears.

5. Scroll down, if necessary, click anywhere in the next paragraph in the document, which begins "These days, it's not hard to know...," and then drag the **First Line Indent** marker to the right, to the .5-inch mark on the horizontal ruler. As you move the indent marker, you can use the vertical guide line to ensure that you match the first line indent of the preceding paragraph.

 You could continue to drag the indent marker to indent the first line of the remaining body paragraphs, but it's faster to use the Repeat button on the Quick Access Toolbar.

6. Scroll down and click in the paragraph below the heading "Early News Media," and then on the Quick Access Toolbar, click the **Repeat** button.

7. Click in the next paragraph, at the top of page 2, which begins "Early news media took many forms," and then click the **Repeat** button.

8. Continue using the **Repeat** button to indent the first line of all of the remaining body paragraphs. Take care not to indent the headings, which in this document are formatted just like the body text.

9. Scroll to the top of the document, verify that you have correctly indented the first line of each body paragraph, and then save the document.

Next, you need to insert page numbers.

Inserting and Modifying Page Numbers

When you insert page numbers in a document, you don't have to type a page number on each page. Instead, you insert a **page number field**, which is an instruction that tells Word to insert a page number on each page, no matter how many pages you eventually add to the document. Word inserts page number fields above the top margin, in the blank area known as the **header**, or below the bottom margin, in the area known as the **footer**. You can also insert page numbers in the side margins, although for business or academic documents, it's customary to place them in the header or footer.

After you insert a page number field, Word switches to Header and Footer view. In this view, you can add your name or other text next to the page number field, or use the HEADER & FOOTER TOOLS DESIGN tab to change various settings related to headers and footers.

The MLA style requires a page number preceded by the student's last name in the upper-right corner of each page. If you prefer (or if your instructor requests it), you can omit the page number from the first page by selecting the Different First Page check box on the DESIGN tab.

To add page numbers to the research paper:

1. Press the **Ctrl+Home** keys to move the insertion point to the beginning of the document.

2. On the ribbon, click the **INSERT** tab. The ribbon changes to display the Insert options, including options for inserting page numbers.

3. In the Header & Footer group, click the **Page Number** button to open the Page Number menu. Here you can choose where you want to position the page numbers in your document—at the top of the page, at the bottom of the page, in the side margins, or at the current location of the insertion point.

4. Point to **Top of Page**. A gallery of page number styles opens. You can scroll the list to review the many styles of page numbers. Because the MLA style calls for a simple page number in the upper-right corner, you will use the Plain Number 3 style. See Figure 2-25.

TIP

To remove page numbers from a document, click the Remove Page Numbers command on the Page Number menu.

Figure 2-25 **Gallery of page number styles**

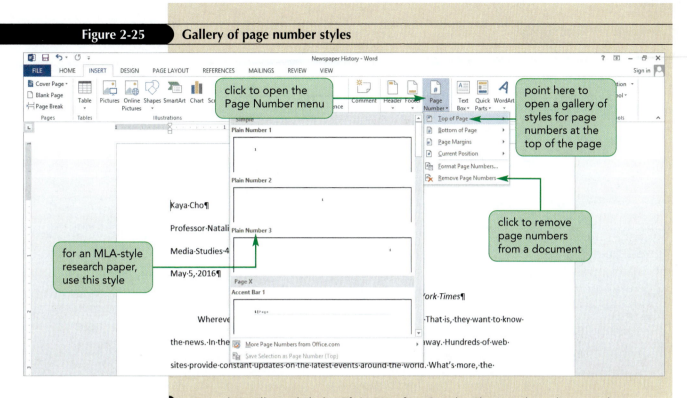

5. In the gallery, click the **Plain Number 3** style. The Word window switches to Header and Footer view, with the page number for the first page in the upper-right corner. The page number has a gray background, indicating that it is actually a page number field and not simply a number that you typed.

The HEADER & FOOTER TOOLS DESIGN tab is displayed on the ribbon, giving you access to a variety of formatting options. The insertion point blinks to the left of the page number field, ready for you to add text to the header if you wish. Note that in Header and Footer view, you can only type in the header or footer areas. The text in the main document area is a lighter shade of gray, indicating that it cannot be edited in this view.

6. Type your last name, and then press the **spacebar**. If you see a wavy red line below your last name, right-click your name, and then click **Ignore** on the Shortcut menu. See Figure 2-26.

Figure 2-26 Last name inserted next to the page number field

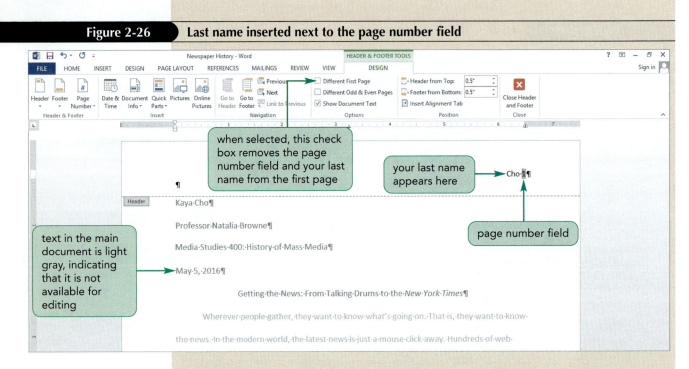

7. Scroll down and observe the page number (with your last name) at the top of pages 2, 3, and 4. As you can see, whatever you insert in the header on one page appears on every page of the document by default.

8. Press the **Ctrl+Home** keys to return to the header on the first page.

9. On the HEADER & FOOTER TOOLS DESIGN tab, in the Options group, click the **Different First Page** check box to insert a check. The page number field and your last name are removed from the first page header. The insertion point blinks at the header's left margin in case you want to insert something else for the first page header. In this case, you don't.

TIP

After you insert page numbers, you can reopen Header and Footer view by double-clicking a page number in Print Layout view.

10. In the Close group, click the **Close Header and Footer** button. You return to Print Layout view, and the HEADER & FOOTER TOOLS DESIGN tab is no longer displayed on the ribbon.

11. Scroll down to review your last name and the page number in the headers for pages 2, 3, and 4. In Print Layout view, the text in the header is light gray, indicating that it is not currently available for editing.

You have finished all the tasks related to formatting the MLA-style research paper. Now Kaya wants your help with creating the essential parts of any research paper—the citations and the bibliography.

Creating Citations and a Bibliography

A bibliography (or, as it is called in the MLA style, the works cited list) is an alphabetical list of all the books, magazine articles, websites, movies, and other works referred to in a research paper. The items listed in a bibliography are known as **sources**. The entry for each source includes information such as the author, the title of the work, the publication date, and the publisher.

Within the research paper itself, you include a parenthetical reference, or citation, every time you quote or refer to a source. Every source included in your citations then has a corresponding entry in the works cited list. A citation should include enough information to identify the quote or referenced material so the reader can easily locate the source in the accompanying works cited list. The exact form for a citation varies depending on the style guide you are using and the type of material you are referencing.

Some style guides are very rigid about the form and location of citations, but the MLA style offers quite a bit of flexibility. Typically, though, you insert an MLA citation at the end of a sentence in which you quote or refer to material from a source. For books or journals, the citation itself usually includes the author's last name and a page number. However, if the sentence containing the citation already includes the author's name, you only need to include the page number in the citation. Figure 2-27 provides some sample MLA citations for books and journals. For detailed guidelines, you can consult the *MLA Handbook for Writers of Research Papers, Seventh Edition*, which includes many examples.

Figure 2-27 **MLA guidelines for citing a book or journal**

Citation Rule	Example
If the sentence includes the author's name, the citation should only include the page number.	Peterson compares the opening scene of the movie to a scene from Shakespeare (188).
If the sentence does not include the author's name, the citation should include the author's name and the page number.	The opening scene of the movie has been compared to a scene from Shakespeare (Peterson 188).

© 2014 Cengage Learning

Word greatly simplifies the process of creating citations and a bibliography. You specify the style you want to use, and then Word takes care of setting up the citation and the works cited list appropriately. Every time you create a citation for a new source, Word prompts you to enter the information needed to create the corresponding entry in the works cited list. If you don't have all of your source information available, Word also allows you to insert a temporary, placeholder citation, which you can replace later with a complete citation. When you are finished creating your citations, Word generates the bibliography automatically. Note that placeholder citations are not included in the bibliography.

PROSKILLS

Written Communication: Acknowledging Your Sources

A research paper is a means for you to explore the available information about a subject and then present this information, along with your own understanding of the subject, in an organized and interesting way. Acknowledging all the sources of the information presented in your research paper is essential. If you fail to do this, you might be subject to charges of plagiarism, or trying to pass off someone else's thoughts as your own. Plagiarism is an extremely serious accusation for which you could suffer academic consequences ranging from failing an assignment to being expelled from school.

To ensure that you don't forget to cite a source, you should be careful about creating citations in your document as you type. It's very easy to forget to go back and cite all your sources correctly after you've finished typing a research paper. Failing to cite a source could lead to accusations of plagiarism and all the consequences that entails. If you don't have the complete information about a source, you should at least insert a placeholder citation. But take care to go back later and substitute complete citations for any placeholders.

Creating Citations

Before you create citations, you need to select the style you want to use, which in the case of Kaya's paper is the MLA style. Then, to insert a citation, you click the Insert Citation button in the Citations & Bibliography group on the REFERENCES tab. If you are citing a source for the first time, Word prompts you to enter all the information required for the source's entry in the bibliography or works cited list. If you are citing an existing source, you simply select the source from the Insert Citation menu.

By default, an MLA citation includes only the author's name in parentheses. However, you can use the Edit Citation dialog box to add a page number. You can also use the Edit Citation dialog box to remove, or suppress, the author's name, so only the page number appears in the citation. However, in an MLA citation, Word will replace the suppressed author name with the title of the source, so you need to suppress the title as well, by selecting the Title check box in the Edit Citation dialog box.

Creating Citations

REFERENCE

- On the ribbon, click the REFERENCES tab. In the Citations & Bibliography group, click the Style button arrow, and then select the style you want.
- Click in the document where you want to insert the citation. Typically, a citation goes at the end of a sentence, before the ending punctuation.
- To add a citation for a new source, click the Insert Citation button in the Citations & Bibliography group, click Add New Source, enter information in the Create Source dialog box, and then click the OK button.
- To add a citation for an existing source, click the Insert Citation button, and then click the source.
- To add a placeholder citation, click the Insert Citation button, click Add New Placeholder, and then, in the content control, type placeholder text, such as the author's last name, that will serve as a reminder about which source you need to cite. Note that a placeholder citation cannot contain any spaces.
- To add a page number to a citation, click the citation in the document, click the Citation Options button, click Edit Citation, type the page number, and then click the OK button.
- To display only the page number in a citation, click the citation in the document, click the Citation Options button, and then click Edit Citation. In the Edit Citation dialog box, select the Author and Title check boxes to suppress this information, and then click the OK button.

So far, Kaya has referenced information from two different sources in her research paper. You'll select a style and then begin adding the appropriate citations.

To select a style for the citation and bibliography:

1. On the ribbon, click the **REFERENCES** tab. The ribbon changes to display references options.

2. In the Citations & Bibliography group, click the **Style button arrow**, and then click **MLA Seventh Edition** if it is not already selected.

3. Press the **Ctrl+F** keys to open the Navigation pane.

4. Use the Navigation pane to find the phrase "As at least one historian has observed," which appears on page 1, and then click in the document at the end of that sentence (between the end of the word "medium" and the closing period).

5. Close the Navigation pane, and then click the **REFERENCES** tab on the ribbon, if necessary. You need to add a citation that informs the reader that historian Adam Taylor made the observation described in the sentence. See Figure 2-28.

Figure 2-28 MLA style selected and insertion point positioned for new citation

selected citation and bibliography style

As at least one historian has observed, the ability to distribute news to a geographically diverse group of people depends on the availability of a reliable medium. But what is a medium exactly? Leona Sanford defines "medium" as a way or a means of accomplishing something.

citation will appear at the insertion point

extension, then, a news medium is a way or means of delivering news to other people.¶

6. In the Citations & Bibliography group, click the **Insert Citation** button to open the menu. At this point, you could click Add New Placeholder on the menu to insert a temporary, placeholder citation. However, because you have all the necessary source information, you can go ahead and create a complete citation.

7. On the menu, click **Add New Source**. The Create Source dialog box opens, ready for you to add the information required to create a bibliography entry for Adam Taylor's book.

8. If necessary, click the **Type of Source** arrow, scroll up or down in the list, and then click **Book**.

9. In the Author box, type **Adam Taylor**.

10. Click in the **Title** box, and then type **Newspapers as Modern Media in a Modern Media World**.

11. Click in the **Year** box, and then type **2005**. This is the year the book was published. Next, you need to enter the name and location of the publisher.

12. Click the **City** box, type **New York**, click the **Publisher** box, and then type **Warrington and Reeves Academy Press**.

Finally, you need to indicate the medium used to publish the book. In this case, Kaya used a printed copy, so the medium is "Print." For books or journals published online, the correct medium would be "Web."

13. Click the **Medium** box, and then type **Print**. See Figure 2-29.

TIP

When entering information in a dialog box, you can press the Tab key to move the insertion point from one box to another.

Figure 2-29 Create Source dialog box with information for the first source

14. Click the **OK** button. Word inserts the parenthetical "(Taylor)" at the end of the sentence in the document.

Although the citation looks like ordinary text, it is actually contained inside a content control, a special feature used to display information that is inserted automatically and that may need to be updated later. You can only see the content control itself when it is selected. When it is unselected, you simply see the citation. In the next set of steps, you will select the content control, and then edit the citation to add a page number.

To edit the citation:

TIP

To delete a citation, click the citation to display the content control, click the tab on the left side of the content control, and then press the Delete key.

1. In the document, click the citation **(Taylor)**. The citation appears in a content control, which is a box with a tab on the left and an arrow button on the right. The arrow button is called the Citation Options button.

2. Click the **Citation Options** button . A menu of options related to editing a citation opens, as shown in Figure 2-30. To edit the information about the source, you click Edit Source. To change the information that is displayed in the citation itself, you use the Edit Citation option.

Figure 2-30 **Citation Options menu**

3. On the Citation Options menu, click **Edit Citation**. The Edit Citation dialog box opens, as shown in Figure 2-31.

Figure 2-31 **Edit Citation dialog box**

To add a page number for the citation, you type the page number in the Pages box. If you want to display only the page number in the citation (which would be necessary if you already mentioned the author's name in the same sentence in the text), then you would also select the Author and Title check boxes in this dialog box to suppress this information.

▶ **4.** Type **45** to insert the page number in the Pages box, click the **OK** button to close the dialog box, and then click anywhere in the document outside the citation content control. The revised citation now reads "(Taylor 45)."

Next, you will add two more citations, both for the same journal article.

To insert two more citations:

▶ **1.** Click at the end of the second-to-last sentence of the current paragraph (which begins "Leona Sanford defines…"), between the word "something" and the period. This sentence mentions historian Leona Sanford; you need to add a citation to one of her journal articles.

▶ **2.** In the Citations & Bibliography group, click the **Insert Citation** button to open the Insert Citation menu. Notice that Adam Taylor's book is now listed as a source on this menu. You could click Taylor's book on the menu to add a citation to it, but right now you need to add a new source.

▶ **3.** Click **Add New Source** to open the Create Source dialog box, click the **Type of Source** arrow, and then click **Journal Article**.

The Create Source dialog box displays the boxes, or fields, appropriate for a journal article. The information required to cite a journal article differs from the information you entered earlier for the citation for the Taylor book. For journal articles, you are prompted to enter the page numbers for the entire article. If you want to display a particular page number in the citation, you can add it later.

By default, Word displays boxes, or fields, for the information most commonly included in a bibliography. In this case, you also want to include the volume and issue numbers for Leona Sanford's article, so you need to display more fields.

▶ **4.** In the Create Source dialog box, click the **Show All Bibliography Fields** check box to select this option. The Create Source dialog box expands to allow you to enter more detailed information. Red asterisks highlight the fields that are recommended, but these recommended fields don't necessarily apply to every source.

▶ **5.** Enter the following information, scrolling down to display the necessary boxes:

Author: **Leona Sanford**

Title: **News Media in History: A Study of Newsgathering from the Roman Empire to the Modern Day**

Journal Name: **Journal of Media Policy Studies International**

Year: **2008**

Pages: **122–145**

Volume: **30**

Issue: **5**

Medium: **Web**

When you are finished, your Create Source dialog box should look like the one shown in Figure 2-32.

| Figure 2-32 | Create Source dialog box with information for the journal article |

which·we·live.¶

Early·News·Media

As·at·least·

diverse·group·of·p

is·a·medium·exactl

something.·By·exte

people.¶

Create Source

Type of Source: Journal Article

Bibliography Fields for MLA

Month		
Day		
★ Pages	122-145	
Editor		[Edit]
Publisher		
Volume	30	
Issue	5	
Short Title		
Standard Number		
Comments		
★ Medium	Web	

☑ Show All Bibliography Fields ★ Recommended Field

Tag name Example: Document

12230 [OK] [Cancel]

Callouts:
- new citation will appear here
- select this check box to display more fields
- scroll up or down to display more boxes

6. Click the **OK** button. The Create Source dialog box closes, and the citation "(Sanford)" is inserted in the text. Because the sentence containing the citation already includes the author's name, you will edit the citation to include the page number and suppress the author's name.

7. Click the **(Sanford)** citation to display the content control, click the **Citation Options** button, and then click **Edit Citation** to open the Edit Citation dialog box.

8. In the Pages box, type **142**, and then click the **Author** and **Title** check boxes to select them. You need to suppress both the author's name and the title because otherwise Word will replace the suppressed author name with the title. When using the MLA style, you don't ever have to suppress the year because the year is never included as part of an MLA citation. When working in other styles, however, you might need to suppress the year.

9. Click the **OK** button to close the Edit Citation dialog box, and then click anywhere outside the content control to deselect it. The end of the sentence now reads "…accomplishing something (142)."

10. Use the Navigation pane to find the sentence that begins "Throughout history…" on the second page. Click at the end of the sentence, to the left of the period after "news," and then close the Navigation pane.

11. On the REFERENCES tab, in the Citations & Bibliography group, click the **Insert Citation** button, and then click the **Sanford, Leona** source at the top of the menu. You want the citation to refer to the entire article instead of just one page, so you will not edit the citation to add a specific page number.

12. Save the document.

You have entered the source information for two sources.

Generating a Bibliography

Once you have created a citation for a source in a document, you can generate a bibliography. When you do, Word scans all the citations in the document, collecting the source information for each citation, and then it creates a list of information for each unique source. The format of the entries in the bibliography will reflect the style you specified when you created your first citation, which in this case is the MLA style. The bibliography itself is a **field**, similar to the page number field you inserted earlier in this session. In other words, it is really an instruction that tells Word to display the source information for all the citations in the document. Because it is a field and not actual text, you can update the bibliography later to reflect any new citations you might add.

You can choose to insert a bibliography as a field directly in the document, or you can insert a bibliography enclosed within a content control that also includes the heading "Bibliography" or "Works Cited." Inserting a bibliography enclosed in a content control is best because the content control includes a useful button that you can use to update your bibliography if you make changes to the sources.

In the MLA style, the bibliography (or works cited list) starts on a new page. So your first step is to insert a manual page break. A **manual page break** is one you insert at a specific location; it doesn't matter if the previous page is full or not. To insert a manual page break, use the Page Break button in the Pages group on the INSERT tab.

To insert a manual page break:

1. Press the **Ctrl+End** keys to move the insertion point to the end of the document.

2. On the ribbon, click the **INSERT** tab.

3. In the Pages group, click the **Page Break** button. Word inserts a new, blank page at the end of the document, with the insertion point blinking at the top. Note that you could also use the Ctrl+Enter keyboard shortcut to insert a manual page break.

4. Scroll up to see the dotted line with the words "Page Break" at the bottom of the text on page 4. See Figure 2-33.

TIP

Use the Blank Page button to insert a new, blank page in the middle of a document.

Figure 2-33 **Manual page break inserted into the document**

Now you can insert the bibliography on the new page 5.

To insert the bibliography:

1. Scroll down so you can see the insertion point at the top of page 5.

2. On the ribbon, click the **REFERENCES** tab.

3. In the Citations & Bibliography group, click the **Bibliography** button. The Bibliography menu opens, displaying three styles with preformatted headings—"Bibliography," "References," and "Works Cited." The Insert Bibliography command at the bottom inserts a bibliography without a preformatted heading. See Figure 2-34.

Figure 2-34 | **Bibliography menu**

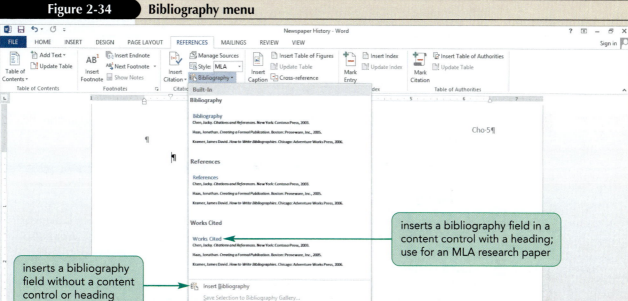

inserts a bibliography field in a content control with a heading; use for an MLA research paper

inserts a bibliography field without a content control or heading

4. Click **Works Cited**. Word inserts the bibliography, with two entries, below the "Works Cited" heading.

 The bibliography text is formatted in Calibri, the default font for the Office theme. The "Works Cited" heading is formatted with the Heading 1 style. To see the content control that contains the bibliography, you need to select it.

5. Click anywhere in the bibliography. Inside the content control, the bibliography is highlighted in gray, indicating that it is a field and not regular text. The content control containing the bibliography is also now visible in the form of a rectangular border and a tab with two buttons. See Figure 2-35.

Figure 2-35 **Bibliography displayed in a content control**

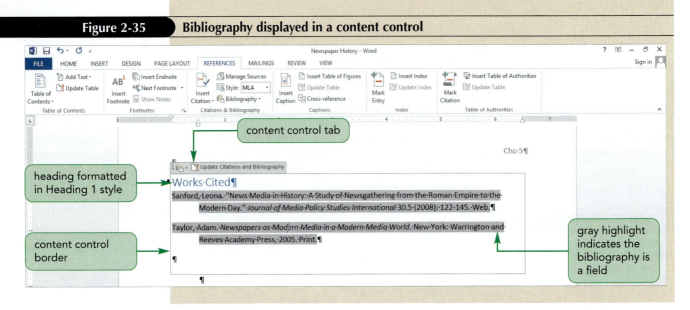

As Kaya looks over the works cited list, she realizes that she misspelled the last name of one of the authors. You'll correct the error now, and then update the bibliography.

INSIGHT

Managing Sources

When you create a source, Word adds it to a Master List of sources, which is available to any document created using the same user account on that computer. Word also adds each new source to the Current List of sources for that document. Both the Master List and the Current List are accessible via the Source Manager dialog box, which you open by clicking the Manage Sources button in the Citations & Bibliography group on the REFERENCES tab. Using this dialog box, you can copy sources from the Master List into the Current List, and vice versa. As you begin to focus on a particular academic field and turn repeatedly to important works in your chosen field, you'll find this ability to reuse sources very helpful.

Modifying an Existing Source

To modify information about a source, you click a citation to that source in the document, click the Citation Options button on the content control, and then click Edit Source. After you are finished editing the source, Word prompts you to update the master list and the source information in the current document. In almost all cases, you should click Yes to ensure that the source information is correct in all the places it is stored on your computer.

To edit a source in the research paper:

▶ **1.** Click in the blank paragraph below the bibliography content control to deselect the bibliography.

▶ **2.** Scroll up to display the last paragraph on page 2, and then click the **(Sanford)** citation you entered earlier in the first line of the paragraph. The content control appears around the citation.

3. Click the **Citation Options** button ⬚, and then click **Edit Source**. The Edit Source dialog box opens. Note that Word displays the author's last name first in the Author box, just as it would appear in a bibliography.

4. Click the **Author** box, and then add an "e" to the last name "Sanford" to change it to "Sanforde."

5. Click the **OK** button. A message dialog box opens, asking if you want to update the master source list and the current document.

6. Click the **Yes** button, and then click anywhere on the second page to deselect the citation content control. The revised author name in the citation now reads "Sanforde."

7. Scroll up to the last paragraph on page 1, locate "Sanford" in the last paragraph on the page, and then change "Sanford" to "Sanforde."

8. Save the document.

You've edited the document text and the citation to include the correct spelling of "Sanforde," but now you need to update the bibliography to correct the spelling.

Updating and Finalizing a Bibliography

The bibliography does not automatically change to reflect edits you make to existing citations or to show new citations. To incorporate the latest information stored in the citations, you need to update the bibliography. To update a bibliography in a content control, click the bibliography, and then, in the content control tab, click Update Citations and Bibliography. To update a bibliography field that is not contained in a content control, right-click the bibliography, and then click Update Field on the shortcut menu.

To update the bibliography:

1. Scroll down to page 5 and click anywhere in the works cited list to display the content control.

2. In the content control tab, click **Update Citations and Bibliography**. The works cited list is updated, with "Sanford" changed to "Sanforde" in the first entry.

Kaya still has a fair amount of work to do on her research paper. After she finishes writing it and adding all the citations, she will update the bibliography again to include all her cited sources. At that point, you might think the bibliography would be finished. However, a few steps remain to ensure that the works cited list matches the MLA style. To finalize Kaya's works cited list to match the MLA style, you need to make the changes shown in Figure 2-36.

| Figure 2-36 | Steps for finalizing a bibliography to match MLA guidelines for a Works Cited list |

1. Format the "Works Cited" heading to match the formatting of the rest of the text in the document.

2. Center the "Works Cited" heading.

3. Double-space the entire works cited list, including the heading, and remove extra space after the paragraphs.

4. Change the font size for the entire works cited list to 12 points.

To format the bibliography as an MLA style works cited list:

1. Click in the **Works Cited** heading, and then click the **HOME** tab on the ribbon.

2. In the Styles group, click the **Normal** style. The "Works Cited" heading is now formatted in Calibri body font like the rest of the document. The MLA style for a works cited list requires this heading to be centered.

3. In the Paragraph group, click the **Center** button ☰.

4. Select the entire works cited list, including the heading. Change the font size to **12** points, change the line spacing to **2.0**, and then remove the paragraph spacing after each paragraph.

5. Click below the content control to deselect the works cited list, and then review your work. See Figure 2-37.

| Figure 2-37 | MLA-style Works Cited list |

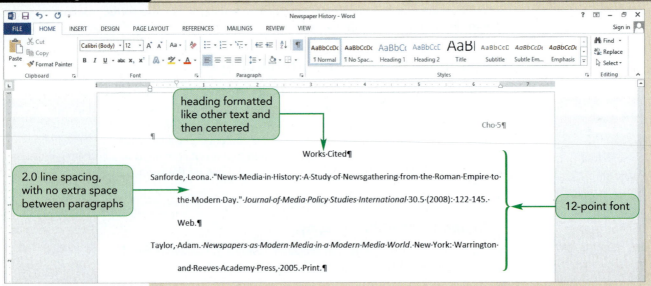

6. Save the document and close it.

Kaya's research paper now meets the MLA style guidelines.

Session 2.2 Quick Check

REVIEW

1. List the five tasks you need to perform to make a default Word document match the MLA style.

2. How do you indent a paragraph one inch from the left margin using an option on the ribbon?

3. Explain how to remove a page number from the first page of a document.

4. What is a bibliography called according to the MLA style?

5. Explain how to create a citation for a new source.

6. Explain how to edit a citation to display only the page number.

SAM Projects

Put your skills into practice with SAM Projects! SAM Projects for this tutorial can be found online. If you have a SAM account, go to www.cengage.com/sam2013 to download the most recent Project Instructions and Start Files.

Review Assignments

Data Files needed for the Review Assignments: Broadcast.docx, Situation.docx

Because the Media Studies document turned out so well, Kaya has been asked to help a student assistant in the Journalism department create a handout describing the classes required for a major in Broadcast Journalism. Kaya asks you to help her revise and format the document. She also asks you to create a document listing the prerequisites and core courses. Finally, as part of her Media Studies class, Kaya is working on a research paper on the history of situation comedy. She asks you to help her format the paper according to the MLA style, and to create some citations and a bibliography. She has inserted the uppercase word "CITATION" wherever she needs to insert a citation. Complete the following steps:

1. Open the file **Broadcast** located in the Word2 ▸ Review folder included with your Data Files, and then save the document as **Broadcast Journalism** in the location specified by your instructor.

2. Read the first comment, which provides an overview of the changes you will be making to the document in the following steps. Perform the task described in the second comment, and then delete both comments.

3. On page 2, in the second paragraph, revise the name of the first public speaking class so that only the first letter of each word is capitalized. Attach a comment to this paragraph that explains the change.

4. On page 2, move the "Senior Project" heading up to position it before the paragraph that begins "This project should incorporate...."

5. Replace the first instance of "journalism" with "media," being sure to match the case.

6. On page 1, format the list of four prerequisite classes as a bulleted list with square bullets. Do the same for the list of core courses, and then indent the three symposium names so they are formatted with an open circle bullet.

7. At the top of page 2, format the list of three public speaking classes as a numbered list, using the "1), 2), 3)" numbering style.

8. In the numbered list, move paragraph 3 ("Broadcast Journalism 220: Video Reporting") up to make it paragraph 2.

9. Format the title "Majoring in Broadcast Journalism" using the Title style. Format the following headings with the Heading 1 style: "Prerequisites," "Core Courses," "Electives," "Public Speaking," and "Senior Project."

10. Change the document theme to the Integral theme.

11. Display the Clipboard task pane. Copy the bulleted list of prerequisites to the Clipboard, and then copy the heading "Prerequisites" to the Clipboard. To ensure that you copy the heading formatting, be sure to select the paragraph mark after "Prerequisites" before you click the Copy button.

12. Open a new, blank document, and then save the document as **Prerequisite List** in the location specified by your instructor.

13. At the beginning of the document, paste the heading "Prerequisites," and then, from the Paste Options menu, apply the Keep Source Formatting option. Below the heading, paste the list of prerequisites, which begins with the text "Journalism 101...."

ASSESS

PRACTICE

14. At the end of the document, insert a new paragraph, and then type **Prepared by:** followed by your first and last names.

15. Save the Prerequisite List document and close it.

16. In the Broadcast Journalism document, clear the contents of the Clipboard task pane, close the Clipboard task pane, save the document, and then close it.

17. Open the file **Situation** located in the Word2 ▸ Review folder included with your Data Files.

18. Save the document as **Situation Comedy** in the location specified by your instructor.

19. In the first paragraph, replace Kaya's name with your own.

20. Adjust the font size, line spacing, paragraph spacing, and paragraph indents to match the MLA style.

21. Insert your last name and a page number on every page except the first.

22. If necessary, select MLA Seventh Edition as the citations and bibliography style.

23. Use the Navigation pane to highlight all instances of the uppercase word "CITATION." Keep the Navigation pane open so you can continue to use it to find the locations where you need to insert citations in Steps 24–28.

24. Delete the first instance of "CITATION" and the space before it, and then create a new source with the following information:
Type of Source: **Book**
Author: **Cecile Webster**
Title: **The Comedy of Situations: A History in Words and Pictures**
Year: **2008**
City: **Boston**
Publisher: **Boston Valley Press**
Medium: **Print**

25. Edit the citation to add **203** as the page number. Display only the page number in the citation.

26. Delete the second instance of "CITATION" and the space before it, and then create a new source with the following information:
Type of Source: **Journal Article**
Author: **Oliver Bernault**
Title: **How Slapstick Conquered the World**
Journal Name: **Pacific Film Quarterly: Criticism and Comment**
Year: **2011**
Pages: **68–91**
Volume: **11**
Issue: **2**
Medium: **Web**

27. Edit the citation to add "80" as the page number.

28. Delete the third instance of "CITATION" and the space before it, and then insert a citation for the book by Cecile Webster.

29. At the end of the document, start a new page and insert a bibliography in a content control with the heading "Works Cited."

30. In the second source you created, add an "e" to change the last name "Bernault" to "Bernaulte," and then update the bibliography.

31. Finalize the bibliography to create an MLA-style Works Cited list.

32. Save the **Situation Comedy** document and close it.

33. Close any other open documents.

Case Problem 1

APPLY

Data File needed for this Case Problem: Yoga.docx

Green Willow Yoga Studio and Spa Karl Boccio, the manager of Green Willow Yoga Studio and Spa, created a flyer to inform clients of the studio's move to a new location. The flyer also lists classes for the summer session and explains the registration process. It's your job to format the flyer to make it look professional and easy to read. Karl included comments in the document explaining what he wants you to do. Complete the following steps:

1. Open the file **Yoga** located in the Word2 ▸ Case1 folder included with your Data Files, and then save the file as **Yoga Flyer** in the location specified by your instructor.

2. Format the document as directed in the comments. After you complete a task, delete the relevant comment. Respond "Yes" to the comment asking if twenty is the correct number of years. When you are finished with the formatting, the comment with the question and the comment with your reply should be the only remaining comments.

3. Move the third bulleted item (which begins "Yoga for Relaxation...") up to make it the first bulleted item in the list.

4. Change the theme to the Ion theme, and then attach a comment to the title listing the heading and body fonts applied by the Ion theme.

5. Save the document and then close it.

Case Problem 2

APPLY

Data File needed for this Case Problem: Hamlet.docx

South Valley Community College Jaleel Reynolds is a student at South Valley Community College. He's working on a research paper about Shakespeare's tragic masterpiece, *Hamlet*. The research paper is only partly finished, with notes in brackets indicating the material Jaleel still plans to write. He also inserted the uppercase word "CITATION" wherever he needs to insert a citation. Jaleel asks you to help him format this early draft to match the MLA style. He also asks you to help him create some citations and a first attempt at a bibliography. He will update the bibliography later, after he finishes writing the research paper. Complete the following steps:

1. Open the file **Hamlet** located in the Word2 ▸ Case2 folder included with your Data Files, and then save the document as **Hamlet Paper** in the location specified by your instructor.

2. In the first paragraph, replace "Jaleel Reynolds" with your name, and then adjust the font size, line spacing, paragraph spacing, and paragraph indents to match the MLA style.

3. Insert your last name and a page number in the upper-right corner of every page except the first page in the document.

4. If necessary, select MLA Seventh Edition as the citations and bibliography style.

5. Use the Navigation pane to find three instances of the uppercase word "CITATION."

6. Delete the first instance of "CITATION" and the space before it, and then create a new source with the following information:
 Type of Source: **Book**
 Author: **Andre Kahn**
 Title: **Tragic Drama in a Tragic Age**
 Year: **2000**
 City: **Chicago**
 Publisher: **Houghton University Press**
 Medium: **Print**

7. Edit the citation to add **127** as the page number.

8. Delete the second instance of "CITATION" and the space before it, and then create a new source with the following information:

 Type of Source: **Sound Recording**

 Performer: **Avery Pohlman**

 Title: **Live From New York's Golden Arch Theater**

 Production Company: **Prescott**

 Year: **1995**

 Medium: **CD**

 City: **New York**

9. Edit the citation to suppress the Author and the Year, so that it displays only the title.

10. Delete the third instance of "CITATION" and the space before it, and then insert a second reference to the book by Andre Kahn.

11. Edit the citation to add **35** as the page number.

12. At the end of the document, start a new page, and then insert a bibliography with the preformatted heading "Works Cited."

13. Edit the first source you created, changing the last name from "Kahn" to **Klann.**

14. Update the bibliography so it shows the revised name "Klann."

15. Finalize the bibliography so that it matches the MLA style.

16. Save the Hamlet Paper document and close it.

Case Problem 3

Data Files needed for this Case Problem: Capital.docx, Sarah.docx

CREATE

Sports Training Sarah Vang has more than a decade of experience as an athletic trainer in several different settings. After moving to a new city, she is looking for a job as a trainer in a hospital. She has asked you to edit and format her resume. As part of the application process, she will have to upload her resume to the hospitals' employee recruitment websites. Because these sites typically request a simple page design, Sarah plans to rely primarily on heading styles and bullets to organize her information. When the resume is complete, she wants you to remove any color applied by the heading styles. She also needs help formatting a document she created for a public health organization for which she volunteers. Complete the following steps:

1. Open the file **Sarah** located in the Word2 ► Case3 folder included with your Data Files, and then save the file as **Sarah Resume** in the location specified by your instructor.

2. Read the comment included in the document, and then perform the task it specifies.

3. Respond to the comment with the response **I think that's a good choice for the theme.**, and then mark Sarah's comment as done.

4. Replace all occurrences of "Mesacrest" with **Mesa Crest**.

5. Format the resume as shown in Figure 2-38. To ensure that the resume fits on one page, pay special attention to the paragraph spacing settings specified in Figure 2-38.

Figure 2-38 **Formatting for Sarah Vang's resume**

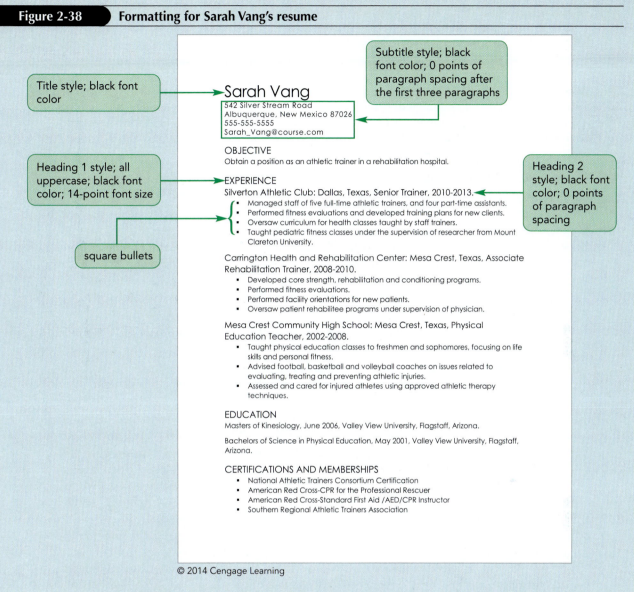

Title style; black font color

Subtitle style; black font color; 0 points of paragraph spacing after the first three paragraphs

Heading 1 style; all uppercase; black font color; 14-point font size

Heading 2 style; black font color; 0 points of paragraph spacing

square bullets

Sarah Vang
542 Silver Stream Road
Albuquerque, New Mexico 87026
555-555-5555
Sarah_Vang@course.com

OBJECTIVE
Obtain a position as an athletic trainer in a rehabilitation hospital.

EXPERIENCE
Silverton Athletic Club: Dallas, Texas, Senior Trainer, 2010-2013.
- Managed staff of five full-time athletic trainers, and four part-time assistants.
- Performed fitness evaluations and developed training plans for new clients.
- Oversaw curriculum for health classes taught by staff trainers.
- Taught pediatric fitness classes under the supervision of researcher from Mount Clareton University.

Carrington Health and Rehabilitation Center: Mesa Crest, Texas, Associate Rehabilitation Trainer, 2008-2010.
- Developed core strength, rehabilitation and conditioning programs.
- Performed fitness evaluations.
- Performed facility orientations for new patients.
- Oversaw patient rehabilitee programs under supervision of physician.

Mesa Crest Community High School: Mesa Crest, Texas, Physical Education Teacher, 2002-2008.
- Taught physical education classes to freshmen and sophomores, focusing on life skills and personal fitness.
- Advised football, basketball and volleyball coaches on issues related to evaluating, treating and preventing athletic injuries.
- Assessed and cared for injured athletes using approved athletic therapy techniques.

EDUCATION
Masters of Kinesiology, June 2006, Valley View University, Flagstaff, Arizona.

Bachelors of Science in Physical Education, May 2001, Valley View University, Flagstaff, Arizona.

CERTIFICATIONS AND MEMBERSHIPS
- National Athletic Trainers Consortium Certification
- American Red Cross-CPR for the Professional Rescuer
- American Red Cross-Standard First Aid /AED/CPR Instructor
- Southern Regional Athletic Trainers Association

6. In the email address, replace "Sarah_Vang" with your first and last names, separated by an underscore, and then save the document and close it.

7. Open the file **Capital** located in the Word2 ▶ Case4 folder included with your Data Files, and then save the file as **Capital Campaign** in the location specified by your instructor. Search for the text "Your Name", and then replace it with your first and last names.

8. Select the three paragraphs below your name, and then decrease the indent for the selected paragraphs so that they align at the left margin. Create a .5-inch hanging indent for the selected paragraphs instead.

9. Change the document theme to Ion, and then add a comment to the first word in the document that reads "I changed the theme to Ion."

10. Use the Advanced Find dialog box to search for bold formatting. Remove the bold formatting from the fourth bold element in the document, and then add a comment to that element that reads "I assumed bold here was a mistake, so I removed it."

11. Save and close the document.

CHALLENGE

Case Problem 4

Data File needed for this Case Problem: Movie.docx

Winona College Tristan Giroux is a student at Winona College. She's working on a research paper about disaster movies for Film Studies 105, taught by Professor Douglas Fischer. The research paper is only partly finished, but before she does more work on it, she asks you to help format this early draft to match the MLA style. She also asks you to help her create some citations, add a placeholder citation, and manage her sources. Complete the following steps:

1. Open the file **Movie** located in the Word2 ▸ Case4 folder included with your Data Files, and then save the document as **Movie Paper** in the location specified by your instructor.

2. Revise the paper to match the MLA style, seventh edition. Instead of Tristan's name, use your own. Also, use the current date.

3. Locate the sentences in which the authors Dana Someya and Peter Williams are mentioned. At the end of the appropriate sentence, add a citation for page 135 in the following book and one for page 152 in the following journal article:

 Someya, Dana. *Society and Disaster in the Silent Era: A Modern Analysis.* New York: Movie House Academy Press, 1997. Print.

 Williams, Peter. "Romance in the Shadow of Disaster." *New England Journal of Cinema Studies* (2012): 133–155. Web.

4. At the end of the second-to-last sentence in the document, insert a placeholder citation that reads "Candela." At the end of the last sentence in the document, insert a placeholder citation that reads "Goldman."

⊕ **Explore** 5. Use Word Help to look up the topic "Create a bibliography," and then, within that article, read the sections titled "Find a source" and "Edit a citation placeholder."

⊕ **Explore** 6. Open the Source Manager, and search for the name "Someya." From within the Current List in the Source Manager, edit the Dana Someya citation to delete "Society and" from the title, so that the title begins "Disaster in the Silent Era...." Click Yes when asked if you want to update the source in both lists. When you are finished, delete "Someya" from the Search box to redisplay all the sources in both lists.

⊕ **Explore** 7. From within the Source Manager, copy a source not included in the current document from the Master List to the Current List. Examine the sources in the Current List and note the checkmarks next to the two sources for which you have already created citations, and the question marks next to the placeholder sources. Sources in the Current list that are not actually cited in the text have no symbol next to them in the Current List. For example, if you copied a source from the Master List into your Current List, that source has no symbol next to it in the Current List.

8. Close the Source Manager, create a bibliography in the MLA style, and note which works appear in it.

⊕ **Explore** 9. Open the Source Manager, and then edit the Goldman placeholder source to include the following information about a journal article:

 Goldman, Simon. "Attack of the Killer Disaster Movie." *Cinema International Journal* (2009): 72–89. Web.

10. Update the bibliography.

⊕ **Explore** 11. Open Internet Explorer and use the Web to research the difference between a works cited list and a works consulted list. If necessary, open the Source Manager, and then delete any uncited sources from the Current List to ensure that your document contains a true works cited list, as specified by the MLA style, and not a works consulted list. (Tristan will create a full citation for the "Candela" placeholder later.)

12. Update the bibliography, finalize it so it matches the MLA style, save the document and close it.

WORD

OBJECTIVES

Session 3.1
- Review document headings in the Navigation pane
- Reorganize document text using the Navigation pane
- Collapse and expand body text in a document
- Create and edit a table
- Sort rows in a table
- Modify a table's structure
- Format a table

Session 3.2
- Set tab stops
- Turn on automatic hyphenation
- Create footnotes and endnotes
- Divide a document into sections
- Create a SmartArt graphic
- Create headers and footers
- Insert a cover page
- Change the document's theme
- Review a document in Read Mode

Creating Tables and a Multipage Report

Writing a Recommendation

Case | *Orchard Street Art Center*

Katherine Hua is the facilities director for Orchard Street Art Center, a nonprofit organization that provides performance, rehearsal, and classroom space for arts organizations in St. Louis, Missouri. The center's facilities include a 300-seat indoor theater, a 200-seat outdoor theater, public terraces and lobbies, five classrooms, 20 rehearsal rooms, and several offices. Katherine hopes to improve the wireless network that serves the center's staff and patrons through a process known as a wireless site survey. She has written a multiple-page report for the center's board of directors summarizing basic information about wireless site surveys. She has asked you to finish formatting the report. Katherine also needs your help with adding a table and a diagram to the end of the report.

In this tutorial, you'll use the Navigation pane to review the document headings and reorganize the document. You will also insert a table, modify it by changing the structure and formatting, set tab stops, create footnotes and endnotes, hyphenate the document, and insert a section break. In addition, you'll create a SmartArt graphic and add headers and footers. Finally, you will insert a cover page and review the document in Read Mode.

STARTING DATA FILES

Word3 →	Tutorial	Review	Case1
	Site.docx	Security.docx	Greenware.docx
	Case2	Case3	Case4
	Evaluation.docx	(none)	(none)

Session 3.1 Visual Overview:

You can organize text or numerical data in a document using the Table button in the Tables group on the INSERT tab.

A **table** consists of information arranged in a grid made up of horizontal rows and vertical columns.

When you first insert a table into a document, it looks like this, with black **borders** defining the rows and columns.

This table has been formatted with one of the Table Styles available on the TABLE TOOLS DESIGN tab.

The AutoFit button makes it easy to quickly adjust the width of table columns to match the cell contents or the width of the page.

The area where a row and a column intersect is called a **cell**.

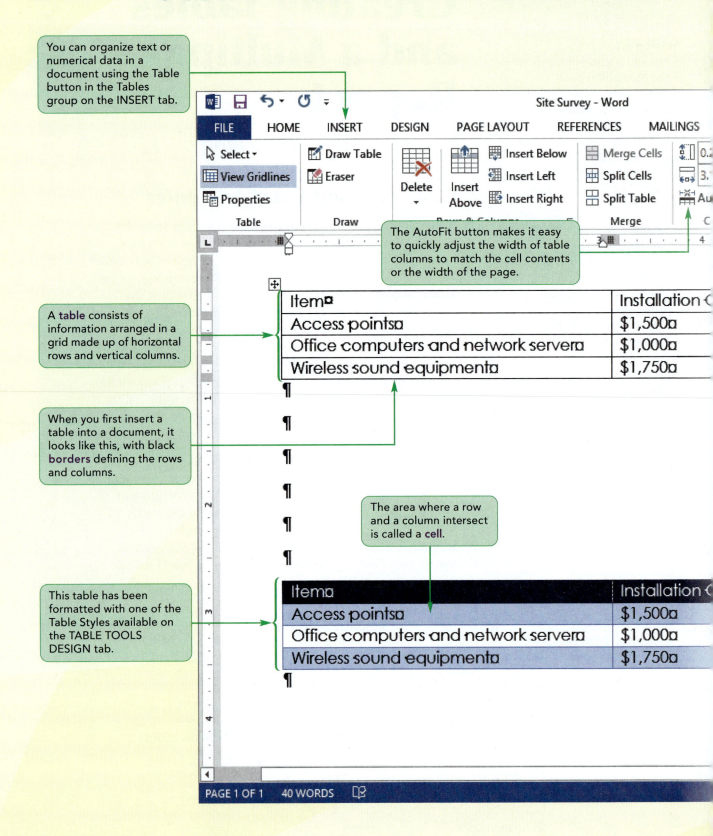

Organizing Information in Tables

The TABLE TOOLS contextual tabs are visible when the insertion point is located inside a table cell, or when the table or part of the table is selected.

The options on the TABLE TOOLS LAYOUT tab help you control both the overall structure of the table and the arrangement of data inside the table cells.

The TABLE TOOLS DESIGN tab gives you access to a variety of formatting options, including Table Styles, which apply a predesigned set of formatting options with one click.

You can use the Sort button to rearrange the rows of a table according to the contents of a particular column. For example, you could sort the table shown here alphabetically by the contents of the "Item" column, or numerically by the contents of the "Installation Cost" column.

The top row of the table, called the **header row**, contains headings that identify the type of information in each column.

Working with Headings in the Navigation Pane

When used in combination with the Navigation pane, Word's heading styles make it easier to navigate through a long document and to reorganize a document. You start by formatting the document headings with heading styles, displaying the Navigation pane, and then clicking the Headings link. This displays a hierarchy of all the headings in the document, allowing you to see, at a glance, an outline of the document headings.

Paragraphs formatted with the Heading 1 style are considered the highest level headings and are aligned at the left margin of the Navigation pane. Paragraphs formatted with the Heading 2 style are considered **subordinate** to Heading 1 paragraphs, and are indented slightly to the right below the Heading 1 paragraphs. Subordinate headings are often referred to as **subheadings**. Each successive level of heading styles (Heading 3, Heading 4, and so on) is indented farther to the right. To simplify your view of the document outline in the Navigation pane, you can choose to hide lower-level headings from view, leaving only the major headings visible.

From within the Navigation pane, you can **promote** a subordinate heading to the next level up in the heading hierarchy. For example, you can promote a Heading 2 paragraph to a Heading 1 paragraph. You can also do the opposite—that is, you can **demote** a heading to a subordinate level. You can also click and drag a heading in the Navigation pane to a new location in the document's outline. When you do so, any subheadings—along with their subordinate body text—move to the new location in the document.

Working with Headings in the Navigation Pane

- Format the document headings using Word's heading styles.
- On the ribbon, click the HOME tab.
- In the Editing group, click the Find button, or press the Ctrl+F keys, to display the Navigation pane.
- In the Navigation pane, click the HEADINGS link to display a list of the document headings, and then click a heading to display that heading in the document window.
- In the Navigation pane, click a heading, and then drag it up or down in the list of headings to move that heading and the body text below it to a new location in the document.
- In the Navigation pane, right-click a heading, and then click Promote to promote the heading to the next-highest level. To demote a heading, right-click it, and then click Demote.
- To hide subheadings in the Navigation pane, click the Collapse arrow next to the higher level heading above them. To redisplay the subheadings, click the Expand arrow next to the higher level heading.

Katherine saved the draft of her report as a Word document named Site. You will use the Navigation pane to review the outline of Katherine's report and make some changes to its organization.

To review the document headings in the Navigation pane:

1. Open the document named **Site** located in the Word3 ▶ Tutorial folder included with your Data Files, and then save the file with the name **Site Survey Report** in the location specified by your instructor.

2. Verify that the document is displayed in Print Layout view, and that the rulers and nonprinting characters are displayed.

3. Make sure the Zoom level is set to **120%**, and that the HOME tab is selected on the ribbon.

4. Press the **Ctrl+F** keys. The Navigation pane opens to the left of the document.

5. In the Navigation pane, click the **HEADINGS** link. The document headings are displayed in the Navigation pane, as shown in Figure 3-1. The blue highlighted heading ("Summary") indicates which part of the document currently contains the insertion point.

Figure 3-1 **Headings displayed in the Navigation pane**

6. In the Navigation pane, click the **What Is a Wireless Site Survey?** heading. Word displays the heading in the document window, with the insertion point at the beginning of the heading. "The What Is a Wireless Site Survey?" heading is highlighted in blue in the Navigation pane.

7. In the Navigation pane, click the **Paying for the Wireless Site Survey** heading. Word displays the heading in the document window. In the Navigation pane, you can see that there are subheadings below this heading.

8. In the Navigation pane, click the **Collapse** arrow next to the "Paying for the Wireless Site Survey" heading. The subheadings below this heading are no longer visible in the Navigation pane. This has no effect on the text in the actual document. See Figure 3-2.

| Figure 3-2 | Heading 2 and Heading 3 text hidden in Navigation pane |

9. In the Navigation pane, click the **Expand** arrow next to the "Paying for the Wireless Site Survey" heading. The subheadings are again visible in the Navigation pane.

Now that you have had a chance to review the report, you need to make a few organizational changes. Katherine wants to promote the Heading 3 text "Anticipated Upgrades" to Heading 2 text. Then she wants to move the "Anticipated Upgrades" heading and its body text up, so it precedes the "Probable Expenditures" section.

To use the Navigation pane to reorganize text in the document:

1. In the Navigation pane, right-click the **Anticipated Upgrades** heading to display the shortcut menu.

2. Click **Promote**. The heading moves to the left in the Navigation pane, aligning below the "Probable Expenditures" heading. In the document window, the text is now formatted with the Heading 2 style, with its slightly larger font.

3. In the Navigation pane, click and drag the **Anticipated Upgrades** heading up. As you drag the heading, the pointer changes to , and a blue guideline is displayed. You can use the guideline to position the heading in its new location.

4. Position the guideline directly below the "Paying for the Wireless Site Survey" heading, as shown in Figure 3-3.

Figure 3-3 **Moving a heading in the Navigation pane**

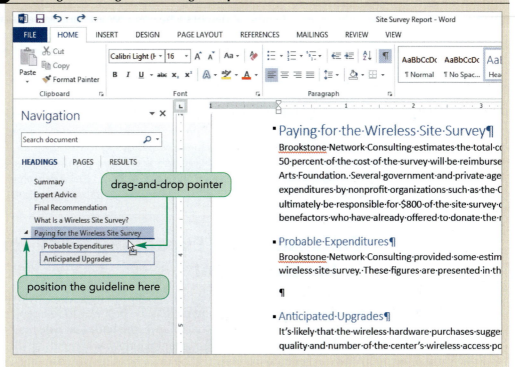

5. Release the mouse button. The "Anticipated Upgrades" heading is displayed in its new position in the Navigation pane, as the second-to-last heading in the outline. The heading and its body text are displayed in their new location in the document, before the "Probable Expenditures" heading. See Figure 3-4.

Figure 3-4 **Heading and body text in new location**

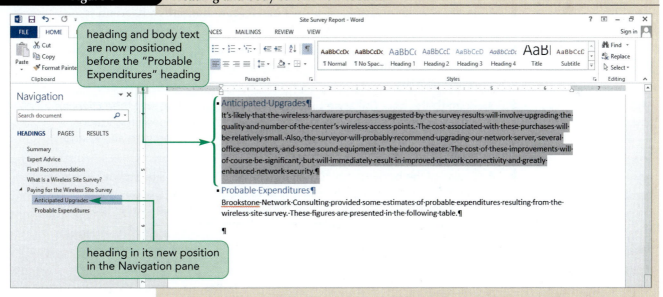

6. Click anywhere in the document to deselect the text, and then save the document.

Katherine also wants you to move the "Final Recommendation" heading and its accompanying body text. You'll do that in the next section, using a different method.

Promoting and Demoting Headings

When you promote or demote a heading, Word applies the next higher or lower level heading style to the heading paragraph. You could accomplish the same thing by using the Style gallery to apply the next higher or lower level heading style, but it's easy to lose track of the overall organization of the document that way. By promoting and demoting headings from within the Navigation pane, you ensure that the overall document outline is right in front of you as you work.

You can also use Outline view to display, promote, and demote headings, and to reorganize a document. Turn on Outline view by clicking the VIEW tab, and then clicking the Outline button in the Views group to display the OUTLINING tab on the ribbon. To hide the OUTLINING tab and return to Print Layout view, click the Close Outline View button on the ribbon or the Print Layout button in the status bar.

Collapsing and Expanding Body Text in the Document

The Navigation pane gives you an overview of the entire document, and dragging headings within the Navigation pane is the best way to reorganize a document. However, you can also hide, or collapse, the body text below a heading in a document. You do this from within the document window, without using the Navigation pane. After you collapse the body text below a heading, you can drag the heading to a new location in the document. When you do, the body text moves along with the heading, just as if you had dragged the heading in the Navigation pane. You'll use this technique now to move the "Final Recommendation" heading and its body text.

To collapse and move a heading in the document:

1. In the Navigation pane, click the **Final Recommendation** heading to display it in the document window.

2. In the document window, place the mouse pointer over the **Final Recommendation** heading to display the gray Collapse button ◢ to the left of the heading.

3. Point to the gray **Collapse** button ◢ until it turns blue, and then click the **Collapse** button ◢. The body text below the "Final Recommendation" heading is now hidden. The Collapse button is replaced with an Expand button.

4. Collapse the body text below the "What Is a Wireless Site Survey?" heading. The body text below that heading is no longer visible. Collapsing body text can be helpful when you want to hide details in a document temporarily, so you can focus on a particular part. See Figure 3-5.

| Figure 3-5 | Body text collapsed in the document |

5. Select the **Final Recommendation** heading.

6. Click and drag the heading down. As you drag, a dark black insertion point moves along with the mouse pointer.

7. Position the dark black insertion point to the left of the "P" in the "Paying for the Wireless Site Survey" heading, and then release the mouse button. The "Final Recommendation" heading and its body text move to the new location, before the "Paying for the Wireless Site Survey" heading.

 Finally, you need to expand the body text below the two collapsed headings.

8. Click anywhere in the document to deselect the text.

9. Point to the **Expand** button ▷ to the left of the "Final Recommendation" heading until it turns blue, and then click the **Expand** button ▶ to redisplay the body text below the heading.

10. Point to the **Expand** button ▷ to the left of the "What Is a Wireless Site Survey?" heading until it turns blue, and then click the **Expand** button ▶ to redisplay the body text below the heading.

11. Save the document.

The document is now organized the way Katherine wants it. Next, you need to create a table summarizing her data on probable expenditures.

Inserting a Blank Table

TIP

The terms "table," "field," and "record" are also used to discuss information stored in database programs, such as Microsoft Access.

A table is a useful way to present information that is organized into categories, or **fields**. For example, you could use a table to organize contact information for a list of clients. For each client, you could include information in the following fields: first name, last name, street address, city, state, and zip code. The complete set of information about a particular client is called a **record**. In a typical table, each column is a separate field, and each row is a record. A header row at the top contains the names of each field.

The sketch in Figure 3-6 shows what Katherine wants the table in her report to look like.

Figure 3-6 Table sketch

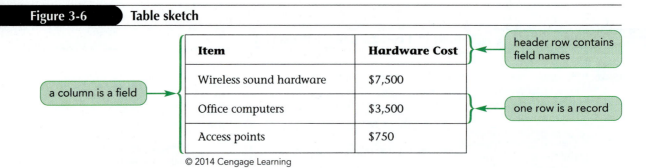

© 2014 Cengage Learning

Katherine's table includes two columns, or fields—"Item" and "Hardware Cost." The header row contains the names of these two fields. The three rows below contain the records.

Creating a table in Word is a three-step process. First, you use the Table button on the INSERT tab to insert a blank table structure. Then you enter information into the table. Finally, you format the table to make it easy to read.

Before you begin creating the table, you'll insert a page break before the "Probable Expenditures" heading. This will move the heading and its body text to a new page, with plenty of room below for the new table. As a general rule, you should not use page breaks to position a particular part of a document at the top of a page. If you add or remove text from the document later, you might forget that you inserted a manual page break, and you might end up with a document layout you didn't expect. By default, Word heading styles are set up to ensure that a heading always appears on the same page as the body text paragraph below it, so you'll never need to insert a page break just to move a heading to the same page as its body text. However, in this case, a page break is appropriate because you need the "Probable Expenditures" heading to appear at the top of a page with room for the table below.

To insert a page break and insert a blank table:

1. In the Navigation pane, click **Probable Expenditures** to display the heading in the document, with the insertion point to the left of the "P" in "Probable."

2. Close the Navigation pane, and then press the **Ctrl+Enter** keys to insert a page break. The "Probable Expenditures" heading and the body text following it move to a new, third page.

3. Scroll to position the "Probable Expenditures" heading at the top of the Word window, and then press the **Ctrl+End** keys to move the insertion point to the blank paragraph at the end of the document.

4. On the ribbon, click the **INSERT** tab.

TIP

You can use the Quick Tables option to choose from preformatted tables that contain placeholder text.

5. In the Tables group, click the **Table** button. A table grid opens, with a menu at the bottom.

6. Use the mouse pointer to point to the upper-left cell of the grid, and then move the mouse pointer down and across the grid to highlight **two columns** and **four rows**. (The outline of a cell turns orange when it is highlighted.) As you move the pointer across the grid, Word indicates the size of the table (columns by rows) at the top of the grid. A Live Preview of the table structure is displayed in the document. See Figure 3-7.

Figure 3-7 **Inserting a blank table**

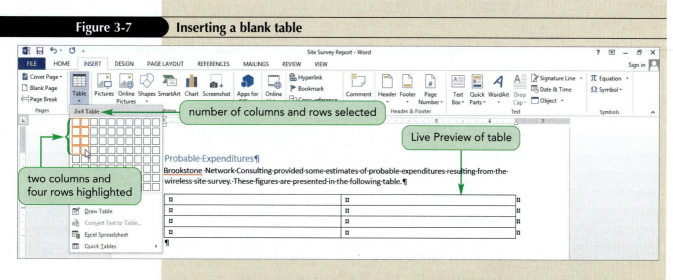

7. When the table size is 2×4, click the lower-right cell in the block of selected cells. An empty table consisting of two columns and four rows is inserted in the document, with the insertion point in the upper-left cell. See Figure 3-8.

Figure 3-8 **Blank table inserted in document**

The two columns are of equal width. Because nonprinting characters are displayed in the document, each cell contains an end-of-cell mark, and each row contains an end-of-row mark, which are important for selecting parts of a table. The Table Select handle ⊞ is displayed at the table's upper-left corner. You can click the Table Select handle ⊞ to select the entire table, or you can drag it to move the table. You can drag the Table Resize handle ☐, which is displayed at the lower-right corner, to change the size of the table. The TABLE TOOLS DESIGN and LAYOUT contextual tabs appear on the ribbon.

Trouble? If you inserted a table with the wrong number of rows or columns, click the Undo button ↻ on the Quick Access Toolbar to remove the table, and then repeat Steps 4 through 7.

The blank table is ready for you to begin entering information.

Entering Data in a Table

You can enter data in a table by moving the insertion point to a cell and typing. If the data takes up more than one line in the cell, Word automatically wraps the text to the next line and increases the height of that row. To move the insertion point to another cell in the table, you can click in that cell, use the arrow keys, or use the Tab key.

To enter information in the header row of the table:

▶ **1.** Verify that the insertion point is located in the upper-left cell.

▶ **2.** Type **Item**. As you type, the end-of-cell mark moves right to accommodate the text.

▶ **3.** Press the **Tab** key to move the insertion point to the next cell to the right.

 Trouble? If Word created a new paragraph in the first cell rather than moving the insertion point to the second cell, you pressed the Enter key instead of the Tab key. Press the Backspace key to remove the paragraph mark, and then press the Tab key to move to the second cell in the first row.

▶ **4.** Type **Hardware Cost** and then press the **Tab** key to move to the first cell in the second row.

You have finished entering the header row—the row that identifies the information in each column. Now you can enter the information about the various expenditures.

To continue entering information in the table:

▶ **1.** Type **wireless sound hardware** and then press the **Tab** key to move to the second cell in the second row. Notice that the "w" in "wireless" is capitalized, even though you typed it in lowercase. By default, AutoCorrect capitalizes the first letter in a cell entry.

▶ **2.** Type **$7,500** and then press the **Tab** key to move the insertion point to the first cell in the third row.

▶ **3.** Enter the following information in the bottom two rows, pressing the **Tab** key to move from cell to cell:

 Office computers; **$3,500**

 Access points; **$750**

At this point, the table consists of a header row and three records. Katherine realizes that she needs to add one more row to the table. You can add a new row to the bottom of a table by pressing the Tab key when the insertion point is in the rightmost cell in the bottom row.

To add a row to the table:

▶ **1.** Verify that the insertion point is in the lower-right cell (which contains the value "$750") and then press the **Tab** key. A new, blank row is added to the bottom of the table.

▶ **2.** Type **Network server**, press the **Tab** key, and then type **$2,200**. When you are finished, your table should look like the one shown in Figure 3-9.

| Figure 3-9 | Table with all data entered |

Trouble? If a new row is added to the bottom of your table, you pressed the Tab key after entering "$2,200". Click the Undo button ↻ on the Quick Access Toolbar to remove the extra row from the table.

The table you've just created presents information about expenditures in an easy-to-read format. To make it even easier to read, you can format the header row in bold so it stands out from the rest of the table. To do that, you need to first select the header row.

Selecting Part of a Table

When selecting part of a table, you need to make sure you select the end-of-cell mark in a cell or the end-of-row mark at the end of a row. If you don't, the formatting changes you make next might not have the effect you expect. The foolproof way to select part of a table is to click in the cell, row, or column you want to select; click the Select button on the TABLE TOOLS LAYOUT contextual tab; and then click the appropriate command—Select Cell, Select Column, or Select Row. (You can also click Select Table to select the entire table.) To select a row, you can also click in the left margin next to the row. Similarly, you can click just above a column to select it. After you've selected an entire row, column, or cell, you can drag the mouse to select adjacent rows, columns, or cells.

Note that in the following steps, you'll position the mouse pointer until it takes on a particular shape so that you can then perform the task associated with that type of pointer. Pointer shapes are especially important when working with tables and graphics; in many cases, you can't perform a task until the pointer is the right shape. It takes some patience to get accustomed to positioning the pointer until it takes on the correct shape, but with practice you'll grow to rely on the pointer shapes as a quick visual cue to the options currently available to you.

To select and format the header row:

1. Position the mouse pointer in the selection bar, to the left of the header row. The pointer changes to a right-facing arrow ⇗.

2. Click the mouse button. The entire header row, including the end-of-cell mark in each cell and the end-of-row mark, is selected. See Figure 3-10.

Figure 3-10) **Header row selected**

3. Press the **Ctrl+B** keys to apply bold to the text in the header row. You can also use the formatting options on the HOME tab to format selected text in a table, including adding italics, changing the font, aligning text within cells, or applying a style.

4. Click anywhere in the table to deselect the header row, and then save the document.

INSIGHT

Formatting a Multipage Table

In some documents, you might have a long table that extends across multiple pages. To make a multipage table easier to read, you can format the table header row to appear at the top of every page. To do so, click in the header row, click the TABLE TOOLS LAYOUT tab, and then click the Properties button in the Table group. In the Table Properties dialog box, click the Row tab, and then select the "Repeat as header row at the top of each page" check box.

Now that you have created a very basic table, you can sort the information in it and improve its appearance.

Sorting Rows in a Table

The term **sort** refers to the process of rearranging information in alphabetical, numerical, or chronological order. You can sort a series of paragraphs, including the contents of a bulleted list, or you can sort the rows of a table.

When you sort a table, you arrange the rows based on the contents of one of the columns. For example, you could sort the table you just created based on the contents of the "Item" column—either in ascending alphabetical order (from *A* to *Z*) or in descending alphabetical order (from *Z* to *A*). Alternatively, you could sort the table based on the contents of the "Hardware Cost" column—either in ascending numerical order (lowest to highest) or in descending numerical order (highest to lowest).

Clicking the Sort button in the Data group on the TABLE TOOLS LAYOUT tab opens the Sort dialog box, which provides a number of options for fine-tuning the sort, including options for sorting a table by the contents of more than one column. This is useful if, for example, you want to organize the table rows by last name, and then by first name within each last name. By default, Word assumes your table includes a header row that should remain at the top of the table—excluded from the sort.

REFERENCE

Sorting the Rows of a Table

- Click anywhere within the table.
- On the ribbon, click the TABLE TOOLS LAYOUT tab.
- In the Data group, click the Sort button.
- In the Sort dialog box, click the Sort by arrow, and then select the header for the column you want to sort by.
- In the Type box located to the right of the Sort by box, select the type of information stored in the column you want to sort by; you can choose Text, Number, or Date.
- To sort in alphabetical, chronological, or numerical order, verify that the Ascending option button is selected. To sort in reverse order, click the Descending option button.
- To sort by a second column, click the Then by arrow, and then click a column header. If necessary, specify the type of information stored in the Then by column, and the sort order.
- At the bottom of the Sort dialog box, make sure the Header row option button is selected. This indicates that the table includes a header row that should not be included in the sort.
- Click the OK button.

Katherine would like you to sort the contents of the table in ascending numerical order based on the contents of the "Hardware Cost" column.

To sort the information in the table:

1. Make sure the insertion point is located somewhere in the table.

2. On the ribbon, click the **TABLE TOOLS LAYOUT** tab.

3. In the Data group, click the **Sort** button. The Sort dialog box opens. Take a moment to review its default settings. The leftmost column in the table, the "Item" column, is selected in the Sort by box, indicating the sort will be based on the contents in this column. Because the "Item" column contains text, "Text" is selected in the Type box. The Ascending option button is selected by default, indicating that Word will sort the contents of the "Item" column from A to Z. The Header row option button is selected in the lower-left corner of the dialog box, ensuring the header row will not be included in the sort. You want to sort the column by the contents of the "Hardware Cost" column, so you need to change the Sort by setting.

4. Click the **Sort by** button arrow, and then click **Hardware Cost**. Because the "Hardware Cost" column contains numbers, the Type box now displays "Number". The Ascending button is still selected, indicating that Word will sort the numbers in the "Hardware Cost" column from lowest to highest. See Figure 3-11.

Figure 3-11 Sort dialog box

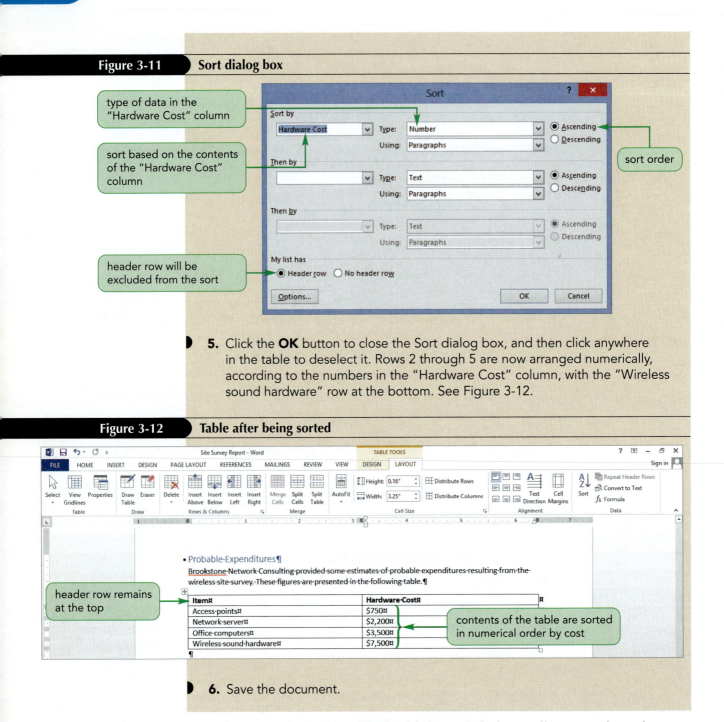

type of data in the "Hardware Cost" column

sort based on the contents of the "Hardware Cost" column

sort order

header row will be excluded from the sort

5. Click the **OK** button to close the Sort dialog box, and then click anywhere in the table to deselect it. Rows 2 through 5 are now arranged numerically, according to the numbers in the "Hardware Cost" column, with the "Wireless sound hardware" row at the bottom. See Figure 3-12.

Figure 3-12 Table after being sorted

header row remains at the top

contents of the table are sorted in numerical order by cost

6. Save the document.

Katherine decides that the table should also include the installation cost for each item. She asks you to insert an "Installation Cost" column.

Inserting Rows and Columns in a Table

To add a column to a table, you can use the tools in the Rows & Columns group on the TABLE TOOLS LAYOUT tab, or you can use the Add Column button in the document window. To use the Add Column button, make sure the insertion point is located somewhere within the table. When you position the mouse pointer at the top of the table, pointing to the border between two columns, the Add Column button appears. When you click that button, a new column is inserted between the two existing columns.

To insert a column in the table:

▶ **1.** Verify that the insertion point is located anywhere in the table.

▶ **2.** Position the mouse pointer at the top of the table, so that it points to the border between the two columns. The Add Column button ⊕ appears at the top of the border. A blue guideline shows where the new column will be inserted. See Figure 3-13.

Figure 3-13	Inserting a column

Add Column button appears when the mouse pointer is positioned over the column border

guideline shows where the column will be inserted

▶ **3.** Click the **Add Column** button ⊕. A new, blank column is inserted between the "Item" and "Hardware Cost" columns. The three columns in the table are narrower than the original two columns, but the overall width of the table remains the same.

▶ **4.** Click in the top cell of the new column, and then enter the following header and data. Use the ↓ key to move the insertion point down through the column.

Installation Cost

$1,500

$850

$1,000

$1,750

Your table should now look like the one in Figure 3-14.

TIP

You can also use the buttons in the Rows & Columns group on the TABLE TOOLS LAYOUT tab to insert a column or row.

Figure 3-14 New "Installation Cost" column

Because you selected the entire header row when you formatted the original headers in bold, the newly inserted header, "Installation Cost," is also formatted in bold.

Katherine just learned that the costs listed for office computers actually cover both office computers and the network server. Therefore, she would like you to delete the "Network server" row from the table.

Deleting Rows and Columns

When you consider deleting a row, you need to be clear about whether you want to delete the *contents* of the row, or the contents and the *structure* of the row. You can delete the contents of a row by selecting the row and pressing the Delete key. This removes the information from the row but leaves the row structure intact. The same is true for deleting the contents of an individual cell, a column, or the entire table. To delete the structure of a row, a column, or the entire table—including its contents—you select the row (or column or the entire table) and then use the Delete button in the Rows & Columns group, or on the Mini toolbar. To delete multiple rows or columns, start by selecting all the rows or columns you want to delete.

Before you delete the Network server row, you need to edit the contents in the last cell in the first column to indicate that the items in that row are for office computers and a server.

To delete the Network server row:

1. In the cell containing the text "Office computers," click to the right of the "s," press the **spacebar**, and then type **and network server**. The cell now reads "Office computers and network server." Part of the text wraps to a second line within the cell. Next, you can delete the Network server row, which is no longer necessary.

2. Click in the selection bar to the left of the **Network server** row. The row is selected, with the Mini toolbar displayed on top of the selected row.

▶ **3.** On the Mini toolbar, click the **Delete** button. The Delete menu opens, displaying options for deleting cells, columns, rows, or the entire table. See Figure 3-15.

Figure 3-15 | **Deleting a row**

▶ **4.** Click **Delete Rows**. The "Network server" row is removed from the table, and the Mini toolbar disappears.

▶ **5.** Save your work.

The table now contains all the information Katherine wants to include. Next, you'll adjust the widths of the three columns.

Changing Column Widths

Columns that are too wide for the material they contain can make a table hard to read. You can change a column's width by dragging the column's right border to a new position. Or, if you prefer, you can double-click a column border to make the column width adjust automatically to accommodate the widest entry in the column. To adjust the width of all the columns to match their widest entries, click anywhere in the table, click the AutoFit button in the Cell Size group on the TABLE TOOLS LAYOUT tab, and then click AutoFit Contents. To adjust the width of the entire table to span the width of the page, click the AutoFit Contents button and then click AutoFit Window.

You'll adjust the columns in Katherine's table by double-clicking the right column border. You need to start by making sure that no part of the table is selected. Otherwise, when you double-click the border, only the width of the selected part of the table will change.

To change the width of the columns in the table:

▶ **1.** Verify that no part of the table is selected, and then position the mouse pointer over the right border of the "Installation Cost" column until the pointer changes to ◄‖►. See Figure 3-16.

Figure 3-16 **Adjusting the column width**

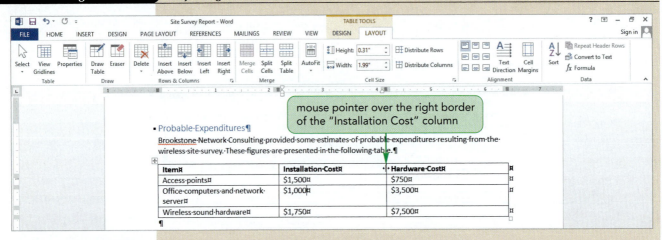

mouse pointer over the right border of the "Installation Cost" column

Item	Installation Cost	Hardware Cost
Access points	$1,500	$750
Office computers and network server	$1,000	$3,500
Wireless sound hardware	$1,750	$7,500

▶ **2.** Double-click the mouse button. The right column border moves left so that the "Installation Cost" column is just wide enough to accommodate the widest entry in the column.

▶ **3.** Verify that no part of the table is selected, and that the insertion point is located in any cell in the table.

▶ **4.** Make sure the TABLE TOOLS LAYOUT tab is selected on the ribbon.

▶ **5.** In the Cell Size group, click the **AutoFit** button, and then click **AutoFit Contents**. All of the table columns adjust so that each is just wide enough to accommodate its widest entry. The text "Office computers and network server" in the lower-left cell no longer wraps to a second line.

To finish the table, you will add some formatting to improve the table's appearance.

Formatting Tables with Styles

To adjust a table's appearance, you can use any of the formatting options available on the HOME tab. To change a table's appearance more dramatically, you can use table styles, which allow you to apply a collection of formatting options, including shading, color, borders, and other design elements, with a single click.

By default, a table is formatted with the Table Grid style, which includes only black borders between the rows and columns, no paragraph spacing, no shading, and the default black font color. You can select a more colorful table style from the Table Styles group on the TABLE TOOLS DESIGN tab. Whatever table style you choose, you'll give your document a more polished look if you use the same style consistently in all the tables in a single document.

Some table styles format rows in alternating colors, called **banded rows**, while others format the columns in alternating colors, called **banded columns**. You can choose a style that includes different formatting for the header row than for the rest of the table. Or, if the first column in your table is a header column—that is, if it contains headers identifying the type of information in each row—you can choose a style that instead applies different formatting to the first column.

Formatting a Table with a Table Style

- Click in the table you want to format.
- On the ribbon, click the TABLE TOOLS DESIGN tab.
- In the Table Styles group, click the More button to display the Table Styles gallery.
- Position the mouse pointer over a style in the Table Styles gallery to see a Live Preview of the table style in the document.
- In the Table Styles gallery, click the style you want.
- To apply or remove style elements (such as special formatting for the header row, banded rows, or banded columns), select or deselect check boxes as necessary in the Table Style Options group.

Katherine wants to use a table style that emphasizes the header row with special formatting, does not include column borders, and uses color to separate the rows.

To apply a table style to the Probable Expenditures table:

1. Click anywhere in the table, and then scroll to position the table at the very bottom of the Word window. This will make it easier to see the Live Preview in the next few steps.

2. On the ribbon, click the **TABLE TOOLS DESIGN** tab. In the Table Styles group, the plain Table Grid style is highlighted, indicating that it is the table's current style.

3. In the Table Styles group, click the **More** button. The Table Styles gallery opens. The default Table Grid style now appears under the heading "Plain Tables." The more elaborate styles appear below, in the "Grid Tables" section of the gallery.

4. Use the gallery's vertical scroll bar to view the complete collection of table styles. When you are finished, scroll up until you can see the "Grid Tables" heading again.

5. Move the mouse pointer over the style located in the fourth row of the Grid Tables section, second column from the right. See Figure 3-17.

Figure 3-17 Table Styles gallery

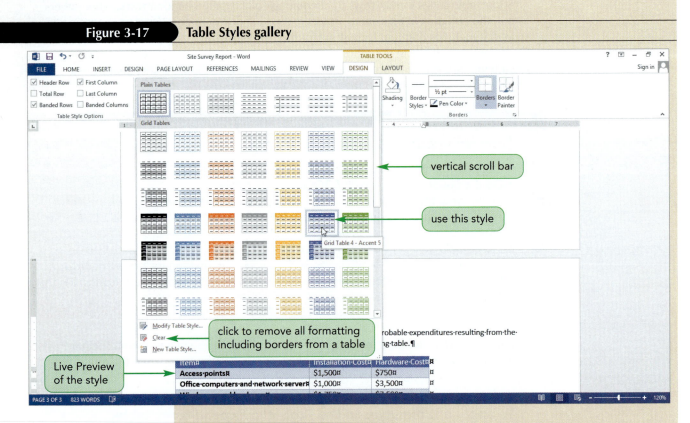

A ScreenTip displays the style's name, "Grid Table 4 - Accent 5." The style consists of a dark blue heading row, with alternating rows of light blue and white below. A Live Preview of the style is visible in the document.

6. Click the **Grid Table 4 - Accent 5** style. The Table Styles gallery closes.

7. Scroll to position the table at the top of the Word window, so you can review it more easily. The table's header row is formatted with dark blue shading and white text. The rows below appear in alternating colors of light blue and white.

The only problem with the newly formatted table is that the text in the first column is formatted in bold. In tables where the first column contains headers, bold would be appropriate—but this isn't the case with Katherine's table. You'll fix this by deselecting the First Column check box in the Table Style Options group.

To remove the bold formatting from the first column:

1. In the Table Style Options group, click the **First Column** check box to deselect this option. The bold formatting is removed from the entries in the Item column. Note that the Header Row check box is selected. This indicates that the table's header row is emphasized with special formatting (dark blue shading with white text). The Banded Rows check box is also selected because the table is formatted with banded rows of blue and white. Figure 3-18 shows the finished table.

Figure 3-18	Completed table

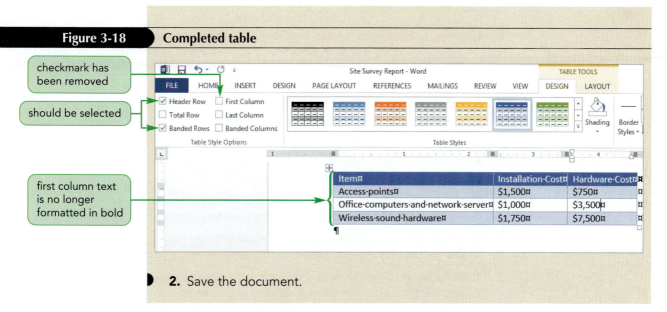

checkmark has been removed

should be selected

first column text is no longer formatted in bold

2. Save the document.

After you apply a table style, it's helpful to know how to remove it in case you want to start over from scratch. The Clear option on the menu below the Table styles gallery removes the current style from a table, including the borders between cells. When a table has no borders, the rows and columns are defined by **gridlines**, which are useful as guidelines but do not appear when you print the table.

In the following steps, you'll experiment with clearing the table's style, displaying and hiding the gridlines, and removing the table's borders.

To experiment with table styles, gridlines, and borders:

1. In the Table Styles group, click the **More** button, and then click **Clear** in the menu below the gallery. Next, you need to make sure the table gridlines are displayed.

2. On the ribbon, click the **TABLE TOOLS LAYOUT** tab.

3. In the View group, click the **View Gridlines** button, if necessary, to select it. The table now looks much simpler, with no shading or font colors. Instead of the table borders, dotted gridlines separate the rows and columns. The text in the table is spaced farther apart because removing the table style restored the default paragraph and line spacing of the Normal style. The bold formatting that you applied earlier, which is not part of a table style, is visible again.

 It is helpful to clear a table's style and view only the gridlines if you want to use a table to lay out text and graphics on a page, but you want no visible indication of the table itself. You'll have a chance to try this technique in the Case Problems at the end of this tutorial.

 Another option is to remove only the table borders, leaving the rest of the table style applied to the table. To do this, you have to select the entire table. But first you need to undo the style change.

4. On the Quick Access Toolbar, click the **Undo** button to restore the Grid Table 4 - Accent 5 style, so that your table looks like the one in Figure 3-18.

5. In the upper-left corner of the table, click the **Table Select** handle to select the entire table, and then click the **TABLE TOOLS DESIGN** tab.

6. In the Borders group, click the **Borders button arrow** to open the Borders gallery, click **No Borders**, and then click anywhere in the table to deselect it. The borders are removed from the table, leaving only the nonprinting gridlines to separate the rows and columns. To add borders of any color to specific parts of a table, you can use the Border Painter.

7. In the Borders group, click the **Border Painter** button, and then click the **Pen Color** button to open the Pen Color gallery.

8. In the Pen Color gallery, click the **Orange, Accent 2** square in the sixth column of the first row of the gallery.

9. Use the Border Painter pointer to click any gridline in the table. An orange border is added to the cell where you clicked.

10. Continue experimenting with the Border Painter pointer, and then press the **Esc** key to turn off the Border Painter pointer when you are finished.

11. Reapply the Grid Table 4 - Accent 5 table style to make your table match the one shown earlier in Figure 3-18.

12. Save the document and then close it.

PROSKILLS

Problem Solving: Fine-Tuning Table Styles

After you apply a table style to a table, you might like the look of the table but find that it no longer effectively conveys your information or is not quite as easy to read. To solve this problem, you might be inclined to go back to the Table Styles gallery to find another style that might work better. Another method to correct problems with a table style is to identify the table elements with problematic formatting, and then manually make formatting adjustments to only those elements using the options on the TABLE TOOLS DESIGN tab. For example, you can change the thickness and color of the table borders using the options in the Borders group, and you can add shading using the Shading button in the Table Styles group. Also, if you don't like the appearance of table styles in your document, consider changing the document's theme and previewing the table styles again. The table styles have a different appearance in each theme. When applying table styles, remember there are many options for attractively formatting the table without compromising the information being conveyed.

In the next session, you'll complete the rest of the report by organizing information using tab stops, creating footnotes and endnotes, dividing the document into sections, inserting headers and footers, and finally inserting a cover page.

REVIEW

Session 3.1 Quick Check

1. What must you do before you can display document headings in the Navigation pane?
2. Explain how to insert a table in a document.
3. After you enter data in the last cell in the last row in a table, how can you insert a new row?
4. Explain how to insert a new column in a table.
5. What button do you use to sort a table?
6. To adjust the width of a table's column to fit its widest entry, would you use the AutoFit Contents option or the AutoFit Window option?
7. How can you adjust a table style so that the first column in the table is formatted like all the others?

Session 3.2 Visual Overview:

You can click the Go to Header and Go to Footer buttons to move easily between the headers and footers in your document.

You can click the Page Number button to insert page numbers in the header or footer. This button is also available in the Header & Footer group on the INSERT tab.

Click the Previous and Next buttons to navigate between header and footer sections in a document.

A **footer** is text that is printed at the bottom of every page.

You can work in the header or footer section of any page in the document. By default, the changes you make on one page apply to the headers or footers on every page in the document.

A **header** is text that is printed at the top of every page.

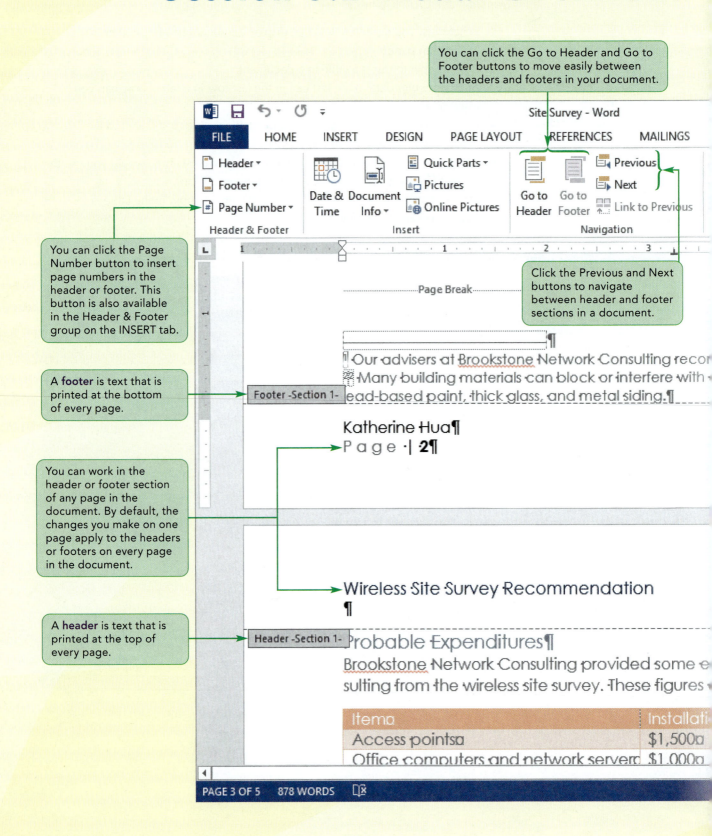

Working with Headers and Footers

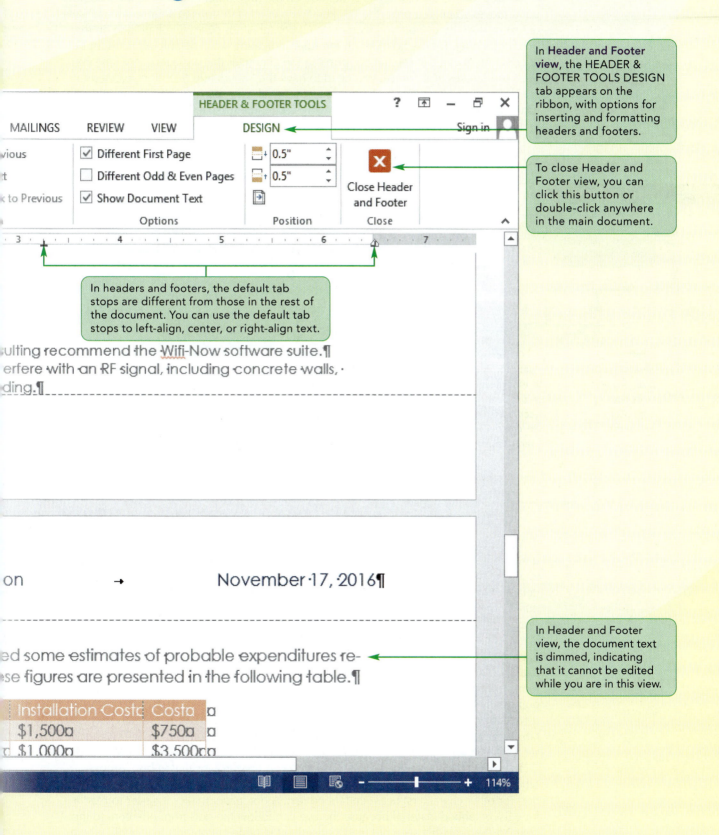

In **Header and Footer view**, the HEADER & FOOTER TOOLS DESIGN tab appears on the ribbon, with options for inserting and formatting headers and footers.

To close Header and Footer view, you can click this button or double-click anywhere in the main document.

In headers and footers, the default tab stops are different from those in the rest of the document. You can use the default tab stops to left-align, center, or right-align text.

In Header and Footer view, the document text is dimmed, indicating that it cannot be edited while you are in this view.

...ulting recommend the Wifi-Now software suite.¶
...erfere with an RF signal, including concrete walls, ·
...ding.¶

on → November·17,·2016¶

...ed some estimates of probable expenditures re-
...se figures are presented in the following table.¶

Installation Cost	Cost
$1,500	$750
$1,000	$3,500

Setting Tab Stops

A **tab stop** (often called a **tab**) is a location on the horizontal ruler where the insertion point moves when you press the Tab key. You can use tab stops to align small amounts of text or data. By default, a document contains tab stops every one-half inch on the horizontal ruler. There's no mark on the ruler indicating these default tab stops, but in the document you can see the nonprinting Tab character that appears every time you press the Tab key. (Of course, you need to have the Show/Hide ¶ button selected to see these nonprinting characters.) A nonprinting tab character is just like any other character you type; you can delete it by pressing the Backspace key or the Delete key.

The five major types of tab stops are Left, Center, Right, Decimal, and Bar, as shown in Figure 3-19. The default tab stops on the ruler are all left tab stops because that is the tab style you'll probably use most often.

Figure 3-19 Tab stop alignment styles

You can use tab stops a few different ways. The simplest is to press the Tab key until the insertion point is aligned where you want it, and then type the text you want to align. Each time you press the Tab key, the insertion point moves right to the next default tab stop, with the left edge of the text aligning below the tab stop. To use a different type of tab stop, or to use a tab stop at a location other than the default tab stop locations (every half-inch on the ruler), first select an alignment style from the tab alignment selector, located at the left end of the horizontal ruler, and then click the horizontal ruler where you want to insert the tab stop. This process is called setting a tab stop. When you set a new tab stop, all of the default tab stops to its left are removed. This means you have to press the Tab key only once to move the insertion point to the newly created tab stop. To set a new tab stop in text you have already typed, select the text including the nonprinting tab stop characters, and then set the tab stop by selecting an alignment style and clicking on the ruler where you want to set the tab stop.

To create more complicated tab stops, you can use the Tabs dialog box. Among other things, the Tabs dialog box allows you to insert a **dot leader**, which is a row of dots (or other characters) between tabbed text. A dot leader makes it easier to read a long list of tabbed material because the eye can follow the dots from one item to the next. You've probably seen dot leaders used in the table of contents in a book, where the dots separate the chapter titles from the page numbers.

To create a left tab stop with a dot leader, click the Dialog Box Launcher in the Paragraph group on the HOME tab, click the Indents and Spacing tab, if necessary, and then click the Tabs button at the bottom of the dialog box. In the Tab stop position box in the Tabs dialog box, type the location on the ruler where you want to insert the tab. For example, to insert a tab stop at the 4-inch mark, type 4. Verify that the Left option button is selected in the Alignment section, and then, in the Leader section, click the option button for the type of leader you want. Click the Set button and then click the OK button.

REFERENCE

Setting, Moving, and Clearing Tab Stops

- To set a tab stop, click the tab alignment selector on the horizontal ruler until the appropriate tab stop alignment style is displayed, and then click the horizontal ruler where you want to position the tab stop.
- To move a tab stop, drag it to a new location on the ruler. If you have already typed text that is aligned by the tab stop, select the text before dragging the tab stop to a new location.
- To clear a tab stop, drag it off the ruler.

In the Site Survey Report document you have been working on, you need to type the list of consultants and their titles. You can use tab stops to quickly format this small amount of information in two columns. As you type, you'll discover whether Word's default tab stops are appropriate for this document or whether you need to set a new tab stop. Before you get started working with tabs, you'll take a moment to explore Word's Resume Reading feature.

To enter the list of consultants using tabs:

1. Open the **Site Survey Report** document. The document opens with the "Summary" heading at the top of the Word window. In the lower-right corner, a "Welcome back!" message is displayed briefly, and is then replaced with the Resume Reading button ▓.

2. Point to the **Resume Reading** button ▓ to expand its "Welcome back!" message. See Figure 3-20.

Figure 3-20 "Welcome back!" message displayed in reopened document

3. Click the **Welcome back!** message. The document window scrolls down to display the table, which you were working on just before you closed the document.

4. Scroll up to display the "Expert Advice" heading on page 1.

5. Confirm that the ruler and nonprinting characters are displayed, and that the document is displayed in Print Layout view, zoomed to 120%.

6. Click to the right of the last "e" in "Lyn Luzerne."

7. Press the **Tab** key. An arrow-shaped tab character appears, and the insertion point moves to the first tab stop after the last "e" in "Luzerne." This tab stop is the default tab located at the 1-inch mark on the horizontal ruler. See Figure 3-21.

Figure 3-21 **Tab character**

8. Type **Associate Engineer**, and then press the **Enter** key to move the insertion point to the next line.

9. Type **Dean Armstrong**, and then press the **Tab** key. The insertion point moves to the next available tab stop, this time located at the 1.5-inch mark on the rule.

10. Type **Senior Engineer**, and then press the **Enter** key to move to the next line. Notice that Dean Armstrong's title does not align with Lyn Luzerne's title on the line above it. You'll fix this after you type the last name in the list.

11. Type **Suzanne J. Sheffield-Harper**, press the **Tab** key, and then type **Project Manager**. See Figure 3-22.

Figure 3-22 **List of consultants**

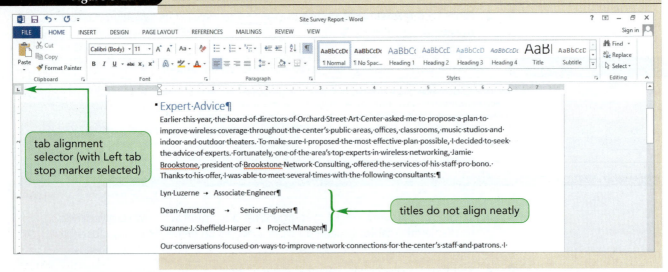

The list of names and titles is not aligned properly. You can fix this by inserting a new tab stop.

To add a new tab stop to the horizontal ruler:

1. Make sure the HOME tab is displayed on the ribbon, and then select the list of consultants and their titles.

2. On the horizontal ruler, click at the 2.5-inch mark. Because the current tab stop alignment style is Left tab, Word inserts a left tab stop at that location. Remember that when you set a new tab stop, all the default tab stops to its left are removed. The column of titles shifts to the new tab stop. See Figure 3-23.

Figure 3-23 **Titles aligned at new tab stop**

To complete the list, you need to remove the paragraph spacing after the first two paragraphs in the list, so the list looks like it's all one paragraph. You can quickly reduce paragraph and line spacing to 0 points by clicking the No Spacing style in the Styles group. In this case, you want to reduce only the paragraph spacing to 0 points, so you'll use the Line and Paragraph Spacing button instead.

3. Select the first two paragraphs in the list, which contain the names and titles for Lyn and Dean.

4. In the Paragraph group, click the **Line and Paragraph Spacing** button, and then click **Remove Space After Paragraph**.

5. Click anywhere in the document to deselect the list, and then save your work.

Decision Making: Choosing Between Tabs and Tables

When you have information that you want to align in columns in your document, you need to decide whether to use tabs or tables. Whatever you do, don't try to align columns of data by adding extra spaces with the spacebar. Although the text might seem precisely aligned on the screen, it probably won't be aligned when you print the document. Furthermore, if you edit the text, the spaces you inserted to align your columns will be affected by your edits; they get moved just like regular text, ruining your alignment.

So what is the most efficient way to align text in columns? It depends. Inserting tabs works well for aligning small amounts of information in just a few columns and rows, such as two columns with three rows, but tabs become cumbersome when you need to organize a lot of data over multiple columns and rows. In this case, using a table to organize columns of information is better. Unlike with tabbed columns of data, it's easy to add data to tables by inserting columns. You might also choose tables over tab stops when you want to take advantage of the formatting options available with table styles. As mentioned earlier, if you don't want the table structure itself to be visible in the document, you can clear its table style and then hide its gridlines.

Katherine would like to add two footnotes that provide further information about topics discussed in her report. You will do that next.

Creating Footnotes and Endnotes

A **footnote** is an explanatory comment or reference that appears at the bottom of a page. When you create a footnote, Word inserts a small, superscript number (called a **reference marker**) in the text. The term **superscript** means that the number is raised slightly above the line of text. Word then inserts the same number in the page's bottom margin and positions the insertion point next to it so you can type the text of the footnote. **Endnotes** are similar, except that the text of an endnote appears at the end of a section or, in the case of a document without sections, at the end of the document. (You'll learn about dividing a document into sections later in this tutorial.) By default, the reference marker for an endnote is a lowercase Roman numeral.

Word automatically manages the reference markers for you, keeping them sequential from the beginning of the document to the end, no matter how many times you add, delete, or move footnotes or endnotes. For example, if you move a paragraph containing footnote 4 so that it falls before the paragraph containing footnote 1, Word renumbers all the footnotes in the document to keep them sequential.

Inserting a Footnote or an Endnote

- Click the location in the document where you want to insert a footnote or an endnote.
- On the ribbon, click the REFERENCES tab.
- In the Footnotes group, click the Insert Footnote button or the Insert Endnote button.
- Type the text of the footnote in the bottom margin of the page, or type the text of the endnote at the end of the document.
- When you are finished typing the text of a footnote or an endnote, click in the body of the document to continue working on the document.

Katherine asks you to insert a footnote that explains the phrase "barriers to RF signal propagation."

To add a footnote to the report:

1. Use the Navigation pane to find the phrase "barriers to RF signal propagation" near the bottom of page 1, and then click to the right of the period after "propagation."

2. Close the Navigation pane.

3. On the ribbon, click the **REFERENCES** tab.

4. In the Footnotes group, click the **Insert Footnote** button. A superscript "1" is inserted to the right of the period after "propagation." Word also inserts the number "1" in the bottom margin below a separator line. The insertion point is now located next to the number in the bottom margin, ready for you to type the text of the footnote.

5. Type **Many building materials can block or interfere with an RF signal, including concrete walls, lead-based paint, thick glass, and metal siding.** See Figure 3-24.

Figure 3-24	Inserting a footnote

Now, Katherine would like you to insert a second footnote.

To insert a second footnote:

1. In the third line of the same paragraph, click at the end of the second sentence to position the insertion point to the right of the period after "signal."

2. In the Footnotes group, click the **Insert Footnote** button, and then type **Our advisers at Brookstone Network Consulting recommend the Wifi-Now software suite.** Because this footnote is placed earlier in the document than the one you just created, Word inserts a superscript "1" for this footnote, and then renumbers the other footnote as "2." See Figure 3-25.

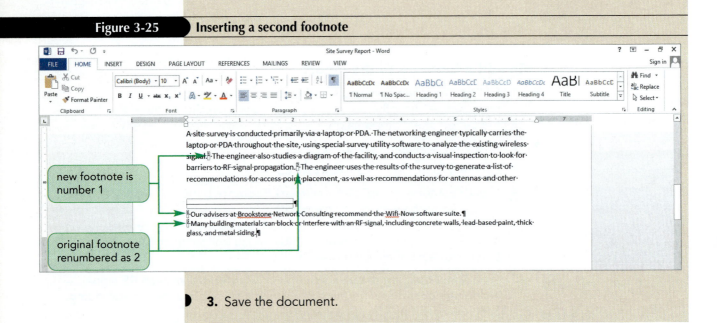

Figure 3-25 **Inserting a second footnote**

▶ **3.** Save the document.

INSIGHT

Understanding Endnotes, Footnotes, and Citations

It's easy to confuse footnotes with endnotes, and endnotes with citations. Remember, a footnote appears at the bottom, or foot, of a page, and always on the same page as its reference marker. You might have one footnote at the bottom of page 3, three footnotes at the bottom of page 5, and one at the bottom of page 6. By contrast, an endnote appears at the end of the document or section, with all the endnotes compiled into a single list. Both endnotes and footnotes can contain any kind of information you think might be useful to your readers. Citations, however, are only used to list specific information about a book or other source you refer to or quote from in the document. A citation typically appears in parentheses at the end of the sentence containing information from the source you are citing, and the sources for all of the document's citations are listed in a bibliography, or a list of works cited, at the end of the document.

Now you're ready to address some other issues with the document. First, Katherine has noticed that the right edges of most of the paragraphs in the document are uneven, and she'd like you to try to smooth them out. You'll correct this problem in the next section.

Hyphenating a Document

By default, hyphenation is turned off in Word documents. That means if you are in the middle of typing a word and you reach the end of a line, Word moves the entire word to the next line instead of inserting a hyphen and breaking the word into two parts. This can result in ragged text on the right margin. To ensure a smoother right margin, you can turn on automatic hyphenation—in which case, any word that ends within the last .25 inch of a line will be hyphenated.

To turn on automatic hyphenation in the document:

1. Review the paragraph above the footnotes on page 1. The text on the right side of this paragraph is uneven. Keeping an eye on this paragraph will help you see the benefits of hyphenation.

2. On the ribbon, click the **PAGE LAYOUT** tab.

3. In the Page Setup group, click the **Hyphenation** button to open the Hyphenation menu, and then click **Automatic**. The Hyphenation menu closes. Throughout the document, the text layout shifts to account for the insertion of hyphens in words that break near the end of a line. For example, in the last paragraph on page 1, the word "recommendations" is now hyphenated. See Figure 3-26.

Figure 3-26 **Hyphenated document**

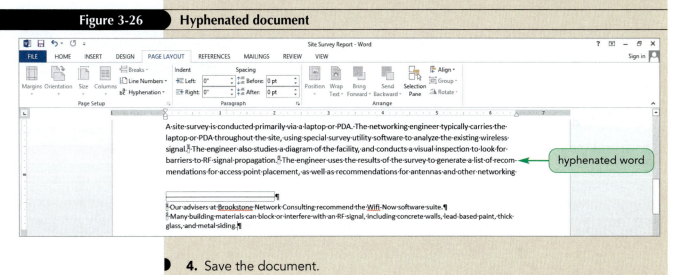

4. Save the document.

Katherine plans to post a handout on the bulletin board at the art center to help inform the staff about the upcoming site survey, and she wants to include a sample handout in the report. Before you can add the sample of the handout, you need to divide the document into sections.

Formatting a Document into Sections

A **section** is a part of a document that can have its own page orientation, margins, headers, footers, and so on. In other words, each section is like a document within a document. To divide a document into sections, you insert a **section break**. You can select from a few different kinds of section breaks. One of the most useful is a Next page section break, which inserts a page break and starts the new section on the next page. Another commonly used kind of section break, a Continuous section break, starts the section at the location of the insertion point without changing the page flow. To insert a section break, you click the Breaks button in the Page Setup group on the PAGE LAYOUT tab and then select the type of section break you want to insert.

Katherine wants to format the handout in landscape orientation, but the report is currently formatted in portrait orientation. To format part of a document in an orientation different from the rest of the document, you need to divide the document into sections.

To insert a section break below the table:

1. Press the **Ctrl+End** keys to move the insertion point to the end of the document, just below the table.

2. In the Page Setup group, click the **Breaks** button. The Breaks gallery opens, as shown in Figure 3-27.

Figure 3-27	Breaks gallery

inserts a page break, like the Page Break button on the INSERT tab

starts a section on a new page

starts a section on the same page, immediately after the insertion point

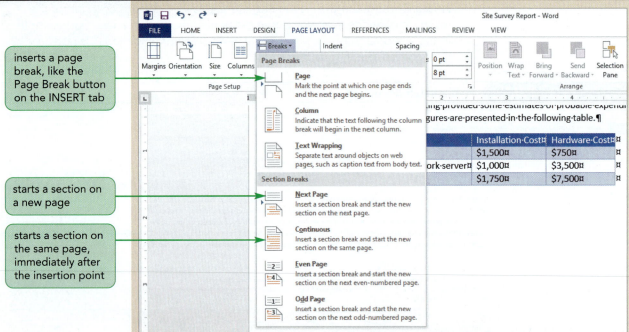

The Page Breaks section of the gallery includes options for controlling how the text flows from page to page. The first option, Page, inserts a page break. It has the same effect as pressing the Page Break button on the INSERT tab or pressing the Ctrl+Enter keys. The Section Breaks section of the gallery includes four types of section breaks. The two you'll use most often are Next Page and Continuous.

3. Under "Section Breaks," click **Next Page**. A section break is inserted, and the insertion point moves to the top of the new page 4.

4. Scroll up until you can see the double-dotted line and the words "Section Break (Next Page)" below the table on page 3. This line indicates that a new section begins on the next page.

5. Save the document.

TIP

To delete a section break, click to the left of the line representing the break, and then press the Delete key.

You've created a new page that is a separate section from the rest of the report. The sections are numbered consecutively. The first part of the document is section 1, and the new page is section 2. Now you can format section 2 in landscape orientation without affecting the rest of the document.

To format section 2 in landscape orientation:

1. Scroll down and verify that the insertion point is positioned at the top of the new page 4.

2. Change the Zoom level to **30%** so you can see all four pages of the document displayed side-by-side.

3. On the ribbon, click the **PAGE LAYOUT** tab.

4. In the Page Setup group, click the **Orientation** button, and then click **Landscape**. Section 2, which consists solely of page 4, changes to landscape orientation, as shown in Figure 3-28. Section 1, which consists of pages 1–3, remains in portrait orientation.

| **Figure 3-28** | **Page 4 formatted in landscape orientation** |

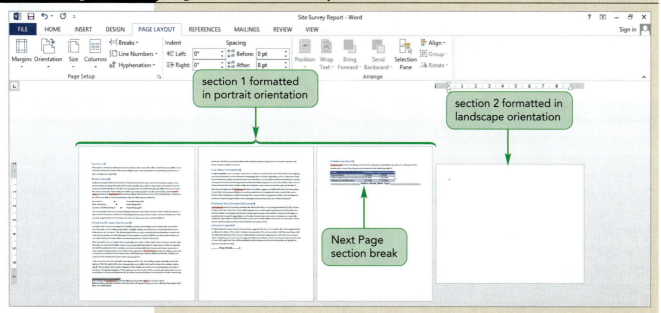

5. Change the Zoom level back to **120%**, and then save the document.

Page 4 is now formatted in landscape orientation, ready for you to create Katherine's handout, which will consist of a graphic that shows the benefits of a site survey. You'll use Word's SmartArt feature to create the graphic.

Creating SmartArt

A **SmartArt** graphic is a diagram of shapes, such as circles, squares, or arrows. A well-designed SmartArt graphic can illustrate concepts that might otherwise require several paragraphs of explanation. To create a SmartArt graphic, you switch to the INSERT tab and then, in the Illustrations group, click the SmartArt button. This opens the Choose a SmartArt Graphic dialog box, where you can select from eight categories of graphics, including graphics designed to illustrate relationships, processes, and hierarchies. Within each category, you can choose from numerous designs. Once inserted into your document, a SmartArt graphic contains placeholder text that you replace with your own text. When a SmartArt graphic is selected, the SMARTART TOOLS DESIGN AND FORMAT tabs appear on the ribbon.

To create a SmartArt graphic:

1. Verify that the insertion point is located at the top of page 4, which is blank.

2. On the ribbon, click the **INSERT** tab.

3. In the Illustrations group, click the **SmartArt** button. The Choose a SmartArt Graphic dialog box opens, with categories of SmartArt graphics in the left panel. The middle panel displays the graphics associated with the category currently selected in the left panel. The right panel displays a larger image of the graphic that is currently selected in the middle panel, along with an explanation of the graphic's purpose. By default, All is selected in the left panel.

4. Explore the Choose a SmartArt Graphic dialog box by selecting categories in the left panel and viewing the graphics displayed in the middle panel.

5. In the left panel, click **Relationship**, and then scroll down in the middle panel and click the **Converging Radial** graphic (in the first column, seventh row from the top), which shows three rectangles with arrows pointing to a circle. In the right panel, you see an explanation of the Converging Radial graphic. See Figure 3-29.

Figure 3-29	Selecting a SmartArt graphic

6. Click the **OK** button. The Converging Radial graphic, with placeholder text, is inserted at the top of page 4. The graphic is surrounded by a rectangular border, indicating that it is selected. The SMARTART TOOLS contextual tabs appear on the ribbon. To the left or right of the graphic, you also see the Text pane, a small window with a title bar that contains the text "Type your text here." See Figure 3-30.

Figure 3-30 SmartArt graphic with Text pane displayed

if the Text pane does not appear on your screen, click this button to select it

Text pane; the width of your Text pane may vary

whatever you type here, at the insertion point…

border indicates the SmartArt graphic is selected

…will appear here, in the selected circle

Trouble? If you do *not* see the Text pane, click the Text Pane button in the Create Graphic group on the SMARTART TOOLS DESIGN tab to select it.

The insertion point is blinking next to the first bullet in the Text pane, which is selected with an orange rectangle. The circle at the bottom of the SmartArt graphic is also selected, as indicated by the border with handles. At this point, anything you type next to the selected bullet in the Text pane will also appear in the selected circle in the SmartArt graphic.

Trouble? If you see the Text pane but the first bullet is not selected as shown in Figure 3-30, click next to the first bullet in the Text pane to select it.

Now you are ready to add text to the graphic.

To add text to the SmartArt graphic:

1. Type **Better Wireless Network**. The new text is displayed in the Text pane and in the circle in the SmartArt graphic. Now you need to insert text in the three rectangles.

2. Press the ↓ key to move the insertion point down to the next placeholder bullet in the Text pane, and then type **Site Survey**. The new text is displayed in the Text pane and in the blue rectangle on the left. See Figure 3-31.

Figure 3-31 **New text in Text pane and in SmartArt graphic**

Figure 3-31 **New text in Text pane and in SmartArt graphic**

3. Press the ↓ key to move the insertion point down to the next placeholder bullet in the Text pane, and then type **Network Upgrades**. The new text appears in the middle rectangle and in the Text pane. You don't need the third rectangle, so you'll delete it.

4. Press the ↓ key to move the insertion point down to the next placeholder bullet in the Text pane, and then press the **Backspace** key. The rectangle on the right is deleted from the SmartArt graphic. The two remaining rectangles and the circle enlarge and shift position.

5. Make sure the SMARTART TOOLS DESIGN tab is still selected on the ribbon.

6. In the Create Graphic group, click the **Text Pane** button to deselect it. The Text pane closes.

7. Click in the white area inside the SmartArt border.

Next, you need to resize the SmartArt graphic so it fills the page.

To adjust the size of the SmartArt graphic:

1. Zoom out so you can see the entire page. As you can see on the ruler, the SmartArt is currently six inches wide. You could drag the SmartArt border to resize it, just as you can with any graphic, but you will get more precise results using the Size button on the SMARTART TOOLS FORMAT tab.

2. On the ribbon, click the **SMARTART TOOLS FORMAT** tab.

3. On the right side of the SMARTART TOOLS FORMAT tab, click the **Size** button to display the Height and Width boxes.

4. Click the **Height** box, type **6.5**, click the **Width** box, type **9**, and then press the **Enter** key. The SmartArt graphic resizes, so that it is now 9 inches wide and 6.5 inches high, taking up most of the page. See Figure 3-32.

Figure 3-32 **Resized SmartArt**

click to type the exact height and width measurements

Trouble? If one of the shapes in the SmartArt graphic was resized, rather than the entire SmartArt graphic, the insertion point was located within the shape rather than in the white space. On the Quick Access Toolbar, click the Undo button, click in the white area inside the SmartArt border, and then repeat Steps 3 and 4.

5. Click outside the SmartArt border to deselect it, and then review the graphic centered on the page.

Next, you need to insert a header at the top of each page in the report and a footer at the bottom of each page in the report.

Adding Headers and Footers

The first step to working with headers and footers is to open Header and Footer view. You can do that in three ways: (1) insert a page number using the Page Number button in the Header & Footer group on the INSERT tab; (2) double-click in the header area (in a page's top margin) or in the footer area (in a page's bottom margin); or (3) click the Header button or the Footer button on the INSERT tab.

By default, Word assumes that when you add something to the header or footer on any page of a document, you want the same text to appear on every page of the document. To create a different header or footer for the first page, you select the Different First Page check box in the Options group on the HEADER & FOOTER TOOLS DESIGN tab. When a document is divided into sections, like the Site Survey Report document, you can create a different header or footer for each section.

For a simple header or footer, double-click the header or footer area, and then type the text you want directly in the header or footer area, formatting the text as you would any other text in a document. To choose from a selection of predesigned header or footer styles, use the Header and Footer buttons on the HEADER & FOOTER TOOLS DESIGN tab (or on the INSERT tab). These buttons open galleries that you can use to select from a number of header and footer styles, some of which include page numbers and graphic elements such as horizontal lines or shaded boxes.

Some styles also include document controls that are similar to the kinds of controls that you might encounter in a dialog box. Any information that you enter in a document control is displayed in the header or footer as ordinary text, but it is also stored in the Word file so that Word can easily reuse it in other parts of the document. For example, later in this tutorial you will create a cover page for the report. Word's predefined cover pages include document controls similar to those found in headers and footers. So if you use a document control to enter the document title in the header, the same document title will show up on the cover page; there's no need to retype it.

In the following steps, you'll create a footer for the whole document (sections 1 and 2) that includes the page number and your name. As shown in Katherine's plan in Figure 3-33, you'll also create a header for section 1 only (pages 1 through 3) that includes the document title and the date. You'll leave the header area for section 2 blank.

Figure 3-33	Plan for headers and footers in Katherine's report

© 2014 Cengage Learning

First you will create the footer on page 1, so you can see how the footer fits below the footnotes at the bottom of the page.

To create a footer for the entire document:

1. Change the Zoom level to **120%**, and then scroll up until you can see the bottom of page 1 and the top of page 2.

2. Double-click in the white space below the footnotes on page 1. The document switches to Header and Footer view. The HEADER & FOOTER TOOLS DESIGN tab is displayed on the ribbon. The insertion point is positioned on the left side of the footer area, ready for you to begin typing. The label "Footer -Section 1-" tells you that the insertion point is located in the footer for section 1. The document text (including the footnotes) is gray,

indicating that you cannot edit it in Header and Footer view. The header area for section 1 is also visible on top of page 2. The default footer tab stops (which are different from the default tab stops in the main document) are visible on the ruler. See Figure 3-34.

Figure 3-34	Creating a footer

document text is unavailable for editing

default footer tab stops

insertion point in the footer for section 1

header area for section 1

HEADER & FOOTER TOOLS DESIGN tab

3. Type your first and last name, and then press the **Enter** key. The insertion point moves to the second line in the footer, aligned along the left margin. This is where you will insert the page number.

4. In the Header & Footer group, click the **Page Number** button. The Page Number menu opens. Because the insertion point is already located where you want to insert the page number, you'll use the Current Position option.

5. Point to **Current Position**. A gallery of page number styles opens. Katherine wants to use the Accent Bar 2 style.

6. Click the **Accent Bar 2** style (the third style from the top). The word "Page," a vertical bar, and the page number are inserted in the footer.

 Next, you'll check to make sure that the footer you just created for section 1 also appears in section 2. To move between headers or footers in separate sections, you can use the buttons in the Navigation group on the HEADER & FOOTER TOOLS DESIGN tab.

7. In the Navigation group, click the **Next** button. Word displays the footer for the next section in the document—that is, the footer for section 2, which appears at the bottom of page 4. The label at the top of the footer area reads "Footer -Section 2-" and it contains the same text (your name and the page number) in this footer as in section 1. Word assumes, by default, that when you type text in one footer, you want it to appear in all the footers in the document.

TIP

To change the numbering style or to specify a number to use as the first page number, click the Page Number button in the Header & Footer group, and then click Format Page Numbers.

Now you need to create a header for section 1. Katherine does not want to include a header in section 2 because it would distract attention from the SmartArt graphic. So you will first separate the header for section 1 from the header for section 2.

To separate the headers for section 1 and section 2:

▶ **1.** Verify that the insertion point is located in the section 2 footer area at the bottom of page 4, and that the HEADER & FOOTER TOOLS DESIGN tab is selected on the ribbon. To switch from the footer to the header in the current section, you can use the Go to Header button in the Navigation group.

▶ **2.** In the Navigation group, click the **Go to Header** button. The insertion point moves to the section 2 header at the top of page 4. See Figure 3-35.

Figure 3-35 — Section 2 header is currently the same as the previous header, in section 1

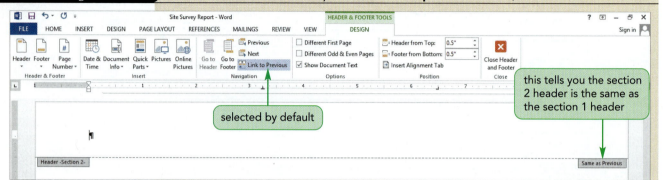

selected by default

this tells you the section 2 header is the same as the section 1 header

Header -Section 2- Same as Previous

Notice that in the Navigation group, the Link to Previous button is selected. In the header area in the document window, the gray tab on the right side of the header border contains the message "Same as Previous," indicating that the section 2 header is set up to display the same text as the header in the previous section, which is section 1. To make the section 2 header a separate entity, you need to break the link between the section 1 and section 2 headers.

TIP

When you create a header for a section, it doesn't matter what page you're working on as long as the insertion point is located in a header in that section.

▶ **3.** In the Navigation group, click the **Link to Previous** button to deselect it. The Same as Previous tab is removed from the right side of the section 2 header border.

▶ **4.** In the Navigation group, click the **Previous** button. The insertion point moves up to the nearest header in the previous section, which is the section 1 header at the top of page 3. The label "Header -Section 1-" identifies this as a section 1 header.

▶ **5.** In the Header & Footer group, click the **Header** button. A gallery of header styles opens.

▶ **6.** Scroll down and review the various header styles, and then click the **Grid** style (eighth style from the top). The placeholder text "[Document title]" is aligned at the left margin. The placeholder text "[Date]" is aligned at the right margin.

▶ **7.** Click the **[Document title]** placeholder text. The placeholder text is now selected within a document control. See Figure 3-36.

Figure 3-36 **Adding a header to section 1**

- **8.** Type **Wireless Site Survey Recommendation**. The text you just typed is displayed in the document control instead of the placeholder text. Next, you need to add the date. The header style you selected includes a date picker document control, which allows you to select the date from a calendar.

- **9.** Click the **[Date]** placeholder text to display an arrow in the document control, and then click the arrow. A calendar for the current month appears, as shown in Figure 3-37. In the calendar, the current date is outlined in dark blue.

Figure 3-37 **Adding a date to the section 1 header**

- **10.** Click the current date. The current date, including the year, is inserted in the document control.

- **11.** Scroll up slightly and click anywhere in the Section 1 footer (on the preceding page) to deselect the date document control. You are finished creating the header and footer for Katherine's report, so you can close Header and Footer view and return to Print Layout view.

- **12.** In the Close group, click the **Close Header and Footer** button, or double-click anywhere in the main document, and then save your work.

> **13.** Change the Zoom level to **30%** so you can see all four pages of the document, including the header at the top of pages 1–3 and the footer at the bottom of pages 1–4. Take a moment to compare your completed headers and footers with Katherine's plan for the headers and footers shown earlier in Figure 3-33.

Finally, you need to insert a cover page for the report.

Inserting a Cover Page

A document's cover page typically includes the title and the name of the author. Some people also include a summary of the report on the cover page, which is commonly referred to as an abstract. In addition, you might include the date, the name and possibly the logo of your company or organization, and a subtitle. A cover page should not include the document header or footer.

To insert a preformatted cover page at the beginning of the document, you use the Cover Page button on the INSERT tab. You can choose from a variety of cover page styles, all of which include document controls in which you can enter the document title, the document's author, the date, and so on. These document controls are linked to any other document controls in the document. For example, you already entered "Wireless Site Survey Recommendation" into a document control in the header of Katherine's report. So if you use a cover page that contains a similar document control, "Wireless Site Survey Recommendation" will be displayed on the cover page automatically. Note that document controls sometimes display information entered when either Word or Windows was originally installed on your computer. If your computer has multiple user accounts, the information displayed in some document controls might reflect the information for the current user. In any case, you can easily edit the contents of a document control.

To insert a cover page at the beginning of the report:

> **1.** Verify that the document is still zoomed so that you can see all four pages, and then press the **Ctrl+Home** keys. The insertion point moves to the beginning of the document.

> **2.** On the ribbon, click the **INSERT** tab.

> **3.** In the Pages group, click the **Cover Page** button. A gallery of cover page styles opens.
>
> Notice that the names of the cover page styles match the names of the preformatted header styles you saw earlier. For example, the list includes a Grid cover page, which is designed to match the Grid header used in this document. To give a document a uniform look, it's helpful to use elements with the same style throughout.

> **4.** Scroll down the gallery to see the cover page styles, and then locate the Grid cover page style.

> **5.** Click the **Grid** cover page style. The new cover page is inserted at the beginning of the document.

> **6.** Change the Zoom level to **120%**, and then scroll down to display the report title in the middle of the cover page. The only difference between the title "Wireless Site Survey Recommendation" here and the title you entered in the document header is that here the title is displayed in all uppercase. The cover page also includes document controls for a subtitle and an abstract. See Figure 3-38.

TIP

To delete a cover page that you inserted from the Cover Page gallery, click the Cover Page button in the Pages group, and then click Remove Current Cover Page.

Figure 3-38 **Newly inserted cover page**

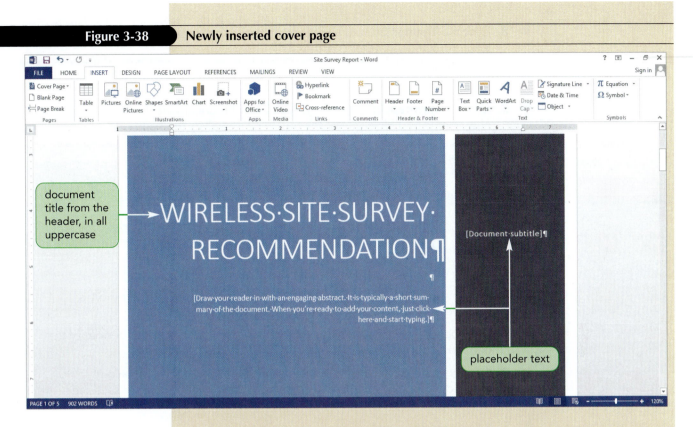

You need to type a subtitle in the subtitle document control on the right side of the page.

7. Click the **[Document subtitle]** placeholder text, and then type **Orchard Street Art Center**. Next, you will remove the abstract document control because you do not need an abstract for this report.

8. Below the document title, right-click the placeholder text that begins **[Draw your reader in…** to display the shortcut menu, and then click **Remove Content Control**. The content control is removed from the cover page.

9. Save the document.

Changing the Theme

The report now contains several formatting elements that are controlled by the document's theme, so changing the theme will affect the document's overall appearance. Katherine suggests that you apply a different theme to the document.

To change the document's theme:

1. Change the Zoom level to **40%** so you can see the first four pages side-by-side, with part of the fifth page visible on the bottom.

2. On the ribbon, click the **DESIGN** tab.

▶ **3.** Click the **Themes** button, select any theme you want, and then review the results in the document.

▶ **4.** Apply three or four more different themes of your choice and review the results of each in the document.

▶ **5.** Click the **Retrospect** theme, and then save the document. The cover page is now orange and olive green, the headings as well as the header and footer text are orange, and the table is formatted with an olive green header row and gray shading.

Your work on the report is finished. You should preview the report before closing it.

To preview the report:

▶ **1.** On the ribbon, click the **FILE** tab.

▶ **2.** In the navigation bar, click the **Print** tab. The cover page of the report is displayed in the document preview in the right pane.

▶ **3.** Examine the document preview, using the arrow buttons at the bottom of the pane to display each page.

▶ **4.** If you need to make any changes to the report, return to Print Layout view, edit the document, preview the document again, and then save the document.

▶ **5.** Display the document in Print Layout view.

▶ **6.** Change the Zoom level back to **120%**, and then press the **Ctrl+Home** keys to make sure the insertion point is located on the first page.

Reviewing a Document in Read Mode

The members of the board of directors might choose to print the report, but some might prefer to read it on their computers instead. In that case, they can take advantage of **Read Mode**, a document view designed to make reading on a screen as easy as possible. Unlike Print Layout view, which mimics the look of the printed page with its margins and page breaks, Read Mode focuses on the document's content. Read Mode displays as much content as possible on the screen at a time, with buttons that allow you to display more. Note that you can't edit text in Read Mode. To do that, you need to switch back to Page Layout view.

To display the Site Survey document in Read Mode:

▶ **1.** In the status bar, click the **Read Mode** button 📖. The document switches to Read Mode, with a reduced version of the cover page on the left and the first part of the document text on the right. On the left edge of the status bar, the message "SCREENS 1-2 OF 8" explains that you are currently viewing the first two screens out of a total of 8.

Trouble? If your status bar indicates that you have a different number of screens, change the Zoom level as needed so that the document is split into 8 screens.

The title page on the left is screen 1. The text on the right is screen 2. To display more of the document, you can click the arrow button on the right. See Figure 3-39.

Figure 3-39 **Document displayed in Read Mode**

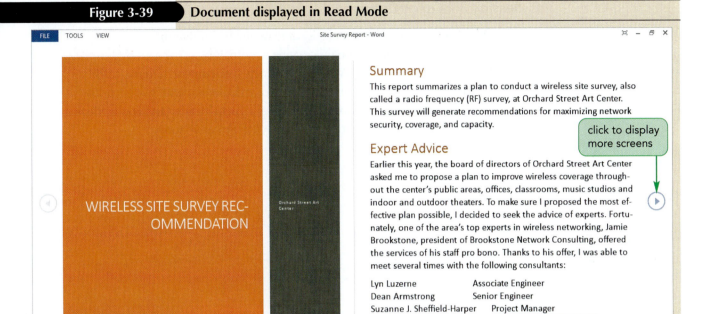

2. Click the **right arrow** button ▶ on the right to display screens 3 and 4. A left arrow button now appears on the left side of the screen. You could click it to move back to the previous screens.

3. Click the **right arrow** button ▶ to display screens 5 and 6, and then click the **right arrow** button ▶ again to display the final two screens. To zoom in on the SmartArt graphic, you can double-click it.

4. Double-click the SmartArt graphic. An object zoom window opens, with the SmartArt graphic displayed. You can display an object zoom window like this for any graphic.

5. In the upper-right corner of the object zoom window, click the **magnifying glass** button 🔍 to zoom in on the SmartArt graphic even more.

6. Click the **magnifying glass** button 🔍 to return to the previous zoom level.

7. Click anywhere outside the object zoom window to return to screens 7 and 8 in Read Mode.

8. Click the **left arrow** button ◀ on the left as necessary to return to screens 1 and 2, and then click the **Print Layout** button 📄 in the status bar to return to Page Layout view.

9. Close the document.

You now have a draft of the Site Survey Report document, including a cover page, the report text, a nicely formatted table, and the SmartArt graphic (in landscape orientation).

REVIEW

Session 3.2 Quick Check

1. Where are the default tab stops located on the horizontal ruler?
2. What tab do you click to begin creating a footnote?
3. Explain how to configure Word to hyphenate a document automatically.
4. Explain how to create separate headers for a document with two sections.
5. List three ways to switch from Page Layout view to Header and Footer view.
6. Explain how to make a graphic easier to view in Read Mode.

ASSESS

SAM Projects

Put your skills into practice with SAM Projects! SAM Projects for this tutorial can be found online. If you have a SAM account, go to www.cengage.com/sam2013 to download the most recent Project Instructions and Start Files.

PRACTICE

Review Assignments

Data File needed for the Review Assignments: Security.docx

The wireless site survey has been completed, and the Orchard Street Art Center has upgraded its network. Now, Katherine Hua is organizing a series of network security training classes for the art center staff. She has begun working on a report for the board that outlines basic information about the training. You need to format the report, add a table at the end containing a preliminary schedule, and create a sample graphic that Katherine could use in a handout announcing the training. Complete the following steps:

1. Open the file **Security** located in the Word3 ▶ Review folder included with your Data Files, and then save it as **Security Training Report** in the location specified by your instructor.
2. Promote the "Training Schedule" and "Level 1 Equipment Needs" headings from Heading 2 text to Heading 1 text, and then move the "Level 1 Equipment Needs" heading and its body text up above the "Training Schedule" heading.
3. Insert a page break before the "Training Schedule" heading. Insert a blank paragraph at the end of the new page 2, and then insert a table using the information shown in Figure 3-40. Format the header row in bold.

Figure 3-40 Information for training schedule table

Date	Topic
April 21	Applications
March 16	User account permissions
April 28	Firewall procedures
April 6	Wireless devices
March 3	Password security

© 2014 Cengage Learning

4. Sort the table by the contents of the "Date" column in ascending order.
5. In the appropriate location in the table, insert a new row for a **User privacy** class on **March 23**.
6. Delete the "Applications" row from the table.
7. Modify the widths of both columns to accommodate the widest entry in each.
8. Apply the Grid Table 4 - Accent 2 style to the table.
9. On page 1, replace the text "[instructor names]" with a tabbed list of instructors and their specialties, using the following information: **Jackie Fuhrman-Dunaway, Wireless security; Marcolo Jimenez, Multimedia wireless security; Surila Jin, Web privacy; Elizabeth Lawson, User support**. Insert a tab after each name, and don't include any punctuation in the list.
10. Use a left tab stop to align the instructors' specialities 2.5 inches from the left margin, and then adjust the list's paragraph spacing so it appears to be a single paragraph.

11. Locate the first sentence below the "Level 1 Equipment Needs" heading. At the end of that sentence, insert a footnote that reads **Some board members mentioned the possibility of holding classes in the concert hall, but the instructors prefer the smaller lecture hall, where microphones are unnecessary**.

12. Hyphenate the document using the default settings.

13. After the training schedule table on page 2, insert a section break that starts a new, third page, and then format the new page in landscape orientation. Insert a SmartArt graphic that illustrates the advantages of computer classes. Use the Equation graphic from the Process category, and, from left to right, include the following text in the SmartArt diagram: **User Education**, **Good Network Management**, and **Secure Wireless Network.** Do not include any punctuation in the SmartArt. Size the SmartArt graphic to fill the page.

14. Create a footer for sections 1 and 2 that aligns your first and last names at the left margin. Insert the page number, without any design elements and without the word "Page," below your name.

15. Separate the section 1 header from the section 2 header, and then create a header for section 1 using the Retrospect header style. Enter **SECURITY TRAINING** as the document title, and select the current date. Note that the document title will be displayed in all uppercase no matter how you type it.

16. Insert a cover page using the Retrospect style. If you typed the document title in all uppercase in the header, it will be displayed in all uppercase here. If you used a mix of uppercase and lowercase in the header, you'll see a mix here. Revise the document title as necessary to make it all uppercase, and then add the following subtitle: **A REPORT FOR THE ORCHARD STREET ART CENTER BOARD OF DIRECTORS**. Enter your name in the Author document control (you might have to replace a default name inserted by Word), and then delete the Company Name and Company Address document controls.

17. Change the document theme to Integral, save and preview the report, and then close it.

Case Problem 1

APPLY

Data File needed for this Case Problem: Greenware.docx

Greenware Consortium You are the assistant business manager of Greenware Consortium, a professional organization for LEED contractors in Seattle, Washington and the surrounding area. LEED, which is short for Leadership in Energy and Environmental Design, is a certification system designed to encourage environmentally friendly building construction and maintenance. Contractors join the Greenware Consortium to make professional contacts with like-minded vendors and customers. You have been asked to help prepare an annual report for the board of directors. The current draft is not complete, but it contains enough for you to get started. Complete the following steps:

1. Open the file **Greenware** located in the Word3 ▶ Case1 folder included with your Data Files, and then save it as **Greenware Report** in the location specified by your instructor.

2. Adjust the heading levels so that the "Greenware Faire" and "Green Tech Fest" headings are formatted with the Heading 2 style.

3. Move the "Membership Forecast" heading and its body text down to the end of the report.

4. Format the Board of Directors list using a left tab stop with a dot leader at the 2.2-inch mark. (*Hint*: Use the Dialog Box Launcher in the Paragraph group on the PAGE LAYOUT tab to open the Paragraph dialog box, and then click the Tabs button at the bottom of the Indents and Spacing tab to open the Tabs dialog box.)

5. At the end of the first paragraph below the "Going Green Walking Tours" heading, insert the following footnote: **The Going Green walking tours are sponsored by the Seattle Public Works Department in association with the Seattle Green for Life Foundation**.

6. Locate the "Purpose" heading on page 1. At the end of the body text below that heading, insert the following footnote: **We recently signed a ten-year contract renewal with our website host, NetMind Solutions**.

7. Insert a page break that moves the "Membership Forecast" heading to the top of a new page, and then, below the body text on the new page, insert a table consisting of three columns and four rows.

8. In the table, enter the information shown in Figure 3-41. Format the column headings in bold.

Figure 3-41 Information for membership forecast table

Membership Type	2016	Projected 2017
Contractor	260	285
Vendor	543	670
Building Owner/Operator	350	400

© 2014 Cengage Learning

9. Sort the table in ascending order by membership type.

10. In the appropriate location in the table, insert a row for a **Student/Apprentice** membership type, with **250** members in 2016, and **300** projected members in 2017.

11. Adjust the column widths so each column accommodates the widest entry.

12. Format the table using the Grid Table 4 - Accent 1 table style without banded rows or a first column.

13. Hyphenate the document using the default settings.

14. Insert a Blank footer, and then type your name to replace the selected placeholder text in the footer's left margin. In the right margin, insert a page number using the Accent Bar 3 style. (*Hint:* Press the Tab key twice to move the insertion point to the right margin before inserting the page number, and then insert the page number at the current location.)

15. Insert a cover page using the Sideline style. Enter the company name, **Greenware Consortium**, and the title, **Annual Report**, in the appropriate document controls. In the subtitle document control, enter **Prepared by [Your Name]** (but replace "[Your Name]" with your first and last names). Delete the Author document control, which might contain a default name inserted by Word, and then insert the current date in the Date document control.

16. Change the document theme to Ion.

17. Save, preview, and then close the document.

TROUBLESHOOT

Case Problem 2

Data File needed for this Case Problem: Evaluation.docx

Customer Evaluation Report Academy Art Tours specializes in European tours emphasizing art and architecture. After managing this year's Masters of Architecture tour, Lisa Marisca has begun writing a report summarizing the customer evaluation forms. She asks you to review her incomplete draft and fix some problems. Complete the following steps:

1. Open the file named **Evaluation** located in the Word3 ▸ Case2 folder included with your Data Files, and then save it as **Evaluation Report** in the location specified by your instructor.

⚙ **Troubleshoot** 2. Adjust the document so that the following are true:
- The heading "Problems Acquiring Updated Passports," its body text, and the SmartArt graphic appear on the last page in landscape orientation, with the rest of the report in portrait orientation.
- In section 1, the heading "Summary" is displayed at the top of page 2.
- The document header contains your first and last names but not a content control for the document title.
- Neither the header nor the footer is displayed on page 1.
- The footer is not displayed on the last page of the document. (*Hint:* After you break the link between sections, you'll need to delete the contents of the footer in one section.)

⚙ **Troubleshoot** 3. On pages 2 and 3, promote headings as necessary so all the headings are on the same level.

4. Increase the paragraph spacing before the first paragraph, "Masters of Architecture," on page 1 as much as necessary so that the paragraph is located at about the 2-inch mark on the vertical ruler. When you're finished, the text should be centered vertically on the page, so it looks like a cover page.

⚙ **Troubleshoot** 5. On page 2, remove any extra rows and columns in the table, and sort the information in a logical way. When you are finished, format it with a style that applies green (Accent 6) shading to the header row, with banded rows below, and remove any bold formatting as necessary.

6. Add a fourth shape to the SmartArt Graphic with the text **Submit completed form, photo, and fee to post office clerk**. Resize the graphic to fill the white space below the document text.

7. Save the document, review it in Read Mode, preview it, and then close it.

Case Problem 3

There are no Data Files needed for this Case Problem.

CREATE

"Aiden Eats" Blog and Newsletter Aiden Malloy publishes his reviews of Minneapolis restaurants both in his blog, Aiden Eats, and in a printed newsletter of the same name. These publications have become so popular that Aiden has decided to try selling advertising space in both venues to local businesses. A colleague has just emailed him a list of potential advertisers. Aiden asks you to create and format a table containing the list of advertisers. When you're finished with that project, you'll create a table detailing some of his recent expenses. Complete the following steps:

1. Open a new, blank document, and then save it as **Advertiser Table** in the location specified by your instructor.

2. Create the table shown in Figure 3-42.

Figure 3-42 Advertiser table

Business	Contact	Phone
Allenton Knife Sharpening	Peter Allenton	555-5555
Bizmark Restaurant Supply	Nolan Everdeen	555-5555
Spices Boutique	Sigrid Larson	555-5555
WestMark Kitchen Design	Sheryl Wu	555-5555

© 2014 Cengage Learning

For the table style, start with the Grid Table 4 - Accent 1 table style, and then make any necessary changes. Use the Blue, Accent 1 color for the borders. The final table should be about 6.5 inches wide and 2.5 inches tall, as measured on the horizontal and vertical rulers. (*Hint:* Remember that you can drag the Table Resize handle to increase the table's overall size.)

3. Replace "Peter Allenton" with your first and last names.

4. Save, preview, and then close the Advertiser Table document.

5. Open a new, blank document, and then save it as **Expense Table** in the location specified by your instructor.

6. Create the table shown in Figure 3-43.

Figure 3-43 Expense table

Restaurant	Date	Expense
Beverly Coffee and Bake Shoppe	2/3/16	$13.50
Vietnam Noodle House	2/10/16	$23.00
The Everett Club	2/23/16	$45.50
	Total	$82.00

© 2014 Cengage Learning

For the table style, start with the Grid Table 4 - Accent 1 table style, and then make any necessary changes. Use the Blue, Accent 1 color for the borders. Note that in the bottom row, you'll need to merge two cells and right-align text within the new, merged cell.

7. For the total, use a formula instead of simply typing the amount. (*Hint:* Click in the cell where you want to insert a formula to sum the values, click the TABLE TOOLS LAYOUT tab, and then click the Formula button in the Data group to open the Formula dialog box, and then click the OK button.)

8. Save, preview, and then close the Expense Table document.

Case Problem 4

There are no Data Files needed for this Case Problem.

Friends of Triangle Beach Kate Chomsky coordinates volunteers who monitor and protect native plant species on Triangle Beach, a nature preserve on the eastern coast of Florida. She needs a flyer to hand out at an upcoming neighborhood festival, where she hopes to recruit more volunteers. You can use Word's table features to lay out the flyer as shown in Kate's sketch in Figure 3-44. At the very end, you'll remove the table borders.

Figure 3-44 Sketch for Triangle Beach flyer

© 2014 Cengage Learning

Complete the following steps:

1. Open a new, blank document, and then save it as **Triangle Beach** in the location specified by your instructor.

2. Change the document's orientation to landscape.

✛ **Explore** 3. Use the Table button on the INSERT tab, to access the Insert Table menu, and then click Draw Table at the bottom of the menu to activate the Draw Table pointer (which looks like a pencil). Click in the upper-left corner of the document (near the paragraph mark), and, using the rulers as guides, drag down and to the right to draw a rectangle that is 9 inches wide and 6 inches high. After you draw the rectangle, you can adjust its height and width using the Height and Width boxes in the Cell Size group on the TABLE TOOLS LAYOUT tab, if necessary. (*Hint*: If the Draw Table pointer disappears after you change the table's height and width, you can turn it back on by clicking the Draw Table button in the Draw group on the TABLE TOOLS LAYOUT tab.)

✛ **Explore** 4. Use the Draw Table pointer to draw the columns and rows shown in Figure 3-44. For example, to draw the column border for the "Friends of Triangle Beach" column, click the top of the rectangle at the point where you want the right column border to be located, and then drag down to the bottom of the rectangle. Use the same technique to draw rows. (*Hint:* To delete a border, click the Eraser button in the Draw group on the TABLE TOOLS LAYOUT tab, click anywhere on the border you want to erase, and then click the Eraser button again to turn it off.)

5. When you are finished drawing the table, press the Esc key to turn off the Draw Table pointer.

✛ **Explore** 6. In the left column, type the text **Friends of Triangle Beach**. With the pointer still in that cell, click the TABLE TOOLS LAYOUT tab, and then in the Alignment group, click the Text Direction button twice to position the text vertically so that it reads from bottom to top. Using the formatting options on the HOME tab, format the text in 36-point font. Use the Align Center button in the Alignment group to center the text in the cell. (*Hint:* You will probably have to adjust and readjust the row and column borders throughout these steps until all the elements of the table are positioned properly.)

7. Type the remaining text as shown in Figure 3-44. Replace "Kate Chomsky" with your own name, remove the hyperlink formatting from the email address, and format it in bold. Change the font size for "Volunteers Needed" to 36 points, and center align the text in that cell. Use the Heading 1 style for the following text—"Remove Invasive Species," "Protect Native Species," "Mission," and "Contact." Change the font size for this text to 20 points. For the remaining text, use the Normal style, and then change the font size to 16 points. If the table expands to two pages, drag a row border up slightly to reduce the row's height. Repeat as necessary until the table fits on one page.

✛ **Explore** 8. On the INSERT tab, use the Shapes button in the Illustrations group to draw the Isosceles Triangle shape, similar to the way you drew the table rectangle, by dragging the pointer. Draw the triangle in the blank cell in the top row. If the triangle isn't centered neatly in the cell, click the Undo button and try again until you draw a triangle that has the same proportions as the one in Figure 3-44. Until you change the theme in the next step, the triangle will be blue.

9. Change the document theme to Facet.

10. Remove the table borders. When you are finished, your flyer should match the table shown in Figure 3-44, but without the table borders.

11. Save your work, preview the document, and then close it.

Enhancing Page Layout and Design

Creating a Newsletter

OBJECTIVES

Session 4.1
- Use continuous section break for page layout
- Format text in columns
- Insert symbols and special characters
- Distinguish between inline and floating objects
- Wrap text around an object
- Insert and format text boxes
- Insert drop caps

Session 4.2
- Create and modify WordArt
- Insert and crop a picture
- Add clip art to a document
- Rotate and adjust a picture
- Remove a photo's background
- Balance columns
- Add a page border
- Save a document as a PDF
- Open a PDF in Word

Case | *Williamson Health Care*

Estefan Silva is a public outreach specialist at Williamson Health Care, a health maintenance organization located in Carson City, Nevada. He has written the text of a newsletter describing an upcoming series of wellness classes. Now he needs you to transform the text into an eye-catching publication with a headline, photos, drop caps, and other desktop publishing elements. Estefan's budget doesn't allow him to hire a professional graphic designer to create the document using desktop publishing software. But there's no need for that because you can do the work for him using Word's formatting, graphics, and page layout tools. After you finish the newsletter, Estefan wants you to save the newsletter as a PDF so he can email it to the printing company. You also need to make some edits to a document that is currently available only as a PDF.

STARTING DATA FILES

Word4 → **Tutorial**
Chart.png
Classes.docx
Registration.docx
Webinar.pdf
Wellness.docx

Review
Exercise.docx
Habits.png
On the Move.docx
Take it Easy.docx

Case1
Green.docx
Sidebar.docx

Case2
Facts.docx
Rights.docx

Case3
Audio.pdf
Shape.docx

Case4
(none)

Microsoft product screenshots used with permission from Microsoft Corporation.

Session 4.1 Visual Overview:

Desktop publishing is the process of preparing commercial-quality printed material, such as the newsletter shown here, using a personal computer. Using Word, you can create documents that have elements of desktop publishing, such as special font treatments, graphics, and page layout options, as well as design elements such as page borders.

This specially formatted text is an example of **WordArt**, which is created using the WordArt button in the Text group on the INSERT tab.

These are examples of text boxes, which are like mini documents within a document.

This photo and the drawing of the woman in a yoga pose under a tree (on the next page) are examples of clip art from Office.com. **Clip art** consists of premade electronic illustrations, photographs, and other graphics. Audio and video clip art are also available.

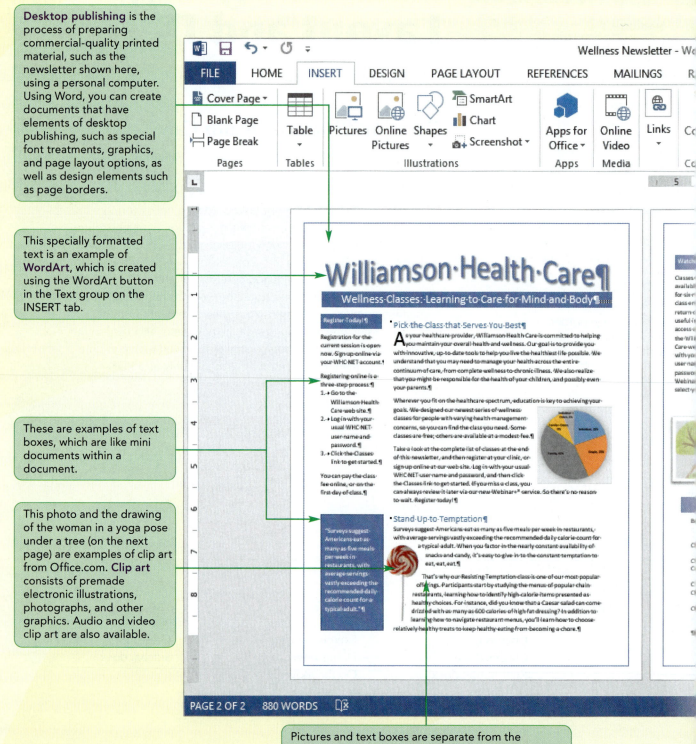

Pictures and text boxes are separate from the document text; you need to adjust the way text flows, or **wraps**, around them. Here, the Tight text wrap option is used to make text flow as closely as possible around the shape of the lollipop.

Elements of Desktop Publishing

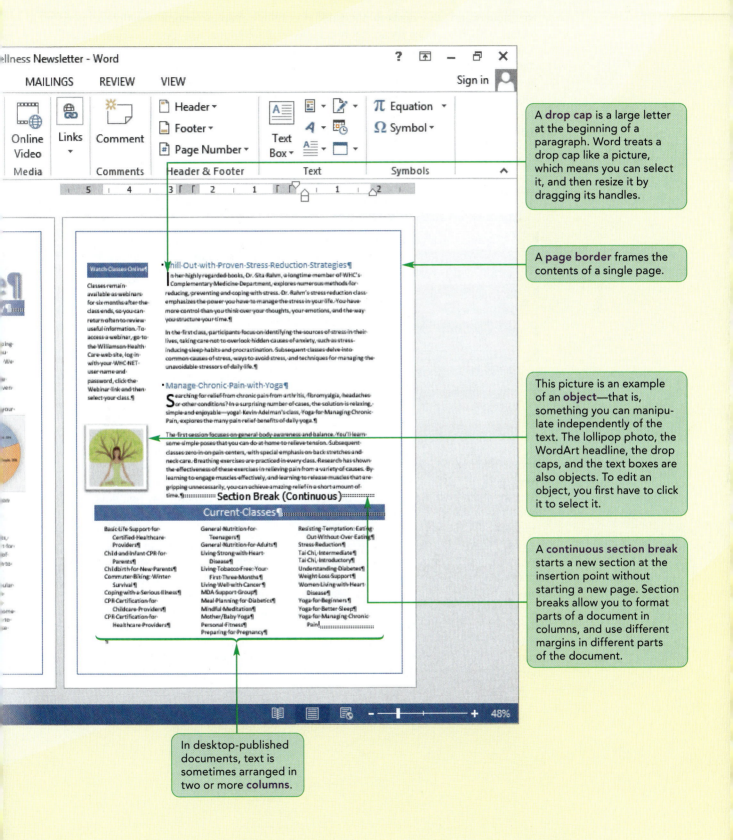

A **drop cap** is a large letter at the beginning of a paragraph. Word treats a drop cap like a picture, which means you can select it, and then resize it by dragging its handles.

A **page border** frames the contents of a single page.

This picture is an example of an **object**—that is, something you can manipulate independently of the text. The lollipop photo, the WordArt headline, the drop caps, and the text boxes are also objects. To edit an object, you first have to click it to select it.

A **continuous section break** starts a new section at the insertion point without starting a new page. Section breaks allow you to format parts of a document in columns, and use different margins in different parts of the document.

In desktop-published documents, text is sometimes arranged in two or more **columns**.

Using Continuous Section Breaks to Enhance Page Layout

Newsletters and other desktop-published documents often incorporate multiple section breaks, with the various sections formatted with different margins, page orientations, column settings, and other page layout options. Continuous section breaks, which start a new section without starting a new page, are especially useful when creating a newsletter because they allow you to apply different page layout settings to different parts of a single page. To create the newsletter shown in the Session 4.1 Visual Overview, the first step is to insert a series of section breaks that will allow you to use different margins for different parts of the document. Section breaks will also allow you to format some of the text in multiple columns.

You'll start by opening and reviewing the document.

To open and review the document:

1. Open the document **Wellness** from the Word4 ▸ Tutorial folder included with your Data Files, and then save it as **Wellness Newsletter** in the location specified by your instructor.

2. Display nonprinting characters and the rulers, and switch to Print Layout view, if necessary.

3. On the ribbon, click the **VIEW** tab.

4. In the Zoom group, click **Multiple Pages** so you can see both pages of the document side-by-side.

5. Compare the document to the completed newsletter shown in the Session 4.1 Visual Overview.

The document is formatted with the Office theme, using the default margins. The first paragraph is formatted with the Title style, and the remaining headings are formatted either with the Heading 1 style, or with blue paragraph shading, center alignment, and white font color. The document doesn't yet contain any text boxes or other desktop publishing elements. The list of classes at the end of the document appears as a standard, single column of text.

To make room for the text boxes, you need to change the left margin to 2.5 inches for all of the text between the "Wellness Classes: Learning to Care for Mind and Body" heading and the "Current Classes" heading. To accomplish this, you'll insert a section break after the "Wellness Classes: Learning to Care for Mind and Body" heading and another one before the "Current Classes" heading. You'll eventually format the list of current classes, at the end of the document, in three columns. To accomplish that, you need to insert a third section break after the "Current Classes" heading. Because you don't want any of the section breaks to start new pages, you will use continuous sections breaks for all three. See Figure 4-1.

Figure 4-1 **Wellness Newsletter document before adding section breaks**

To insert continuous section breaks in the document:

1. Change the Zoom level to **120%**.

2. In the document, click at the beginning of the third paragraph, which contains the heading "Pick the Class that Serves You Best."

3. On the ribbon, click the **PAGE LAYOUT** tab.

4. In the Page Setup group, click the **Breaks** button, and then click **Continuous**. A short dotted line, indicating a continuous section break, appears in the blue shading at the end of the preceding paragraph. If the paragraph text were shorter, you would see a longer line with the words "Section Break (Continuous)." You'll be able to see the section break text more clearly when you insert the next one.

5. Scroll down to page 2, click at the beginning of the shaded paragraph "Current Classes," and then insert a continuous section break. A dotted line with the words "Section Break (Continuous)" appears at the end of the preceding paragraph.

6. Click at the beginning of the next paragraph, which contains the first class title "Basic Life Support for Certified Healthcare Providers," and then insert a continuous section break. A dotted line with the words "Section Break (Continuous)" appears in the blue shading at the end of the preceding paragraph.

Now that you have created sections within the Wellness Newsletter document, you can format the individual sections as if they were separate documents. In the following steps, you'll format the first and third sections by changing their left and right margins to .75 inch. Then, you'll format the second section by changing its left margin to 2.5 inches.

To set custom margins for sections 1, 2, and 3:

1. Press the **Ctrl+Home** keys to position the insertion point in section 1.

2. In the Page Setup group, click the **Margins** button, and then click **Custom Margins** to open the Page Setup dialog box.

3. Change the Left and Right margin settings to **.75** inch, and then click the **OK** button. The blue shading expands slightly on both sides of the paragraph.

4. On page 1, click anywhere in the heading "Pick the Class that Serves You Best" to position the insertion point in section 2.

5. In the Page Setup group, click the **Margins** button, and then click **Custom Margins** to open the Page Setup dialog box.

6. Change the Left margin setting to **2.5** inches, and then click the **OK** button. The text in section 2 shifts to the right, and the document text flows to a third page. Throughout this tutorial, as you add and resize various elements, the text will occasionally expand from two pages to three or four. But by the time you are finished, the newsletter will consist of only two pages.

7. Scroll down to page 2, click in the shaded heading "Current Classes" to position the insertion point in section 3, and then change the Left and Right margin settings to **.75** inch.

8. On the ribbon, click the **VIEW** tab.

9. In the Zoom group, click **Multiple Pages** so you can see all three pages of the document side-by-side. See Figure 4-2.

Figure 4-2 Sections 1, 2, and 3 with new margins

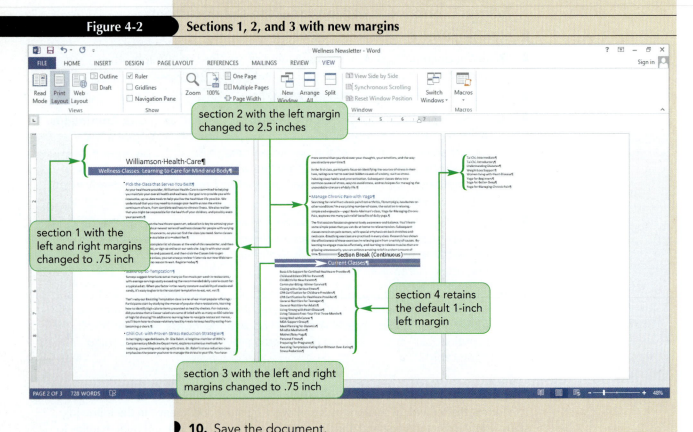

10. Save the document.

In addition to allowing you to format parts of a document with different margins, section breaks allow you to format part of a document in columns. You'll add some columns to section 4 next.

Formatting Text in Columns

Text meant for quick reading is often laid out in columns, with text flowing down one column, continuing at the top of the next column, flowing down that column, and so forth. To get started, click the Columns button in the Page Setup group on the PAGE LAYOUT tab, and then click the number of columns you want in the Columns gallery. For more advanced column options, you can use the More Columns command to open the Columns dialog box. In this dialog box, you can adjust the column widths and the space between columns, and choose to format either the entire document in columns or just the section that contains the insertion point.

As shown in the Session 4.1 Visual Overview, Estefan wants section 4 of the newsletter document, which consists of the class list, to be formatted in three columns.

To format section 4 in three columns:

1. Click anywhere in the list of classes at the end of the document to position the insertion point in section 4.

2. On the ribbon, click the **PAGE LAYOUT** tab.

3. In the Page Setup group, click the **Columns** button to display the Columns gallery. At this point, you could simply click Three to format section 4 in three columns of equal width. However, it's helpful to take a look at the columns dialog box so you can get familiar with some more advanced column options.

4. Click **More Columns** to open the Columns dialog box, and then in the Presets section, click **Three**. See Figure 4-3.

Figure 4-3	**Columns dialog box**

change this setting to create four or more columns

these settings adjust the width of individual columns and the space between them

creates columns of the same width

columns will only be applied to the section that currently contains the insertion point

To format text in four or more columns, you can change the setting in the Number of columns box instead of selecting an option in the Presets section. By default, the Apply to box, in the lower-left corner, displays "This section," indicating that the three-column format will be applied only to the current section. To apply columns to the entire document, you could click the Apply to

arrow and then click Whole document. To change the width of the individual columns or the spacing between the columns, you can use the settings in the Width and spacing section of the Columns dialog box.

5. Click the **OK** button. Section 4 is now formatted in three columns of the default width. See Figure 4-4.

Figure 4-4 **Section 4 formatted in three columns**

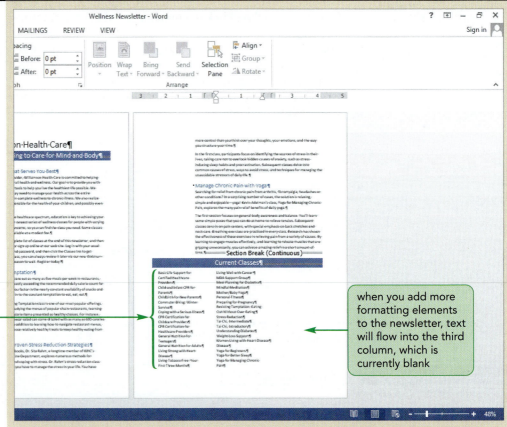

column format applied to only this section

when you add more formatting elements to the newsletter, text will flow into the third column, which is currently blank

Note that the third column is currently blank. This will change when you add more formatting elements to the newsletter. The newsletter text now fits on two pages.

6. Change the document Zoom level to **120%**, scroll down so you can see the entire list of classes, and then save the document.

Keep in mind that you can restore a document or a section to its original format by formatting it as one column. You can also adjust paragraph indents within columns, just as you would in normal text. In fact, Estefan would like you to format the columns in section 4 with hanging indents so that it's easier to read the class titles that take up more than one line.

To indent the class names, you first need to select the three columns of text. Selecting columns of text by dragging the mouse can be tricky. It's easier to use the Shift+click method instead.

To format the columns in section 4 with hanging indents:

1. Make sure the **PAGE LAYOUT** tab is selected on the ribbon.

2. Click at the beginning of the first class name ("Basic Life Support for Certified Healthcare Providers"), press and hold the **Shift** key, and then click at the end of the last class name ("Yoga for Managing Chronic Pain"). The entire list of classes is selected.

3. In the Paragraph group, click the **Dialog Box Launcher** to open the Paragraph dialog box with the Indents and Spacing tab displayed.

4. In the Indentation section, click the **Special** arrow, click **Hanging**, and then change the By setting to **0.2"**.

5. Click the **OK** button to close the Paragraph dialog box, and then click anywhere in the list to deselect it. The class list is now formatted with a hanging indent, so the second line of each paragraph is indented .2 inches. See Figure 4-5.

Figure 4-5 **Text formatted in columns with hanging indent**

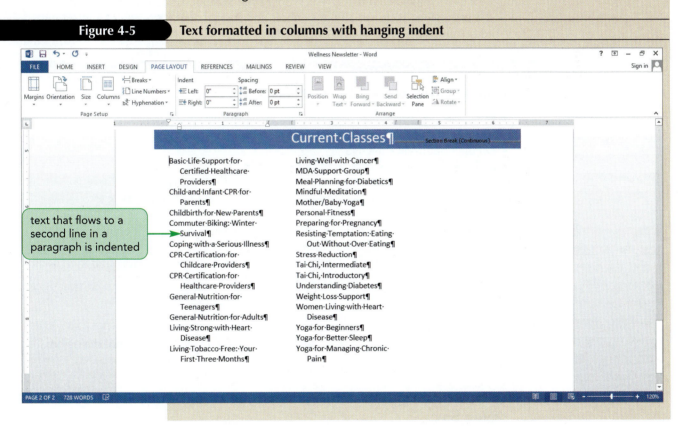

Inserting Symbols and Special Characters

When creating documents in Word, you can change some of the characters available on the standard keyboard into special characters or symbols called **typographic characters**. Word's AutoCorrect feature automatically converts some standard characters into typographic characters as you type. In some cases, you need to press the spacebar and type more characters before Word inserts the appropriate typographic character. If Word inserts a typographic character that you don't want, you can click the Undo button to revert to the characters you originally typed. See Figure 4-6.

Figure 4-6 Common typographic characters

To insert this symbol or character	Type	Word converts to
Em dash	word--word	word—word
Smiley face	:)	☺
Copyright symbol	(c)	©
Trademark symbol	(tm)	TM
Registered trademark symbol	(r)	®
Fractions	1/2, 1/4	½, ¼
Arrows	<-- or -->	← or →

© 2014 Cengage Learning

Most of the typographic characters in Figure 4-6 can also be inserted using the Symbol button on the INSERT tab, which opens a gallery of commonly used symbols, and the More Symbols command, which opens the Symbol dialog box. The Symbol dialog box provides access to all the symbols and special characters you can insert into a Word document.

REFERENCE

Inserting Symbols and Special Characters from the Symbol Dialog Box

- Move the insertion point to the location in the document where you want to insert a particular symbol or special character.
- On the ribbon, click the INSERT tab.
- In the Symbols group, click the Symbol button.
- If you see the symbol or character you want in the Symbol gallery, click it to insert it in the document. For a more extensive set of choices, click More Symbols to open the Symbol dialog box.
- In the Symbol dialog box, locate the symbol or character you want on either the Symbols tab or the Special Characters tab.
- Click the symbol or special character you want, click the Insert button, and then click the Close button.

Estefan forgot to include a registered trademark symbol (®) after "Webinar+" on page 1. He asks you to add one now. After you do, you'll explore the Symbol dialog box.

To insert the registered trademark symbol and explore the Symbol dialog box:

1. Use the Navigation pane to find the term **Webinar+** in the document, and then close the Navigation pane.

2. Click to the right of the plus sign to position the insertion point between the plus sign and the space that follows it.

3. Type **(r)**. AutoCorrect converts the "r" in parentheses into the superscript ® symbol.

 If you don't know which characters to type to insert a symbol or special character, you can review the AutoCorrect replacements in the AutoCorrect: English (United States) dialog box.

4. On the ribbon, click the **FILE** tab.

5. In the navigation bar, click **Options** to open the Word Options dialog box.

6. In the left pane, click **Proofing**, and then click the **AutoCorrect Options** button. The AutoCorrect: English (United States) dialog box opens, with the AutoCorrect tab displayed.

7. Review the table at the bottom of the AutoCorrect tab. The column on the left shows the characters you can type, and the column on the right shows what AutoCorrect inserts as a replacement. See Figure 4-7.

Figure 4-7 **AutoCorrect: English (United States) dialog box**

when you type the characters shown in this column…

…Word inserts the typographic characters shown in this column

8. Scroll down to review the AutoCorrect replacements, click the **Cancel** button to close the AutoCorrect: English (United States) dialog box, and then click the **Cancel** button to close the Word Options dialog box.

Now you can explore the Symbol dialog box, which offers another way to insert symbols and special characters.

9. On the ribbon, click the **INSERT** tab.

10. In the Symbols group, click the **Symbol** button, and then click **More Symbols**. The Symbol dialog box opens with the Symbols tab displayed.

11. Scroll down the gallery of symbols on the Symbols tab to review the many symbols you can insert into a document. To insert one, you would click it, and then click the Insert button.

12. Click the **Special Characters** tab. The characters available on this tab are often used in desktop publishing. Notice the shortcut keys that you can use to insert many of the special characters.

13. Click the **Cancel** button to close the Symbol dialog box.

Introduction to Working with Objects

An object is something that you can manipulate independently of the document text. In desktop publishing, you use objects to illustrate the document or to enhance the page layout. To complete the newsletter for Estefan, you'll need to add some text boxes, drop caps, and pictures. These are all examples of objects in Word.

Inserting Graphic Objects

Objects used for illustration purposes or to enhance the page layout are sometimes called **graphic objects**, or simply **graphics**. The INSERT tab is the starting point for adding graphics to a document. After you insert a graphic object, you typically need to adjust its position on the page. Your ability to control the position of an object depends on whether it is an inline object or a floating object.

Distinguishing Between Inline and Floating Objects

An **inline object** behaves as if it were text. Like an individual letter, it has a specific location within a line of text, and its position changes as you add or delete text. You can align an inline object just as you would align text, using the alignment buttons in the Paragraph group on the HOME tab. However, inline objects are difficult to work with because every time you add or remove paragraphs of text, the object moves to a new position.

In contrast, you can position a **floating object** anywhere on the page, with the text flowing, or wrapping, around it. Unlike an inline object, which has a specific position in a line of text, a floating object has a more fluid connection to the document text. It is attached, or **anchored**, to an entire paragraph—so if you delete that paragraph, you will also delete the object. However, you can also move the object independently of that paragraph. An anchor symbol next to an object tells you that the object is a floating object rather than an inline object, as illustrated in Figure 4-8.

Figure 4-8	Inline objects compared to floating objects

you can use the Page Layout button to wrap text around an object, thereby transforming an inline object into a floating object

this inline object is positioned after the "e" in "care" and before the "B" in "Breathing"

anchor symbol indicates that this picture is a floating object

text wraps around a floating object

Image used with permission of Microsoft Corporation

You'll typically want to transform all inline objects into floating objects because floating objects are far more flexible.

Wrapping Text Around an Object

To transform an inline object into a floating object, you apply a **text wrapping setting** to it. First, click the object to select it, click the Layout Options button next to the object, and then click an option in the Layout Options gallery. For example, you can select Square text wrapping to make the text follow a square outline as it flows around the object, or you can select Tight text wrapping to make the text follow the shape of the object more exactly. Figure 4-9 describes the different types of wrapping.

Figure 4-9		Text wrapping options in the Layout Options gallery

Menu Icon	Type of Wrapping	Description
	Square	Text flows in a square outline around the object, regardless of the shape of the object; by default, Square text wrapping is applied to preformatted text boxes inserted via the Text Box button on the INSERT tab.
	Tight	Text follows the exact outline of the object; if you want the text to flow around an object, this is usually the best option.
	Through	Text flows through the object, filling up any open areas; this type is similar to Tight text wrapping.
	Top and Bottom	Text stops above the object and then starts again below the object.
	Behind Text	The object is layered behind the text, with the text flowing over it.
	In Front of Text	The object is layered in front of the text, with the text flowing behind it; if you want to position an object in white space next to the text, this option gives you the greatest control over its exact position. By default, In Front of Text wrapping is applied to any shapes inserted via the Shapes button in the Illustrations group on the INSERT tab.

© 2014 Cengage Learning

Most graphic objects, including photos and SmartArt, are inline by default. All text boxes and shapes are floating by default. Objects that are inserted as floating objects by default have a specific text wrapping setting assigned to them, but you can change the default setting to any text wrapping setting you want.

INSIGHT

Displaying Gridlines

When formatting a complicated document like a newsletter, you'll often have to adjust the position of objects on the page until everything looks the way you want. To make it easier to see the relative position of objects, you can display the document's gridlines. These vertical and horizontal lines are not actually part of the document. They are simply guidelines you can use when positioning text and objects on the page. By default, when gridlines are displayed, objects align with, or **snap to**, the nearest intersection of a horizontal and vertical line. The figures in this tutorial do not show gridlines because they would make the figures difficult to read. However, you will have a chance to experiment with gridlines in the Case Problems at the end of this tutorial. To display gridlines, click the VIEW tab on the ribbon, and then click the Gridlines check box to insert a check.

Inserting Text Boxes

You can choose to add a preformatted text box to a document, or you can create your own text box from scratch and adjust its appearance. To insert a preformatted text box, you use the Text Box button in the Text group. Text boxes inserted this way include placeholder text that you can replace with your own text. Preformatted text boxes come with preset font and paragraph options that are designed to match the text box's overall look. However, you can change the appearance of the text in the text box by using the options on the HOME tab, just as you would for ordinary text. The text box, as a whole, is designed to match the document's current theme. You could alter its appearance by using the Shape Styles options on the DRAWING TOOLS FORMAT tab, but there's typically no reason to do so.

Because the preformatted text boxes are so professional looking, they are usually a better choice than creating your own. However, if you want a very simple text box, you can use the Shapes button in the Illustrations group to draw a text box. After you draw the text box, you can adjust its appearance by using the Shape Styles options on the DRAWING TOOLS FORMAT tab. You can type any text you want inside the text box at the insertion point. When you are finished, you can format the text using the options on the HOME tab.

Inserting a Text Box

- To insert a preformatted, rectangular text box, click in the document where you want to insert the text box.
- On the ribbon, click the INSERT tab.
- In the Text group, click the Text Box button to open the Text Box gallery, and then click a text box style to select it.
- In the text box in the document, delete the placeholder text, type the text you want to include, and then format the text using the options on the HOME tab.

or

- To insert and format your own rectangular text box, click the INSERT tab on the ribbon.
- In the Text group, click the Shapes button to open the Shapes gallery, and then click Text Box.
- In the document, position the pointer where you want to insert the text box, press and hold the mouse button, and then drag the pointer to draw the text box.
- In the text box, type the text you want to include, and then format the text using the options on the HOME tab.
- Format the text box using the options in the Shape Styles group on the DRAWING TOOLS FORMAT tab.

Inserting a Preformatted Text Box

Estefan's newsletter requires three text boxes. You need to insert the first text box on page 1, to the left of the "Pick the Class that Serves You Best" heading. For this text box, you'll insert one that is preformatted to work as a sidebar. A **sidebar** is a text box designed to look good positioned to the side of the main document text. A sidebar is typically used to draw attention to important information.

To insert a preformatted text box in the document:

1. Scroll up to the top of page 1, and then click anywhere in the "Pick the Class that Serves You Best" heading.

2. Change the Zoom level to **Multiple Pages** so you can see both pages of the document.

3. On the ribbon, click the **INSERT** tab.

4. In the Text group, click the **Text Box** button to display the Text Box gallery, and then use the scroll bar to scroll down the gallery to locate the Ion Sidebar 1 text box.

5. Click **Ion Sidebar 1**. The text box is inserted in the left margin of page 1. See Figure 4-10.

Figure 4-10	Text box inserted on page 1

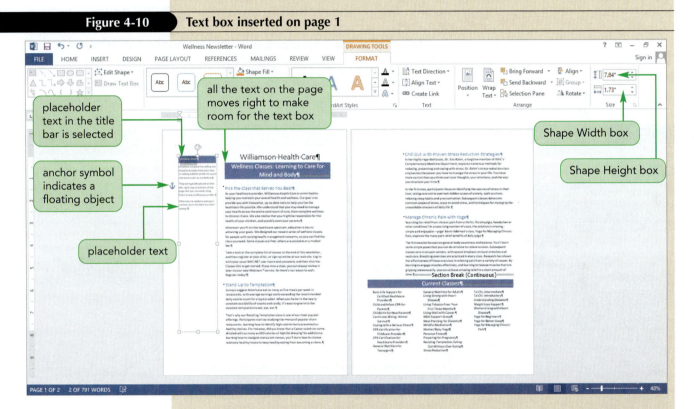

All the text on page 1 moves right to make room for the text box. Later, after you resize and move the text box, the first two paragraphs will resume their original positions, centered at the top of the page. The anchor symbol next to the text box tells you it is a floating object.

The text box consists of a blue title bar at the top that contains placeholder text, with additional placeholder text below the title bar. The dotted outline with handles indicates the borders of the text box. When you first insert a text box, the placeholder text in the title bar is selected, ready for you to type your own title. In this case, however, before you add any text, you'll resize and reposition the text box.

6. On the ribbon, click the **DRAWING TOOLS FORMAT** tab, if necessary.

7. In the Size group, click the **Shape Height** box, type **4.3**, click the **Shape Width** box, type **1.5**, and then press the **Enter** key. The text box is now shorter and narrower.

8. Change the Zoom level to **120%**.

 Next, you need to drag the text box down below the first two paragraphs. Currently, only the placeholder text in the text box title bar is selected. Before you can move it, you need to select the entire text box.

9. Position the pointer somewhere over the text box border until the pointer changes to ⬚.

10. Click the text box border to select the entire text box. The text box border changes from dotted to solid, and the Layout Options button appears to the right of the text box.

11. Position the pointer ⬚ over the text box's title bar, press and hold the mouse button, and then drag the text box down so that the top of the text box aligns with the first line of text below the "Pick the Class that Serves You Best" heading. The left edge of the text box should align with the left edge of the blue shaded heading "Wellness Classes: Learning to Care for Mind and Body." The anchor symbol remains in its original position, next to the shaded paragraph.

12. When you are sure the text box is positioned correctly, release the mouse button. See Figure 4-11.

Figure 4-11	Resized and repositioned text box

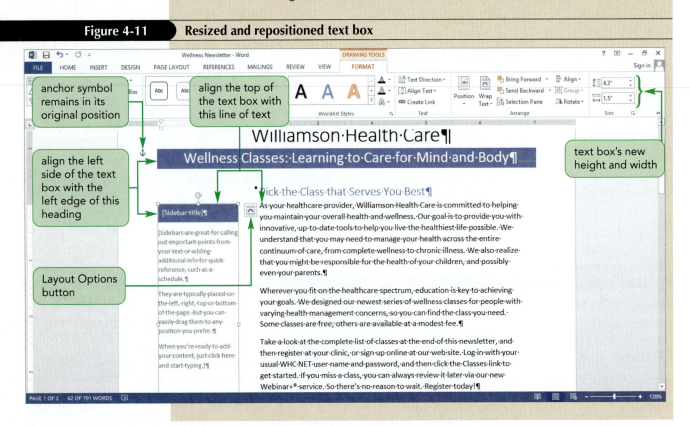

After you insert a text box or other object, you usually need to adjust its relationship to the surrounding text; that is, you need to adjust its text wrapping setting.

Changing the Text Wrapping Setting for the Text Box

A preformatted text box inserted via the Text box button on the INSERT tab is, by default, a floating object formatted with Square text wrapping. You will verify whether this is true when you open the Layout Options gallery in the following steps. Then you'll select the In Front of Text option instead to gain more control over the exact position of the text box on the page.

To open the Layout Options gallery and change the wrapping option:

▶ 1. Change the Zoom level to **One Page** so you can see the text box's position relative to the text on page 1.

▶ 2. Click the **Layout Options** button. The Layout Options gallery opens with the Square option selected. See Figure 4-12.

Figure 4-12 Square text wrapping currently applied to text box

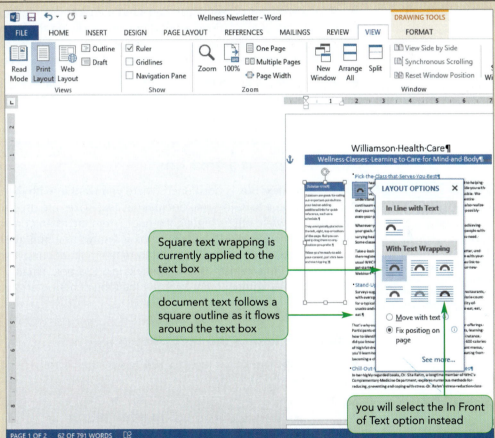

Square text wrapping is currently applied to the text box

document text follows a square outline as it flows around the text box

you will select the In Front of Text option instead

Square text wrapping is currently applied to the text box. You can see evidence of Square text wrapping where the document text flows around the lower-right corner of the text box. You'll have a chance to see some more dramatic examples of text wrapping later in this tutorial, but it's important to be able to identify subtle examples of it.

Trouble? If the Layout Options button is not visible, click the text box border to select the entire text box and display the Layout Options button.

3. Click any of the other options in the Layout Options gallery and observe how the document text and the text box shift position. Continue exploring the Layout Options gallery, trying out several of the options.

4. Click the **In Front of Text** option 🖼 and then click the **Close** button ✖ in the upper-right corner of the Layout Options gallery to close the gallery. The document text shifts so that it now flows directly down the left margin, without wrapping around the text box.

 Your next formatting task is to make sure the text box is assigned a fixed position on the page. You could check this setting on the Layout Options button, but you'll use the Wrap Text button in the Arrange group instead.

5. On the ribbon, click the **DRAWING TOOLS FORMAT** tab.

6. In the Arrange group, click the **Wrap Text** button. The Wrap Text menu gives you access to all the options in the Layout Options gallery, plus some more advanced settings.

7. Verify that Fix Position on Page has a checkmark next to it. To avoid having graphic objects move around unexpectedly on the page as you add or delete other elements, it's a good idea to check this setting either in the Wrap Text menu or in the Layout Options menu for every graphic object.

8. Click anywhere in the document to close the gallery, and then save the document.

Adding Text to a Text Box

Now that the text box is positioned where you want it, with the correct text wrapping, you can add text to it. In some documents, text boxes are used to present new information, while others highlight a quote from the main document. A direct quote from a document formatted in a text box is known as a **pull quote**. To create a pull quote text box, you can copy the text from the main document, and then paste it into the text box. You can also simply type text in a text box. Finally, you can insert text from another Word document by using the Object button arrow on the INSERT tab.

To insert text in the text box:

1. Change the Zoom level to **120%**, and then scroll as necessary so you can see the entire text box.

2. In the text box's title bar, click the placeholder text **[Sidebar title]** to select it, if necessary, and then type **Register Today!**

3. Click the placeholder text below the title bar to select it. See Figure 4-13.

Figure 4-13 **Text box with placeholder text selected**

new text in the title bar

placeholder text is selected and ready to be replaced

4. Press the **Delete** key to delete the placeholder text. Now you can insert new text from another Word document.

5. On the ribbon, click the **INSERT** tab.

6. In the Text group, click the **Object button arrow** to open the Object menu, and then click **Text from File**. The Insert File dialog box opens. Selecting a Word document to insert is just like selecting a document in the Open dialog box.

7. Navigate to the Word4 ▶ Tutorial folder included with your Data Files, click **Registration** to select the file, and then click the **Insert** button. The registration information contained in the Registration document is inserted directly into the text box. The inserted text was formatted in 9-point Calibri in the Registration document, and it retains that formatting when you paste it into the Wellness Newsletter document. To make the text easier to read, you'll increase the font size to 11 points.

8. With the insertion point located in the last paragraph in the text box (which is blank), press the **Backspace** key to delete the blank paragraph, and then click and drag the mouse pointer to select all the text in the text box, including the title in the shaded title box.

9. On the ribbon, click the **HOME** tab.

10. In the Font group, click the **Font Size** arrow, and then click **11**. The size of the text in the text box increases to 11 points. See Figure 4-14.

Figure 4-14 **Registration information inserted in text box**

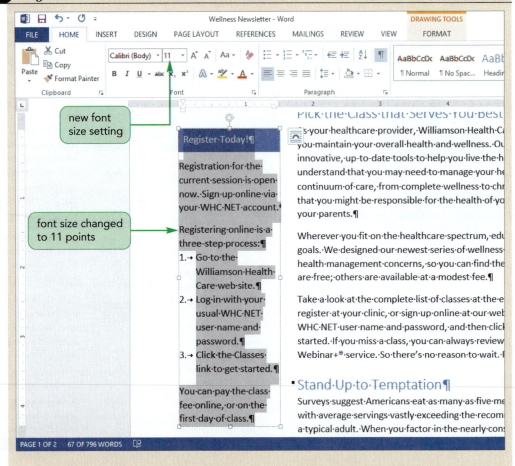

Trouble? Don't be concerned if the text in your text box wraps slightly differently from the text shown in Figure 4-14. The same fonts can vary slightly from one computer to another, causing slight differences in the way text wraps within and around text boxes.

▶ **11.** Click anywhere outside the text box to deselect it, and then save the document.

The first text box is complete. Now you need to add one more on page 1, and another on page 2. Estefan wants the second text box on page 1 to have a different look from the first one, so he asks you to use the Shapes button to draw a text box.

Drawing and Formatting a Text Box Using the Shapes Menu

A text box is considered a shape, just like the other shapes you can insert via the Shapes button on the INSERT tab. This is true whether you insert a text box via the Text Box button or via the Shapes button. While text boxes are typically rectangular, you can actually turn any shape into a text box. Start by using the Shapes button to draw a shape of your choice, and then, with the shape selected, type any text you want. You won't see an insertion point inside the shape, but you can still type text inside it and then format it. You can format the shape itself by using the Shape Styles options on the DRAWING TOOLS FORMAT tab.

To draw and format a text box:

1. Scroll down to display the bottom half of page 1.

2. On the ribbon, click the **INSERT** tab.

3. In the Illustrations group, click the **Shapes** button to display the Shapes gallery. See Figure 4-15.

Figure 4-15 **Shapes gallery**

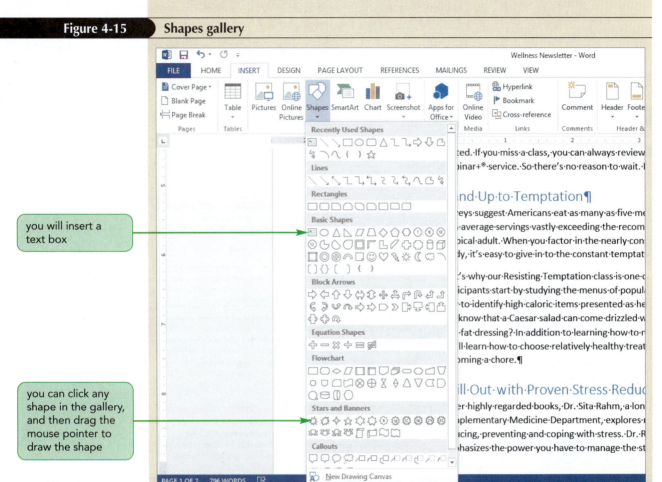

you will insert a text box

you can click any shape in the gallery, and then drag the mouse pointer to draw the shape

At this point, you could click any shape in the gallery, and then drag the pointer in the document to draw that shape. Then, after you finish drawing the shape, you could start typing in the selected shape to insert text.

4. In the Basic Shapes section of the Shapes gallery, click the **Text Box** icon . The gallery closes and the mouse pointer turns to a black cross ✚.

5. Position the pointer in the blank area in the left margin at about the 6-inch mark (according to the vertical ruler), and then click and drag down and to the right to draw a text box approximately **1.5** inches wide and **2.5** inches tall. When you are satisfied with the text box, release the mouse button.

Don't be concerned about the text box's exact dimensions or position on the page. For now, just make sure it fits in the blank space to the left of the last two paragraphs on the page.

The new text box is selected, with handles on its border and the insertion point blinking inside. The Layout Options button is visible and the text box's anchor symbol is positioned to the left of the paragraph below the heading "Stand Up to Temptation." By default, a shape is always anchored to the nearest paragraph that begins above the shape's top border. It doesn't matter where the insertion point is located.

▶ **6.** Use the Shape Height and Shape Width boxes on the DRAWING TOOLS FORMAT tab to set the height to **2.7** inches and the width to **1.5** inches.

▶ **7.** Drag the text box as necessary to align its bottom border with the last line of text on the page, and its left border with the left edge of the text box above. See Figure 4-16.

Figure 4-16 **Text box created using the Shapes button**

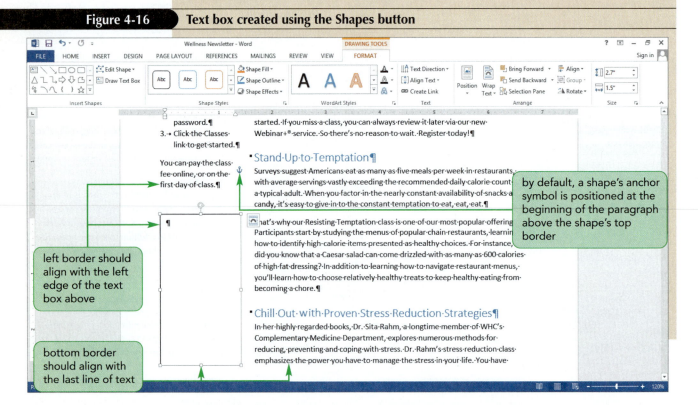

left border should align with the left edge of the text box above

bottom border should align with the last line of text

by default, a shape's anchor symbol is positioned at the beginning of the paragraph above the shape's top border

Now you need to add some text to the blank text box. Instead of inserting text from another Word document, you will copy a sentence from the newsletter and paste it into the text box to create a pull quote. After you add the text, you'll format the text box to make it match the one shown earlier in the Session 4.1 Visual Overview.

To copy text from the newsletter and paste it into the text box:

▶ **1.** Select the first sentence after the heading "Stand Up to Temptation," which begins "Surveys suggest…," and then press the **Ctrl+C** keys to copy it to the Office Clipboard.

▶ **2.** Click in the blank text box, and then press the **Ctrl+V** keys to paste the copied sentence into the text box. The newly inserted sentence is formatted in 11-point Calibri, just as it was in the main document.

3. Add quotation marks at the beginning and end of the sentence, so it's clear the text box is a pull quote. Your next task is to center the sentence between the top and bottom borders of the text box. Then you'll add some color.

4. On the ribbon, click the **DRAWING TOOLS FORMAT** tab, if necessary.

5. In the Text group, click the **Align Text** button to display the Align text menu, and then click **Middle**. The text is now centered between the top and bottom borders of the text box. Next, you'll change the text's font color and add a background color.

6. In the Shape Styles group, click the **More** button to display the Shape Styles gallery. Like the text styles you have used to format text, shape styles allow you to apply a collection of formatting options, including font color and shading, with one click.

7. Move the mouse pointer over the various options in the Shape Styles gallery and observe the Live Previews in the document. When you are finished, position the mouse pointer over the Colored Fill - Blue, Accent 5, style, which is a dark blue box, the second from the right in the second row. See Figure 4-17.

Figure 4-17 **Shape Styles gallery**

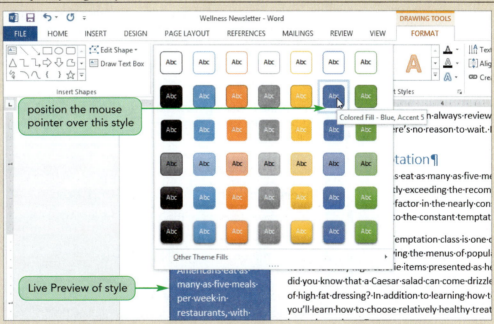

8. In the Shape Styles gallery, click the **Colored Fill - Blue, Accent 5** style. The style is applied to the text box, and the Shape Styles gallery closes.

Trouble? Don't be concerned if the text in your text box wraps slightly differently from the text shown in Figure 4-17. The same fonts can vary slightly from one computer to another, causing slight differences in the way text wraps within and around text boxes.

Now, you need to make sure the text box is located in a fixed position on the page. In the following steps, you'll also experiment with making some changes involving the text box's anchor symbol. It's important to understand the role the anchor symbol plays in the document's overall layout.

To fix the text box's position on the page and experiment with the anchor symbol:

▶ 1. Verify that the text box is still selected, with the DRAWING TOOLS FORMAT tab displayed on the ribbon.

▶ 2. In the Arrange group, click the **Wrap Text** button. A checkmark appears next to Move with Text because that is the default setting for shapes.

▶ 3. Click **Fix Position on Page** to add a checkmark and close the Wrap Text menu. This setting helps ensure that the text box will remain in its position on page 1, even if you add text above the paragraph it is anchored to. However, if you add so much text that the paragraph moves to page 2, then the text box will also move to page 2, but it will be positioned in the same location on the page that it occupied on page 1—that is, in the bottom, lower-left corner.

 If you select the entire paragraph to which the text box is anchored, you will also select the text box, as you'll see in the next step.

▶ 4. Triple-click the paragraph below the "Stand Up to Temptation" heading. The entire paragraph and the text box are selected. If you pressed the Delete key at this point, you would delete the paragraph of text and the text box. If you ever need to delete a paragraph but not the graphic object that is anchored to it, you should first drag the anchor to a different paragraph.

▶ 5. Click anywhere in the document to deselect the text and the text box, and then save the document.

You've finished creating the second text box on page 1. Estefan wants you to add a third text box at the top of page 2. For this text box, you'll again use the preformatted Ion Side Bar 1 text box.

To insert another preformatted text box:

▶ 1. Scroll down to display the top half of page 2, and then click in the first line on page 2.

▶ 2. On the ribbon, click the **INSERT** tab.

▶ 3. In the Text group, click the **Text Box** button to display the menu, scroll down, and then click **Ion Sidebar 1**.

▶ 4. Click the border of the text box to select the entire text box and display the Layout Options button.

▶ 5. Click the **Layout Options** button 🖼, click the **In Front of Text** 🖼 option, verify that the Fix position on page button is selected, and then close the Layout Options gallery.

▶ 6. Drag the text box left to center it in the blank space to the left of the document text, with the top of the text box aligned with the first line of text on page 2.

▶ 7. Change the text box's height to **3.5** inches and the width to **1.5** inches.

▶ 8. In the title bar, replace the placeholder text with **Watch Classes Online**.

▶ 9. In the main text box, click the placeholder text to select it, and then press the **Delete** key.

10. On the ribbon, click the **INSERT** tab.

11. In the Text group, click the **Object button arrow**, and then click **Text from File**.

12. Navigate to the Word4 ▸ Tutorial folder, if necessary, and then insert the document named **Classes**.

13. Delete the extra paragraph at the end of the text box, increase the font size for the text to **11** points, and then make sure your text box is positioned like the one shown in Figure 4-18.

Figure 4-18 Completed text box on page 2

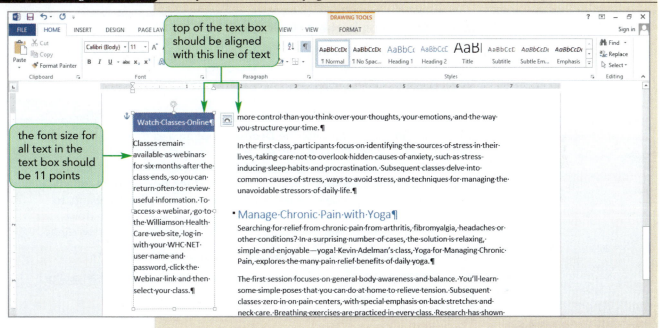

top of the text box should be aligned with this line of text

the font size for all text in the text box should be 11 points

14. Click anywhere in the document to deselect the text box, and then save the document.

INSIGHT

Linking Text Boxes

If you have a large amount of text that you want to place in different locations in a document, with the text continuing from one text box to another, you can use linked text boxes. For example, in a newsletter, you might have an article that starts in a text box on page 3 of the newsletter and continues in a text box on page 4. To flow the text automatically from one text box to a second, blank text box, click the first text box to select it (this text box should already contain some text). Next, on the ribbon, click the DRAWING TOOLS FORMAT tab, click the Create Link button in the Text group, and then click the empty text box. The text boxes are now linked. You can resize the first text box without worrying about how much text fits in the box. The text that no longer fits in the first text box is moved to the second text box. Note that you'll find it easier to link text boxes if you use simple text boxes without title bars.

To make the main document text look more polished, you will add some drop caps.

Inserting Drop Caps

As you saw in the Session 4.1 Visual Overview, a drop cap is a graphic that replaces the first letter of a paragraph. Drop caps are commonly used in newspapers, magazines, and newsletters to draw the reader's attention to the beginning of an article. You can place a drop cap in the margin or next to the paragraph, or you can have the text of the paragraph wrap around the drop cap. By default, a drop cap extends down three lines, but you can change that setting in the Drop Cap dialog box.

Estefan asks you to create a drop cap for some of the paragraphs that follow the headings. He wants the drop cap to extend two lines into the paragraph, with the text wrapping around it.

To insert drop caps in the newsletter:

1. Scroll up to page 1, and then click anywhere in the paragraph below the "Pick the Class that Serves You Best" heading.

2. On the ribbon, click the **INSERT** tab.

3. In the Text group, click the **Drop Cap** button. The Drop Cap gallery opens.

4. Move the mouse pointer over the **Dropped** option and then the **In margin** option, and observe the Live Preview of the two types of drop caps in the document. The default settings applied by these two options are fine for most documents. Clicking Drop Cap Options, at the bottom of the menu, allows you to select more detailed settings. In this case, Estefan wants to make the drop cap smaller than the default. Instead of extending down through three lines of text, he wants the drop cap to extend only two lines.

5. Click **Drop Cap Options**. The Drop Cap dialog box opens.

6. Click the **Dropped** icon, click the **Lines to drop** box, and then change the setting to **2**. See Figure 4-19.

Figure 4-19 Drop Cap dialog box

selected Position option

drop cap will extend down two lines

7. Click the **OK** button. Word formats the first character of the paragraph as a drop cap "A," as shown in the Session 4.1 Visual Overview. The dotted box with selection handles around the drop cap indicates it is selected.

8. Near the bottom of page 1, insert a similar drop cap in the paragraph following the "Chill Out with Proven Stress Reduction Strategies" heading. You skipped the paragraph following the "Stand Up to Temptation" heading because you'll eventually insert a graphic there. Including a drop cap there would make the paragraph look too cluttered.

9. On page 2, insert a similar drop cap in the paragraph following the "Manage Chronic Pain with Yoga" heading.

10. Click anywhere in the text to deselect the drop cap, and then save your work.

PROSKILLS

Written Communication: Writing for a Newsletter

Clip art, WordArt, and other design elements can make a newsletter very appealing to readers. They can also be a lot of fun to create and edit. But don't let the design elements in your desktop-published documents distract you from the most important aspect of any document—clear, effective writing. Because the newsletter format feels less formal than a report or letter, some writers are tempted to use a casual, familiar tone. If you are creating a newsletter for friends or family, that's fine. But in most other settings—especially in a business or academic setting—you should strive for a professional tone, similar to what you find in a typical newspaper. Avoid jokes; you can never be certain that what amuses you will also amuse all your readers. Worse, you risk unintentionally offending your readers. Also, space is typically at a premium in any printed document, so you don't want to waste space on anything unessential. Finally, keep in mind that the best writing in the world will be wasted in a newsletter that is overburdened with too many design elements. You don't have to use every element covered in this tutorial in a single document. Instead, use just enough to attract the reader's attention to the page, and then let the text speak for itself.

REVIEW

Session 4.1 Quick Check

1. Explain how to format a document in two columns of the default width.
2. Explain how to insert the ® symbol in a document.
3. What symbol tells you that an object is a floating object?
4. How do you convert an inline object to a floating object?
5. Which text wrapping option gives you the greatest control over an object's exact position, and is also the default text wrapping applied to shapes inserted via the Shapes button?
6. Explain how to insert a preformatted text box designed to match the current theme.

Session 4.2 Visual Overview:

You can only use the Remove Background button for photos. For all other pictures, you need to crop instead.

You can click the Crop button arrow to access more advanced cropping options, including cropping to a shape such as an oval or an arrow.

The gray area represents the part of the picture that has been cropped.

The term "picture" refers to a photo, drawing, or other image.

This photo of the lollipop was inserted into the document, with the text wrapping around its rectangular, white background.

You can **crop**, or cut off, part of a picture by clicking the Crop button and then dragging a sizing handle on the picture border.

Editing Pictures

Clicking the Remove Background button in the Adjust group on the PICTURE TOOLS FORMAT tab displays the BACKGROUND REMOVAL tab, with tools for removing a photo's background.

The photo of the lollipop is displayed here with its background removed, which allows the text to wrap around the shape of the lollipop itself.

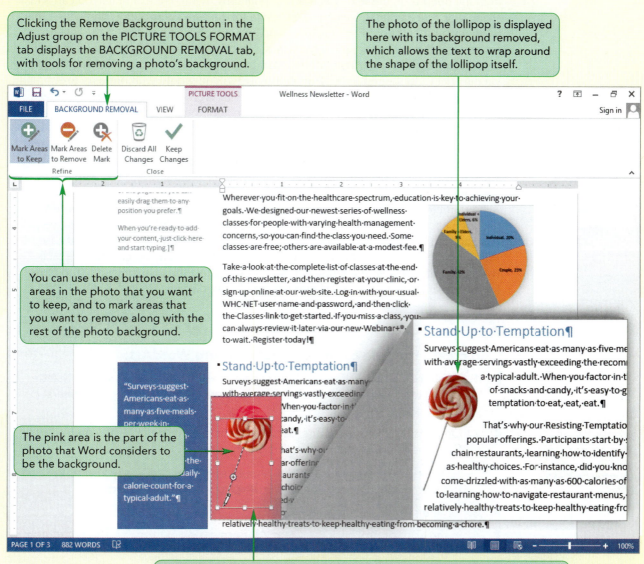

You can use these buttons to mark areas in the photo that you want to keep, and to mark areas that you want to remove along with the rest of the photo background.

The pink area is the part of the photo that Word considers to be the background.

This border helps Word distinguish between the background and the parts of the image you want to keep. Any area of the image outside the border will be automatically excluded. In this case, part of the lollipop spiral lies outside the border, so Word considers it part of the background. To fix that, you can drag one of the border handles to expand the border until the entire lollipop spiral is inside the border.

Formatting Text with WordArt

To create special text elements such as a newspaper headline, you can use decorative text known as WordArt. Essentially, WordArt is text in a text box that is formatted with a text effect. Before you move on to learning about WordArt, it's helpful to review the formatting options available with text effects.

To begin applying a text effect, you select the text you want to format. Then you can choose from several preformatted text effects via the Text Effects and Typography button in the Font group on the HOME tab. You can also modify a text effect by choosing from the options on the Text Effects and Typography menu. For example, you can add a shadow or a glow effect. You can also change the **outline color** of the characters—that is, the exterior color of the characters—and you can change the style of the outline by making it thicker or breaking it into dashes, for example. To change the character's **fill color**—that is, the interior color of the characters—you just select a different font color via the Font Color button in the Font group, just as you would with ordinary text.

All of these text effect options are available with WordArt. However, the fact that WordArt is in a text box allows you to add some additional effects. You can add rounded, or **beveled**, edges to the letters in WordArt, format the text in 3-D, and transform the text into waves, circles, and other shapes. You can also rotate WordArt text so it stretches vertically on the page. In addition, because WordArt is in a text box, you can use page layout and text wrap settings to place it anywhere you want on a page, with text wrapped around it.

To start creating WordArt, you can select text you want to transform into WordArt, and then click the WordArt button in the Text group on the INSERT tab. Alternatively, you can start by clicking the WordArt button without selecting text first. In that case, Word inserts a text box with placeholder WordArt text, which you can then replace with something new. In the following steps, you'll select the first paragraph and format it as WordArt to create the newsletter title that Estefan wants.

To create the title of the newsletter using WordArt:

1. If you took a break after the last session, make sure the Wellness Newsletter is open and zoomed to 120%, with the rulers and nonprinting characters displayed.

2. On page 1, select the entire paragraph containing the "Williamson Health Care" heading, including the paragraph mark.

 To avoid unexpected results, you should start by clearing any formatting from the text you want to format as WordArt, so you'll do that next.

3. On the ribbon, click the **HOME** tab.

4. In the Font group, click the **Clear All Formatting** button ⧉. The paragraph reverts to the Normal style. Now you can convert the text to WordArt.

5. On the ribbon, click the **INSERT** tab.

6. In the Text group, click the **WordArt** button. The WordArt gallery opens.

7. Position the mouse pointer over the WordArt style that is second from the left in the top row. A ScreenTip describes some elements of this WordArt style—"Fill - Blue, Accent 1, Shadow." See Figure 4-20.

> Be sure to select the paragraph mark so the page layout in your newsletter matches the figures.

Figure 4-20 **WordArt gallery**

8. Click the WordArt style **Fill - Blue, Accent 1, Shadow**. The gallery closes, and a text box containing the formatted text is displayed in the document. See Figure 4-21.

Figure 4-21 **WordArt text box inserted in document**

Because the WordArt text box is formatted with Tight text wrapping by default, the shaded paragraph "Wellness Classes: Learning to Care for Mind and Body" wraps to the right of and below the WordArt text box. The DRAWING TOOLS FORMAT tab appears as the active tab on the ribbon, displaying a variety of tools that you can use to edit the WordArt. Before you change the look of the WordArt, you need to fix its position on the page and change its text wrap setting.

9. Make sure the **DRAWING TOOLS FORMAT** tab is selected on the ribbon.

10. In the Arrange group, click the **Wrap Text** button to open the Wrap Text menu, click **Fix Position on Page** to insert a checkmark, and then close the Wrap Text menu.

▶ **11.** Click the **Wrap Text** button again, and then click **Top and Bottom**. The Wrap Text menu closes, and the shaded paragraph moves down below the WordArt text box.

▶ **12.** Save the document.

Now that the document text is wrapped below the WordArt text box, you can modify the WordArt in several ways.

Modifying WordArt

Your first task is to resize the WordArt. When resizing WordArt, you need to consider both the font size of the text and the size of the text box that contains the WordArt. You change the font size for WordArt text just as you would for ordinary text—by selecting it and then choosing a new font size using the Font size box in the Font group on the HOME tab. If you choose a large font for a headline, you might also need to resize the text box to ensure that the resized text appears on a single line. Estefan is happy with the font size of the new WordArt headline, so you only need to adjust the size of the text box so it spans the width of the page. The larger text box will then make it possible for you to add some more effects.

To resize the WordArt text box and add some effects:

▶ **1.** Make sure the **DRAWING TOOLS FORMAT** tab is selected on the ribbon.

▶ **2.** Change the width of the text box to **7** inches. The text box height should remain at the default .93 inches.

By default, the text is centered within the text box, which is what Estefan wants. Note, however, that you could use the alignment buttons on the HOME tab to align the text any way you wanted within the text box borders. You could also increase the text's font size so that it expands to span the full width of the text box. Instead, you will take advantage of the larger text box to apply a transform effect, which will expand and change the overall shape of the WordArt text. Then you'll make some additional modifications.

▶ **3.** Make sure the WordArt text box is selected.

▶ **4.** In the WordArt Styles group, click the **Text Effects** button [A ▾] to display the Text Effects gallery, and then point to **Transform**. The Transform menu displays options for changing the WordArt's shape.

▶ **5.** Move the mouse pointer over the options in the Transform menu and observe the Live Previews in the WordArt text box. Note that you can always remove a transform effect that has been previously applied by clicking the option in the No Transform section, at the top of the gallery. When you are finished, position the mouse pointer over the Chevron Up effect. See Figure 4-22.

Figure 4-22 Applying a Transform text effect

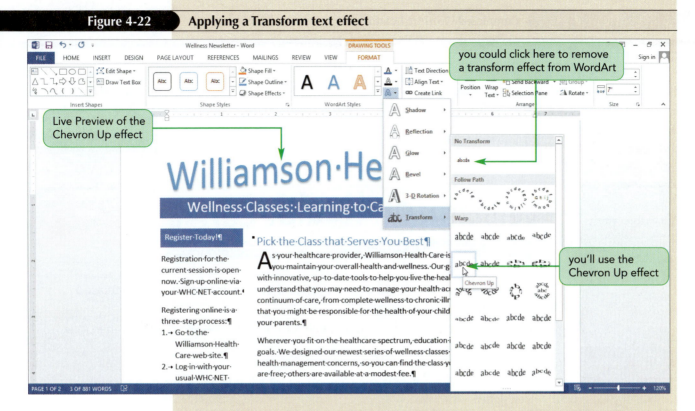

Trouble? If you don't see the Live Preview of the transform effect, that's okay. Continue with these steps.

6. Click the **Chevron Up** effect. The Transform menu closes, and the effect is applied to the WordArt. Now you will make some additional changes using the options in the WordArt Styles group. You'll start by changing the fill color.

7. In the WordArt Styles group, click the **Text Fill button arrow** [A▾] to display the Text Fill color gallery.

8. In the Theme Colors section of the gallery, click the square that is second from the right in the top row to select the **Blue, Accent 5** color. The Text Fill gallery closes, and the WordArt is formatted in a shade of blue that matches the shading in the paragraph below. Next, you'll add a shadow to make the headline more dramatic.

9. In the WordArt Styles group, click the **Text Effects** button [A▾] to display the Text Effects menu, and then point to **Shadow** to display the Shadow gallery. This menu is divided into several sections.

10. In the Outer section, point to the top-left option to display a ScreenTip that reads "Offset Diagonal Bottom Right."

11. Click the **Offset Diagonal Bottom Right** shadow style. A shadow is added to the WordArt text. See Figure 4-23.

Figure 4-23 **Completed WordArt headline**

Note that the height of the text box that contains the WordArt increased slightly, to 0.94 inches.

12. Click a blank area of the document to deselect the WordArt, and then save the document.

The WordArt headline is complete. Your next job is to add some pictures to the newsletter.

Working with Pictures

In Word, a picture is a photo, drawing, or other image. Although you can copy and paste pictures into a document from other documents, you'll typically insert pictures via either the Pictures button or the Online Pictures button, both of which are located in the Illustrations group on the INSERT tab. You use the Pictures button to insert a picture from a file stored on your computer. You use the Online Pictures button to insert clip art. A variety of clip art is available for Office users from the Office.com Website. As you saw in the Session 4.1 Visual Overview, the final version of the Wellness Newsletter document will contain two pieces of clip art—a photograph of a lollipop and a drawing of a woman doing yoga. The newsletter will also contain a picture of a chart, which Estefan's coworker created earlier and saved as a separate file.

After you insert a picture into a document, it functions as an object that you can move, resize, wrap text around, and edit in other ways using the appropriate contextual tab on the ribbon. In general, the skills you used when modifying text boxes apply to pictures as well.

Written Communication: Understanding Copyright Laws

The ownership of all forms of media, including text, line drawings, photographs, and video, is governed by copyright laws. You should assume that anything you find on the web is owned by someone who has a right to control its use. It's your responsibility to make sure you understand copyright laws and to abide by them. The U.S. Copyright Office maintains a Frequently Asked Questions page that should answer any questions you might have: www.copyright.gov/help/faq.

Generally, copyright laws allow a student to reuse a photo, drawing, or other item for educational purposes, on a one-time basis, without getting permission from the owner. However, to avoid charges of plagiarism, you need to acknowledge the source of the item in your work. You don't ever want to be accused of presenting someone else's work as your own. Businesses face much more stringent copyright restrictions. To reuse any material, you must request permission from the owner, and you will often need to pay a fee.

All the images on Office.com are available for use in your Word documents, as long as you don't use them for commercial purposes. To determine the copyright holder for a particular Office.com image, use a browser to go to Office.com, search for the image, and then click the image. If no copyright holder is listed, you should assume the image is owned by Microsoft and cannot be used for commercial purposes. Images owned by other sources, such as Shutterstock, are probably available for purchase, but it's up to you to contact the copyright holder and make the necessary arrangements.

Inserting and Cropping a Picture

You can use the Chart button in the Illustrations group on the INSERT tab to enter data into a data sheet and then create a chart that illustrates the data. However, the chart Estefan wants to insert in the newsletter was created by a coworker using a different program, and then saved as a PNG file named Chart.png. That means you can insert the chart as a picture using the Pictures button in the Illustrations group.

Estefan asks you to insert the chart picture on page 1.

To insert the chart picture on page 1:

1. On page 1, click at the end of the first paragraph below the "Pick the Class that Serves You Best" heading to position the insertion point between "…your parents." and the paragraph mark. Normally, there's no need to be so precise about where you click before inserting a picture, but doing so here will ensure that your results match the results described in these steps exactly.

2. On the ribbon, click the **INSERT** tab.

3. In the Illustrations group, click the **Pictures** button to open the Insert Pictures dialog box.

4. Navigate to the Word4 ▸ Tutorial folder included with your Data Files, and then insert the picture file named **Chart.png**. The chart picture is inserted in the document as an inline object. It is selected, and the PICTURE TOOLS FORMAT tab is displayed on the ribbon.

5. Scroll down if necessary so you can see the entire chart.

The chart is wider than it needs to be and would look better as a square. So you'll need to cut off, or crop, part of it. In addition to the ability to crop part of a picture, Word offers several more advanced cropping options. The one you'll probably use most often is cropping to a shape, which means trimming the edges of a picture so it fits into a star, an oval, an arrow, or another shape. You can also crop to a specific ratio of height to width.

Whatever method you use, once you crop a picture, the part you cropped is hidden from view. However, it remains a part of the picture in case you change your mind and want to restore the cropped picture to its original form.

Before you crop off the sides of the chart, you'll try cropping it to a specific shape.

To crop the chart picture:

▶ 1. In the Size group, click the **Crop button arrow** to display the Crop menu, and then click **Crop to Shape**. A gallery of shapes is displayed, similar to the gallery you saw in Figure 4-15.

▶ 2. In the Basic Shapes section of the gallery, click the **Lightning Bolt** shape ✏️ (third row down, sixth from the right). The chart picture takes on the shape of a lightning bolt, with everything outside the lightning bolt shape cropped off.

 Obviously, this isn't a useful option for the chart, but cropping to shapes can be very effective with photos in informal documents such as party invitations or posters, especially if you then use the Behind Text wrapping option, so that the document text flows over the photo.

▶ 3. Press the **Ctrl+Z** keys to undo the cropping.

▶ 4. In the Size group, click the **Crop** button (not the Crop button arrow). Dark black sizing handles appear around the picture borders.

▶ 5. Position the pointer directly over the middle sizing handle on the right border. The pointer changes to ├.

▶ 6. Press and hold down the mouse button. The pointer changes to +.

▶ 7. Drag the pointer toward the left until the chart border aligns with the 3.75-inch mark on the horizontal ruler, as shown in Figure 4-24.

Figure 4-24	Cropping a picture

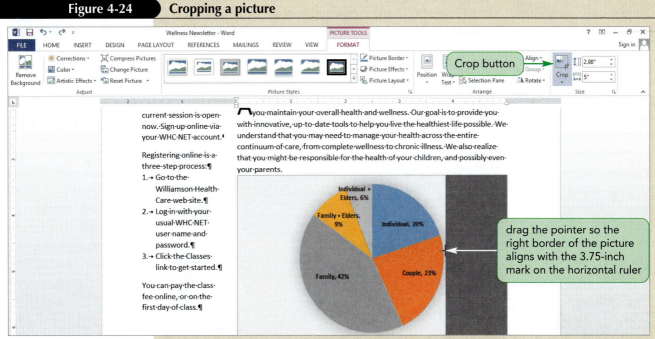

© 2014 Cengage Learning

8. When the chart looks like the one shown in Figure 4-24, release the mouse button. The right portion of the chart picture is no longer visible. The original border remains, indicating that the cropped portion is still saved as part of the picture in case you want to undo the cropping.

9. Drag the middle handle on the left border to the right until the left border aligns with the 2-inch mark on the horizontal ruler.

The chart now takes up much less space, but it's not exactly a square. To ensure a specific ratio, you can crop the picture by changing its **aspect ratio**—that is, the ratio of width to height. You'll try that next. But first, you'll restore the picture to its original state.

10. In the Adjust group, click the **Reset Picture button arrow** to display the Reset Picture menu, and then click **Reset Picture & Size**. The chart picture returns to its original state.

11. In the Size group, click the **Crop button arrow**, and then point to **Aspect Ratio** to display the Aspect Ratio menu, which lists various ratios of width to height. A square has a 1-to-1 ratio of width to height.

12. Under "Square," click **1:1**. The chart is cropped to a square shape. See Figure 4-25.

Figure 4-25 **Chart cropped to a 1:1 aspect ratio**

© 2014 Cengage Learning

▶ **13.** Click anywhere outside the chart to deselect it and complete the cropping procedure.

Next, you need to change the chart from an inline object to a floating object by wrapping text around it. You also need to position it on the page. You can complete both of these tasks at the same time by using the Position button in the Arrange group.

To change the chart's position and wrapping:

▶ **1.** Change the Zoom level to **One Page**, and then click the chart to select it.

▶ **2.** On the ribbon, click the **PICTURE TOOLS FORMAT** tab.

▶ **3.** In the Arrange group, click the **Position** button to display the Position gallery. You can click an icon in the "With Text Wrapping" section to move the selected picture to one of nine preset positions on the page. As with any gallery, you can see a Live Preview of the options before you actually select one.

▶ **4.** Move the mouse pointer over the various icons and observe the changing Live Preview in the document, with the chart picture moving to different locations on the page and the text wrapping around it.

▶ **5.** Point to the icon in the middle row on the far right side to display a ScreenTip that reads "Position in Middle Right with Square Text Wrapping," and then click the **Position in Middle Right with Square Text Wrapping** icon. The chart picture moves to the middle of the page along the right margin. By default, it is formatted with Tight text wrapping, so the text wraps to its left, following its square outline.

Your final step is to resize the chart picture to make it a bit smaller.

6. In the Size group, click the **Shape Height** box, type **1.8**, and then press the **Enter** key. The settings in both the Shape Height and Shape Width boxes change to 1.8 inches. For most types of graphics, the aspect ratio is locked, meaning that when you change one dimension, the other changes to match. In this case, because the aspect ratio of the chart is 1:1, when you changed the height to 1.8 inches, the width also changed to 1.8 inches, ensuring that the chart retained its square shape.

7. Click anywhere outside the chart picture to deselect it, and then save the document.

INSIGHT

Aligning Graphic Objects and Using the Selection Task Pane

The steps in this tutorial provide precise directions about where to position graphic objects in the document. However, when you are creating a document on your own, you might find it helpful to use the Align button in the Arrange group on the PICTURE TOOLS FORMAT tab to align objects relative to the margin or the edge of the page. Aligning a graphic relative to the margin, rather than the edge of the page, is usually the best choice because it ensures that you don't accidentally position a graphic outside the page margins, causing the graphic to get cut off when the page is printed.

After you choose whether to align to the page or margin, you can open the Align menu again and choose an alignment option. For example, you can align the top of an object at the top of the page, or align the bottom of an object at the bottom of the page. You can also choose to have Word distribute multiple objects evenly on the page. To do this, it's helpful to open the Selection task pane first by clicking the PAGE LAYOUT tab and then clicking Selection Pane. Press and hold the Ctrl key, and then in the Selection task pane, click the objects you want to select. After the objects are selected, there's no need to switch back to the PICTURE TOOLS FORMAT tab. Instead, you can take advantage of the Align button in the Arrange group on the PAGE LAYOUT tab to open the Align menu, where you can then click Distribute Horizontally or Distribute Vertically.

The chart picture is finished. Next, Estefan asks you to insert the lollipop clip art near the bottom of page 1.

Searching for and Inserting Clip Art

The first step in using clip art is finding the clip art you want. Most clip art websites include a search box where you can type some descriptive keywords to help you narrow the selection down to a smaller range. To find clip art on Office.com, you can type your keywords in the search box in the Insert Pictures window.

To search for clip art and insert it in the Wellness Newsletter document:

1. Zoom in so you can read the document text at the bottom of page 1, and then click at the end of the first paragraph below the "Stand Up to Temptation" heading to position the insertion point between "…eat, eat." and the paragraph mark.

2. Change the Zoom level to **Multiple Pages** so you can see the entire document.

3. On the ribbon, click the **INSERT** tab.

4. In the Illustrations group, click the **Online Pictures** button to display the Insert Pictures window. See Figure 4-26.

| Figure 4-26 | Insert Pictures window |

Here you can choose to search for clip art at Office.com, or you can use Microsoft's Bing search engine to search the entire web. Note that, despite the label "Royalty-free photos and illustrations" below the "Office.com Clip Art" heading, not all of the clip art available on Office.com is available for free. Some of it is offered by companies, such as Shutterstock, that require you to pay a fee.

5. In the search box to the right of "Office.com Clip Art," type **striped lollipop** and then press the **Enter** key. An image of a red and white striped lollipop appears in the search results window.

6. Click the red and white lollipop image to select it. Once selected, its border changes to blue. In the lower-left corner of the window, you see all the keywords associated with the picture ("Striped lollipop sucker") and its size in pixels (604 × 1024). See Figure 4-27.

TIP

A pixel is the smallest possible element in a graphic image.

Figure 4-27 **Selected clip art photo**

Image used with permission of Microsoft Corporation

7. In the lower-right corner of the search results window, click the **Insert** button. The clip art is inserted as an inline object at the current location of the insertion point. See Figure 4-28.

Figure 4-28 **Clip art photo inserted as inline object**

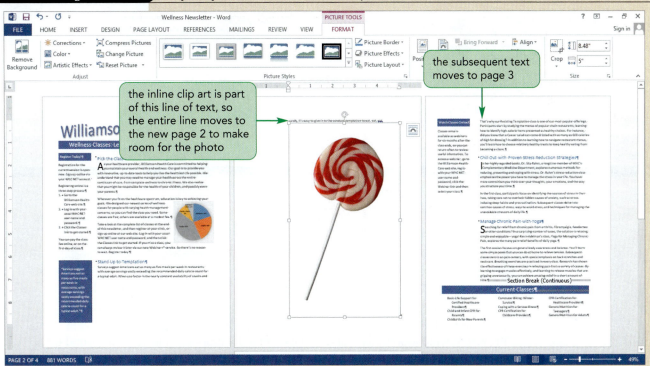

© 2014 Cengage Learning; Image used with permission of Microsoft Corporation

Because the photo is too large to fit on page 1, the line of text that contains the insertion point jumps to page 2, with the photo displayed below the text. The rest of the document text starts on page 3 and flows to page 4. The clip art photo is selected, as indicated by its border with handles. The PICTURE TOOLS FORMAT tab is displayed on the ribbon. Now you can reduce the photo's size, wrap text around it, and position it on the page.

8. In the Size group, click the **Shape Height** box, type **2**, and then press the **Enter** key. To maintain the photo's preset aspect ratio, Word changes the photo's width to 1.18 inches. Some of the text from page 3 moves up to fill the space below the smaller photo on page 2.

9. In the Arrange group, click the **Wrap Text** button, and then click **Tight**. The photo, which is now a floating object, moves to the top of page 1, with text wrapping to its right.

10. Drag the photo down to position it so the first line of the paragraph under "Stand Up to Temptation" wraps above it. See Figure 4-29. The anchor symbol for the photo is not visible because it's covered by the blue text box.

Figure 4-29	Resized clip art photo as a floating object

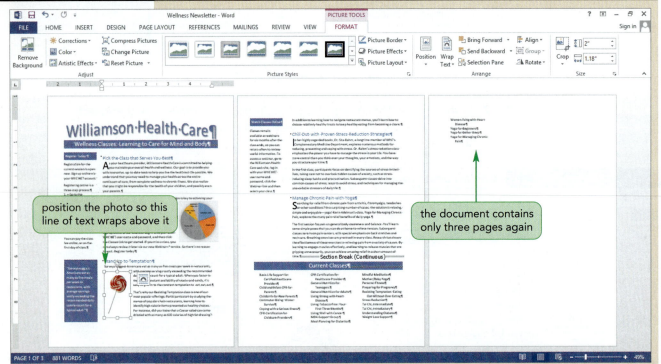

© 2014 Cengage Learning; Image used with permission of Microsoft Corporation

Trouble? Don't be concerned if you can't get the text to wrap around the lollipop photo exactly as shown in Figure 4-29.

11. Click the **Layout Options** button, click **Fix position on page**, and then close the Layout Options menu.

Estefan likes the photo, but he asks you to make a few changes. First, he wants you to rotate the lollipop to the left to position it vertically on the page. Also, Estefan wants the text to wrap around the curved shape of the lollipop itself, instead of around its rectangular outline. To accomplish that, you need to remove the photo's background.

Rotating a Picture

You can quickly rotate a picture by dragging the Rotation handle that appears on the photo's border when the photo is selected. To access some preset rotation options, you can click the Rotate button in the Arrange group to open the Rotate menu. To quickly rotate a picture 90 degrees, click Rotate Right 90° or Rotate Left 90° in the Rotate menu. You can

also flip a picture, as if the picture were printed on both sides of a card and you wanted to turn the card over. To do this, click Flip Vertical or Flip Horizontal in the Rotate menu.

Estefan only wants to rotate the lollipop picture slightly. You can do that by dragging the Rotation handle.

To rotate the clip art photo:

1. Change the document Zoom level to **120%**, and then scroll down so you can see the bottom half of page 1.

2. Click the lollipop picture, if necessary, to select it, and then position the mouse pointer over the circular rotation handle above the middle of the photo's top border. The mouse pointer changes to ↻.

3. Drag the mouse pointer down and to the left, until the lollipop rotates to a vertical position. See Figure 4-30.

Figure 4-30 **Dragging the Rotation handle**

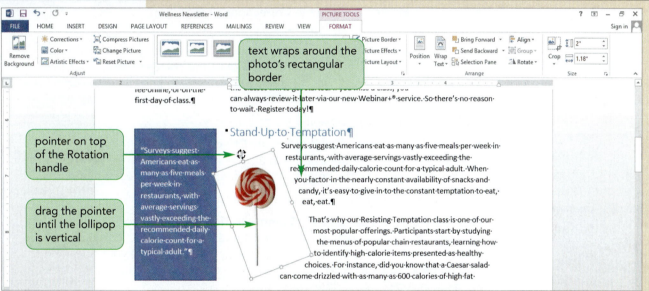

Image used with permission of Microsoft Corporation

Don't be concerned if the text wrapping around your rotated picture looks different from the text wrapping in Figure 4-30.

4. Release the mouse button. The lollipop is displayed in the new, rotated position, with the text wrapped around the photo's tilted, rectangular border.

5. Save the document.

You're almost finished editing the lollipop photo. Your last task is to remove its background so the text wraps around the shape of the lollipop itself. But before you remove the background from the lollipop photo, you'll explore the options in the Adjust group.

Adjusting a Picture

The Adjust group on the PICTURE TOOLS FORMAT tab provides several tools for adjusting a picture's overall look. Some, such as the Remove Background button, only work for photos. Others, such as the Color button, provide some options that work only for photos and some that work for both photos and line drawings. You'll explore some of these options in the following steps.

To try out some options in the Adjust group:

1. Make sure that the lollipop photo is still selected, and that the **PICTURE TOOLS FORMAT** tab is selected on the ribbon.

2. In the Adjust group, click the **Corrections** button, and then move the mouse pointer over the various options in the Corrections gallery and observe the Live Preview in the document. You can use the Corrections gallery to sharpen or soften a photo's focus, or to adjust the brightness of a photo or line drawing.

3. Press the **Esc** key to close the Corrections gallery.

4. In the Adjust group, click the **Color** button, and then move the mouse pointer over the options in the Color gallery and observe the Live Preview in the document. For photos, you can adjust the color saturation and tone. For photos and line drawings, you can use the Recolor options to completely change the picture's colors.

5. Press the **Esc** key to close the Color gallery.

6. In the Adjust group, click the **Artistic Effects** button, and then move the mouse pointer over the options in the Artistic Effects gallery and observe the Live Preview in the document. Artistic Effects can only be used on photos.

7. Press the **Esc** key to close the Artistic Effects gallery.

8. In the Adjust group, click the **Compress Pictures** button to open the Compress Pictures dialog box. In the Target output portion of the dialog box, you can select the option that reflects the purpose of your document. Compressing pictures reduces the file size of the Word document, but can result in some loss of detail.

9. Click the **Cancel** button to close the Compress Pictures dialog box.

Now you are ready to remove the white background from the lollipop photo.

Removing a Photo's Background

Removing a photo's background can be tricky, especially if you are working on a photo with a background that is not clearly differentiated from the foreground image. For example, you might find it difficult to remove a white, snowy background from a photo of an equally white snowman. You start by clicking the Remove Background button in the Adjust group, and then making changes to help Word distinguish between the background that you want to exclude and the image you want to keep.

REFERENCE

Removing a Photo's Background

- Select the photo, and then on the PICTURE TOOLS FORMAT tab, in the Adjust group, click the Remove Background button.
- Drag the handles on the border as necessary to include any parts of the photo that have been incorrectly marked for removal.
- To mark areas to keep, click the Mark Areas to Keep button in the Refine group on the BACKGROUND REMOVAL tab, and then use the drawing pointer to select areas of the photo to keep.
- To mark areas to remove, click the Mark Areas to Remove button in the Refine group on the BACKGROUND REMOVAL tab, and then use the drawing pointer to select areas of the photo to remove.
- Click the Keep Changes button in the Close group.

You'll start by zooming in so you can clearly see the photo as you edit it.

To remove the white background from the lollipop photo:

1. On the Zoom slider, drag the **slider button** to change the Zoom level to **180%**, and then scroll as necessary to display the selected lollipop photo.

2. In the Adjust group, click the **Remove Background** button. See Figure 4-31.

Figure 4-31 Removing the background of a photo

Image used with permission of Microsoft Corporation

The part of the photo that Word considers to be the background turns pink, and the BACKGROUND REMOVAL tab appears on the ribbon. A blue border with white handles surrounds the lollipop. The blue border helps Word narrow the area of focus as it tries to distinguish between the background and the parts

of the image you want to keep. Word will automatically remove any part of the image outside the blue border when you click the Keep Changes button.

Trouble? If you don't see the blue border with the white handles, click the Mark Areas to Remove button in the Refine group on the BACKGROUND REMOVAL tab, and then click in the pink background, in the upper-right corner of the picture. This will insert a small white circle with a negative sign inside it, which you can ignore. The blue border with the white handles should now be displayed.

Notice that the lollipop stick is pink, indicating that Word considers it to be part of the background. The same might also be true for a small section at the top of the lollipop spiral, although this can vary from one computer to another. To ensure that Word keeps the entire lollipop spiral, you need to expand the blue border with the white handles. Then you can make additional adjustments using the tools on the BACKGROUND REMOVAL tab.

3. If necessary, drag the square handle in the upper-right corner of the blue border up slightly until the border contains the entire red and white lollipop spiral. The entire red and white spiral should now be visible in its original colors, with no pink shading, indicating that Word no longer considers any part of the spiral to be part of the background. The only problem is that Word still considers the lollipop stick part of the background. You can fix that problem by marking the stick as an area to keep.

4. On the BACKGROUND REMOVAL tab, click the **Mark Areas to Keep** button in the Refine group, and then move the drawing pointer 𝒫 over the lollipop. You can use this pointer to draw a line on the lollipop stick.

5. Position the mouse pointer at the top of the stick, and then press and hold the mouse button down as you drag the pointer down to the bottom of the stick. The pointer changes to a white arrow, and a dotted line appears as you drag the pointer. See Figure 4-32.

Figure 4-32 **Marking an area to keep**

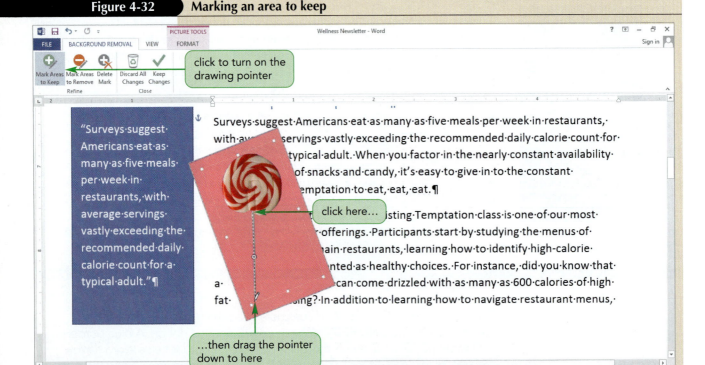

Image used with permission of Microsoft Corporation

6. Release the mouse button. A plus sign in a white circle appears on the dotted line, indicating that you have marked that part of the photo as an area to keep. The stick now appears in its original color, without pink shading. Now you will accept the changes you made to the photo.

Trouble? If Word uncovers a line of white from the background rather than the lollipop stick, you didn't draw the line precisely down the middle of the stick. Use the Undo button to reverse the change, and then begin again with Step 4.

7. In the Close group, click the **Keep Changes** button. The background is removed from the photo, leaving only the image of the lollipop. Now the text wrapping follows the curved shape of the lollipop, just as Estefan requested. Depending on exactly where you positioned the lollipop, some of the text might now wrap to the left of the lollipop stick.

8. Change the Zoom level to **100%** so that you can see the entire lollipop, as well as the top of page 2, and then drag the lollipop as necessary so the text wraps similarly to the text shown in Figure 4-33.

Figure 4-33 **Lollipop with background removed**

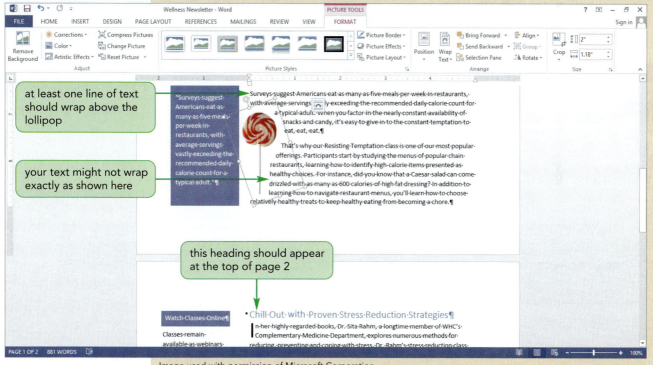

Image used with permission of Microsoft Corporation

Don't be concerned if you can't get the text wrapping to match exactly. The most important thing is that when you are finished, the "Chill Out with Proven Stress Reduction Strategies" heading should be positioned at the top of page 2. Also, at least one line of text should wrap above the lollipop.

9. Click outside the picture to deselect it, and then save the document.

You're finished with your work on the lollipop photo. Now Estefan asks you to add one more piece of clip art—the yoga drawing on page 3.

Inserting and Editing a Clip Art Drawing

You can insert the clip art drawing the same way you inserted the clip art photo—by clicking the Online Pictures button in the Illustrations group on the INSERT tab and then typing some keywords. In the following steps, after you insert the yoga drawing, you'll add a picture style to it from the Picture Styles gallery.

To insert and add a style to the yoga clip art drawing:

1. Change the Zoom level to **120%**, and then scroll to display the middle of page 2. You'll insert the yoga drawing in the blank space below the text box.

2. Click at the end of the paragraph below the "Manage Chronic Pain with Yoga" heading to position the insertion point between "…daily yoga." and the paragraph mark.

3. On the ribbon, click the **INSERT** tab.

4. In the Illustrations group, click the **Online Pictures** button, type **yoga under tree** in the Office.com Clip Art search box, and then press the **Enter** key. The drawing of the woman in a yoga pose under a tree, shown earlier in the Session 4.1 Visual Overview, is displayed in the search results window.

5. Click the drawing to select it, and then click the **Insert** button. The picture is inserted as an inline object below the line containing the insertion point because there is not enough room for it at the end of that line. See Figure 4-34.

Figure 4-34 | Clip art drawing inserted in document

Image used with permission of Microsoft Corporation

Next, you need to resize the drawing, apply a picture style, wrap text around it, and then position it on the page.

6. In the Size group, click the **Shape Height** box, type **1.4**, and then press the **Enter** key. To maintain the picture's preset aspect ratio, the width automatically adjusts to 1.39 inches. The picture moves up to the preceding line because it's now small enough to fit.

7. In the Arrange group, click the **Wrap Text** button to open the Wrap Text menu. The In line with Text option is selected. Because the picture is still an inline picture, the Move with Text and Fix Position on Page options are grayed out, indicating that they are not available.

8. Click **In Front of Text** to select it and close the Wrap Text menu.

9. Click the **Wrap Text** button again, and then click **Fix Position on Page**. The yoga picture appears layered on top of the document text. Keep in mind that even though you selected Fix Position on Page, the picture is not stuck in one place. You can drag it anywhere you want. The point of the Fix Position on Page setting is that it prevents the picture from moving unexpectedly as you make changes to other parts of the document.

10. In the Picture Styles group, click the **Simple Frame, White** style, which is the first style in the visible row of the Picture Styles gallery. A frame and a shadow are applied to the yoga drawing.

11. Drag the picture to center it in the white space below the text box in the margin, deselect it, and then save the document. See Figure 4-35.

TIP

To add a simple border without adding a style, click the Picture Border button, and then click a color in the color gallery.

Figure 4-35 Resized yoga picture with picture style

Image used with permission of Microsoft Corporation

INSIGHT

Working with Digital Picture Files

Digital picture files come in two main types—vector graphics and raster graphics. A vector graphics file stores an image as a mathematical formula, which means you can increase or decrease the size of the image as much as you want without affecting its overall quality. Vector graphics are often used for line drawings and, because they tend to be small, are widely used on the web. File types for vector graphics are often proprietary, which means they only work in specific graphics programs. In Word, you will sometimes encounter files with the .wmf file extension, which is short for Windows Metafiles. A .wmf file is a type of vector graphics file created specifically for Windows.

In most cases, though, you'll work with raster graphics, also known as bitmap graphics. A **bitmap** is a grid of square colored dots, called **pixels**, that form a picture. A bitmap graphic, then, is essentially a collection of pixels. The most common types of bitmap files are:

- BMP—These files, which have the .bmp file extension, tend to be very large, so it's best to resave them in a different format before using them in a Word document.
- GIF—These files are suitable for most types of simple line art, without complicated colors. A GIF file is compressed, so it doesn't take up much room on your computer. A GIF file has the file extension .gif.
- JPEG—These files are suitable for photographs and drawings. Files stored using the JPEG format are even more compressed than GIF files. A JPEG file has the file extension .jpg. If conserving file storage space is a priority, use JPEG graphics for your document.
- PNG—These files are similar to GIF files, but suitable for art containing a wider array of colors.
- TIFF—These files are commonly used for photographs or scanned images. TIFF files are usually much larger than GIF or JPEG files, but smaller than BMP files. A TIFF file has the file extension .tif.

Now that you are finished arranging the graphics in the newsletter, you need to make sure the columns are more or less the same length.

Balancing Columns

To **balance** columns on a page—that is, to make them equal length—you insert a continuous section break at the end of the last column. Word then adjusts the flow of content between the columns so they are of equal or near-equal length. The columns remain balanced no matter how much material you remove from any of the columns later. The columns also remain balanced if you add material that causes the columns to flow to a new page; the overflow will also be formatted in balanced columns.

To balance the columns:

1. Press the **Ctrl+End** keys to move the insertion point to the end of the document, if necessary.
2. Insert a continuous section break. See Figure 4-36.

Figure 4-36 Newsletter with balanced columns

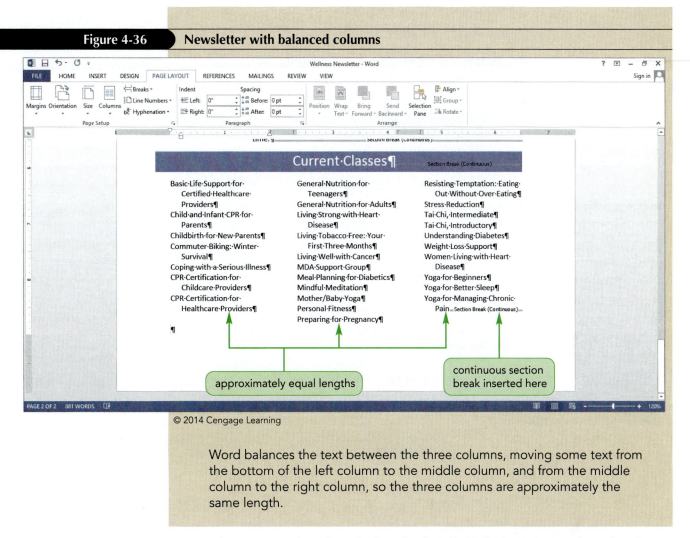

© 2014 Cengage Learning

Word balances the text between the three columns, moving some text from the bottom of the left column to the middle column, and from the middle column to the right column, so the three columns are approximately the same length.

Note that you can also adjust the length of a column by inserting a column break using the Breaks button in the Page Setup group on the PAGE LAYOUT tab. A column break moves all the text and graphics following it to the next column. Column breaks are useful when you have a multipage document formatted in three or more columns, with only enough text on the last page to fill some of the columns. In that case, balancing columns on the last page won't work. Instead, you can use a column break to distribute an equal amount of text over all the columns on the page. However, as with page breaks, you need to be careful with column breaks because it's easy to forget that you inserted them. Then, if you add or remove text from the document, or change it in some other significant way, you might end up with a page layout you didn't expect.

Inserting a Border Around a Page

The newsletter is almost finished. Your last task is to add a border around both pages. The default style for a page border is a simple black line that forms a box around each page in the document. However, you can choose more elaborate options, including a dotted line, double lines, and, for informal documents, a border of graphical elements such as stars or trees. In this case, Estefan prefers the default line style, but he wants it to be blue.

To insert a border around both pages of the newsletter:

1. Change the Zoom level to **Multiple Pages**.

2. On the ribbon, click the **DESIGN** tab.

3. In the Page Background group, click the **Page Borders** button. The Borders and Shading dialog box opens with the Page Border tab displayed. You can use the Setting options on the left side of this tab to specify the type of border you want. Because a document does not normally have a page border, the default setting is None. The Box setting is the most professional and least distracting choice, so you'll select that next.

4. In the Setting section, click the **Box** setting.

 At this point, you could scroll the Style box and select a line style for the border, such as a dotted line, but Estefan prefers the default style—a simple line. He's also happy with the default width of 1/2 pt. For very informal documents, you could click the Art arrow and select a predesigned border consisting of stars or other graphical elements. However, the only change Estefan wants to make is to change the border color to blue.

5. Click the **Color** arrow to open the Color gallery, and then click the **Blue, Accent 5** square, which is the second square from the right in the top row of the Theme Colors section. The Color gallery closes and the Blue, Accent 5 color is displayed in the Color box. See Figure 4-37.

> Be sure to select the Box setting before you select other options for the border. Otherwise, when you click OK, your document won't have a page border, and you'll have to start over.

| Figure 4-37 | Adding a border to the newsletter |

use the default line style

use a simple Box border

select the Blue, Accent 5 color

use the default width for the line style

apply to the whole document

6. In the lower-right corner of the Borders and Shading dialog box, click the **Options** button. The Border and Shading Options dialog box opens.

 By default, the border is positioned 24 points from the edges of the page. If you plan to print your document on an older printer, it is sometimes necessary to change the Measure from setting to Text, so that the border is positioned relative to the outside edge of the text rather than the edge of the page. Alternatively, you can increase the settings in the Top, Bottom, Left, and Right boxes to move the border closer to the text. For most modern printers, however, the default settings are fine.

▶ **7.** In the Border and Shading Options dialog box, click the **Cancel** button, and then click the **OK** button in the Borders and Shading dialog box. The newsletter now has a simple, blue border, as shown earlier in the Session 4.1 Visual Overview.

▶ **8.** Save the document. Finally, to get a better sense of how the document will look when printed, it's a good idea to review it with nonprinting characters turned off.

▶ **9.** On the ribbon, click the **HOME** tab.

▶ **10.** In the Paragraph group, click the **Show/Hide** button to turn off nonprinting characters. Notice that the WordArt headline increases slightly in size to take up the space formerly occupied by the nonprinting paragraph mark.

▶ **11.** Change the Zoom level to **120%**, and then scroll to display page 2.

▶ **12.** On page 2, in the first line below the heading, replace "Dr. Sita Rahm" with your first and last name, and then save the document.

Estefan plans to have the newsletter printed by a local printing company. Betsy, his contact at the printing company, has asked him to email her the newsletter as a PDF.

Saving a Document as a PDF

A **PDF**, or **Portable Document Format file**, contains an image showing exactly how a document will look when printed. Because a PDF can be opened on any computer, saving a document as a PDF is a good way to ensure that it can be read by anyone. This is especially useful when you need to email a document to people who might not have Word installed on their computers. All PDFs have a file extension of .pdf. By default, PDFs open in Adobe Acrobat Reader, a free program installed on most computers for reading PDFs, or in Adobe Acrobat, a PDF-editing program available for purchase from Adobe.

To save the Wellness Newsletter document as a PDF:

▶ **1.** On the ribbon, click the **FILE** tab to display Backstage view.

▶ **2.** In the navigation bar, click **Export** to display the Export screen with Create PDF/XPS Document selected.

▶ **3.** Click the **Create PDF/XPS Document** button. The Publish as PDF or XPS dialog box opens.

▶ **4.** If necessary, navigate to the location specified by your instructor for saving your files, and then verify that "Wellness Newsletter" appears in the File name box. Below the Save as type box, the "Open file after publishing" check box is selected. By default, the "Standard (publishing online and printing)" button is selected. This generates a PDF suitable for printing. If you plan to distribute a PDF only via email or over the web, you should select the "Minimum size (publishing online)" button instead. See Figure 4-38.

TIP

To save a document as a PDF and attach it to an email message in Outlook, click the FILE tab, click Share in the navigation bar, click Email, and then click Send as PDF.

Figure 4-38 **Publish as PDF or XPS dialog box**

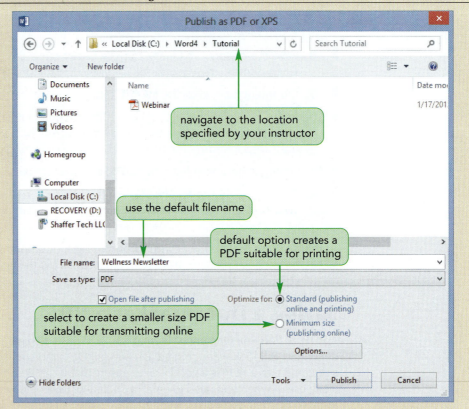

5. Click the **Publish** button. The Publish as PDF or XPS dialog box closes, and, after a pause, either Adobe Acrobat Reader or Adobe Acrobat opens with the Wellness Newsletter PDF displayed.

 Trouble? If the Wellness Newsletter PDF does not open, your computer might not have Acrobat Reader or Acrobat installed. In that case, skip Step 6.

6. Scroll down and review the PDF, and then close Adobe Acrobat Reader or Adobe Acrobat.

7. In Word, close the Wellness Newsletter document, but keep Word running.

In addition to saving a Word document as a PDF, you can convert a PDF to a Word document.

Converting a PDF to a Word Document

TIP

If the PDF's creator restricted the file's security using settings available in Adobe Acrobat, you will not be able to copy text from the PDF or convert it to a Word document.

You may sometimes need to use text from a PDF in your own Word documents. Before you can do this, of course, you need to make sure you have permission to do so. Assuming you do, you can open the PDF in Acrobat or Acrobat Reader, drag the mouse pointer to select the text you want to copy, press the Ctrl+C keys, return to your Word document, and then press the Ctrl+V keys to paste the text into your document. If you need to reuse or edit the entire contents of a PDF, it's easier to convert it to a Word document. This is a very useful option with PDFs that consist mostly of text. For more complicated PDFs, such as the Wellness Newsletter.pdf file you just created, the results are less predictable.

Estefan has a PDF containing some text about the Webinar+ service. He asks you to open it in Word and make some minor edits before converting it back to a PDF.

To open the Webinar PDF in Word:

▶ **1.** On the ribbon, click the **FILE** tab to display Backstage view.

▶ **2.** In the navigation bar, click **Open**, if necessary, to display the Open screen, and then navigate to the Word4 ▶ Tutorial folder included with your Data Files.

▶ **3.** If necessary, click the arrow to the right of the File name box, and then click **All Files**.

▶ **4.** In the file list, click **Webinar**, click the **Open** button, and then, if you see a dialog box explaining that Word is about to convert a PDF to a Word document, click the **OK** button. The PDF opens as a Word document, with the name "Webinar" in the title bar. At this point, the Webinar.docx file is a temporary file stored in the temporary folder on your computer. If you want to retain a copy of the document, you need to save it.

▶ **5.** Save the document as **Webinar Revised** in the location specified by your instructor.

▶ **6.** Turn on nonprinting characters, set the Zoom level to **120%**, and then review the document, which consists of a WordArt headline and two paragraphs formatted in italic. If you see some extra spaces at the end of the paragraphs, they were added during the conversion from a PDF to a Word document. In a more complicated document, you might see graphics overlaid on top of text, or columns broken across multiple pages.

▶ **7.** Delete any extra spaces, remove the italic formatting from both paragraphs, and then save the document. You are finished editing the document, so now you can convert it back to a PDF.

▶ **8.** On the ribbon, click the **FILE** tab to display Backstage view.

▶ **9.** In the navigation bar, click **Export**.

▶ **10.** Click the **Create PDF/XPS Document** button.

▶ **11.** If necessary, navigate to the location specified by your instructor for saving your files, verify that "Webinar Revised" appears in the File name box, and then click the **Publish** button.

▶ **12.** Review the PDF in Acrobat or Acrobat Reader, close Acrobat or Acrobat Reader, and then close the Webinar Revised document in Word.

REVIEW

Session 4.2 Quick Check

1. What is WordArt?

2. Name five types of bitmap files.

3. Is all the clip art offered by Office.com available for free, with no copyright restrictions?

4. When cropping a picture, how can you maintain a specific ratio of width to height?

5. How do you rotate a picture?

6. Explain how to balance columns in a document.

7. What is a PDF?

SAM Projects

ASSESS

PRACTICE

Review Assignments

Data Files needed for the Review Assignments: Exercise.docx, Habits.png, On the Move.docx, Take it Easy.docx

Estefan is working on another newsletter. This one provides information about the benefits of exercise and good nutrition, and includes a list of exercise and nutrition classes. He has already written the text, and he asks you to transform it into a professional-looking newsletter. He also asks you to save the newsletter as a PDF so he can email it to the printer, and to edit some text currently available only as a PDF. The finished newsletter should match the one shown in Figure 4-39.

Figure 4-39 **Completed Exercise Newsletter document**

Williamson Health Care
Exercise and Healthy Eating at Every Age

On the Move

The Surgeon General suggests adults get at least thirty minutes of physical activity five days a week. How about a quick walk after dinner instead of stretching out on the couch?

Try Our New Exercise and Nutrition Classes

Wherever you fit on the health care spectrum, education is key to achieving your health goals. We designed our newest series of nutrition and exercise classes for people with varying health management concerns, so you can find the class you need. Some classes are free; others are available at a modest fee.

Take a look at the complete list of classes at the end of this newsletter, and then register at your clinic, or sign up online at our website. Log in with your usual WHC NET user name and password, and then click the Classes link to get started. If you miss a class, you can always review it later via our new Webinar+ service. So there's no reason to wait. Register today!

Preventing Type 2 Diabetes

Diabetes is a disease in which the body fails to produce or properly use insulin. Between 5 and 10% of the country's 20 million diabetes sufferers have type 1 diabetes. Most type 1 diabetics are children and young adults. So far, we know of no way to prevent the onset of type 1 diabetes. However, the more common variety, type 2 diabetes, can be delayed or prevented—if you act in time. The secrets to preventing type 2 diabetes are a healthy diet and regular exercise.

Every first Monday of the month, our Lakeside clinic offers free diabetes risk assessments. We'll check your blood pressure and weight and help you fill out a health questionnaire. Your results will be analyzed by HealthLife®, our new health data app, which you can download to your smart phone, tablet or computer.

"Every first Monday of the month, our Lakeside clinic offers free diabetes risk assessments."

If you have already been diagnosed with diabetes, keep in mind that Williamson Health Care is committed to helping you maintain your overall health and wellness. Our goal is to provide you with innovative, up-to-date tools to help you live the healthiest life possible. We understand that you may need to manage your health challenges, while also caring for the health of your children, and possibly even your parents.

WHC Members: Exercise Habits

Take it Easy

Start by making some easy changes. On your way to work or school, hop off the bus one stop earlier than usual. When you go to the mall, park at the edge of the lot, instead of right by the door. The walk will do you good.

Eating Well in a Busy World

It's hard to eat well if you're always on the run. Studies show that people who fail to sit down for regular meals eat far more than they think. For help dining well in a busy world, check out "20 Fast Food Friends," a list of healthy options available at national fast food franchises. You'll find the list on the Williamson Health Care website, and at the front desk at all Williamson Health Care clinics.

It's surprisingly easy to make healthy changes in your diet. For starters, try switching from whole milk to skim milk in your morning latte. Over a year's time, even small improvements have a cumulative effect, leaving you lighter and feeling better.

Fresh is Better

If you can only do one thing to improve your diet, eat more fresh fruits and vegetables. They're packed with vitamins and fiber, which, in a well-managed diet, can help ward off heart disease, diabetes, and other debilitating conditions. Experts suggest eating at least five servings of fruits and vegetables a day.

A healthy serving of meat for a single meal is 3 ounces. That's about the size of a deck of cards. But most restaurants serve meat in 8 to 12 ounce portions—far more than any adult should eat in one sitting. To find out if your portions are healthy, make friends with your measuring cups. Devote a week or two to measuring your servings at every meal. And remember, you don't have to worry about measuring fresh fruits and vegetables. Make an apple or carrot your go-to snack, and you'll never have to worry about snack portions again!

Nutrition and Exercise Classes

Balance and Fitness
Basic Nutrition for Childcare Providers
Cardio Training for All Ages
Child and Infant Nutrition for Parents
College Cooking for Healthy-Minded Cooks
Commuter Cooking: Eating on the Road
Cooking for Kids
Cooking for the Diabetic in Your Family

Cooking Italian the Healthy Way
General Nutrition for Adults
General Nutrition for Teenagers
High Impact Cardio Training
Meal Planning for Diabetics
Mindful Meditation
Mother/Baby Yoga
Personal Fitness
Resisting Temptation: Eating Out Without Over Eating
Strength Training for New Mothers

Strength Training for Teens
Strength Training in Your Golden Years
Stress Reduction
Tai Chi, Intermediate
Tai Chi, Introductory
Triathlon Training
Water Aerobics for All Ages
Water Aerobics for Teens
Water Walking
Yoga for Beginners
Yoga for During Pregnancy
Yoga for Better Sleep

Complete the following steps:

1. Open the file **Exercise** from the Word4 ▸ Review folder included with your Data Files, and then save the document as **Exercise Newsletter** in the location specified by your instructor.

2. Insert continuous section breaks in the following locations:
 - On page 1, at the beginning of the "Try Our New Exercise and Nutrition Classes" heading, to the left of the "T" in "Try"
 - On page 2, at the beginning of the shaded heading "Nutrition and Exercise Classes," to the left of the "N" in "Nutrition"
 - On page 2, at the beginning of the first class name, to the left of the "B" in "Balance"

3. In sections 1 and 3, change the left and right margins to .75 inches. In section 2, change the left margin to 2.5 inches.

4. Format section 4 in three columns of equal width, and then format the entire list of class names with a 0.2-inch hanging indent.

5. Search for the term **HealthLife**, and then add the ® symbol to the right of the final "e."

6. On page 1, click anywhere in the "Try Our New Exercise and Nutrition Classes" heading, and then insert a preformatted text box using the Retrospect Sidebar option.

7. Change the text wrapping setting for the text box to In Front of Text. Change the height of the text box to 4.4 inches and its width to 1.2 inches, and then drag it left to position it in the white space in the left margin, with its top edge aligned with the first line of text below the "Try Our New Exercise and Nutrition Classes" heading. The left border of the text box should align with the left edge of the shaded paragraph above. Verify that the text box's position is fixed on the page, but note that its placement will shift slightly as you add other elements to the newsletter.

8. Delete all the placeholder text in the text box, and then insert the text of the Word document **On the Move**, which is located in the Word4 ▸ Review folder included with your Data Files. Delete any extra paragraph marks at the end of the text, if necessary.

9. On the INSERT tab, use the Shapes button to draw a rectangular text box that roughly fills the blank space in the lower-left margin of page 1. When you are finished, adjust the height and width as necessary to make the text box 2.5 inches tall and 1.3 inches wide.

10. Make sure the text wrap setting for the text box is set to In Front of Text, and that the text box has a fixed position on the page. Drag the text box's anchor up next to the "Preventing Type-2 Diabetes" heading to keep the text box from moving to page 2 later, when you add a graphic to page 1.

11. On page 1, in the second paragraph below the "Preventing Type 2 Diabetes" heading, select the first sentence (which begins "Every first Monday…"), and then copy it to the Office Clipboard.

12. Paste the copied sentence into the text box at the bottom of page 1, and then add quotation marks at the beginning and end.

13. Use the Align Text button to align the text in the middle of the text box, and then apply the Intense Effect - Orange, Accent 2 shape style (the orange style option in the bottom row of the Shape Styles gallery).

14. On page 2, click in the first paragraph, and then insert a preformatted text box using the Retrospect Sidebar option.

15. Change the text wrapping setting for the text box to In Front of Text. Change the height of the text box to 5.2 inches and its width to 1.2 inches, and then drag it left to position it in the white space in the left margin, with its top edge aligned with the first line of text. Verify that its position is fixed on the page. Don't be concerned that it overlaps the shaded paragraph below. This will change as you add more elements to the newsletter.

16. Delete all the placeholder text in the text box, and then insert the text of the Word document **Take it Easy**, which is located in the Word4 ▸ Review folder included with your Data Files. Delete any extra paragraph marks at the end of the text, if necessary.

17. After each of the four headings formatted with orange font, insert a drop cap that drops two lines.

18. On page 1, select the entire first paragraph, "Williamson Health Care," including the paragraph mark. Clear the formatting from the paragraph, and then format the text as WordArt, using the Fill - Orange, Accent 2, Outline - Accent 2 style.

19. Use the Position button to place the WordArt in the top center of the document, with square text wrapping, and make sure the WordArt has a fixed position on the page.

20. Change the text box width to 7 inches and retain the default height of .87 inches.

21. Apply the Chevron Up transform text effect, change the text fill to Orange, Accent 2 (the orange square in the top row of the Theme Colors section), and then add a shadow using the Offset Diagonal Bottom Right style (the first option in the top row of the Outer section).

22. Click at the end of the paragraph below the "Try Our New Exercise and Nutrition Classes" heading, and then insert the picture file named **Habits.png** from the Word4 ▸ Review folder included with your Data Files.

23. Practice cropping the chart to a shape, and then try cropping it by dragging the cropping handles. Use the Reset Picture button as necessary to restore the picture to its original appearance. When you are finished, crop the picture using a square aspect ratio, and then change its height and width to 1.8 inches. Use the Position button to place the chart picture in the middle of the right side of page 1 with square text wrapping.

24. On page 1, click at the end of the second paragraph below the "Preventing Type 2 Diabetes" heading, and then insert a clip art picture from Office.com that shows a woman in a pink headband, with a yellow towel around her neck, drinking from a water bottle, as shown in Figure 4-39. Search for the clip art using the keywords **exercising with water**.

25. Apply Square text wrapping, change the picture's height to 1.7 inches, retain the default width of 1.13 inches, and position the picture as shown in Figure 4-39. When the picture is properly positioned, the heading "Eating Well in a Busy World" should be positioned at the top of page 2, as shown in Figure 4-39.

26. On page 2, click at the end of the first paragraph below the "Fresh is Better" heading, and then insert a clip art photo from Office.com that shows a pineapple with green leaves, as shown in Figure 4-39. Search for the clip art using the keywords **pineapple photo**. When displayed in the search results, the photo will have a light blue background, with the pineapple tilted on its side.

27. Change the photo's width to 2 inches and retain the default height of 1.34 inches. Apply Tight text wrapping, fix its position on the page, and then remove the photo's background.

28. Rotate the photo so the pineapple is positioned vertically, with the leaves on top, and then drag the photo to position it as shown in Figure 4-39.

29. Balance the columns at the bottom of page 2.

30. Insert a simple box outline of the default style and width for the entire document. For the border color, use Blue, Accent 1 (the fifth square from the left in the top row of the Theme Colors).

31. In the top text box on page 1, replace "The surgeon general" with your first and last name. If you can't fit your entire name on the first two lines of the text box, use your first initial and your last name. Make any additional adjustments necessary to ensure that your newsletter matches the one shown in Figure 4-39.

32. Save the document, and then save it again as a PDF named **Exercise Newsletter.pdf** in the location specified by your instructor. Wait for the PDF to open, review it, and then close the program in which it opened. Close the **Exercise Newsletter.docx** document, but leave Word open.

33. In Word, open the **Exercise Newsletter.pdf** file, save it as a Word document named **Exercise Newsletter from PDF.docx**, review its appearance, note the problems with the formatting that you would have to correct if you actually wanted to use this new DOCX file, and then close it.

Case Problem 1

Data Files needed for this Case Problem: Green.docx, Sidebar.docx

Green Commission, Morelos, Arizona Clarice Stephan is the coordinator for the Green Commission in Morelos, Arizona, a citizen committee charged with encouraging environmentally friendly practices such as recycling, LEED construction, and water conservation. She has written the text of the commission's bimonthly newsletter. Now she needs your help to finish it. The newsletter must fit on one page so the commission's recycling guidelines can be printed on the other side. The finished newsletter should match the one shown in Figure 4-40.

Figure 4-40 **Completed Green Newsletter document**

Recycle, Reuse, Renew
Green Commission Updates

Recycling Review

Each household is entitled to one recycling bin. You can recycle an unlimited amount of materials, with no extra fee for materials that exceed the limit of your household's recycling bin. Please place extra materials in a clean box that is clearly labeled "Recycling," and place it next to your bin.

See the complete recycling guidelines on the other side of this newsletter.

Morelos Receives $5000 Recycling Grant

We're extremely happy to announce that the Morelos Green Commission has been awarded a $5000 Change It Up grant from the Arizona Department of Public Works. The money will pay for new recycling bins at all city parks. Many thanks go to Suzette Orleans, who spent many hours completing the grant application, along with James Suarez and Leah Chang.

The recycling bins will be installed at the end of the summer. The Department of Sanitation will be responsible for emptying them twice a week during the summer, and once a week the rest of the year. The Morelos High School Honor Society has offered to clean the bins once a month as part of their student volunteer program.

Hazardous Waste Collection

The next city-wide hazardous waste collection is scheduled for the week of July 15. Sanitation workers will retrieve the items from the curb next to your trash bins on your usual trash pickup day. Please keep all hazardous waste items indoors until the morning of your scheduled trash pickup. For a list of all accepted items, go to the City of Morelos web site, and click Hazardous Waste Pickup.

Many household hazardous wastes can be recycled cleanly and effectively by recycling professionals. Aren't sure what's considered hazardous waste? The labels of most products will provide helpful clues. Look for the following words: caution, warning, toxic, pesticide, keep away from children, flammable, and warning. Acceptable materials include antifreeze, brake fluid, kerosene, oil-based paint, furniture polish, pesticides, herbicides, household batteries, pool chemicals and fertilizers.

Winners of the Citizen Green Award

Kendra Ann Ramirez-Beech
Michael Paul Bernault
Beatrice Cai
Emma Comerez
Jonathan Carnala
Laydra Carole
Samuel Butler

Aralee Erbe
Henry Douglas
Jose Caruccio
Sophie Carrucio
Krista Dennis
Seamus Van Buren
Jacqueline Fey-Esperanza
Haiyan Jiang

Marcos Jeschke
Jaques Lambeau
Maria Morelo-Jimenez
Elizabeth Juarez
Mario Mondre
Helena Pentakota Roys
Maximillian Del Rio

Harriet Soles
Micah Schwerz
Alyssa Tonette
Pamela Twist-Chamberlain
Roberto Oriel

Complete the following steps:

1. Open the file **Green** located in the Word4 ▸ Case1 folder included with your Data Files, and then save it as **Green Newsletter** in the location specified by your instructor.

2. Change the document margins to Narrow, and then, where indicated in the document, insert continuous section breaks. Remember to delete each instance of the highlighted text "[INSERT SECTION BREAK]" before you insert a section break.

3. In section 2, change the left margin to 3 inches, and then format section 4 in four columns, with a 0.3-inch hanging indent.

4. Format the second paragraph in the document ("Green Commission Updates") as WordArt, using the Gradient Fill - Dark Green, Accent 1, Reflection style (second from the left in the middle row of the WordArt gallery). Change the text box height to 0.7 inches and the width to 7 inches. If necessary, drag the WordArt text box to center it between the left and right margins.

5. Insert drop caps that drop two lines in the first paragraph after the "Morelos Receives $5000 Recycling Grant" heading, and in the first paragraph after the "Hazardous Waste Collection" heading.

6. Click in the fourth paragraph in the document (the one with the drop cap "W"), and then insert a preformatted text box using the Ion Sidebar 1 option. Change the text wrapping setting for the text box to In Front of Text, and then change its height to 3 inches and its width to 2 inches.

7. Drag the text box down, and then align its top border with the "Morelos Receives $5000 Recycling Grant" heading.

8. Delete the title placeholder text in the text box, and type **Recycling Review**. In the main text box, delete the placeholder text and insert the text of the Word document **Sidebar** from the Word4 ▸ Case1 folder included with your Data Files. Change the font size for all the text in the text box, including the title, to 11 points.

9. In the blank space below the "Recycling Review" text box, draw a rectangular text box. When you are finished, adjust the height and width to make the text box 1.3 inches tall and 2 inches wide. Apply the Moderate Effect - Blue, Accent 2 shape style (third from the left in the second row from the bottom), and then position the text box as shown in Figure 4-40, leaving room for the recycling bin graphic you will add later.

10. In the text box, type **See the complete recycling guidelines on the other side of this newsletter**. Align the text in the middle of the text box, and then use the Center button to center the text between the text box's left and right borders.

11. At the end of the fifth paragraph (which begins "The recycling bins will be…"), insert a clip art picture from Office.com that shows a boy in an orange shirt and blue pants placing a tan bag in a green recycling bin. Search for the clip art using the keywords **boy putting trash in recycling**. Crop the picture to an oval shape, apply Tight text wrapping, fix its position on the page, and then change its height to 1 inch. Drag the picture to position it so the first line in the fifth paragraph wraps above it, as shown in Figure 4-40.

12. At the end of the first paragraph below the "Hazardous Waste Collection" heading, insert a clip art picture from Office.com that shows a green recycling bin. Search for the clip art using the keywords **recycling symbol on bin**. Change the picture's height to 1.3 inches, apply In Front of Text text wrapping, add the Center Shadow Rectangle picture style (second from right in the second row of the Picture Styles gallery), and then position the picture in the left margin, centered between the two text boxes, with a fixed position on the page, as shown in Figure 4-40.

13. Add a box page border using a line style with a thick exterior line and a thinner interior line, in the default width, and in the same color as the font for the "Morelos Receives $5000 Recycling Grant" heading.

14. In the last paragraph, replace "Roberto Oriel" with your first and last names.

15. Make any adjustments necessary so that your newsletter matches the one shown in Figure 4-40, and then save the document.

16. Save the document as a PDF named **Green Newsletter** in the location specified by your instructor. Review the PDF and then close the program in which it opened.

17. In Word, open the PDF named **Green Newsletter.pdf**, save it as **Green Newsletter from PDF.docx**, review its contents, note the corrections you would have to make if you actually wanted to use this document, and then close it.

Case Problem 2

Data Files needed for this Case Problem: Facts.docx, Rights.jpg

Alexander Hamilton High School Paula McQuiddy teaches American history at Alexander Hamilton High School in Ruby Falls, Wisconsin. She has decided to create a series of handouts about important historical documents. Each handout will contain the text of the historical document, with red and blue accent colors, along with a picture of the American flag and a text box with essential facts about the document. Paula has asked you to help her complete her first handout, which is about the Bill of Rights. You will create the handout shown in Figure 4-41.

Figure 4-41 Completed Bill of Rights handout

© 2014 Cengage Learning; Image used with permission of Microsoft Corporation

Complete the following steps:

1. Open the file **Rights** located in the Word4 ▶ Case2 folder included with your Data Files, and then save it as **Bill of Rights** in the location specified by your instructor.
2. Display the document gridlines.
3. Change the document margins to Narrow, change the theme to Facet, and format all the heading text using the Dark Blue font color in the Standard Colors section of the Font Color gallery.
4. At the top of the document, add the text **The Bill of Rights** as a new paragraph, and then format it as WordArt, using the Gradient Fill - Red, Accent 1, Reflection style (the second from the left in the middle row). Add Top and Bottom text wrapping, and then fix the text box's position on the page. If the position of the WordArt shifts, drag it back up to the top of the page. Change its height to 1.3 inches and its width to 7 inches. Apply the Square transform text effect (the first effect in the top row of the Warp section). Remove the reflection effect. Drag the WordArt as necessary to center it at the top of the page. The top edge of the text box should align with the top gridline.

5. At the end of the paragraph below the WordArt, insert a clip art photo of the American flag from Office.com. Search for the clip art using the keywords **waving American flag hanging on a pole**.

6. Apply Tight text wrapping to the photo, change the height to 2 inches, remove the photo's background, and then position it along the left margin, so the first two lines of regular text wrap above it, as shown in Figure 4-41.

7. Format the list of amendments in two columns. Use column breaks to format the amendments as shown in Figure 4-41, with Amendment IV at the top of the second column on page 1, and Amendment VIII at the top of the second column on page 2.

8. At the end of the last paragraph on page 2, insert a preformatted text box using the Grid Sidebar style. Apply In Front of Text text wrapping, and then change the height to 5.3 inches and the width to 7 inches. Position the text box at the bottom of page 2, centered in the white space, with a fixed position on the page.

9. Delete the placeholder text in the text box, and then insert the text of the Word document named **Facts** from the Word4 ▶ Case2 folder included with your Data Files. If necessary, delete any extra paragraph marks.

10. Add a box page border, using the default style, in the default width, and in the same color as the headings with the amendment numbers.

11. Make any adjustments necessary so that your newsletter matches the one shown in Figure 4-41, and then hide the gridlines.

12. At the end of the text box on page 2, insert a new, bulleted paragraph, remove the bullet formatting, right-align the paragraph, and then insert the text **Prepared by Student Name**, with your first and last names replacing the text "Student Name." Save the document.

13. Save the document as a PDF named **Bill of Rights.pdf** in the location specified by your instructor. Review the PDF in Acrobat or Acrobat Reader.

14. From within Acrobat or Acrobat Reader, use the appropriate keyboard shortcut to copy the bulleted paragraphs in the blue text box, open a new, blank Word document, and then paste the copied text into it. In a new bulleted list at the end of the document, list three differences between the formatting of the bulleted list in the current document and in the Bill of Rights.pdf file. Format the new paragraphs in red so they are easy to spot.

15. Save the Word document as **Facts from PDF** in the location specified by your instructor and then close it. Close Acrobat or Acrobat Reader.

TROUBLESHOOT

Case Problem 3

Data Files needed for this Case Problem: Audio.pdf, Shape.docx

Shape Crafter 3D Printing You have recently been hired as an assistant in the Human Resources department at Shape Crafter 3D Printing in Indianapolis, Indiana. Your supervisor explains that while working on the company's monthly newsletter, he left his laptop briefly unattended. His young daughter took advantage of the opportunity to make some unwelcome changes to his Word document. You've offered to troubleshoot the document and format the newsletter to look like the one shown in Figure 4-42. Your second task is to open a PDF containing a newsletter announcing a new program for employees, and edit the text to remove any irregularities that occurred in the conversion from a PDF to a Word document.

Figure 4-42 Completed Shape Crafter newsletter

change the left margin to 1.75 inches

change the WordArt text direction setting to Rotate all text 270°; change its height to 9.94 inches and its width to 1.3 inches; and then change the font size to 72 points

for the border, use the Dark Red, Accent 1 color and the default line style and width

find this image at Office.com by searching for "tennis ball sitting next to a tennis racquet"

use the Blue - Gray, Accent color 5 Dark option in the Recolor section of the Color gallery

square text box shape with 1.5-inch sides; use the Light 1 Outline, Colored Fill - Dark Red, Accent 1 shape style

for the headings' shading, use the Dark Red, Accent 1 color; switch to white font

text is hyphenated

change spacing between columns to 0.2"

square text box shape with 1.25-inch sides

Shape Crafter News

CTO Tonella Desantes Honored

Chief Technology Officer, **Tonella Desantes**, achievements but also her community service. She began her career as an accountant at First Light Systems in Milwaukee, where she helped design and implement technical audits and became its first chief quality officer. She joined Shape Crafter 3D Printing in 2001 and was named CTO in 2006.

A valued member of many civic organizations, Desantes serves on the board of directors of the Foundation for Public Schools, the Prairieland Community Restoration Association, and the Wayton University Alumni Association. She was one of the founders and charter members of the governing board of The Phoenix House, a local community organization that helps unemployed single mothers re-enter the job market.

Tennis Team Wins Third Place

Are you surprised to learn that Shape Crafter 3D Printing fields a prize-winning tennis team? Many participants in the Seventh Annual Indian Tennis Association's Executive Team Championships were. Not only did Shape Crafter 3D Printing field a team, but it finished third behind teams from Cottingham Investments (First Place) and Bryerly Pharmaceuticals (Second Place). On the other hand, tennis aficionados throughout the state wouldn't have been surprised at all with Shape Crafter 3D Printing's success. After all, playing for the Shape Crafter

3D Print[...] the ma[...] who als[...] sota Sta[...] The four-person team boasts two other tennis pros, **Maya Lapata**, who is Director of Internal Auditing at Shape Crafter 3D Printing and who finished fifth last year in the U.S. Women's Senior Invitational held in New York City, and **Juan Carlos Rica**, mer tennis pro at Earlham Wood Country Club. Way to go, team!

"Are you surprised to learn that Shape Crafter 3D Printing fields a prize-winning tennis team?"

Take a Chance on Getting Away

First prize is a trip to the gorgeous San Juan Islands in Puget Sound. The San Juan Islands consist of three main islands—Orcas, Lopez, and San Juan. They are famous for stunning scenery, great biking and hiking, and miles of quiet beaches. Visitors to San Juan Island will find quaint and historic fishing villages, and, if they're lucky, spot some of the magnificent orca whales that frequent the western side of the island. Orcas Island, with its many galleries, is the perfect destination for art and pottery lovers. Lopez attracts thousands of bikers and h[...]

The raffle winner will receive round-trip air fare for two, one week accommodation at the Blackberry Bed and Breakfast on Orcas Island, and free daily passes for the San Juan Islands ferry, which travels to all three islands.

Don't forget to buy your ticket for the Get-Away Raffle.

© 2014 Cengage Learning; Photos courtesy of Ann Shaffer

Complete the following steps:

1. Open the file **Shape** located in the Word4 ▸ Case3 folder included with your Data Files, and then save it as **Shape Crafter Newsletter** in the location specified by your instructor.

⚙ **Troubleshoot** 2. Revise the document to match the newsletter shown in Figure 4-42. Start by fixing the border, changing the left margin, and resetting the pictures. Keep in mind that you can use the Selection Task Pane to select a picture, and remember to crop the photos so they match the ones shown in Figure 4-42. Also, you'll need to flip two of the pictures horizontally. You should be able to size the pictures appropriately by looking at their sizes relative to the text in Figure 4-42.

⚙ **Troubleshoot** 3. In the Arrange group, use the Selection task pane and the Align Objects button to align the photo of Tonella Desantes and the tennis racquet with the left margin. Also, align the two text boxes with the right margin.

4. Replace the double hyphens with an em dash.

5. In the middle of the second column, replace "Juan Carlos Rica" with your first and last names.

⚙ **Troubleshoot** 6. Make any adjustments necessary so that your newsletter matches the one shown in Figure 4-42. You might need to drag the WordArt text box left slightly to keep all the text on one page. Save the document.

7. Save the document as a PDF named **Shape Crafter Newsletter.pdf** in the location specified by your instructor. Review the PDF in Acrobat or Acrobat Reader, and then close Acrobat or Acrobat Reader.

8. Open the PDF **Audio.pdf** located in the Word4 ▸ Case3 folder included with your Data Files, and then save it as a Word document named **Audio Download Program** in the location specified by your instructor.

⚙ **Troubleshoot** 9. Edit the text to remove the picture, the WordArt, and the shaded text. Format the blue headings using the Heading 1 style, and then remove any extra spaces and paragraph breaks. Make any other edits necessary so that the text is formatted with consistent paragraph and line spacing throughout.

10. Save the document, and then close it. Close any other open documents.

Case Problem 4

There are no Data Files needed for this Case Problem.

Glenfield Graphic Design You are an intern at Glenfield Graphic Design, a firm that specializes in designing fund-raising materials, including newsletters, for nonprofit organizations. As part of your training, your supervisor asks you to review examples of newsletter designs on the web, and then re-create the design of one of those newsletters in a Word document. Instead of writing the complete text of a newsletter, you can use placeholder text. Complete the following steps:

1. Open a new, blank document, and then save it as **Newsletter Design** in the location specified by your instructor.

2. Open your browser and search online for images of sample newsletters by searching for the keywords **newsletter image**. Review at least a dozen images of newsletters before picking a style that you want to re-create in a Word document. The style you choose should contain at least two pictures. Keep the image of the newsletter you select visible in your browser so you can return to it for reference as you work.

3. In your Word document, create the first page of the newsletter. To generate text that you can use to fill the page, type **=lorem()** and then press the Enter key.

4. Add at least two pictures to the newsletter, using clip art from Office.com. Rotate or flip pictures and remove the background from photos as necessary to make them work in the newsletter layout.

5. Make any other changes necessary so that the layout and style of your document match the newsletter example that you found online.

6. Somewhere in the document, attach a comment that reads **I used the following webpage as a model for this newsletter design:**, and then include the URL for the newsletter image you used as a model. To copy a URL from a browser window, click the URL in the browser's Address box, and then press the Ctrl+C keys.

7. Save the document, close it, and then close your browser.

Written Communication

Writing Clear and Effective Business Documents

Whether it's a simple email message sent to a group, a memo to provide information on an upcoming event, or a press release introducing a new product to the market, the quality of your written communication tells the world how prepared, informed, and detail-oriented you are. When searching for a job, the ability to write clearly and effectively is essential. After all, your first contact with a company is often a cover letter and resume. For a prospective employer, these documents provide the first indicators of the kind of employee you might be. To make the best possible impression, follow these important rules in all types of business communication.

Rule One: Identify Your Audience

Who will read your document? What do they already know about your subject? For starters, you can assume your audience is made up of busy people who will only take the time to read what is important and relevant to them. They don't want to be entertained. They just want to read the information as quickly as possible. In the case of a resume and cover letter, your audience is typically one or more professional people who don't know you. Therefore, the goal of your resume and cover letter should be to introduce yourself quickly and efficiently.

Rule Two: Do Your Research

Provide all the information the reader will need to make a decision or take action. Be absolutely certain that the facts you present are correct. Don't assume that something is true just because a friend told you it was, or because you read it online. Verify all your facts using reputable sources. Remember, your goal as a writer is to make the reader trust you. Nothing alienates a reader faster than errors or misleading statements. When applying for a job, make sure you are knowledgeable about the company so that you can mention relevant and accurate details in your cover letter.

Rule Three: State Your Purpose

At the beginning of the document, explain why you are writing. The reader shouldn't have to wonder. Are you writing to inform, or do you want action to be taken? Do you hope to change a belief or simply state your position? In a cover letter accompanying your resume, state clearly that you are writing to apply for a job, and then explain exactly what job you are applying for. That might sound obvious, but many job applicants forget about directness in their efforts to come across as clever or interesting. This only hurts their chances because prospective employers typically have many cover letters to read, with no time to spare for sorting through irrelevant information.

Rule Four: Write Succinctly

Use as few words as possible. Don't indulge in long, complicated words and sentences because you think they make you sound smart. The most intelligent writing is usually short and to the point. Keep in mind that hiring a new employee is a very time-consuming process. In small companies, people in charge of hiring often have to do it while performing their regular duties. Thus, the more succinct your resume and cover letter, the greater the chances that a potential employer will actually read both documents.

Rule Five: Use the Right Tone

Be professional and courteous. In the case of writing to a prospective employer, don't make the mistake of being overly friendly because it might indicate to the reader that you are not taking the job application process seriously.

Rule Six: Revise, Revise, Revise

After you finish a document, set it aside for a while, and then proofread it when it's no longer fresh in your mind. Even a small grammar or punctuation error can cause a potential employer to set aside your resume in favor of a more polished one with no errors. Remember, the best writers in the world seek out readers who can provide constructive suggestions, so consider having a friend or colleague read it and provide feedback. If someone points out an unclear passage, make every attempt to improve it.

Following these basic rules will help to ensure that you develop strong, professional written communication skills.

PROSKILLS

Create a Resume and Cover Letter

You've seen how Microsoft Word 2013 allows you to create polished, professional-looking documents in a variety of business settings. The word-processing skills you've learned will be useful to you in many areas of your life. For example, you could create a Word table to keep track of a guest list for a wedding, or you could use Word's desktop publishing features to create a flyer promoting a garage sale or a concert for a friend's band. In the following exercise, you'll create a table summarizing information about prospective employers, and then you'll use that information to create a resume and a cover letter.

Note: Please be sure *not* to include any personal information of a sensitive nature in the documents you create to be submitted to your instructor for this exercise. Later on, you can update the documents with such information for your own personal use.

1. Pick a career field that interests you, and then go online and look up information about four companies or organizations in that field for which you would like to work.

2. Create a table that summarizes your research. Your table should include one column with information about how to apply for a job. Does the company require you to email your resume and cover letter as PDFs, to submit them as Word documents via a website, to paste them into a form on a website, or to mail printed copies? The process of applying for a job can vary widely from one company to another—and from one industry to another—so make sure you clearly explain the process for each company in your table and include any relevant website addresses. Include three columns in your table with general information that would be useful for you in a job interview. For example, you might include a "Most Important Product" column and a "Facts About Company Founder" column. Create a complete record for each company, and then sort the table alphabetically by company name.

3. Create a resume that you could use to apply for jobs at the four companies you researched. To ensure that your resume is suitable for your chosen field, search the web for sample resumes in your field. Find a resume design that you like, and then adapt the design for your resume. Your goal should be to create the most elegant, professional-looking resume you can, using advanced page layout options as necessary. For example, you could use a table to organize the page layout.

4. After creating your resume, proofread it for any errors, and then revise it for proper tone and clear and succinct content. If possible, ask a classmate or a family member to read it and provide constructive feedback.

5. Create a copy of your resume, and then revise this new version to use the simplest possible formatting. This time, your goal should be to create a resume that you could easily paste into a form on a website.

6. Create a cover letter to accompany your resume. Make sure that your letter clearly states your purpose, and that the letter is formatted correctly and written succinctly. When reviewing your cover letter and revising it, make sure your writing is professional and uses an appropriate tone.

7. Review all your documents carefully in Print Preview, make any necessary changes, and then save the documents.

8. Save your two resumes and your cover letter as PDFs.

Working with Templates, Themes, and Styles

Creating a Summary Report

WORD

OBJECTIVES

Session 5.1
- Create a new document from a template
- Move through a document using Go To
- Use the thesaurus to find synonyms
- Customize a document theme
- Save a custom theme
- Select a style set
- Customize a style
- Change character spacing

Session 5.2
- Create a new style
- Inspect styles
- Reveal and compare text formatting details
- Review line and page break settings
- Generate and update a table of contents
- Create and use a template
- Create a Quick Part

Case | *Department of Cultural Affairs*

In the small city of Westphal, Minnesota, citizen committees often work with city departments to make recommendations regarding municipal issues. A new committee led by Jonah Freiburg, a senior member of the Department of Cultural Affairs, is responsible for recommending a new site for the increasingly popular Blue Spruce Folk Festival. Jonah has asked you to help prepare the report summarizing the committee's preliminary recommendations. He's also interested in learning more about Word templates, so he'd like you to do some research by opening a few templates and examining the styles they offer. Next, he wants you to modify the formatting currently applied to his report document, including modifying the theme and one of the styles, creating a new style, and adding a table of contents. Then he wants you to create a template that can be used for all reports produced by the department, as well as a reusable text box containing the department's address and phone number, which department members can insert into any Word document via the Quick Part gallery.

STARTING DATA FILES

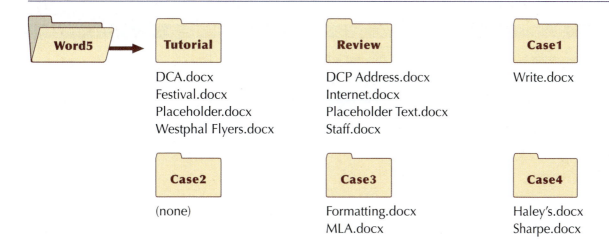

Word5 → **Tutorial**
DCA.docx
Festival.docx
Placeholder.docx
Westphal Flyers.docx

Review
DCP Address.docx
Internet.docx
Placeholder Text.docx
Staff.docx

Case1
Write.docx

Case2
(none)

Case3
Formatting.docx
MLA.docx

Case4
Haley's.docx
Sharpe.docx

Session 5.1 Visual Overview:

The **theme colors** are the colors you see in the Theme Colors section of any color gallery, such as the Font Color gallery. Theme colors are used in the document's styles to format headings, body text, and other elements.

Every document has two **theme fonts**, which are used in the document's styles. The theme fonts appear at the top of the font list when you click the Font arrow in the Font group on the HOME tab.

Collectively, all the styles available in a document are called a **style set**. This style set, named Word 2013, is applied to all new documents by default.

Theme **effects**, such as reflections or shadows, can be used to modify shapes.

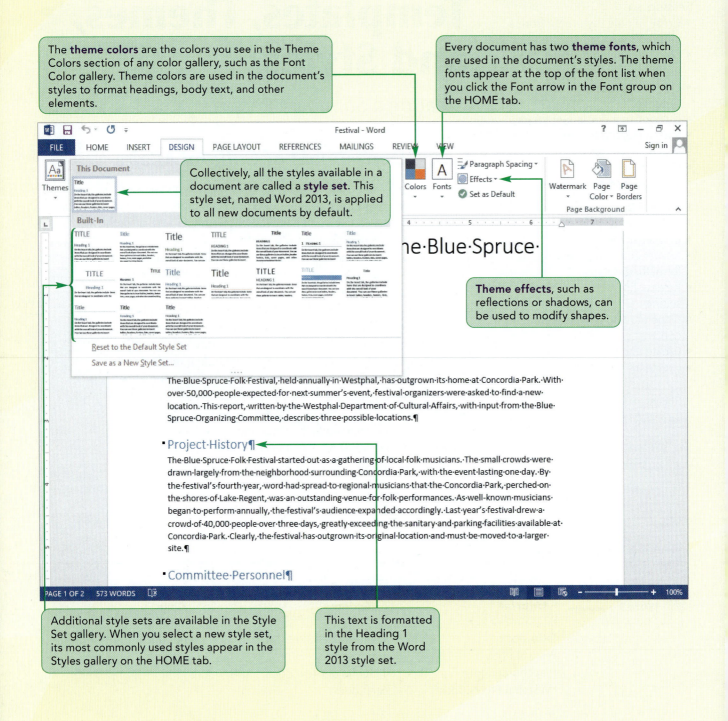

The Blue Spruce Folk Festival, held annually in Westphal, has outgrown its home at Concordia Park. With over 50,000 people expected for next summer's event, festival organizers were asked to find a new location. This report, written by the Westphal Department of Cultural Affairs, with input from the Blue Spruce Organizing Committee, describes three possible locations.¶

Project History¶

The Blue Spruce Folk Festival started out as a gathering of local folk musicians. The small crowds were drawn largely from the neighborhood surrounding Concordia Park, with the event lasting one day. By the festival's fourth year, word had spread to regional musicians that the Concordia Park, perched on the shores of Lake Regent, was an outstanding venue for folk performances. As well-known musicians began to perform annually, the festival's audience expanded accordingly. Last year's festival drew a crowd of 40,000 people over three days, greatly exceeding the sanitary and parking facilities available at Concordia Park. Clearly, the festival has outgrown its original location and must be moved to a larger site.¶

Committee Personnel¶

Additional style sets are available in the Style Set gallery. When you select a new style set, its most commonly used styles appear in the Styles gallery on the HOME tab.

This text is formatted in the Heading 1 style from the Word 2013 style set.

Custom Themes and Style Sets

The Themes gallery displays the available themes on your computer, including any custom themes you have created and saved in the Document Themes folder.

This style set, named Shaded, is applied to the Festival document, shown below. In the Shaded style set, the Heading 1 style formats text with blue paragraph shading and a white font color.

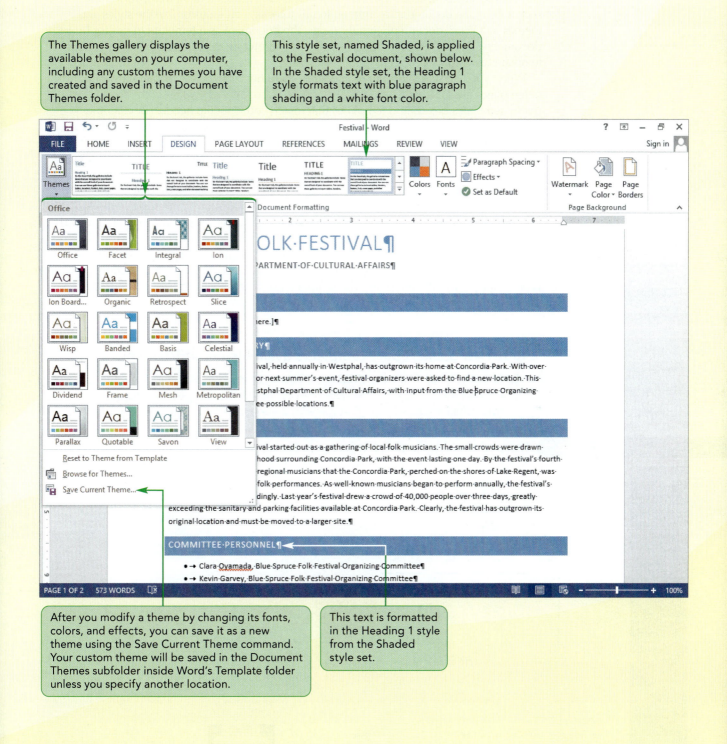

After you modify a theme by changing its fonts, colors, and effects, you can save it as a new theme using the Save Current Theme command. Your custom theme will be saved in the Document Themes subfolder inside Word's Template folder unless you specify another location.

This text is formatted in the Heading 1 style from the Shaded style set.

Creating a New Document from a Template

A template is a file that you use as a starting point for a series of similar documents so that you don't have to re-create formatting and text for each new document. A template can contain customized styles, text, graphics, or any other element that you want to repeat from one document to another. In this tutorial, you'll customize the styles and themes in a Word document, and then save the document as a template to use for future documents. Before you do that, however, you will investigate some of the ready-made templates available at Office.com.

When you first start Word, the Recent screen in Backstage view displays a variety of templates available from Office.com. You can also enter keywords in the Search for online templates box to find templates that match your specific needs. For example, you could search for a calendar template, a birthday card template, or a report template.

Every new, blank document that you open in Word is a copy of the Normal template. Unlike other Word templates, the **Normal template** does not have any text, formatting, or graphics, but it does include all the default settings that you are accustomed to using in Word. For example, the default theme in the Normal template is the Office theme. The Office theme, in turn, supplies the default body font (Calibri) and the default heading font (Calibri Light). The default line spacing and paragraph spacing you are used to seeing in a new document are also specified in the Normal template.

Jonah would like you to review some templates designed for reports. As you'll see in the following steps, when you open a template, Word actually creates a document that is an exact copy of the template. The template itself remains unaltered, so that you can continue to use it as the basis for other documents.

TIP

Templates have the file extension .dotx to differentiate them from regular Word documents, which have the extension .docx.

To review some report templates available on Office.com:

1. On the ribbon, click the **FILE** tab to open Backstage view, and then click **New** in the navigation bar. The New screen in Backstage view displays thumbnail images of the first page of a variety of templates. See Figure 5-1.

Figure 5-1 **Featured templates in the New screen in Backstage view**

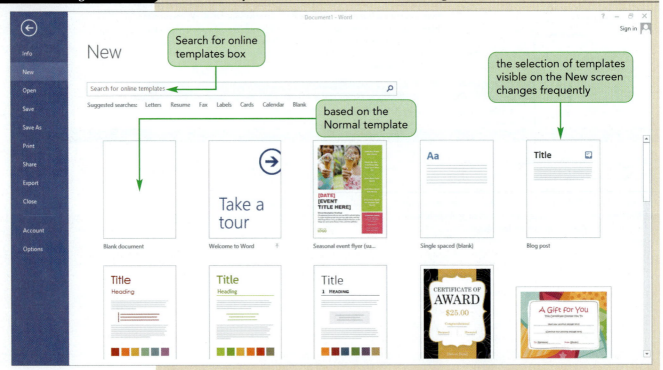

Trouble? If you just started Word, you'll see the list of templates on the Recent screen. You'll be able to complete the next step using the Search for online templates box on the Recent screen.

Below the Search for online templates box are template options available from Office.com. You've already used the Blank document template to open a new, blank document that is based on the Normal template. The list of templates changes frequently as new templates become available, so your screen probably won't match Figure 5-1 exactly.

If your computer has been used to create customized templates, two additional links are displayed below the Search for online templates box—FEATURED and PERSONAL. You can ignore those links for now. In this case, you want to open a document based on a template designed specifically for reports.

▶ 2. Click the **Search for online templates** box, type **report** and then press the **Enter** key. The New screen displays thumbnail images for a variety of report templates. If you scroll down to the bottom, you'll see options for searching for templates to use in other Office applications. The Category pane on the right displays a list of report categories. You could click any category to display only the templates in that category.

▶ 3. Click the first template in the top row. A window opens with a preview of the template. Figure 5-2 shows the Report (Essential design) template. The template that opens on your computer might be different.

| Figure 5-2 | Previewing a template |

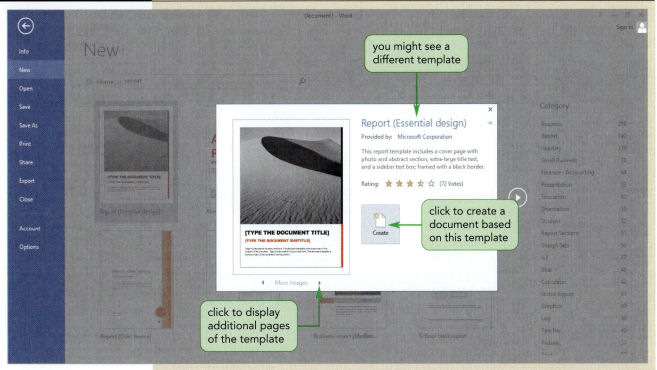

You could click the Close button to close the preview window and browse other report templates, but Jonah asks you to continue investigating the current template.

▸ **4.** Click the **Create** button. A new document opens. A document based on the Essential design report template begins with a cover page and contains a number of content controls designed specifically for the template, similar to the content controls you've seen in other documents. It also contains some placeholder text, a header, a footer, and graphics.

 At this point, you could save the document with a new name and then begin revising it to create an actual report. But since your goal now is to review various templates, you'll close the document.

▸ **5.** Close the document without saving any changes.

▸ **6.** On the ribbon, click the **FILE** tab, and then click **New** in the navigation bar.

▸ **7.** Search online for newsletter templates, open a document based on one of the templates, and then review the document, making note of the various elements it includes.

▸ **8.** Close the newsletter document without saving it.

▸ **9.** Return to the New screen, and search for templates for flyers. Open a new document based on one of the templates, review the document, and then close it without saving it.

PROSKILLS

Decision Making: Using Templates from Other Sources

The Office.com website offers a wide variety of templates that are free to registered Microsoft Office users. Countless other websites offer templates for free, for individual sale, as part of a subscription service, or a combination of all three. However, you need to be wary when searching for templates online. Keep in mind the following when deciding which sites to use:

- Files downloaded from the Internet can infect your computer with viruses and spyware, so make sure your computer has up-to-date antivirus and antispyware software before downloading any templates.
- Evaluate a site carefully to verify that it is a reputable source of virus-free templates. Verifying the site's legitimacy is especially important if you intend to pay for a template with a credit card. Search for the website's name and URL using different search engines (such as Bing and Google) to see what other people say about it.
- Some websites claim to offer templates for free, when in fact the offer is primarily a lure to draw visitors to sites that are really just online billboards, with ads for any number of businesses completely unrelated to templates or Word documents. Avoid downloading templates from these websites.
- Many templates available online were created for earlier versions of Word that did not include themes or many other Word 2013 design features. Make sure you know what you're getting before you pay for an out-of-date template.

Now that you are finished reviewing report templates, you will open the document containing the report about the Blue Spruce Folk Festival.

To open Jonah's report document:

1. Open the document **Festival** from the Word5 ▶ Tutorial folder included with your Data Files, and then save it as **Festival Report** in the location specified by your instructor.

2. Display nonprinting characters and the rulers, switch to Print Layout view, and then change the Zoom level to **120%**, if necessary. See Figure 5-3.

| Figure 5-3 | Festival Report document |

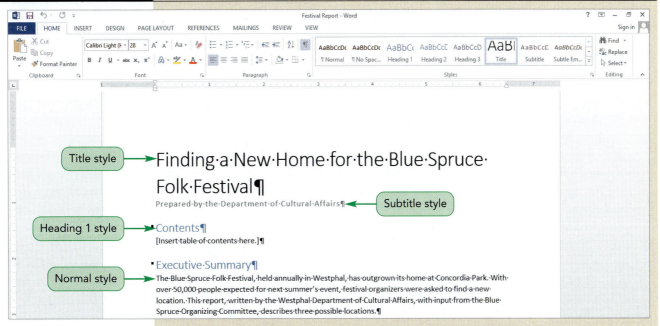

The report is formatted using the default settings of the Normal template, which means its current theme is the Office theme. Text in the report is formatted using the Title, Subtitle, Heading 1, Heading 2, and Normal styles. The document includes a footer containing the department name and a page number field.

Before you begin revising the document, you should review its contents. To get a quick overview of a document, it's helpful to use the Go To feature.

Using Go To

The Go To tab in the Find and Replace dialog box allows you to move quickly among elements in a document. For example, you can use it to move from heading to heading, from graphic to graphic, or from table to table. In a long document, this is an efficient way to review your work. Although the Festival Report document is not very long, you can still review its contents using Go To.

To use the Go To feature to review the Festival Report document:

1. If necessary, press the **Ctrl+Home** keys to move the insertion point to the beginning of the document.

2. On the ribbon, make sure the HOME tab is displayed.

▶ 3. In the Editing group, click the **Find button arrow** to display the Find menu, and then click **Go To**. The Find and Replace dialog box opens, with the Go To tab displayed. See Figure 5-4.

| Figure 5-4 | Go To tab in the Find and Replace dialog box |

type additional information about the document element here

click the document element you want to go to

click to move to the previous or next instance in the document

In the Go to what box, you can click the document element you want to go to. Then click the Next or Previous buttons to move back and forth among instances of the selected element in the document. You can also enter more specific information in the box on the right. For instance, when Page is selected in the Go to what box, you can type a page number in the box, and then click Next to go directly to that page.

Right now, Jonah would like to review all the headings in the document—that is, all the paragraphs formatted with a heading style.

▶ 4. Scroll down to the bottom of the Go to what box, click **Heading**, and then click the **Next** button. The document scrolls down to position the first document heading, "Contents," at the top of the document window.

▶ 5. Click the **Next** button again. The document scrolls down to display the "Executive Summary" heading at the top of the document window.

▶ 6. Click the **Next** button six more times to display the last heading in the document, "Framingham Park," at the top of the document window.

▶ 7. Click the **Previous** button to display the "Metcalfe Farm" heading at the top of the document window, and then close the Find and Replace dialog box.

INSIGHT

Choosing Between Go To and the Navigation Pane

Both the Go To tab in the Find and Replace dialog box and the Navigation pane allow you to move through a document heading by heading. Although you used Go To in the preceding steps, the Navigation pane is usually the better choice for working with headings; it displays a complete list of the headings, which helps you keep an eye on the document's overall organization. However, the Go To tab is more useful when you want to move through a document one graphic at a time, or one table at a time. In a document that contains a lot of graphics or tables, it's a good idea to use the Go To feature to make sure you've formatted all the graphics or tables similarly.

Next, before you begin formatting the document, Jonah asks you to help him find a synonym for a word in the text.

Using the Thesaurus to Find Synonyms

In any kind of writing, choosing the right words to convey your meaning is important. If you need help, you can use Word's thesaurus to look up a list of synonyms, or possible replacements, for a specific word. You can right-click a word to display a shortcut menu with a short list of synonyms, or open the Thesaurus task pane for a more complete list.

Jonah is not happy with the word "sheds" in the paragraph about the Metcalfe Farm site because he thinks it suggests the buildings on the property are shabby or in need of repair. He asks you to find a more appropriate synonym.

To look up a synonym in the thesaurus:

1. In the first line after the "Metcalfe Farm" heading, right-click the word **sheds**. A shortcut menu opens.

2. Point to **Synonyms**. A menu with a list of synonyms for "sheds" is displayed, as shown in Figure 5-5.

Figure 5-5 **Shortcut menu with list of synonyms**

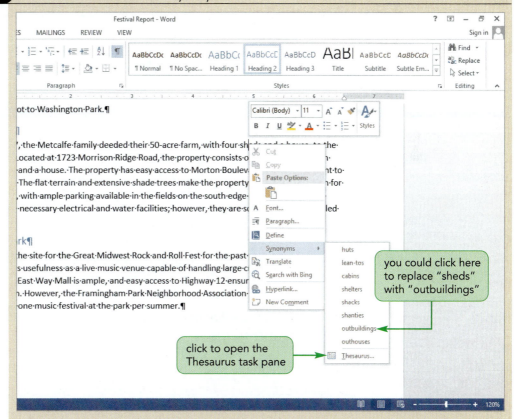

One word in the list, "outbuildings," is a good replacement for "sheds." You could click "outbuildings" to insert it in the document in place of "sheds," but Jonah asks you to check the Thesaurus task pane to see if it suggests a better option.

3. At the bottom of the shortcut menu, click **Thesaurus**. The Thesaurus task pane opens on the right side of the document window, with the word "sheds" at the top, and a more extensive list of synonyms below. The word "sheds" is also selected in the document, ready to be replaced. See Figure 5-6.

Figure 5-6 Thesaurus task pane

The synonym list in the task pane is organized by different shades of meaning, with words related to the idea of a "hut" at the top of the list. You can scroll down the list to see other groups of synonyms, including some that are synonyms for "sheds" when it is used as a verb rather than a noun. Below the list of synonyms, the word "sheds" appears in blue, with a speaker icon next to it. If your computer has a speaker, you can click the speaker icon to hear the word "sheds" pronounced correctly.

4. In the Thesaurus task pane, move the mouse pointer over the list of synonyms to display the scroll bar, scroll down to display other synonyms, and then scroll back up to the top of the list.

5. Right-click **outbuildings**. The word is highlighted in blue, and a menu opens. See Figure 5-7.

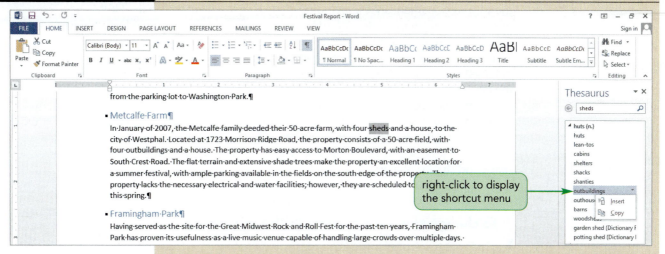

Figure 5-7 Selecting a synonym in the Thesaurus task pane

Trouble? If the Thesaurus task pane changes to display a set of synonyms for the word "outbuildings," you clicked the word "outbuildings" with the left mouse button instead of the right. Click the Back button ← to redisplay the synonyms for "sheds," and then begin again with Step 5.

6. Click **Insert** to replace "sheds" with "outbuildings" in the document, and then close the Thesaurus task pane.

7. Save the document.

Now that the document text is finished, you can get to work on the formatting. You'll start by customizing the document theme.

Customizing the Document Theme

A document theme consists of three main components—theme colors, theme fonts, and theme effects. A specific set of colors, fonts, and effects is associated with each theme, but you can mix and match them to create a customized theme for your document. The theme fonts are the fonts used in a document's styles. You see them at the top of the font list when you click the Font arrow in the Font group on the HOME tab. The theme colors are displayed in the Theme Colors section of any color gallery. The colors used to format headings, body text, and other elements are all drawn from the document's theme colors. Theme effects alter the appearance of shapes. Because they are generally very subtle, theme effects are not a theme element you will typically be concerned with.

When you change the theme colors, fonts, or effects for a document, the changes affect only that document. However, you can also save the changes you make to create a new, custom theme, which you can then use for future documents.

The Festival Report document, which was based on the Normal template, is formatted with the Office theme—which applies a blue font color to the headings by default, and formats the headings in the Calibri Light font. Jonah wants to select different theme colors and theme fonts. He doesn't plan to include any graphics, so there's no need to customize the theme effects. You'll start with the theme colors.

Changing the Theme Colors

The theme colors, which are designed to coordinate well with each other, are used in the various document styles, including the text styles available on the HOME tab. They are also used in shape styles, WordArt styles, and picture styles. So when you want to change the colors in a document, it's always better to change the theme colors rather than selecting individual elements and applying a new color to each element from a color gallery. That way you can be sure colors will be applied consistently throughout the document—for example, the headings will all be shades of the same color.

Reports created by the Department of Cultural Affairs are typically emailed to many recipients, some of whom might choose to print the reports. To keep printing costs as low as possible for all potential readers of his report, Jonah wants to format his document in black and white. He asks you to apply a set of theme colors consisting of black and shades of gray.

To change the theme colors in the document:

1. Press the **Ctrl+Home** keys to display the beginning of the document.

2. On the ribbon, click the **DESIGN** tab.

3. In the Document Formatting group, move the mouse pointer over the **Colors** button. A ScreenTip is displayed, indicating that the current theme colors are the Office theme colors.

4. Click the **Colors** button. A gallery of theme colors opens, with the Office theme colors selected at the top of the gallery. See Figure 5-8.

Figure 5-8 Theme Colors gallery

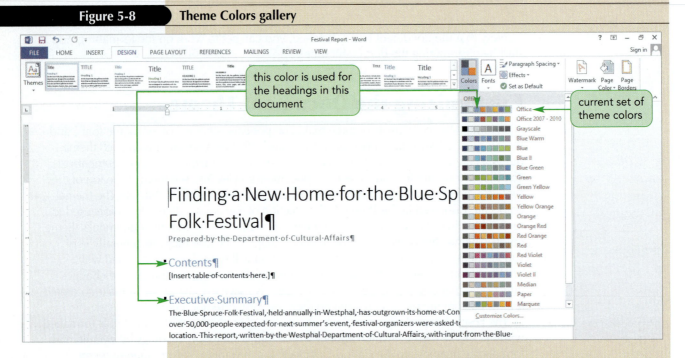

Each set of colors contains eight colors, with each assigned to specific elements. For example, the third color from the left is the color used for headings. The remaining colors are used for other types of elements, such as hyperlinks, page borders, shading, and so on.

Trouble? If you see additional theme colors at the top of the gallery under the "Custom" heading, then custom theme colors have been created and stored on your computer.

> **5.** Move the mouse pointer over the options in the gallery to observe the Live Preview of the colors in the document.

> **6.** Near the top of the gallery, click the **Grayscale** color set, which is the third from the top. The document headings are now formatted in gray.

> **7.** Save the document.

The new colors you selected affect only the Festival Report document. Your changes do not affect the Office theme that was installed with Word. Next, Jonah asks you to customize the document theme further by changing the theme fonts.

Changing the Theme Fonts

As with theme colors, you can change the theme fonts in a document to suit your needs. Each theme uses two coordinating fonts—one for the headings and one for the body text. In some themes, the same font is used for the headings and the body text. When changing the theme fonts, you can select from all the font combinations available in any of the themes installed with Word.

To select a different set of theme fonts for the document:

> **1.** In the Document Formatting group, move the mouse pointer over the **Fonts** button. A ScreenTip is displayed, indicating that the current fonts are Calibri Light for headings and Calibri for body text.

> **2.** Click the **Fonts** button. The Theme Fonts gallery opens, displaying the heading and body font combinations for each theme.

> **3.** Scroll down to review the fonts. Jonah prefers the Franklin Gothic set of theme fonts, which includes Franklin Gothic Medium for headings and Franklin Gothic Book for the body text.

> **4.** In the Theme Fonts gallery, point to **Franklin Gothic** to display a Live Preview in the document. See Figure 5-9.

Figure 5-9 **Theme Fonts gallery**

point to this set of theme fonts to display a Live Preview in the document

▶ **5.** Click **Franklin Gothic**. The Theme Fonts gallery closes, and the new fonts are applied to the document.

▶ **6.** Save the document.

The changes you have made to the theme fonts for the Festival Report document do not affect the original Office theme that was installed with Word and that is available to all documents. To make your new combination of theme fonts and theme colors available to other documents, you can save it as a new, custom theme.

INSIGHT

Creating Custom Combinations of Theme Colors and Fonts

The theme color and font combinations installed with Word were created by Microsoft designers who are experts in creating harmonious-looking documents. It's usually best to stick with these preset combinations rather than trying to create your own set. However, in some situations you might need to create a customized combination of theme colors or fonts. When you do so, that set is saved as part of Word so that you can use it in other documents.

To create a custom set of theme colors, you click the Colors button in the Document Formatting group on the DESIGN tab, and then click Customize Colors to open the Create New Theme Colors dialog box, in which you can select colors for different theme elements, and enter a descriptive name for the new set of theme colors. The custom set of theme colors will be displayed as an option in the Themes Colors gallery. To delete a custom set of colors from the Theme Colors gallery, right-click the custom color set in the gallery, click Delete, and then click Yes.

To create a custom set of heading and body fonts, you click the Fonts button in the Document Formatting group on the DESIGN tab, click Customize Fonts, select the heading and body fonts, and then enter a name for the new set of fonts in the Name box. The custom set of theme fonts is displayed as an option in the Theme Fonts gallery. To delete a custom set of fonts from the Theme Fonts gallery, right-click the custom font set in the gallery, click Delete, and then click Yes.

Saving a Custom Theme

TIP

To delete a custom theme saved in the Document Themes folder, click the Themes button on the DESIGN tab, right-click the theme, click Delete, and then click Yes.

You can save a custom theme to any folder, but when you save a custom theme to the default location—the Document Themes subfolder inside the Templates folder—it is displayed as an option in the Themes gallery.

Jonah asks you to save his combination of theme fonts and theme colors as a new custom theme, using "DCA," the acronym for "Department of Cultural Affairs," as part of the filename.

To save the new custom theme:

▶ **1.** In the Document Formatting group, click the **Themes** button, and then click **Save Current Theme**. The Save Current Theme dialog box opens. See Figure 5-10.

Figure 5-10 Save Current Theme dialog box

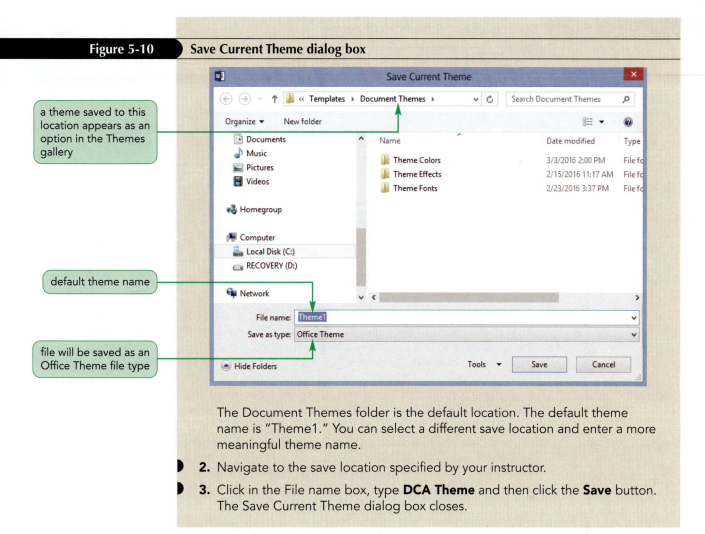

a theme saved to this location appears as an option in the Themes gallery

default theme name

file will be saved as an Office Theme file type

The Document Themes folder is the default location. The default theme name is "Theme1." You can select a different save location and enter a more meaningful theme name.

2. Navigate to the save location specified by your instructor.

3. Click in the File name box, type **DCA Theme** and then click the **Save** button. The Save Current Theme dialog box closes.

Jonah plans to use the new theme to help standardize the look of all documents created in his department. When he is ready to apply it to a document, he can click the Themes button in the Document Formatting group on the DESIGN tab, click Browse for Themes, navigate to the folder containing the custom theme, and then select the theme. If he wants to be able to access his theme from the Themes gallery instead, he will need to save it to the Document Themes folder first.

Jonah likes the document's new look, but he wants to make some additional changes. First, he wants to select a different style set.

Selecting a Style Set

Recall that a style is a set of formatting options that you can apply to a specific text element in a document, such as a document's title, heading, or body text. So far, you have used only the set of styles available in the Style gallery on the HOME tab. However, 16 additional style sets, or groups of styles, are available in the Style Set gallery accessed via the Document Formatting group on the DESIGN tab.

Each style set has a Normal style, a Heading 1 style, a Heading 2 style, and so on, but the formatting settings associated with each style vary from one style set to another. See Figure 5-11.

Figure 5-11 Styles from two different style sets

Word 2013 Style Set	Title Style Heading 1 style Heading 2 style Normal style
Shaded Style Set	TITLE STYLE HEADING 1 STYLE HEADING 2 STYLE Normal style

© 2014 Cengage Learning

In the Shaded style set shown in Figure 5-11, the Heading 1 style includes a thick band of color with a contrasting font color. The main feature of the Heading 1 style of the Word 2013 style set is simply a blue font color. Note that Figure 5-11 shows the styles as they look with the default theme fonts and colors for a new document. The Word 2013 style set is currently applied to the Festival Report document; but because you've changed the theme fonts and colors in the document, the colors and fonts in the document are different from what is shown in Figure 5-11. However, the styles in the document still have the same basic look as the Word 2013 styles shown in the figure.

Jonah asks you to select a style set for the Festival Report document that makes the Heading 1 text darker, so the headings are easier to read. Before you do that, you'll review the styles currently available in the Style gallery on the HOME tab. Then, after you select a new style set, you'll go back to the Style gallery to examine the new styles.

To review the styles in the Style gallery and select a new style set for the document:

1. On the ribbon, click the **HOME** tab.

2. In the Styles group, click the **More** button and then review the set of styles currently available in the Style gallery. Note that the icon for the Heading 1 style indicates that it applies a light gray font color.

3. On the ribbon, click the **DESIGN** tab.

4. In the Document Formatting group, click the **More** button to open the Style Set gallery. Move the mouse pointer across the icons in the gallery to display their ScreenTips and to observe the Live Previews in the document.

5. Point to the **Lines (Stylish)** style set, which is second from the right in the top row. In the Lines (Stylish) style set, the Heading 1 style applies a dark gray font color, with a light gray line that spans the width of the document. See Figure 5-12.

Figure 5-12	Live Preview of the Lines (Stylish) style set

Lines (Stylish) style set

preview of the Heading 1 style in the Lines (Stylish) style set

preview of the Normal style in the Lines (Stylish) style set

Notice that the theme fonts you specified earlier—Franklin Gothic Medium for headings and Franklin Gothic Book for body text—are still applied, as are the Grayscale theme colors.

6. Click the **Lines (Stylish)** style set. The styles in the document change to reflect the styles in the Lines (Stylish) style set. You can verify this by looking at the Style gallery on the HOME tab.

7. On the ribbon, click the **HOME** tab.

8. In the Styles group, click the **More** button to review the styles available in the Style gallery. The icon for the Heading 1 style indicates that it now applies a black font color. The style also applies a light gray underline, although that is not visible in the Style gallery icon.

9. Click anywhere in the document to close the Style gallery, and then save the document.

INSIGHT

The Set as Default Button: A Note of Caution

The Set as Default button in the Document Formatting group on the DESIGN tab saves the document's current formatting settings as the default for any new blank documents you create in Word. In other words, it saves the current formatting settings to the Normal template. You might find this a tempting option, but, as you will learn in Session 5.2, when working with styles, modifying the Normal template is almost never a good idea. Instead, a better option is to save a document with the formatting you like as a new template. You can then use the template for documents that you want to match your current document.

Customizing Styles

The ability to select a new style set gives you a lot of flexibility when formatting a document. However, sometimes you will want to customize an individual style to better suit your needs. To do so, you can modify or update the style. When you modify a style, you open the Modify Style dialog box, where you then select formatting attributes to add to the style. When you update a style, you select text in the document that is already formatted with the style, apply new formatting to the text, and then update the style to incorporate the new formatting. Updating a style is usually the better choice because it allows you to see the results of your formatting choices in the document, before you change the style itself.

Jonah asks you to update the Heading 1 style for the report by expanding the character spacing and applying italic formatting. You will begin by applying these changes to a paragraph that is currently formatted with the Heading 1 style. Then you can update the Heading 1 style to match the new formatting. As a result, all the paragraphs formatted with the Heading 1 style will be updated to incorporate expanded character spacing and italics.

Changing Character Spacing

The term **character spacing** refers to the space between individual characters. To add emphasis to text, you can expand or contract the spacing between characters. As with line and paragraph spacing, space between characters is measured in points, with one point equal to 1/72 of an inch. To adjust character spacing for selected text, click the Dialog Box Launcher in the Font group on the HOME tab, and then click the Advanced tab in the Font dialog box. Of the numerous settings available on this tab, you'll find two especially useful.

First, the Spacing box allows you to choose Normal spacing (which is the default character spacing for the Normal style), Expanded spacing (with the characters farther apart than with the Normal setting), and Condensed spacing (with the characters closer together than with the Normal setting). With both Expanded and Condensed spacing, you can specify the number of points between characters.

Second, the Kerning for fonts check box allows you to adjust the spacing between characters to make them look like they are spaced evenly. Kerning is helpful when you are working with large font sizes, which can sometimes cause evenly spaced characters to appear unevenly spaced. Selecting the Kerning for fonts check box ensures that the spacing is adjusted automatically.

To add expanded character spacing and italics to a paragraph formatted with the Heading 1 style:

1. In the document, scroll down if necessary and select the **Executive Summary** heading, which is formatted with the Heading 1 style.

2. Make sure the HOME tab is selected on the ribbon.

3. In the Font group, click the **Dialog Box Launcher**. The Font dialog box opens.

4. Click the **Advanced** tab. The Character Spacing settings at the top of this tab reflect the style settings for the currently selected text. The Spacing box is set to Normal. The more advanced options, located in the OpenType Features section, allow you to fine-tune the appearance of characters.

5. Click the **Spacing** arrow, and then click **Expanded**. See Figure 5-13.

Figure 5-13 **Changing character spacing in the Font dialog box**

Expanded option selected

the default setting for Expanded spacing is one point of space between characters

preview of expanded characters

The By box next to the Spacing box indicates that each character is separated from the other by one point of space. You could increase the point setting; but in the current document, one point is fine. The Preview section shows a sample of the expanded character spacing.

Next, you need to apply italic formatting, which you could do from the Font group on the HOME tab. But since you have the Font dialog box open, you'll do it from the Font tab in the Font dialog box instead.

6. In the Font dialog box, click the **Font** tab.

Here you can apply most of the settings available in the Font group on the HOME tab, and a few that are not available in the Font group—such as colored underlines and **small caps** (smaller versions of uppercase letters). You can also hide text from view by selecting the Hidden check box.

7. In the Font style box, click **Italic**. The Preview section of the Font tab shows a preview of the italic formatting applied to the "Executive Summary" heading. See Figure 5-14.

Figure 5-14 Applying italic formatting to text using the Font dialog box

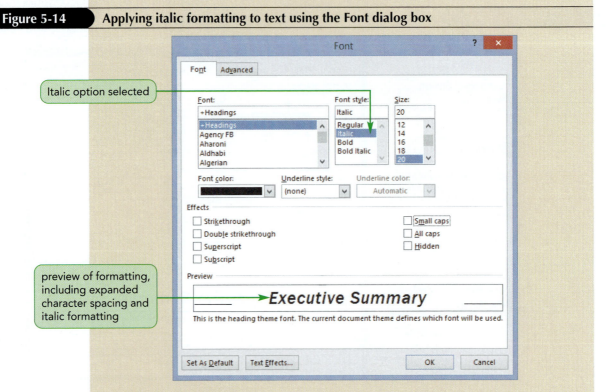

The other font attributes associated with the Heading 1 style are also visible on the Font tab.

8. Click the **OK** button to close the Font dialog box. The selected heading is now italicized, with the individual characters spread slightly farther apart.

9. Click anywhere in the "Executive Summary" heading to deselect the text, and then save the document.

Now that the selected heading is formatted the way you want, you can update the Heading 1 style to match it. When working with styles, it's helpful to open the Styles pane to see more information about the styles in the current style set, so you'll do that next.

Displaying the Styles Pane

The Styles pane shows you more styles than are displayed in the Style gallery. You can click a style in the Styles pane to apply it to selected text, just as you would click a style in the Style gallery.

The Styles pane provides detailed information about each style. In particular, it differentiates between character styles, paragraph styles, and linked styles. A **character style** contains formatting options that affect the appearance of individual characters, such as font style, font color, font size, bold, italic, and underline. When you click a character style, it formats the word that contains the insertion point, or, if text is selected in the document, any selected characters.

A **paragraph style** contains all the character formatting options as well as formatting options that affect the paragraph's appearance—including line spacing, text alignment, tab stops, and borders. When you click a paragraph style, it formats the entire paragraph that contains the insertion point, or, if text is selected in the document, it formats all selected paragraphs (even paragraphs in which just one character is selected).

A **linked style** contains both character and paragraph formatting options. If you click in a paragraph or select a paragraph and then apply a linked style, both the paragraph

styles and character styles are applied to the entire paragraph. If you apply a linked style to a selected word or group of words rather than to an entire paragraph, only the character styles for that linked style are applied to the selected text; the paragraph styles are not applied to the paragraph itself. All of the heading styles in Word are linked styles.

To open the Styles pane to review information about the styles in the current style set:

1. Make sure the HOME tab is selected on the ribbon.

2. In the Styles group, click the **Dialog Box Launcher**. The Styles pane opens on the right side of the document window. See Figure 5-15.

Figure 5-15 Styles pane

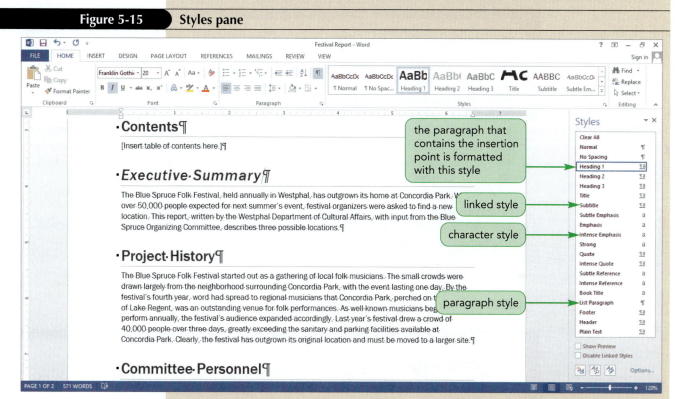

Trouble? If the Styles pane on your computer is floating over the top of the document window, double-click the pane's title bar to dock the Styles pane on the right side of the document window.

The outline around the Heading 1 style in the Styles pane indicates that the insertion point is currently located in a paragraph formatted with the Heading 1 style. A paragraph symbol to the right of a style name indicates a paragraph style, a lowercase letter "a" indicates a character style, and a combination of both a paragraph symbol and a lowercase letter "a" indicates a linked style. You can display even more information about a style by moving the mouse pointer over the style name in the Styles pane.

3. In the Styles pane, move the mouse pointer over **Heading 1**. An arrow is displayed to the right of the Heading 1 style name, and a ScreenTip with detailed information about the Heading 1 style opens below the style name.

The information in the ScreenTip relates only to the formatting applied by default with the Heading 1 style; it makes no mention of italic formatting or expanded character spacing. Although you applied these formatting changes to the "Executive Summary" heading, they are not yet part of the Heading 1 style.

You'll incorporate the new formatting into the Heading 1 style in the next section, when you update the style.

Updating a Style

Word is set up to save all customized styles to the current document by default. In fact, when you update a style, you don't even have a choice about where to save it—the updated style is automatically saved to the current document, rather than to the current template. If for some reason you needed to save a customized style to the current template instead, you would need to modify the style using the Modify Style dialog box, where you could then select the New documents based on this template button to save the modified style to the current template.

INSIGHT

Preserving the Normal Template

Unless you created a document based on an Office.com template, the current template is probably the Normal template. Any changes you make to the Normal template will affect all new, blank documents that you create in Word in the future, so altering the Normal template is not something you should do casually. This is especially important if you are working on a shared computer at school or work. In that case, you should never change the Normal template unless you have been specifically instructed to do so. Many organizations even take the precaution of configuring their networked computers to make changing the Normal template impossible.

If you want to make customized styles available in other document, you can always save the current document as a new template. All future documents based on your new template will contain your new styles. Meanwhile, the Normal template will remain unaffected by the new styles.

Next, you'll use the Styles pane to update the Heading 1 style to include italic formatting with expanded character spacing.

REFERENCE

Updating a Style

- On the ribbon, click the HOME tab.
- In the Styles group, click the Dialog Box Launcher to display the Styles pane.
- In the document, apply formatting to a paragraph or group of characters.
- Click in the formatted paragraph (if you are updating a paragraph or linked style) or in the formatted group of characters (if you are updating a character style).
- In the Styles pane, right-click the style you want to update to display a shortcut menu.
- Click Update *Style* to Match Selection (where *Style* is the name of the style you want to update).

To update the Heading 1 style:

The insertion point must be located in the "Executive Summary" heading to ensure that you update the Heading 1 style with the correct formatting.

1. In the document, make sure the insertion point is located in the paragraph containing the "Executive Summary" heading, which is formatted with the Heading 1 style.

2. In the Styles pane, right-click **Heading 1**. A menu opens with options related to working with the Heading 1 style. See Figure 5-16.

Figure 5-16 **Heading 1 style menu**

italic formatting and expanded character are applied to the paragraph that contains the insertion point

click to save the customized Heading 1 style to the current document

click to open the Modify Style dialog box

3. Click **Update Heading 1 to Match Selection**. The Heading 1 style is updated to reflect the changes you made to the "Executive Summary" heading. As a result, all the headings in the document formatted in the Heading 1 style now have italic formatting with expanded character spacing.

4. Save the document. The updated Heading 1 style is saved along with the document. No other documents are affected by this change to the Heading 1 style.

You can also use the Styles pane to create a new style for a document. You will do that in the next session.

REVIEW

Session 5.1 Quick Check

1. By default, all new, blank documents are based on which template?
2. Which dialog box contains the Go To tab?
3. What are the three components of a document theme?
4. Explain how to select a new style set.
5. Explain how to display the dialog box tab where you can adjust the character spacing for selected text.
6. What is the difference between a character style and a paragraph style?
7. By default, are updated styles saved to the current document or the current template?

Session 5.2 Visual Overview:

You use the options in the Create New Style from Formatting dialog box to create a new style based on the formatting applied to selected text.

By default, each new style is based on the style originally applied to the selected text.

You should give your new style a descriptive name.

The new style will consist of all the formatting applied to the selected text, such as an orange font color and italic formatting.

You can use these options to add additional formatting to the new style.

Clicking the Format button gives you access to more formatting options, including paragraph spacing and border options.

As when modifying an existing style, when creating a new style, it's usually best to save the style only to the current document.

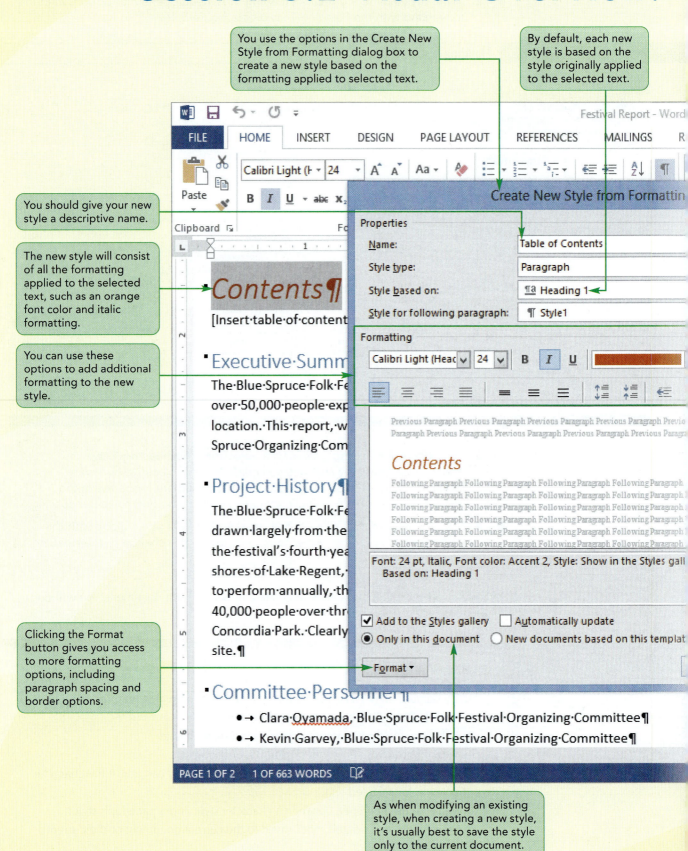

Creating a New Style

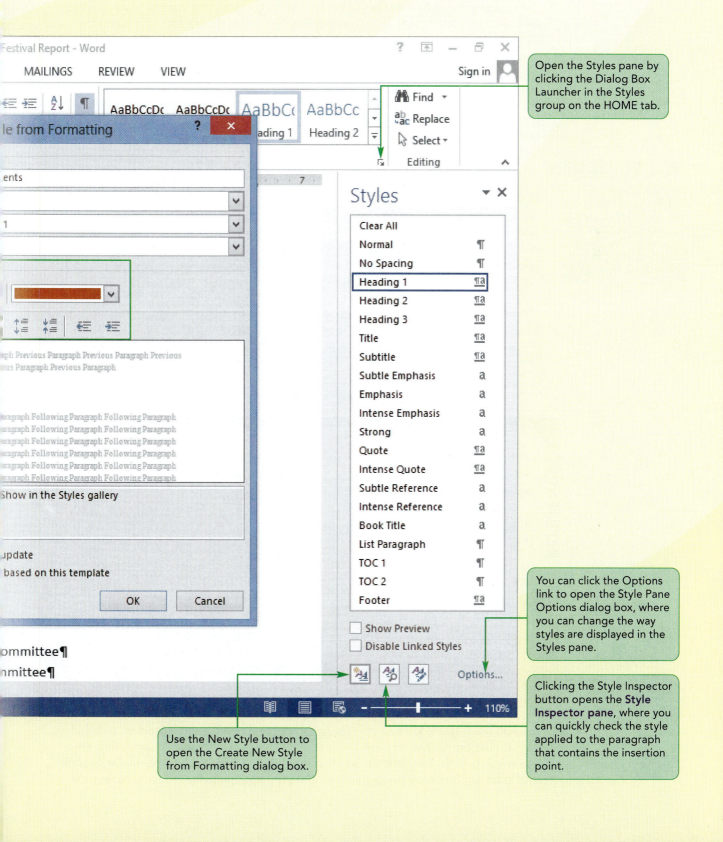

Open the Styles pane by clicking the Dialog Box Launcher in the Styles group on the HOME tab.

You can click the Options link to open the Style Pane Options dialog box, where you can change the way styles are displayed in the Styles pane.

Clicking the Style Inspector button opens the **Style Inspector pane**, where you can quickly check the style applied to the paragraph that contains the insertion point.

Use the New Style button to open the Create New Style from Formatting dialog box.

Creating a New Style

Creating a new style is similar to updating a style, except that instead of updating an existing style to match the formatting of selected text, you save the text's formatting as a new style. By default a new style is saved to the current document. You can choose to save a new style to the current template, but, as explained earlier, that is rarely advisable.

To begin creating a new style, select text with formatting you want to save, and then click the New Style button in the lower-left corner of the Styles pane. This opens the Create New Style from Formatting dialog box, where you can assign the new style a name and adjust other settings.

Remember that all text in your document has a style applied to it, whether it is the default Normal style or a style you applied. When you create a new style based on the formatting of selected text, the new style is based on the style originally applied to the selected text. That means the new style retains a connection to the original style, so that if you make modifications to the original style, these modifications will also be applied to the new style.

TIP

To break the link between a style and the style it is based on, click the Style based on arrow in the Create New Style from Formatting dialog box, and then click (no style).

For example, suppose you need to create a new style that will be used exclusively for formatting the heading "Budget" in all upcoming reports. You could start by selecting text formatted with the Heading 1 style, then change the font color of the selected text to purple, and then save the formatting of the selected text as a new style named "Budget." Later, if you update the Heading 1 style—perhaps by adding italic formatting—the text in the document that is formatted with the Budget style will also be updated to include italic formatting because it is based on the Heading 1 style. Note that the opposite is not true—changes to the new style do *not* affect the style on which it is based.

When creating a new style, you also must consider what will happen when the insertion point is in a paragraph formatted with your new style, and you then press the Enter key to start a new paragraph. Typically, that new paragraph is formatted in the Normal style, but you can choose a different style if you prefer. You make this selection using the Style for following paragraph box in the Create New Style from Formatting dialog box.

In most cases, any new styles you create will be paragraph styles. However, you can choose to make your new style a linked style or a character style instead.

REFERENCE

Creating a New Style

- Select the text with the formatting you want to save as a new style.
- In the lower-left corner of the Styles pane, click the New Style button to open the Create New Style from Formatting dialog box.
- Type a name for the new style in the Name box.
- Make sure the Style type box contains the correct style type. In most cases, Paragraph style is the best choice.
- Verify that the Style based on box displays the style on which you want to base your new style.
- Click the Style for following paragraph arrow, and then click the style you want to use. Normal is usually the best choice.
- To save the new style to the current document, verify that the Only in this document option button is selected; or to save the style to the current template, click the New documents based on this template option button.
- Click the OK button.

Jonah wants you to create a new paragraph style for the "Contents" heading. It should look just like the current Heading 1 style, with the addition of small caps formatting. He asks you to base the new style on the Heading 1 style, and to select the Normal style as the style to be applied to any paragraph that follows a paragraph formatted with the new style.

To format the "Contents" heading in small caps:

1. If you took a break after the last session, make sure the Festival Report document is open in Print Layout view with the nonprinting characters and the ruler displayed. Confirm that the document Zoom level is set at 120% and that the Styles pane is docked on the right side of the document window.

2. Make sure the HOME tab is selected on the ribbon.

3. In the document, select the **Contents** heading.

4. In the Font group, click the **Dialog Box Launcher** and then, in the Font dialog box, click the **Font** tab, if necessary.

5. In the Effects section, click the **Small caps** check box to add a check. See Figure 5-17.

| Figure 5-17 | Formatting the "Contents" heading |

6. Click the **OK** button. The Font dialog box closes, and the "Contents" heading is formatted in small caps.

Now that the text is formatted the way you want, you can save its formatting as a new style.

To save the formatting of the "Contents" heading as a new style:

1. Verify that the **Contents** heading is still selected.

2. In the lower-left corner of the Styles pane, click the **New Style** button ⊞. The Create New Style from Formatting dialog box opens. A default name for the new style, "Style1," is selected in the Name box. The name "Style1" is also displayed in the Style for following paragraph box.

3. Type **Contents** to replace the default style name with the new one. The Style type box contains Paragraph by default, which is the type of style you want to create. The Style based on box indicates that the new Contents style is based on the Heading 1 style, which is also what you want. Notice that the Style for following paragraph box is now blank. You need to select the Normal style.

4. Click the **Style for following paragraph** arrow, and then click **Normal**. See Figure 5-18.

Figure 5-18	Creating a new style

name for the new style

the new style is based on the Heading 1 style

Normal style will be applied to a new paragraph inserted after a paragraph formatted with the new style

leave this check box unselected

5. In the bottom-left corner of the dialog box, verify that the Only in this document button is selected.

Note that, by default, the Automatically update check box is *not* selected. As a general rule, you should not select this check box because it can produce unpredictable results in future documents based on the same template.

If you plan to use a new style frequently, it's helpful to assign a keyboard shortcut to it. Then you can apply the style to selected text simply by pressing the keyboard shortcut.

TIP

To assign a keyboard shortcut to an existing style, right-click the style in the Styles pane, click Modify, click the Format button, and then click Shortcut key.

6. In the lower-left corner of the Create New Style from Formatting dialog box, click the **Format** button, and then click **Shortcut key** to open the Customize Keyboard dialog box. If you wanted to assign a keyboard shortcut to the Contents style, you would click in the Press new shortcut key box, press a combination of keys not assigned to any other function, and then click the Assign button. For now, you can close the Customize Keyboard dialog box without making any changes.

7. Click the **Close** button. You return to the Create New Style from Formatting dialog box.

8. Click the **OK** button. The Create New Style from Formatting dialog box closes. The new Contents style is added to the Style gallery and to the Styles pane. See Figure 5-19.

After you update a style or create a new one, you can create a custom style set that contains the new or updated style.

9. On the ribbon, click the **DESIGN** tab.

10. In the Document Formatting group, click the **More** button, and then click Save as a New Style Set. The Save as a New Style Set dialog box opens, with the QuickStyles folder selected as the save location by default. Only style sets saved to the QuickStyles folder will appear in the Style Set gallery.

In this case, you don't actually want to create a new style set, so you can close the Save as a New Style Set dialog box.

11. Click the **Cancel** button, and then save the document.

Managing Your Styles

INSIGHT

If you create a lot of styles, the Style gallery can quickly become overcrowded. To remove a style from the Style gallery without deleting the style itself, right-click the style in the Styles gallery and then click Remove from Style Gallery.

To delete a style entirely, open the Styles pane, and then right-click the style. What happens next depends on the type of style you are trying to delete. If the style was based on the Normal style, you can click Delete Style (where *Style* is the name of the style you want to delete), and then click Yes. If the style was based on any other style, you can click Revert to *Style* (where *Style* is the style that the style you want to delete was based on), and then click Yes.

If you create a new style and then paste text formatted with your style in a different document, your new style will be displayed in that document's Style gallery and Styles pane. This means that a document containing text imported from multiple documents can end up with a lot of different styles. In that case, you'll probably reformat the document to use only a few styles of your choosing. But what do you do about the remaining, unused styles? You could delete them, but that can be time-consuming. It's sometimes easier to hide the styles that are not currently in use in the document. At the bottom of the Styles pane, click the Options link to open the Style Pane Options dialog box, click the Select styles to show arrow, and then click In current document.

The styles used in the Festival Report document are relatively simple. However, in a long document with many styles, it's easy to lose track of the style applied to each paragraph and the formatting associated with each style. In that case, it's important to know how to display additional information about the document's formatting.

Displaying Information About Styles and Formatting

When you need to learn more about a document's formatting—perhaps because you're revising a document created by someone else—you should start by opening the Styles pane. To quickly determine which style is applied to a paragraph, you can click a paragraph (or select it), and then look to see which style is selected in the Styles pane. To display a brief description of the formatting associated with that style, you can point to the selected style in the Styles pane. However, if you need to check numerous paragraphs in a long document, it's easier to use the Style Inspector pane, which remains open while you scroll through the document and displays only the style for the paragraph that currently contains the insertion point. To see a complete list of all the formatting applied to a paragraph, you can use the **Reveal Formatting pane**. Within the Reveal Formatting pane, you can also choose to compare the formatting applied to two different paragraphs.

Inspecting Styles

You can use the Style Inspector to examine the styles attached to each of the paragraphs in a document. When you are using the Style Inspector, it's also helpful to display the HOME tab on the ribbon so the Style gallery is visible.

To use the Style Inspector pane to examine the styles in the document:

1. On the ribbon, click the **HOME** tab.

2. On page 1, click anywhere in the **[Insert table of contents here.]** paragraph. The Normal style is selected in both the Style gallery and the Styles pane, indicating that the paragraph is formatted with the Normal style.

3. At the bottom of the Styles pane, click the **Style Inspector** button. The Style Inspector pane opens, and is positioned next to the Styles pane. See Figure 5-20.

Figure 5-20 **Style Inspector pane**

Trouble? If the Style Inspector pane on your computer is floating over the top of the document window, double-click the pane's title bar to dock the Style Inspector pane next to the Styles pane.

In the Style Inspector pane, the top box under "Paragraph formatting" displays the name of the style applied to the paragraph that currently contains the insertion point.

4. Press the **Ctrl+↓** keys. The insertion point moves down to the next paragraph, which contains the "Executive Summary" heading. The Style Inspector pane tells you that this paragraph is formatted with the Heading 1 style.

5. Press the **Ctrl+↓** keys as necessary to move the insertion point down through the paragraphs of the document, observing the style names displayed in the Style Inspector pane as well as the styles selected in the Styles pane. Note that the bulleted paragraphs below the "Committee Personnel" heading are formatted with the List Paragraph style. This style is applied automatically when you format paragraphs using the Bullets button in the Paragraph group on the HOME tab.

6. Scroll up and select the paragraph **[Insert table of contents here.]**.

INSIGHT

Finding Styles

Suppose you want to find all the paragraphs in a document formatted with a specific style. One option is to right-click the style in the Styles pane, and then click Select All *Number* Instances, where *Number* is the number of paragraphs in the document formatted with the style.

Another way to find paragraphs formatted with a particular style is by using the Find tab in the Find and Replace dialog box. If necessary, click the More button to display the Format button in the lower-left corner of the Find tab. Click the Format button, click Style, select the style you want in the Find Style dialog box, and then click the OK button. If you want to find specific text formatted with the style you selected, you can type the text in the Find what box on the Find tab, and then click Find Next to find the first instance. If, instead, you want to find any paragraph formatted with the style, leave the Find what box blank.

You can also use the Find and Replace dialog box to find paragraphs formatted with one style and then apply a different style. On the Replace tab, click in the Find what box and use the Format button to select the style you want to find. Then, click in the Replace with box and use the Format button to select the style you want to use as a replacement. Click Find Next to find the first instance of the style, and then click Replace to apply the replacement style. As you've probably guessed, you can also type text in the Find what and Replace with boxes to find text formatted with a specific style and replace it with text formatted in a different style.

Next, Jonah wants you to use the Reveal Formatting panes to learn more about the formatting applied by the Normal and Heading 2 styles.

Examining and Comparing Formatting in the Reveal Formatting Pane

You access the Reveal Formatting pane by clicking a button in the Style Inspector pane. Because the Reveal Formatting pane only describes formatting details without mentioning styles, it's helpful to keep the Style Inspector pane open while you use the Reveal Formatting pane.

To examine formatting details using the Reveal Formatting pane:

1. At the bottom of the Style Inspector pane, click the **Reveal Formatting** button ![Reveal Formatting icon]. The Reveal Formatting pane opens, displaying detailed information about the formatting applied to the selected paragraph. See Figure 5-21.

Figure 5-21 Displaying formatting details in the Reveal Formatting pane

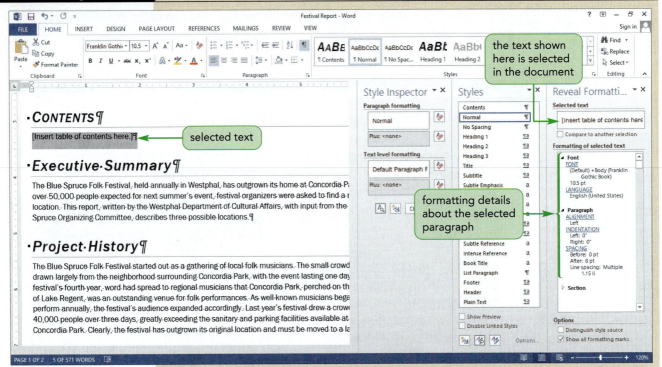

Trouble? If the Reveal Formatting pane on your computer is floating over the top of the document window, double-click the pane's title bar to dock the Reveal Formatting pane next to the other two task panes.

The Formatting of selected text box displays information about the formatting applied to the paragraph that contains the insertion point. Note that this information includes no mention of the style used to apply this formatting, but you can still see the style's name, Normal, displayed in the Style Inspector pane.

Now that you have the Reveal Formatting pane open, you can use it to compare one paragraph's formatting to another's. Jonah asks you to compare text formatted with the Normal style to text formatted with the Heading 2 style.

To compare the formatting of one paragraph to another:

1. In the Reveal Formatting pane, click the **Compare to another selection** check box to select it. The options in the Reveal Formatting pane change to allow you to compare the formatting of one paragraph to that of another. Under Selected text, both text boxes display the selected text, "[Insert table of contents here.]" This tells you that, currently, the formatting applied to the selected text is being compared to itself.

 Now you'll compare this paragraph to one formatted with the Heading 2 style.

2. In the document, scroll down to page 2 and select the text **Washington Park**, which is formatted with the Heading 2 style. The text "Washington Park" is displayed in the Reveal Formatting pane, in the text box below "[Insert table of contents here.]" The Formatting differences section displays information about the formatting applied to the two different paragraphs. See Figure 5-22.

Figure 5-22 Comparing one paragraph's formatting with another's

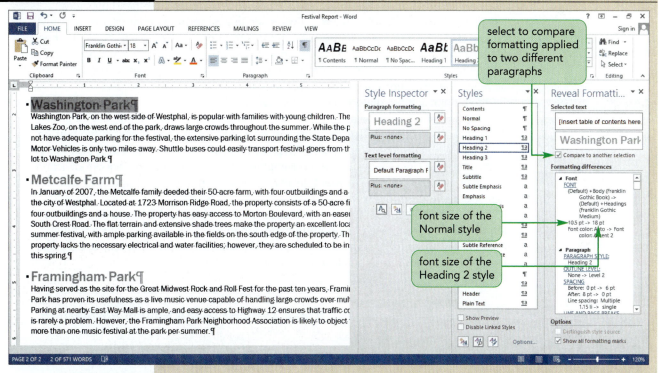

The information in the Reveal Formatting pane is very detailed. But, generally, if you see two settings separated by a hyphen and a greater than symbol, the item on the right relates to the text in the bottom box. For example, in the Font section, you see "10.5 pt -> 18 pt." This tells you that the text in the top text box, "[Insert table of contents here.]," is formatted in a 10.5-point font, whereas the text in the bottom text box, "Washington Park," is formatted in an 18-point font.

The Paragraph section of the Reveal Formatting pane provides some information about two important default settings included with all of Word's heading styles—line and page break settings.

Reviewing Line and Page Break Settings

By default, all of Word's heading styles are set up to ensure that a heading is never separated from the paragraph that follows it. For example, suppose you have a one-page document that includes a heading with a single paragraph of body text after it. Then suppose you add text before the heading that causes the heading and its paragraph of body text to flow down the page so that, ultimately, the entire paragraph of body text moves to page 2. Even if there is room for the heading at the bottom of page 1, it will move to page 2, along with its paragraph of body text. The setting that controls this is the **Keep with next** check box on the Line and Page Breaks tab in the Paragraph dialog box. By default, the Keep with next check box is selected for all headings.

A related setting on the same tab is the **Keep lines together** check box, which is also selected by default for all headings. This setting ensures that if a heading paragraph consists of more than one line of text, the lines of the heading paragraph will never be separated by a page break. This means that if one line of a heading moves from page 1 to page 2, all lines of the heading will move to page 2.

A nonprinting character in the shape of a small black square is displayed next to any paragraph for which either the Keep lines together setting or the Keep with next setting is selected. Because both settings are selected by default for all the heading styles (Heading 1 through Heading 9), you always see this nonprinting character next to text formatted with a heading style. By default, the Keep lines together setting and the Keep with next setting are deselected for all other styles. However, if you have a paragraph of body text that you want to prevent from breaking across two pages, you could apply the Keep lines together setting to that paragraph.

One helpful setting related to line and page breaks—Widow/Orphan control—is selected by default for all Word styles. The term **widow** refers to a single line of text alone at the top of a page. The term **orphan** refers to a single line of text at the bottom of a page. When selected, the **Widow/Orphan control** check box, which is also found on the Line and Page Breaks tab of the Paragraph dialog box, ensures that widows and orphans never occur in a document. Instead, at least two lines of a paragraph will appear at the top or bottom of a page.

You can see evidence of the line and page break settings in the formatting information displayed in the Reveal Formatting pane. Jonah asks you to check these settings for the Festival Report document. You'll start by displaying information about only the paragraph formatted with the Heading 2 style.

To review line and page break settings in the Reveal Formatting pane:

1. In the Reveal Formatting pane, click the **Compare to another selection** check box to deselect it. The Reveal Formatting pane changes to display only information about the formatting applied to "Washington Park," which is currently selected in the document.

 The Style Inspector pane tells you that "Washington Park" is formatted with the Heading 2 style, so all the information in the Reveal Formatting pane describes the Heading 2 style.

2. In the Formatting of selected text box, scroll down to display the entire Paragraph section.

3. Review the information below the blue heading "LINE AND PAGE BREAKS." The text "Keep with next" and "Keep lines together" tells you that these two settings are active for the selected text. The blue headings in the Reveal Formatting pane are actually links that open a dialog box with the relevant formatting settings.

4. In the Formatting of selected text box, click **LINE AND PAGE BREAKS**. The Paragraph dialog box opens, with the Line and Page Breaks tab displayed. See Figure 5-23.

Figure 5-23 **Line and Page Breaks tab in the Paragraph dialog box**

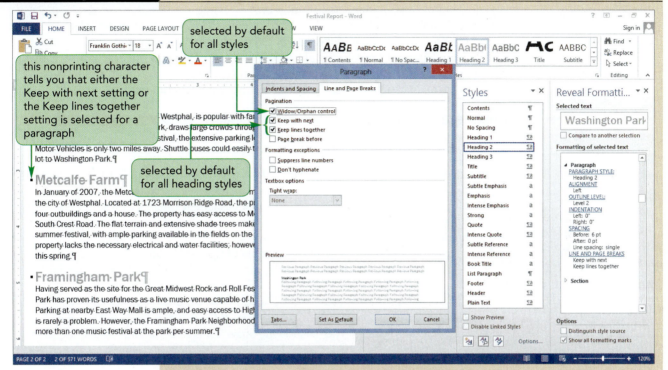

The settings on the tab are the settings for the selected paragraph, which is formatted with the Heading 2 style. The Widow/Orphan control, Keep with next, and Keep lines together check boxes are all selected, as you would expect for a heading style.

You are finished reviewing formatting information, so you can close the Paragraph dialog box and the Reveal Formatting pane.

5. In the Paragraph dialog box, click the **Cancel** button; and then, in the Reveal Formatting pane, click the **Close** button ✕.

6. In the Style Inspector pane, click the **Close** button ✕; and then, in the Styles pane, click the **Close** button ✕.

7. Click anywhere in the document to deselect the "Washington Park" heading.

You are almost finished working on the Festival Report document. Your next task is to add a table of contents.

Generating a Table of Contents

You can use the Table of Contents button in the Table of Contents group on the REFERENCES tab to generate a table of contents that includes any text to which you have applied heading styles. A **table of contents** is essentially an outline of the document. By default, in a table of contents, Heading 1 text is aligned on the left, Heading 2 text is indented slightly to the right below the Heading 1 text, Heading 3 text is indented slightly to the right below the Heading 2 text, and so on.

The page numbers and headings in a table of contents in Word are hyperlinks that you can click to jump to a particular part of the document. When inserting a table of contents, you can insert one of several predesigned formats. If you prefer to select from more options, open the Table of Contents dialog box where, among other settings, you can adjust the level assigned to each style within the table of contents.

REFERENCE

Generating a Table of Contents

- Apply heading styles, such as Heading 1, Heading 2, and Heading 3, to the appropriate text in the document.
- Move the insertion point to the location in the document where you want to insert the table of contents.
- On the ribbon, click the REFERENCES tab.
- In the Table of Contents group, click the Table of Contents button.
- To insert a predesigned table of contents, click one of the Built-In styles in the Table of Contents menu.
- To open a dialog box where you can choose from a variety of table of contents settings, click Custom Table of Contents to open the Table of Contents dialog box. Click the Formats arrow and select a style, change the Show levels setting to the number of heading levels you want to include in the table of contents, verify that the Show page numbers check box is selected, and then click the OK button.

The current draft of Jonah's report is fairly short, but the final document will be much longer. He asks you to create a table of contents for the report now, just after the "Contents" heading. Then, as Jonah adds sections to the report, he can update the table of contents.

To insert a table of contents into the document:

1. Scroll up to display the "Contents" heading on page 1.

2. Below the heading, delete the placeholder text **[Insert table of contents here.]**. Do not delete the paragraph mark after the placeholder text. Your insertion point should now be located in the blank paragraph between the "Contents" heading and the "Executive Summary" heading.

3. On the ribbon, click the **REFERENCES** tab.

4. In the Table of Contents group, click the **Table of Contents** button. The Table of Contents menu opens, displaying a gallery of table of contents formats. See Figure 5-24.

Figure 5-24 Table of Contents menu

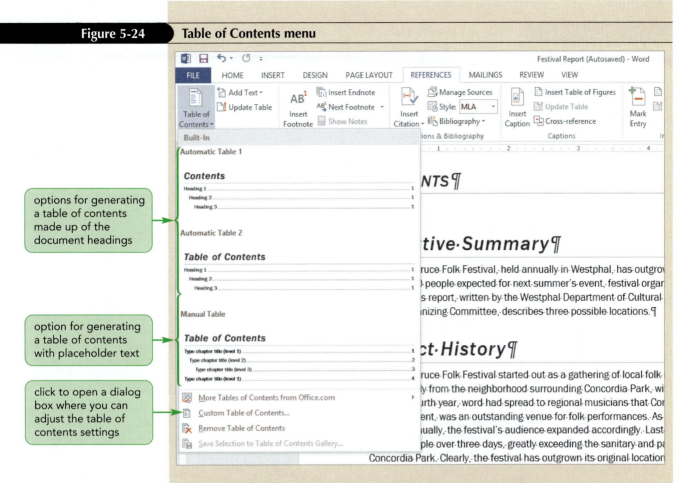

options for generating a table of contents made up of the document headings

option for generating a table of contents with placeholder text

click to open a dialog box where you can adjust the table of contents settings

The Automatic Table 1 and Automatic Table 2 options each insert a table of contents made up of the first three levels of document headings in a predefined format. Each of the Automatic options also includes a heading for the table of contents. Because Jonah's document already contains the heading "Contents," you do not want to use either of these options.

The Manual option is useful only in specialized situations, when you need to type the table of contents yourself—for example, when creating a book manuscript for an academic publisher that requires a specialized format.

You'll use the Custom Table of Contents command to open the Table of Contents dialog box.

5. Below the Table of Contents gallery, click **Custom Table of Contents**. The Table of Contents dialog box opens, with the Table of Contents tab displayed. See Figure 5-25.

Figure 5-25 Table of Contents dialog box

text formatted with the Contents style is included in the table of contents

TOC format will come from the document's template

The Print Preview box on the left shows the appearance of the table of contents in Print Layout view, while the Web Preview box on the right shows what the table of contents would look like if you displayed it in Web Layout view. The Formats box shows the default option, From template, which applies the table of contents styles provided by the document's template.

In the Print Preview section, notice that the Contents heading style, which you created in Session 5.1, appears in the table of contents at the same level as the Heading 1 style.

6. In the lower-right corner of the Table of Contents dialog box, click the **Options** button. The Table of Contents Options dialog box opens. The Styles check box is selected, indicating that Word will compile the table of contents based on the styles applied to the document headings.

7. In the TOC level list, review the priority level assigned to the document's styles, using the vertical scroll bar, if necessary. See Figure 5-26.

Figure 5-26 Checking the styles used in the table of contents

Contents style is assigned the same TOC level as the Heading 1 style

If the box next to a style name is blank, then text formatted with that style does not appear in the table of contents. The numbers next to the Contents, Heading 1, Heading 2, and Heading 3 styles tell you that any text formatted with these styles appears in the table of contents. Heading 1 is assigned to level 1, and Heading 2 is assigned to level 2.

Like Heading 1, the Contents style is assigned to level 1; however, you don't want to include the "Contents" heading in the table of contents itself. To remove any text formatted with the Contents style from the table of contents, you need to delete the Contents style level number.

8. Delete the **1** from the TOC level box for the Contents style, and then click the **OK** button. "Contents" is no longer displayed in the sample table of contents in the Print Preview and Web Preview sections of the Table of Contents dialog box.

9. Click the **OK** button to accept the remaining default settings in the Table of Contents dialog box. Word searches for text formatted with the Heading 1, Heading 2, and Heading 3 styles, and then places those headings and their corresponding page numbers in a table of contents. The table of contents is inserted at the insertion point, below the "Contents" heading. See Figure 5-27.

Figure 5-27 **Table of contents inserted into document**

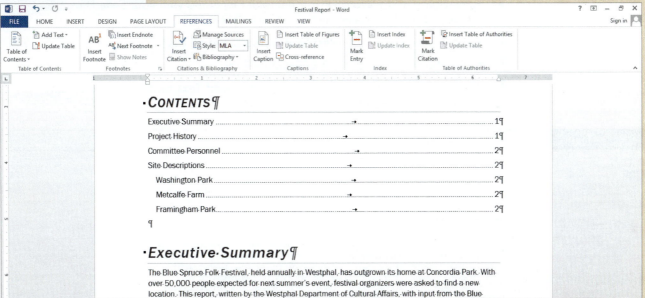

The text in the table of contents is formatted with the TOC styles for the current template. Depending on how your computer is set up, the table of contents might appear on a light gray background.

You can check the hyperlink formatting to make sure the headings really do function as links.

10. Press and hold the **Ctrl** key while you click **Metcalfe Farm** in the table of contents. The insertion point moves to the beginning of the "Metcalfe Farm" heading near the bottom of page 2.

11. Save the document.

Updating a Table of Contents

If you add or delete a heading in the document, or add body text that causes one or more headings to move to a new page, you can quickly update the table of contents by clicking the Update Table button in the Table of Contents group on the REFERENCES tab. To add text that is not formatted as a heading to the table of contents, you can select the text, format it as a heading, and then update the table of contents. However, if you already have the REFERENCES tab displayed, it's more efficient to select the text in the document, use the Add Text button in the Table of Contents group to add a Heading style to the selected text, and then update the table of contents.

Jonah has information on another potential festival site saved as a separate Word file, which he asks you to insert at the end of the Festival Report document. You will do this next, and then add the new heading to the table of contents.

To add a section to the Festival Report document and update the table of contents:

1. Press the **Ctrl+End** keys to move the insertion point to the end of the document, and then press the **Enter** key.

2. On the ribbon, click the **INSERT** tab.

3. In the Text group, click the **Object button arrow**, and then click **Text from File**.

4. Navigate to the Word5 ▸ Tutorial folder included with your Data Files, click **Westphal Flyers**, and then click the **Insert** button.

5. Select the paragraph **Westphal Flyers Baseball Park**.

6. On the ribbon, click the **REFERENCES** tab.

7. In the Table of Contents group, click the **Add Text** button. The Add Text menu opens. See Figure 5-28.

Figure 5-28 Add Text menu

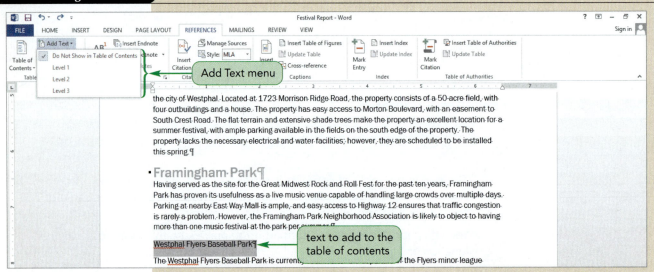

8. Click **Level 2**. The text is formatted with the Heading 2 style to match the headings for the sections about the other possible festival sites. Now that the text is formatted with a heading style, you can update the table of contents.

9. Scroll up so you can see the table of contents, and then, in the Table of Contents group, click the **Update Table** button. The Update Table of Contents dialog box opens.

You can use the Update page numbers only option button if you don't want to update the headings in the table of contents. This option is useful if you add additional content that causes existing headings to move from one page to another. In this case, you want to update the entire table of contents.

10. Click the **Update entire table** option button to select it, and then click the **OK** button. The table of contents is updated to include the "Westphal Flyers Baseball Park" heading. See Figure 5-29.

Figure 5-29 **Updated table of contents**

·CONTENTS¶

Executive·Summary	1¶
Project·History	1¶
Committee·Personnel	2¶
Site·Descriptions	2¶
Washington·Park	2¶
Metcalfe·Farm	2¶
Framingham·Park	2¶
Westphal·Flyers·Baseball·Park	2¶

new heading → Westphal·Flyers·Baseball·Park

11. In the document, scroll down below the "Committee Personnel" heading on page 2, and replace "Jonah Freiburg" with your first and last names.

12. Press the **Ctrl+End** keys to move the insertion point to the last paragraph in the document, which is blank, and then press the **Delete** key to delete the blank paragraph.

13. Save the document.

Now that you are finished working on the Festival Report document, Jonah asks you to use the document to create a template that can be used for all reports issued by the Department of Cultural Affairs.

Saving a Document as a Template

If you frequently need to create a particular type of document, it's a good idea to create your own template for that type of document. Organizations often use templates to ensure that all employees use the same basic format for essential documents. When creating a template, you can save it to any folder on your computer. After you save it, you can open the template to revise it just as you would open any other document. You can also use the Save As option in Backstage view to create a new document based on the template, in which case Word Document will be selected as the file type in the Save As dialog box. If you want to be able to open a new document based on the template from within the New screen, you need to save your template to the Custom Office Templates folder that is installed with Word.

REFERENCE

Saving a Document as a Template

- On the ribbon, click the FILE tab, and then click Export in the navigation bar.
- Click Change File Type, click Template, and then click the Save As button to open the Save As dialog box with Word Template selected in the Save as type box.
- Navigate to the folder in which you want to save the template. To save the template to the Custom Office Templates folder that is installed with Word, click the Documents folder in the Navigation pane of the Save As dialog box, and then click Custom Office Templates.
- In the File name box, type a name for the template.
- Click the Save button.

You will save the new Department of Cultural Affairs template in the location specified by your instructor; however, you'll also save it to the Custom Office Templates folder so you can practice opening a new document based on your template from the New screen in Backstage view.

To save the Festival Report document as a new template:

1. Save the **Festival Report** document to ensure that you have saved your most recent work.

2. On the ribbon, click the **FILE** tab, and then click **Export** in the navigation bar.

3. Click **Change File Type**. The Export screen displays options for various file types you can use when saving a file. For example, you could save a Word document as a Plain Text file that contains only text, without any formatting or graphics. See Figure 5-30.

| Figure 5-30 | Export screen with Change File Type options in Backstage view |

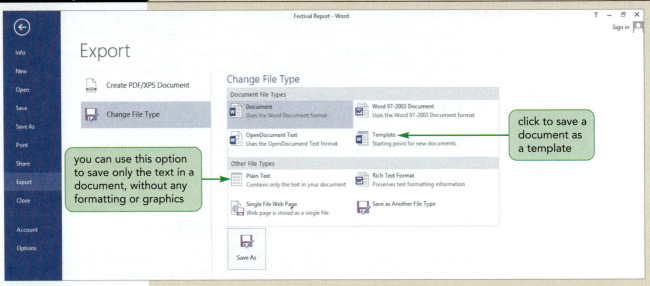

TIP
You can also click the FILE tab, click Save As, and then select Template as the file type.

4. Under Change File Type, click **Template**, and then click the **Save As** button. The Save As dialog box opens with Word Template selected in the Save as type box.

5. If necessary, navigate to the location specified by your instructor. Next, you'll replace the selected, default filename with a new one.

6. In the File name box, type **DCA Report**. See Figure 5-31.

Figure 5-31 Saving a document as a template

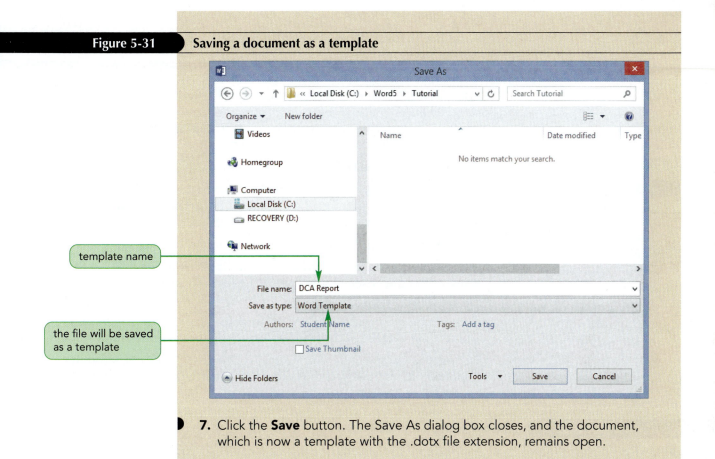

template name

the file will be saved as a template

7. Click the **Save** button. The Save As dialog box closes, and the document, which is now a template with the .dotx file extension, remains open.

PROSKILLS

Written Communication: Standardizing the Look of Your Documents

Large companies often ask their employees to use a predesigned template for all corporate documents. If you work for an organization that does not require you to use a specific template, consider using one anyway in order to create a standard look for all of your documents. A consistent appearance is especially important if you are responsible for written communication for an entire department because it ensures that colleagues and clients will immediately recognize documents from your department.

Be sure to use a professional-looking template. If you decide to create your own, use document styles that make text easy to read, with colors that are considered appropriate in your workplace. Don't try to dazzle your readers with design elements. In nearly all professional settings, a simple, elegant look is ideal.

To make the new DCA Report template really useful to Jonah's colleagues, you need to delete the specific information related to the music festival and replace it with placeholder text explaining the type of information required in each section. In the following steps, you will delete the body of the report and replace it with some placeholder text. Jonah wants to use the current subtitle, "Prepared by the Department of Cultural Affairs," as the subtitle in all department reports, so there's no need to change it. However, the title will vary from one report to the next, so you need to replace it with a suitable placeholder. You'll retain the table of contents. When Jonah's colleagues use the template to create future reports, they can update the table of contents to include any headings they add to their new documents.

To replace the information about the music festival with placeholder text:

1. Scroll up to the top of the document, and then replace the report title "Finding a New Home for the Blue Spruce Folk Festival" with the text **[Insert title here.]**. Be sure to include the brackets so the text will be readily recognizable as placeholder text. To ensure that Jonah's colleagues don't overlook this placeholder, you can also highlight it.

2. On the ribbon, click the **HOME** tab, if necessary.

TIP

To remove highlighting from selected text, click the Text Highlight Color button arrow, and then click No Color.

3. In the Font group, click the **Text Highlight Color** button, and then click and drag the highlight pointer over the text **[Insert title here.]**. The text is highlighted in yellow, which is the default highlight color.

4. Press the **Esc** key to turn off the highlight pointer.

5. Scroll down below the table of contents, and then delete everything in the document after the "Executive Summary" heading so all that remains is the "Executive Summary" heading.

6. Press the **Enter** key to insert a blank paragraph below the heading. Now you can insert a file containing placeholder text for the body of the template.

7. In the blank paragraph under the "Executive Summary" heading, insert the **Placeholder** file from the Word5 ▸ Tutorial folder included with your Data Files. See Figure 5-32.

Figure 5-32 | **Template with placeholder text**

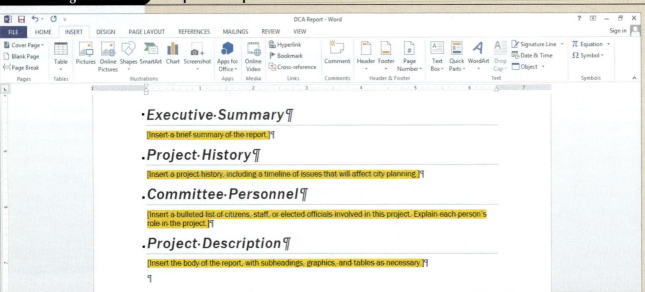

Scroll up to review the document, and notice that the inserted placeholder text is highlighted and the headings are all correctly formatted with the Heading 1 style. When Jonah created the Placeholder document, he formatted the text in the default Heading 1 style provided by the Office theme. But when you inserted the file into the template, Word automatically applied your updated Heading 1 style. Now you can update the table of contents.

8. On the ribbon, click the **REFERENCES** tab.

9. In the Table of Contents group, click the **Update Table** button. The table of contents is updated to include the new headings.

▶ **10.** On the Quick Access Toolbar, click the **Save** button to save your changes to the template just as you would save a document.

At this point, you have a copy of the template stored in the location specified by your instructor. If you closed the template, clicked the FILE tab, and then opened the template again from the same folder, you would be opening the template itself, and not a new document based on the template. If you want to be able to open a new document based on the template from the New screen, you have to save the template to the Custom Office Templates folder. You'll do that next. You can also open a new document based on a template by double-clicking the template file from within File Explorer. You'll have a chance to try that in the Case Problems at the end of this tutorial.

To save the template to the Custom Office Templates folder:

▶ **1.** On the ribbon, click the **FILE** tab, and then click **Save As** in the navigation bar.

▶ **2.** Click **Computer** if necessary, and then click the **Browse** button to open the Save As dialog box.

▶ **3.** In the Navigation pane of the Save As dialog box, click the **Documents** folder, and then, in the file list on the right, double-click **Custom Office Templates**. See Figure 5-33.

Figure 5-33	Saving a template in the Custom Office Templates folder

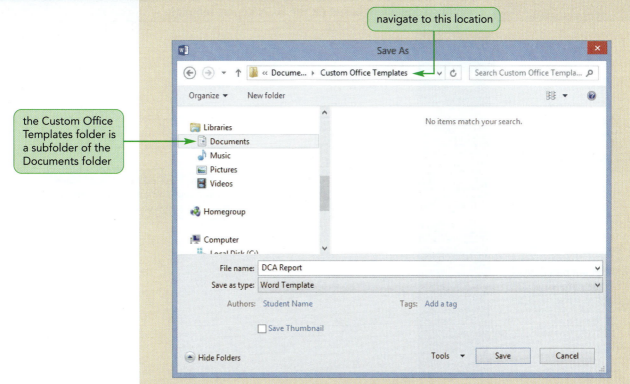

navigate to this location

the Custom Office Templates folder is a subfolder of the Documents folder

▶ **4.** Click the **Save** button to save the template to the Custom Office Templates folder and close the Save As dialog box.

▶ **5.** On the ribbon, click the **FILE** tab, and then click **Close** in the navigation bar to close the template, just as you would close a document.

The template you just created will simplify the process of creating new reports in Jonah's department.

Opening a New Document Based on Your Template

Documents created using a template contain all the text and formatting included in the template. Changes you make to this new document will not affect the template file, which remains unchanged in the Custom Office Templates folder.

Jonah would like you to use the DCA Report template to begin a report on a new literacy program.

To open a new document based on the DCA Report template:

▶ **1.** On the ribbon, click the **FILE** tab, and then click **New** in the navigation bar.

Because you have created and saved a template, the New tab in Backstage view now includes two links—FEATURED and PERSONAL. The FEATURED link is selected by default, indicating that the templates currently featured by Office.com are displayed. To open the template you just saved to the Custom Office Templates folder, you need to display the personal templates instead.

▶ **2.** Click **PERSONAL**. The DCA Report template is displayed as an option on the New screen. See Figure 5-34.

Figure 5-34 **Opening a document based on the DCA Report template**

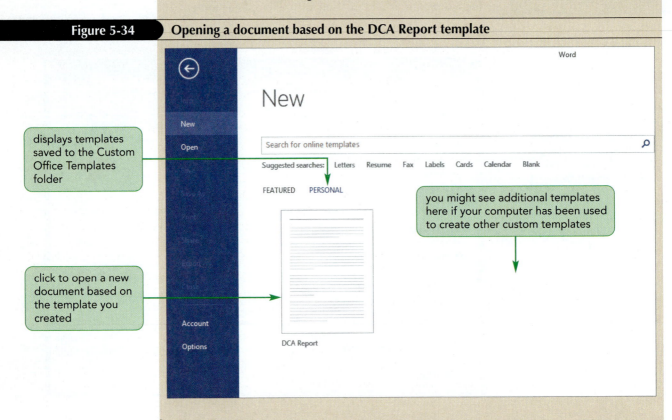

displays templates saved to the Custom Office Templates folder

you might see additional templates here if your computer has been used to create other custom templates

click to open a new document based on the template you created

DCA Report

▶ **3.** Click **DCA Report**. A new document opens containing the text and formatting from the DCA Report template.

▶ **4.** Delete the placeholder **[Insert title here.]** and type **Start Again Literacy Project** in its place.

Jonah and his colleagues will add new material to this report later. For now, you can close it.

5. Save the document as **Literacy Project** in the location specified by your instructor, and then close the document.

Next, to ensure that you can repeat the steps in this tutorial, you will delete the DCA Report template from the Custom Office Templates folder. You can delete it from within the Open dialog box.

6. On the ribbon, click the **FILE** tab, and then in the navigation bar, click **Open**.

7. Click **Computer** if necessary, and then click the **Browse** button.

8. In the navigation pane of the Save As dialog box, click the **Documents** folder, and then double-click **Custom Office Templates**. The DCA Report template is displayed in the file list.

9. Right-click **DCA Report** to display a shortcut menu, and then click **Delete**. The template file is removed from the file list.

10. Click **Cancel** to close the Open dialog box, and then close Backstage view.

Creating a template makes it easy to create a series of similar documents. But what if you want to insert specific text such as an address or email address, or a graphic such as a logo, in many different documents? In that case, you can save the item as a Quick Part.

Creating a New Quick Part

A **Quick Part** is reusable content that you create and that you can then insert into any document later with a single click in the Quick Part gallery. For example, you might create a letterhead with your company's address and logo. To save the letterhead as a Quick Part, you select it and then save it to the Quick Part gallery. Later, you can insert the letterhead into a document by clicking it in the Quick Part gallery.

By default, a new Quick Part appears as an option in the Quick Part gallery. However, you can assign a Quick Part to any gallery you want. For example, you could assign a text box Quick Part to the Text Box gallery so that every time you click the Text Box button on the INSERT tab, you see your text box as one of the options in the Text Box gallery.

Quick Parts are just one type of a larger category of reusable content known as **building blocks**. All of the ready-made items that you can insert into a document via a gallery are considered building blocks. For example, preformatted headers, preformatted text boxes, and cover pages are all examples of building blocks. Some reference sources use the terms "building block" and "Quick Part" as if they were synonyms, but in fact a Quick Part is a building block that you create.

When you save a Quick Part, you always save it to a template; you can't save a Quick Part to an individual document. Which template you save it to depends on what you want to do with the Quick Part. If you want the template to be available to all new documents created on your computer, you should save it to the Building Blocks template. The **Building Blocks template** is a special template that contains all the building blocks installed with Word on your computer, as well as any Quick Parts you save to it. If you want to restrict the Quick Part to only documents based on the current template, or if you want to be able to share the Quick Part with someone else, you should save it to the current template. To share the Quick Part, you simply distribute the template to anyone who wants to use the Quick Part.

REFERENCE

Creating and Using Quick Parts

- Select the text, text box, header, footer, table, graphic, or other item you want to save as a Quick Part. If you want to save only a formatted structure as a Quick Part (such as a formatted text box), delete any text in the item before selecting it.
- On the ribbon, click the INSERT tab.
- In the Text group, click the Quick Parts button, and then click Save Selection to Quick Part Gallery.
- In the Create New Building Block dialog box, replace the text in the Name box with a descriptive name for the Quick Part.
- Click the Gallery arrow, and then choose the gallery to which you want to save the Quick Part.
- To make the Quick Part available to all documents on your computer, select Building Blocks in the Save in box. To restrict the Quick Part to the current template, select the name of the template on which the current document is based.
- Click the OK button.

Jonah has created a text box containing the address and phone number for the Department of Cultural Affairs. He asks you to show him how to save the text box as a Quick Part. He wants the Quick Part to be available to all new documents created on his computer, so you'll need to save it to the Building Blocks template.

To save a text box as a Quick Part:

1. Open the document **DCA** from the Word5 ▶ Tutorial folder included with your Data Files, and then save it as **DCA Address** in the location specified by your instructor.

2. Display nonprinting characters and the rulers, switch to Print Layout view, and then change the Zoom level to **120%**, if necessary.

3. Click the **text box** to select it, taking care to select the entire text box and not the text inside it. When the text box is selected, you'll see the anchor symbol in the left margin.

4. On the ribbon, click the **INSERT** tab.

5. In the Text group, click the **Quick Parts** button. If any Quick Parts have been created on your computer, they will be displayed in the gallery at the top of the menu. Otherwise, you will see only the menu shown in Figure 5-35.

| Figure 5-35 | Quick Parts menu, with no Quick Part gallery visible |

6. At the bottom of the menu, click **Save Selection to Quick Part Gallery**. The Create New Building Block dialog box opens. The name of this dialog box is appropriate because a Quick Part is a type of building block. See Figure 5-36.

Figure 5-36 **Create New Building Block dialog box**

the first word in the text box is used as the name of the new building block by default

the new building block will be saved in the Quick Part gallery by default

the new building block will be saved to the Building Blocks template by default

By default, the first word in the text box, "Department," is used as the default name for the new building block. Also, the default setting in the Gallery box tells you that the new building block will be saved in the Quick Part gallery. You could change this by selecting a different gallery name. The Save in box indicates that the Quick Part will be saved to the Building Blocks template, which means it will be available to all documents on your computer.

Jonah asks you to accept the default settings.

7. Click the **OK** button to accept your changes and close the Create New Building Block dialog box.

You've finished creating the new Quick Part. Now you can try inserting it in the current document.

To insert the new Quick Part into the current document:

1. Press the **Ctrl+End** keys to move the insertion point to the end of the document.

2. In the Text group, click the **Quick Parts** button. This time, the Quick Part gallery is displayed at the top of the menu. See Figure 5-37.

Figure 5-37 **New Quick Part in the Quick Part gallery**

new Quick Part now appears in the gallery at the top of the menu

3. Click the **Department** Quick Part. A copy of the blue text box is inserted at the end of the document, at the insertion point.

4. In the newly inserted text box, replace the phone number with your first and last names, and then save the document.

The new Quick Part is stored in the Quick Part gallery, ready to be inserted into any document. However, after reviewing the Quick Part, Jonah has decided he wants to reformat the address text box and save it as a new Quick Part later. So you'll delete the Quick Part you just created.

To delete a Quick Part:

1. In the Text group, click the Quick Parts button, and then click Building Blocks Organizer to open the Building Blocks Organizer dialog box. Here you see a list of all the building blocks available in your copy of Word, including Quick Parts. See Figure 5-38.

Figure 5-38 Building Blocks Organizer dialog box

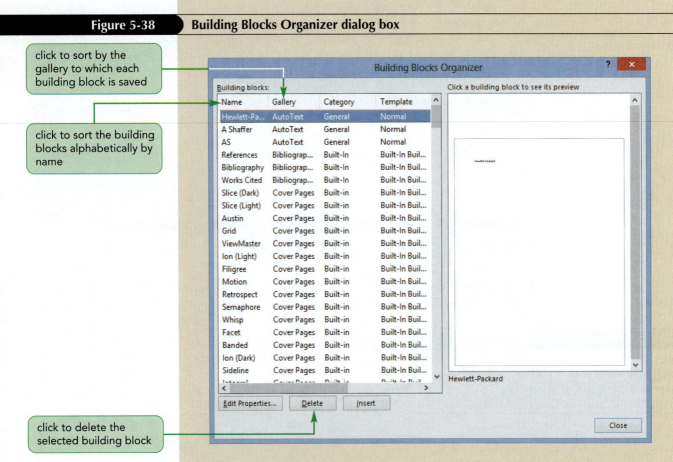

click to sort by the gallery to which each building block is saved

click to sort the building blocks alphabetically by name

click to delete the selected building block

The list on your computer will be somewhat different from the list shown in Figure 5-38.

You can click a building block in the list, and then click the Edit Properties button to open a dialog box where you can rename the building block and make other changes. You can also use the Building Blocks Organizer to delete a building block.

2. Click the **Name** column header to sort the building blocks alphabetically by name, scroll down and click **Department**, click the **Delete** button, and then click the **Yes** button in the warning dialog box. The Department Quick Part is deleted from the list in the Building Blocks Organizer.

3. Click the **Close** button.

4. In the Text group, click the **Quick Parts** button, and then verify that the Department Quick Part is no longer displayed in the Quick Part gallery.

 Finally, to completely delete the Quick Part from the Building Blocks template, you need to save the current document. In the process of saving the document, Word will save your changes to the Building Blocks template, which controls all the building blocks available in your copy of Word. If you don't save the document now, you'll see a warning dialog box later, when you attempt to close the document. It's easy to get confused by the wording of this warning dialog box, and you might end up restoring your Quick Part rather than deleting it. To avoid seeing this warning dialog box entirely, remember to save the current document after you delete a Quick Part.

5. Save the **DCA Address** document and then close it.

Jonah is happy to know how to save Quick Parts to the Building Blocks template. He'll create a new Quick Part later, and save it to a custom template so he can make it available to everyone in his department.

REVIEW

Session 5.2 Quick Check

1. Explain how to create a new style.
2. Is it possible to remove a style from the Style gallery without deleting the style itself?
3. What is the difference between the Style Inspector pane and the Reveal Formatting pane?
4. What must you do if you want to be able to open a new document based on a template you created?
5. What must you do to your document before you can create a table of contents for it?
6. What button can you click to revise a table of contents, and where is that button located?
7. What term is used to refer to all the ready-made items that you can insert into a document via a gallery, such as preformatted headers, preformatted text boxes, and cover pages?
8. What is the relationship between Quick Parts and building blocks?

ASSESS

SAM Projects

Put your skills into practice with SAM Projects! SAM Projects for this tutorial can be found online. If you have a SAM account, go to www.cengage.com/sam2013 to download the most recent Project Instructions and Start Files.

PRACTICE

Review Assignments

Data Files needed for the Review Assignments: DCP Address.docx, Internet.docx, Placeholder Text.docx, Staff.docx

Jonah's DCA Report template is now used for all reports created by employees of the Westphal Department of Cultural Affairs. Inspired by Jonah's success with the template, a project manager in the Department of City Planning (DCP), Suzanne Hansen, wants you to help with a report on expanding high-speed Internet access for city residents. After you format the report, she'd like you to save the document as a new template, and then create a Quick Part. Complete the following steps:

1. Create a new document based on the Oriel report template from Office.com. Replace the [TYPE THE DOCUMENT TITLE] placeholder with your name, and then save the document as **Document from Oriel Template** in the location specified by your instructor. If you see a dialog box explaining that the document is being upgraded to the newest file format, click the OK button.

2. Close the document.

3. Open the document **Internet** from the Word5 ▸ Review folder included with your Data Files, and then save it as **Internet Report** in the location specified by your instructor.

4. Use the Go To feature to review all the headings in the document.

5. In the second line of the "Project Background" section, use the Thesaurus task pane to replace "vital" with a synonym. Use the third synonym in the list of words related to "fundamental."

6. Change the theme colors to Grayscale, and then change the theme's fonts to the Georgia fonts.

7. Save the new colors and fonts as a theme named **DCP Theme** in the location specified by your instructor.

8. Change the style set to Minimalist.

9. Change the formatting of the "Project Background" heading by adding italic formatting and by changing the character spacing so that it is expanded by 1 point between characters.

10. Update the Heading 1 style to match the newly formatted "Project Background" heading.

11. Revise the "Likely Challenges" heading by changing the font size to 16 points, and then update the Heading 2 style to match the newly formatted "Likely Challenges" heading.

12. Create a new paragraph style for the "Contents" heading that is based on the Heading 1 style, but that also includes Gray-25%, Accent 2 paragraph shading and the White, Background 1 font color. Name the new style TOC (short for "Table of Contents"), select Normal as the style for the following paragraph, and then save the new style to the current document.

13. Open the Style Inspector pane, and check the style applied to each paragraph in the document. Then use the Reveal Formatting pane to compare the formatting applied to the "Contents" heading with the formatting applied to the "Project Background" heading.

14. Delete the placeholder below the "Contents" heading, and then insert a custom table of contents that does not include the TOC style. Except for excluding the TOC style, use the default settings in the Table of Contents dialog box.

15. Insert a blank paragraph at the end of the document, and then insert the Word file **Staff** from the Word5 ▸ Review folder included with your Data Files. Add the text **Contributing Staff Members** to the table of contents as a Level 1 heading, and then delete the blank paragraph at the end of the document.

16. At the end of the report, replace "Student Name" with your first and last names.

17. Save your changes to the Internet Report document.

18. Save the Internet Report document as a Word Template named **DCP Report** in the location specified by your instructor.

19. On page 1, replace the title "HIGH-SPEED INTERNET ACCESS FOR ALL RESIDENTS" with the placeholder text **[INSERT TITLE HERE.]**, and then highlight the placeholder in the default yellow color.

20. Delete everything in the report after the table of contents.

21. In the blank paragraph below the table of contents, insert the Word file **Placeholder Text** from the Word5 ▸ Review folder included with your Data Files.

22. At the end of the template, replace "Student Name" with your first and last names, and then update the table of contents.

23. Save the template, save it again to the Custom Office Templates folder, and then close it.

24. Open a new document based on the DCP Report template, enter **New South Side Bike Path** as the document title, save the new document as **Bike Path** in the location specified by your instructor, and then close it.

25. Delete the DCP Report template from the Custom Office Templates folder.

26. Open the document **DCP Address** from the Word5 ▸ Review folder included with your Data Files, and then save it as a Word Template named **DCP Address Box** in the location specified by your instructor.

27. Save the green text box as a Quick Part named **Address**. Save it to the DCP Address Box template, not to the Building Blocks template.

28. Save the template and close it.

Case Problem 1

APPLY

Data File needed for this Case Problem: Write.docx

Write and Wrong Quality Assurance Arshia Husain is the founder and owner of Write and Wrong Quality Assurance, a consulting firm that reviews book manuscripts from a variety of fields for technical accuracy. When one of Arshia's consultants reviews a book, he or she must fill out a report consisting of tables that detail various issues. By the time a consultant finishes reviewing an entire book, the report can be quite long. Therefore, it's important that each report include a table of contents on the first page. Your job is to create a template that Arshia and her consultants can use when reviewing manuscripts. Complete the following steps:

1. Open the document **Write** from the Word5 ▸ Case1 folder included with your Data Files, and then save it as **Write and Wrong** in the location specified by your instructor.

2. Use Go To to review all the tables in the document.

3. Change the document's theme to the View theme, and then change the theme colors to Red Orange. Change the style set to Basic (Simple).

4. Highlight in yellow the four instances of placeholder text below the company name and above the "Contents" heading.

5. Format the "Contents" heading by changing the character spacing to Expanded, with the default amount of space between the expanded characters. Increase the font size to 18 points, add italic formatting, and then change the font color to one shade darker, using the Red, Accent 1, Darker 50% font color. Update the Heading 1 style for the current document to match the newly formatted heading.

6. Create a new paragraph style for the company name at the top of the document that is based on the Heading 1 style, but that also includes Red, Accent 3, Darker 25% paragraph shading; White, Background 1 font color; 20-point font size; and center alignment. Add 16 points of paragraph spacing before the paragraph and 6 points after. Name the new style **Company**. Select the Normal style as the style for the following paragraph, and save the style to the current document.

7. Remove the Company style from the Style Gallery.

8. Below the "Contents" heading, replace the yellow highlighted placeholder text with a custom table of contents that does not include the Company style.

9. In the document, delete the paragraph containing the "Contents" heading, and then update the table of contents to remove "Contents" from it.

10. Click in the paragraph before the table of contents, and increase the spacing after it to 24 points.

11. Add the "General Recommendations" heading, which is above the last table, to the table of contents at the same level as the "Organization" heading.

12. Above the second table, replace "Illustrations" with a synonym. In the Thesaurus task pane, use the fourth synonym in the list of words related to "artworks," and then update the table of contents to include the revised heading.

13. Save your changes to the Write and Wrong document, and then save the Write and Wrong document as a template named **Issue Report** in the location specified by your instructor.

14. Save one of the blank tables as a Quick Part named **Additional Table**. Save the Quick Part to the Issue Report template.

15. Save the template to its current location, and then save the template again to the Custom Office Templates folder. Close the template.

16. Open a document based on your new template, and then save the new document as **System** in the location specified by your instructor.

17. Replace the publication title placeholder with the text **System Management: Theory and Practice**.

18. At the end of the document, insert the text **Special Issues**, format it with the Heading 1 style, and then insert the Additional Table Quick Part in a new paragraph after the heading.

19. Update the table of contents to include the new heading.

20. Save and close the document, and then delete the Issue Report template from the Custom Office Templates folder.

Case Problem 2

There are no Data Files needed for this Case Problem.

CREATE

Blooming Town Beekeepers Paula Spalding is president of Blooming Town Beekeepers, an association of people interested in raising bees in urban settings. The group plans to have a booth at an upcoming gardening exposition, and Paula is preparing a series of handouts to share with people who are interested in becoming beekeepers. Your job is to create a sample handout for Paula based on an Office.com template. In the handout, you'll use drawings from Office.com, which Paula will eventually replace with her own photos. Your completed handout should look like the one shown in Figure 5-39.

Figure 5-39 Handout for Blooming Town Beekeepers

if you can't find these drawings on Office.com, you can use similar drawings

© 2014 Cengage Learning; Images used with permission of Microsoft Corporation

After you finish the handout, Paula would like you to use it as the basis for a new template that she can use for future handouts. Complete the following steps:

1. Open a new document based on the Office.com template named "Seasonal event flyer (summer)."

2. Save the new document as **Beekeepers** in the location specified by your instructor. Notice that the left side of the document is laid out using a table structure. The two colored boxes on the right side are laid out using a separate table structure.

3. Replace the [DATE] placeholder with the text **LIFE IS SWEET**.

4. Replace the [EVENT TITLE HERE] placeholder with the text **BE A BEEKEEPER**.

5. Replace the [Event Description Heading] placeholder with the text **Blooming Town Beekeepers can show you how!**

6. Replace the placeholder text below "Blooming Town Beekeepers can show you how!" with the following text: **Raising bees and harvesting honey in an urban environment is an increasingly popular activity. Our association of friendly apiarists can show you how to get started**.

7. Delete the "replace with LOGO" picture in the lower-left corner of the page, and then replace it with the clip art drawing of a bee shown in Figure 5-39. Find the image by going to Office.com and searching for the keyword **bee**. If you cannot find the image shown in Figure 5-39, choose a similar image. If necessary, resize the inserted picture to make it approximately one-inch square.

8. Replace the remaining placeholder text as follows:
 - [Add Key Event Info Here!]: **Monthly outings to the homes of local apiarists!**
 - [Don't Be Shy—Tell Them Why They Can't Miss It!]: **Free weekly hive health inspections!**
 - [One More Point Here!]: **Meeting schedule at www.beekeepers.cengage.com**
 - [Add More Great Info Here!]: **Sign up for a beekeeper buddy!**
 - [You Have Room for Another One Here!]: **All the honey you can eat!**
 - [COMPANY NAME]: **BLOOMING TOWN BEEKEEPERS**
 - [Street Address][City, ST ZIP Code][Telephone]: **Paula Spalding 555-555-5555**
 - [Web Address]: **paula@bees.cengage.com**

9. Insert a manual line break after Paula's last name, and then delete the extra space before her phone number so the phone number is centered under her name.

10. Replace Paula's first and last names with your name. If you can't fit your entire name, abbreviate it, perhaps by using only your first initial and your last name, so that it fits on one line.

11. Delete the [Dates and Times] placeholders.

12. At the top of the document, replace the photo of the girls holding ice cream cones with a drawing of a beehive from Office.com. Use the beehive drawing shown earlier in Figure 5-39, which you can find by searching for the keyword **hive**. If you cannot locate the image shown in Figure 5-39, choose a similar image. Change its text wrap setting to In Front of Text, and then resize and position it appropriately within the table cell.

13. Attach a comment to the first paragraph in the green column that reads: **This document contains** *number* **paragraph styles,** *number* **linked styles, and** *number* **character styles**. For each type of style, replace *number* with the correct number.

14. Save the document, and then save it again as a template named **Beekeepers Flyer** in the location specified by your instructor.

15. Delete the comment.

16. In the green shaded column, replace the four paragraphs of text with four instances of the placeholder text **[Insert beekeeper information.]**.

17. Save the bee picture as a Quick Part named **Bee** to the Beekeepers Flyer template.

18. Save and close the template.

Case Problem 3

RESEARCH

Data Files needed for this Case Problem: Formatting.docx, MLA.docx

MLA-Style Research Paper Template You are a research assistant for Jasper Leff, a professor of history at a local college. Professor Leff requires his students to write three MLA-style research papers each semester. To ensure that his students use the proper format, he wants to provide them with a Word template for an MLA-style research paper. He asks you to create the template for him. You'll start by doing some research on specifications for the MLA style. Complete the following steps:

1. Open the document **Formatting** from the Word5 ► Case3 folder included with your Data Files, and then save it as **MLA Formatting** in the location specified by your instructor.

2. Change the document's theme to the Slice theme, and then change the theme colors to Violet II. Change the style set to Lines (Simple).

3. Using a source on the web or an up-to-date print publication, research the characteristics of an MLA-style research paper.

4. In the MLA Formatting document, fill in the table with the necessary information about MLA-style research papers.

5. Save the MLA Formatting document, and then use it for reference as you complete the remaining steps in this Case Problem.

6. Open the document **MLA** from the Word5 ► Review folder included with your Data Files, and then save it as a Word template named **MLA Paper** in the location specified by your instructor.

7. Review the template, which contains three paragraphs that Professor Leff generated by typing =lorem() and pressing the Enter key. You can use this text as body text to separate placeholder headings in the template.

8. Edit the comment to insert the appropriate examples after each colon. Format the examples in the comment with yellow highlighting.

9. Add your name in the appropriate location for an MLA-style research paper, and then add place-holder text in square brackets for any missing document elements. For example, for the paper title, you should insert **[Title]**. Format all the placeholder text as it would be formatted if it were text in an actual MLA-style research paper. Include one **[Heading]** placeholder after the first paragraph of body text, and one more after the second paragraph of body text. Include the appropriate title for the bibliography. For the bibliography itself, include the left-aligned placeholder text **[Insert bibliography using Word's bibliography feature.]**.

10. Format the body text appropriately, and then apply the appropriate line and paragraph spacing to the entire template.

11. Save the MLA Paper template, and then close it.

Case Problem 4

CHALLENGE

Data File needed for this Case Problem: Haley's.docx, Sharpe.docx

Sharpe Sustainability Designs You are the assistant to Haley Sachjten, the publications director at Sharpe Sustainability Designs, an engineering firm in New York City. Sharpe specializes in projects that minimize a building's impact on the environment by using as many recycled materials as possible and by maximizing energy efficiency. Haley often uses Word styles in the reports and other publica-tions she creates for the company, and she wants to learn more about managing styles. In particular, she wants to learn how to copy styles from one document to another. She's asked you to help her explore the Style Pane Options, Manage Styles, and Organizer dialog boxes. She would also like your help creating a Quick Part for a memo header. Complete the following steps:

1. Open the document **Sharpe** from the Word5 ▶ Case4 folder included with your Data Files, and then save it as **Sharpe Memo** in the location specified by your instructor. This document contains the text you will eventually save as a Quick Part. It contains all the default styles available in any new Word document, as well as one style, named Memo Header, which Haley created earlier. In the following steps, you will copy styles from another document to this document. For now, you can close it.

2. Close the Sharpe Memo document.

3. Open the document **Haley's** from the Word5 ▶ Case4 folder included with your Data Files, and then save it as **Haley's Styles** in the location specified by your instructor. This document contains styles created by Haley, which you will copy to the Sharpe Memo document. It also includes sample paragraphs formatted with Haley's styles, and one paragraph that you will format with a style later in this Case Problem.

⊕ **Explore** 4. Open the Style Pane Options dialog box, and then change the settings so the Styles pane displays only the styles currently used in the document, in alphabetical order. Before closing this dialog box, verify that these settings will only be applied to the current document rather than to new documents based on this template.

5. Press the Print Screen button on your keyboard to capture a screenshot that shows the Styles pane displaying only the styles used in the current document, in alphabetical order.

6. Paste the screenshot at the end of the document, just as you would paste text that you had previously copied to the Clipboard.

⊕ **Explore** 7. At the bottom of the Styles pane, click the Manage Styles button, and then click the Import/Export button to open the Organizer dialog box. Close the Normal template and open the Sharpe Memo document instead. (*Hint*: On the right, under the In Normal box, click the Close File button, and then click the Open File button. In the Open dialog box, you'll need to display all files.)

⊕ **Explore** 8. Copy the following styles from the Haley's Styles document to the Sharpe Memo document: Company Name, Department, Energy, and Product Description. Then copy the Memo style from the Sharpe Memo document to the Haley's Styles document.

9. Close the Organizer dialog box, and then save your changes to the Sharpe Memo document.

10. In the Haley's Styles document, apply the Memo style to the "Sample of Memo style" paragraph at the end of the document.

11. Save the Haley's Styles document, and then close it.

12. Open the **Sharpe Memo** document, and then review the list of styles in the Styles pane to locate the styles you just copied to this document from the Haley's Styles document.

13. Apply the Company Name style to "Sharpe Sustainability Designs" in the second paragraph.

14. Save the Sharpe Memo document, and then save it again as a template named **Sharpe Memo Template** in the location specified by your instructor.

15. Select all of the text in the document, and then save it as a Quick Part named **Green Memo**. Save the Quick Part to the current template, not to the Building Blocks template.

16. Change the Paragraph shading for the first paragraph to blue, using the Blue, Accent 5 color in the top row of the Shading gallery, and then save the document text as a new Quick Part named **Blue Memo**. Again, save the Quick Part to the current template.

17. Delete all the text from the document, save the Sharpe Memo Template file, and then close it.

⊕ **Explore** 18. Open a File Explorer window, and then navigate to the location where you saved the Sharpe Memo Template file. Open a new document based on the template by double-clicking the template's filename in File Explorer.

19. Save the new document as **Sample Memo** in the location specified by your instructor, insert the Blue Memo Quick Part in the document, and then save and close the document.

WORD

Using Mail Merge

Creating a Form Letter, Mailing Labels, and a Telephone Directory

Case | *Candlestick Artisan Bakery*

Maiya Kandel owns Candlestick Artisan Bakery in Carlyle, Louisiana. The bakery has just moved to a new, expanded location with an attached coffee shop. Maiya hopes to encourage customers to visit the coffee shop by offering a free cup of coffee and pastry. She plans to send a form letter to regular customers announcing the new location and the opening of the coffee shop.

The form letter will also contain specific details for individual customers, such as name, address, and each customer's favorite type of bread and pastry. Maiya has already written the text of the form letter. She plans to use the mail merge process to add the personal information for each customer to the form letter. She asks you to revise the form letter by inserting a date field in the document that will display the current date. Then she wants you to use the Mail Merge feature in Word to create customized letters for her customers. After you create the merged letters, she'd like you to create mailing labels for the envelopes and a directory of employee phone numbers. Finally, you'll convert some text to a table so that it can be used in a mail merge.

STARTING DATA FILES

Word6 → **Tutorial**
Bakery.docx
Customer.docx
Phone.docx

Review
Additional.docx
Business.docx
Free.docx

Case1
Fund.docx

Case2
Client.xlsx
Directory.docx
Labels.docx
New.docx

Case3
Oxford.docx
Springwell.txt

Case4
(none)

Session 6.1 Visual Overview:

Use the Start Mail Merge button to select the type of main document you are creating. Possible types include letters, envelopes, emails, labels, and directories.

The Select Recipients button allows you to select an existing data source or create a new one in the New Address List dialog box.

The MAILINGS tab contains four groups of options that, working left to right, walk you through the process of creating a mail merge.

To complete the mail merge, you click the Finish & Merge button. This creates a new document, the **merged document**, which contains a separate copy of the main document for each record in the data source.

The Edit Recipient List button allows you to make changes to a data source.

A **merge field** tells Word what information you want to retrieve from the data source and display in the main document. For example, a merge field might retrieve a name or a zip code. A merge field is enclosed by angled brackets, or **chevrons**, like this: << >>.

You can use the options in the Write & Insert Fields group to insert merge fields in the main document.

The options in the Preview Results group allow you to see how the data from the data source will look in the merged document.

Mail Merge

A **data source** is a file that contains information, such as names and addresses, that is organized into fields and records; the merge fields cause the information in the data source to be displayed in the main document. You can use a Word table, an Excel spreadsheet, or other types of files as data sources, or you can create a new data source using the New Address List dialog box.

The header row contains the names of the fields in the data source.

A data source stores information in a table.

Each row, or **record**, contains a complete set of information, such as an address for a customer.

main document

data source

The **main document** contains placeholders called merge fields.

merged document

Inserting a Date Field

A **date field** is an instruction that tells Word to display the current date in a document. Although a date field is not a merge field, it's common to use date fields in mail merge documents to ensure that the main document always includes the current date. Every time you open a document containing a date field, it updates to display the current date. To insert a date field, you use the Date and Time dialog box to select from a variety of date formats. In addition to displaying the date with the current day, month, and year, you can include the current time and the day of the week. Word inserts a date field inside a content control; unless the content control is selected, the field looks like ordinary text.

Maiya asks you to insert a date field in her document before beginning the mail merge process.

To open Maiya's document and insert a date field:

▶ 1. Open the document **Bakery** from the Word6 ▸ Tutorial folder included with your Data Files, and then save it as **Bakery Main Document** in the location specified by your instructor.

▶ 2. Display nonprinting characters, switch to Print Layout view, display the rulers, and then set the Zoom level to **120%**.

▶ 3. Review the contents of the letter. Notice that the fourth paragraph includes the placeholder text "[INSERT DATE FIELD]."

▶ 4. Delete the placeholder text **[INSERT DATE FIELD]**, taking care not to delete the paragraph mark after the placeholder text. When you are finished, the insertion point should be located in the second blank paragraph of the document, with two blank paragraphs below it.

▶ 5. On the ribbon, click the **INSERT** tab.

▶ 6. In the Text group, click the **Date & Time** button. The Date and Time dialog box opens. See Figure 6-1.

| Figure 6-1 | Date and Time dialog box |

The Available formats list provides options for inserting the current date and time. In this case, you want to insert the date as a content control in a format that includes the complete name of the month, the date, and the year (for example, March 11, 2016).

▶ **7.** In the Available formats list, click the third format from the top, which is the month, date, and year format.

▶ **8.** Make sure the **Update automatically** check box is selected so the date is inserted as a content control that updates every time you open the document.

▶ **9.** Click the **OK** button. The current date is inserted in the document. At this point, it looks like ordinary text. To see the content control, you have to click the date.

▶ **10.** Click the date to display the content control. If you closed the document and then opened it a day later, the content control would automatically display the new date. See Figure 6-2.

Figure 6-2 **Date field inside content control**

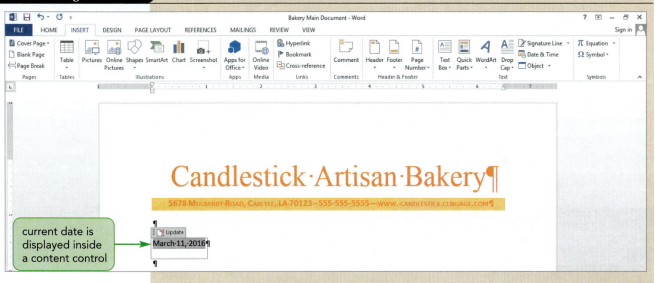

current date is displayed inside a content control

▶ **11.** Scroll down to display the letter's closing, change "Maiya Kandel" to your first and last names, and then scroll back up to the beginning of the letter.

▶ **12.** Save the document.

Now that the document contains the current date, you can begin the mail merge process.

Performing a Mail Merge

When you perform a mail merge, you insert individualized information from a data source into a main document. A main document can be a letter or any other kind of document containing merge fields that tell Word where to insert names, addresses, and other variable information from the data source. When you **merge** the main document with information from the data source, you produce a new document called a merged document. The Session 6.1 Visual Overview summarizes mail merge concepts.

Maiya's main document is the letter shown in the Session 6.1 Visual Overview. In this session, you will insert the merge fields shown in this letter. You'll also create Maiya's data source, which will include the name and address of each customer. The data source will also include information about each customer's favorite bread and pastry.

You can perform a mail merge by using the Mail Merge task pane, which walks you through the steps of performing a mail merge. You access the Mail Merge task pane by clicking the Start Mail Merge button in the Start Mail Merge group, and then clicking the Step-by-Step Mail Merge Wizard command on the menu. You can also use the options on the MAILINGS tab, which streamlines the process and offers more tools. In this tutorial, you'll work with the MAILINGS tab to complete the mail merge for Maiya. The MAILINGS tab organizes the steps in the mail merge process so that you can move from left to right across the ribbon using the buttons to complete the merge.

Starting the Mail Merge and Selecting a Main Document

The first step in the mail merge process is selecting the type of main document. Your choice of main document type affects the commands that are available to you later as you continue through the mail merge process, so it's important to make the correct selection at the beginning. In this case, you will use a letter as the main document.

To start the mail merge process and select a main document:

1. On the ribbon, click the **MAILINGS** tab.

 Notice that most of the buttons in the groups on the MAILINGS tab are grayed out, indicating the options are unavailable. These options only become available after you begin the mail merge process and select a data source.

2. In the Start Mail Merge group, click the **Start Mail Merge** button. The Start Mail Merge menu opens, as shown in Figure 6-3.

| Figure 6-3 | Start Mail Merge menu |

The first five options on the menu allow you to specify the type of main document you will create. Most of the options involve print items, such as labels and letters, but you can also select an email message as the type of main document. In this case, you'll create a letter.

3. Click **Letters**. The Start Mail Merge menu closes.

 Next, you need to select the list of recipients for Maiya's letter; that is, you need to select the data source.

4. In the Start Mail Merge group, click the **Select Recipients** button. The Select Recipients menu allows you to create a new recipient list, use an existing list, or select from Outlook Contacts (the address book in Outlook).

Because Maiya hasn't had a chance to create a data source yet, she asks you to create one.

5. Click **Type a New List**. The New Address List dialog box opens, as shown in Figure 6-4.

| Figure 6-4 | New Address List dialog box |

fields included in the new data source by default

The default fields for a data source are displayed in this dialog box. Before you begin creating the data source, you need to identify the fields and records Maiya wants you to include.

Creating a Data Source

As described in the Session 6.1 Visual Overview, a data source is a file that contains information organized into fields and records. Typically, the data source for a mail merge contains a list of names and addresses, but it can also contain email addresses, telephone numbers, and other data. Various kinds of files can be used as the data source, including several types of files from Office applications, such as a Word table stored in a document file, an Excel workbook, or an Access database. You can also use a file from another kind of database, such as one created by a corporation to store its sales information.

When performing a mail merge, you'll usually select an existing data source file—created in another application—that already contains the necessary information. However, in this tutorial, you'll create a new data source in Word and then enter the data into it so you can familiarize yourself with the basic structure of a data source. After creating the new data source, you'll save the file in its default format as an Access database file, with an .mdb file extension. Microsoft Outlook also uses MDB files to store contact information—in which case they are referred to as Microsoft Office Address Lists files.

When you create a new data source, Word provides a number of default fields, such as First Name, Last Name, and Company. You can customize the data source by adding new fields and removing the default fields that you don't plan to use. When creating a data source, keep in mind that each field name must be unique; you can't have two fields with the same name.

The Microsoft Office Address Lists file you will create in this session will contain information about Maiya's customers, including each customer's name, address, preferred type of bread, and favorite pastry. Maiya collected all the necessary information by asking customers to sign up for the bakery's mailing list. Figure 6-5 shows one of the forms she used to collect the information.

Figure 6-5 Customer comment card

Candlestick Artisan Bakery

Sign up for our mailing list to receive special offers and information about our latest recipes.

First Name_____ Last Name _____

Street Address _____ Apartment _____

City _____ Zip Code _____

Email Address _____

Home delivery customers, please include a phone number (home or cell) _____

Which of our whole grain breads do you like best? _____

Which of our all-butter pastries do you like best? _____

© 2014 Cengage Learning

The information on each form will make up one record in the data source. Each blank on the form translates into one field in the data source as shown in Figure 6-6.

Figure 6-6 Fields to include in the data source

Field Names	Description
First Name	Customer's first name
Last Name	Customer's last name
Address Line 1	Customer's street address
Address Line 2	Additional address information, such as an apartment number
City	City
State	State
ZIP Code	Zip code
E-mail Address	Customer's email address
Phone	Customer's home or cell phone number
Favorite Bread	Customer's favorite type of bread
Favorite Pastry	Customer's favorite pastry

© 2014 Cengage Learning

Even though you won't need the customers' email addresses or phone numbers to complete the mail merge, you can still include them in the data source. That way, Maiya can reuse the data source in future mail merges to send emails to her customers, or when creating a directory of phone numbers for home delivery customers.

Creating a Data Source for a Mail Merge

- On the ribbon, click the MAILINGS tab.
- In the Start Mail Merge group, click the Select Recipients button, and then click Type a New List to open the New Address List dialog box.
- To select the fields for your data source, click the Customize Columns button to open the Customize Address List dialog box.
- To delete an unnecessary field, select it, click the Delete button, and then click the Yes button.
- To add a new field, click the Add button, type the name of the field in the Add Field dialog box, and then click the OK button.
- To rearrange the order of the field names, click a field name, and then click the Move Up button or the Move Down button.
- To rename a field, click a field name, click the Rename button to open the Rename Field dialog box, type a new field name, and then click the OK button to close the Rename Field dialog box.
- Click the OK button to close the Customize Address List dialog box.
- In the New Address List dialog box, enter information for the first record, click the New Entry button, and then enter the information for the next record. Continue until you are finished entering all the information for the data source, and then click the OK button to open the Save Address List dialog box.
- Type a name for the data source in the File name box. By default, Word will save the file to the My Data Sources folder unless you specify another save location. Click the Save button. The file is saved with the .mdb file extension.

You're ready to create the data source for the form letter using information Maiya has given you for three of her customers. However, before you begin entering information, you need to customize the list of fields to include only the fields Maiya requires.

To customize the list of fields before creating the data source:

1. In the New Address List dialog box, click the **Customize Columns** button. The Customize Address List dialog box opens. Here you can delete the fields you don't need, add new ones, and arrange the fields in the order you want. You'll start by deleting fields.

2. In the Field Names box, verify that **Title** is selected, and then click the **Delete** button. A message is displayed asking you to confirm the deletion.

3. Click the **Yes** button. The Title field is deleted from the list of field names.

4. Continue using the Delete button to delete the following fields: **Company Name**, **Country or Region**, and **Work Phone**.

 Next, you need to add some new fields. When you add a new field, it is inserted below the selected field, so you'll start by selecting the last field in the list.

5. In the Field Names box, click **E-mail Address**, and then click the **Add** button. The Add Field dialog box opens, asking you to type a name for your field. See Figure 6-7.

REFERENCE

Figure 6-7	Add Field dialog box

6. Type **Favorite Bread** and then click the **OK** button. The field "Favorite Bread" is added to the Field Names list.

7. Use the Add button to add the **Favorite Pastry** field below the Favorite Bread field.

 Next, you need to move the E-mail Address field up above the Home Phone field, so that the fields are in the same order as they appear on the form shown in Figure 6-5.

8. Click **E-mail Address**, and then click the **Move Up** button. The E-mail Address field moves up, so it is now displayed just before the Home Phone field.

 Finally, because Maiya's form asks customers to fill in a home or cell phone number, you need to change "Home Phone" to simply "Phone."

9. Click **Home Phone**, and then click the **Rename** button to open the Rename Field dialog box.

10. In the To box, replace "Home Phone" with **Phone** and then click the **OK** button to close the Rename Field dialog box and return to the Customize Address List dialog box. See Figure 6-8.

Figure 6-8	Customized list of field names

new merge fields

renamed field

11. Click the **OK** button in the Customize Address List dialog box to close it and return to the New Address List dialog box. This dialog box reflects the changes you just made. For instance, it no longer includes the Title field. The fields are listed in the same order as they appeared in the Customize Address List dialog box.

▶ **12.** Use the horizontal scroll bar near the bottom of the New Address List dialog box to scroll to the right to display the Favorite Bread and Favorite Pastry fields. See Figure 6-9.

Figure 6-9 ▶ **Changes made to New Address List dialog box**

new fields

Organizing Field Names

INSIGHT

Although the order of field names in the data source doesn't affect their placement in the main document, it's helpful to arrange field names logically in the data source so you can enter information quickly and efficiently. For example, you'll probably want the First Name field next to the Last Name field. To make it easier to transfer information from a paper form to a data source, it's a good idea to arrange the fields in the same order as on the form, just like you did in the preceding steps. Also, note that if you include spaces in your field names, Word will replace the spaces with underscores when you insert the fields into the main document. For example, Word transforms the field name "First Name" into "First_Name."

Now that you have specified the fields you want to use, you are ready to enter the customer information into the data source.

Entering Data into a Data Source

Maiya has given you three completed customer information forms and has asked you to enter the information from the forms into the data source. You'll use the New Address List dialog box to enter the information. As you press the Tab key to move right from one field to the next, the dialog box will scroll to display fields that are not currently visible.

To enter data into a record using the New Address List dialog box:

▶ **1.** In the New Address List dialog box, scroll to the left to display the First Name field.

▶ **2.** Click in the **First Name** field, if necessary, and then type **Monica** to enter the first name of the first customer.

Do not press the spacebar after you finish typing an entry in the New Address List dialog box.

TIP

You can press the Shift+Tab keys to move the insertion point to the previous field.

3. Press the **Tab** key to move the insertion point to the Last Name field.

4. Type **Piedmont** and then press the **Tab** key to move the insertion point to the Address Line 1 field.

5. Type **45 Fairet Avenue** and then press the **Tab** key to move the insertion point to the Address Line 2 field.

6. Type **Apartment 5A** and then press the **Tab** key to move the insertion point to the City field.

7. Type **Carlyle** and then press the **Tab** key to move the insertion point to the State field.

8. Type **LA** and then press the **Tab** key to move the insertion point to the ZIP Code field.

9. Type **70129** and then press the **Tab** key to move the insertion point to the E-mail Address field.

10. Type **piedmont@sample.cengage.com** and then press the **Tab** key to move the insertion point to the Phone field.

11. Type **555-555-5555** and then press the **Tab** key to move the insertion point to the Favorite Bread field.

12. Type **sourdough** and then press the **Tab** key. The insertion point is now in the Favorite Pastry field, which is the last field in the data source.

13. Type **profiterole** and then stop. Do *not* press the Tab key.

14. Use the horizontal scroll bar to scroll to the left, and then review the data in the record. See Figure 6-10.

Figure 6-10 **Completed record**

You have finished entering the information for the first record of the data source. Now you're ready to enter information for the next two records. You can create a new record by clicking the New Entry button, or by pressing the Tab key after you have finished entering information into the last field for a record. Note that within a record, you can leave some fields blank. For example, only two of Maiya's three customers included information for the Address Line 2 field.

To add additional records to the data source:

1. In the New Address List dialog box, click the **New Entry** button. A new, blank record is created.

2. Enter the information shown in Figure 6-11 for the next two records. To start the Edward Chavezi record, press the **Tab** key after entering the Favorite Pastry field for the Peter Ahrens record.

Figure 6-11		Information for records 2 and 3								
First Name	Last Name	Address Line 1	Address Line 2	City	State	ZIP Code	E-mail Address	Phone	Favorite Bread	Favorite Pastry
Peter	Ahrens	603 Pine Tree Road	P.O. Box 6375	Baptiste	LA	70128	ahrens@sample.cengage.com	555-555-5555	raisin	cinnamon roll
Edward	Chavezi	278 S. Linder		Carlyle	LA	70123	chavezi@sample.cengage.com	555-555-5555	sesame wheat	kolache

© 2014 Cengage Learning

Note that the Address Line 2 field should be blank in the Edward Chavezi record.

Trouble? If you start a fourth record by mistake, click the Delete Entry button to remove the blank fourth record.

You have entered the records for three customers. Maiya's data source eventually will contain hundreds of records for Candlestick Artisan Bakery customers. The current data source, however, contains the records Maiya wants to work with now. Next, you need to save the data source.

Saving a Data Source

TIP

Within File Explorer, the file type for a Microsoft Office Address Lists file is listed as "Microsoft Access Database."

After you finish entering data for your new data source, you can close the New Address List dialog box. When you do so, the Save Address List dialog box opens, where you can save the data source using the default file type, Microsoft Office Address Lists.

To save the data source:

1. In the New Address List dialog box, click the **OK** button. The New Address List dialog box closes, and the Save Address List dialog box opens, as shown in Figure 6-12.

Figure 6-12 **Saving the data source**

default save location is a subfolder of the My Documents folder

type the filename for your data source here

The Save as type box indicates that the data source will be saved as a Microsoft Office Address Lists file. The File name box is empty; you need to name the file before saving it.

▶ **2.** Click the **File name** box, if necessary, and then type **Bakery Data**.

Unless you specify another save location, Word will save the file to the My Data Sources folder, which is a subfolder of the My Documents folder.

In this case, you'll save the data source in the same location in which you saved the main document.

▶ **3.** Navigate to the location in which you saved the main document, and then click the **Save** button. The Save Address List dialog box closes, and you return to the main document.

The next step in the mail merge process is to add the necessary merge fields to the main document. For Maiya's letter, you need to add merge fields for the inside address, for the salutation, and for each customer's favorite type of pastry and bread.

PROSKILLS

Decision Making: Planning Your Data Source

When creating a data source, think beyond the current mail merge task to possible future uses for your data source. For example, Maiya's data source includes both an E-mail Address field and a Phone field—not because she wants to use that information in the current mail merge project, but because she can foresee needing these pieces of information at a later date to communicate with her customers. Having all relevant customer information in one data source will make it easier to retrieve and use the information effectively.

In some cases, you'll also want to include information that might seem obvious. For example, Maiya's data source includes a State field even though all of her current customers live in or around Carlyle, Louisiana. However, she included a State field because she knows that her pool of addresses could expand sometime in the future to include residents of other states.

Finally, think about the structure of your data source before you create it. Try to break information down into as many fields as seems reasonable. For example, it's always better to include a First Name field and a Last Name field, rather than simply a Name field, because including two separate fields makes it possible to alphabetize the information in the data source by last name. If you entered first and last names in a single Name field, you could only alphabetize by first name.

If you're working with a very small data source, breaking information down into as many fields as possible is less important. However, it's very common to start with a small data source, and then, as time goes on, find that you need to continually add information to the data source, until you have a large file. If you failed to plan the data source adequately at the beginning, the expanded data source could become difficult to manage.

Another important issue is what type of file you use to store your data source. In this session, you created a data source from within Word and saved it as a Microsoft Office Address Lists file. However, in most situations, you should save your data source in a spreadsheet or database file so that you can utilize the data manipulation options a spreadsheet program or database program provides.

Inserting Merge Fields

When inserting merge fields into the main document, you must include proper spacing around the fields so that the information in the merged document will be formatted correctly. To insert a merge field, you move the insertion point to the location where you want to insert the merge field, and then click the Insert Merge Field button arrow in the Write & Insert Fields group.

For Maiya's letter, you will build an inside address by inserting individual merge fields for the address elements. The letter is a standard business letter, so you'll place merge fields for the customer's name and address below the date.

To insert a merge field in the main document:

▶ **1.** Click in the second blank paragraph below the date.

▶ **2.** In the Write & Insert Fields group, click the **Insert Merge Field button arrow**. A menu opens with the names of all the merge fields in the data source. Note that the spaces in the merge field names have been replaced with underscores. See Figure 6-13.

Figure 6-13 Insert Merge Field menu

Figure 6-13 Insert Merge Field menu

menu contains all the merge fields in the data source

space replaced with underscore

Trouble? If the Insert Merge Field dialog box opens, you clicked the Insert Merge Field button instead of the Insert Merge Field button arrow. Close the dialog box and repeat Step 2.

3. Click **First_Name**. The Insert Merge Field menu closes, and the merge field is inserted into the document.

The merge field consists of the field name surrounded by double angled brackets << >>, also called chevrons.

Trouble? If you make a mistake and insert the wrong merge field, click to the left of the merge field, press the Delete key to select the field, and then press the Delete key again to delete it.

4. In the Write & Insert Fields group, click the **Highlight Merge Fields** button. The First_Name merge field is displayed on a gray background, making it easier to see in the document. See Figure 6-14.

TIP

You can only insert merge fields into a main document using the tools on the MAILINGS tab or in the Mail Merge task pane. You cannot type merge fields into the main document—even if you type the angled brackets.

Figure 6-14 First_Name merge field highlighted in main document

merge field is surrounded by chevrons

merge field with gray highlight

Later, when you merge the main document with the data source, Word will replace the First_Name merge field with information from the First Name field in the data source.

Now, you're ready to insert the merge fields for the rest of the inside address. You'll add the necessary spacing and punctuation between the merge fields as well. You might be accustomed to pressing the Shift+Enter keys to start a new line in an inside address without inserting paragraph spacing. However, because your data source includes a record in which one of the fields (the Address Line 2 field) is blank, you need to press the Enter key to start each new line. As you will see later in this tutorial, this ensures that Word hides the Address Line 2 field in the final merged document whenever that field is blank. To maintain the proper spacing in the main document, you'll adjust the paragraph spacing after you insert all the fields.

To insert the remaining merge fields for the inside address:

▶ **1.** Press the **spacebar** to insert a space after the First_Name merge field, click the **Insert Merge Field button arrow**, and then click **Last_Name**.

▶ **2.** Press the **Enter** key to start a new paragraph, click the **Insert Merge Field button arrow**, and then click **Address_Line_1**. Word inserts the Address_Line_1 merge field into the form letter.

▶ **3.** Press the **Enter** key, click the **Insert Merge Field button arrow**, and then click **Address_Line_2**. Word inserts the Address_Line_2 merge field into the form letter.

▶ **4.** Press the **Enter** key, insert the **City** merge field, type **,** (a comma), press the **spacebar** to insert a space after the comma, and then insert the **State** merge field.

▶ **5.** Press the **spacebar**, and then insert the **ZIP_Code** merge field. The inside address now contains all the necessary merge fields. See Figure 6-15.

Figure 6-15 **Main document with merge fields for inside address**

Next, you will adjust the paragraph spacing for the inside address.

▶ **6.** Select the first three paragraphs of the inside address.

▶ **7.** On the ribbon, click the **HOME** tab.

▶ **8.** In the Paragraph group, click the **Line and Paragraph Spacing** button, and then click **Remove Space After Paragraph**. The paragraph spacing is removed, so that the paragraphs of the inside address are now correctly spaced.

You can now add the salutation of the letter, which will contain each customer's first name.

To insert the merge field for the salutation:

▶ **1.** Insert a new paragraph after the ZIP_Code field, type **Dear** and then press the **spacebar**.

▶ **2.** On the ribbon, click the **MAILINGS** tab.

▶ **3.** In the Write & Insert Fields group, click the **Insert Merge Field button arrow**, click **First_Name** to insert this field into the document, and then type **:** (a colon).

▶ **4.** Save the document.

You'll further personalize Maiya's letter by including merge fields that will allow you to reference each customer's favorite type of pastry and bread.

To add merge fields for each customer's favorite type of pastry and bread:

▶ **1.** Scroll down to display the third paragraph in the body of the letter, which begins "Please join us...."

▶ **2.** In the third paragraph in the body of the letter, select the placeholder text **[FAVORITE PASTRY]**, including the brackets. You'll replace this phrase with a merge field. Don't be concerned if you also select the space following the closing bracket.

▶ **3.** Insert the **Favorite_Pastry** merge field. Word replaces the selected text with the Favorite_Pastry merge field.

▶ **4.** Verify that the field has a single space before it and after it. Add a space on either side if necessary.

▶ **5.** Replace the placeholder text "[FAVORITE BREAD]" in the third paragraph in the body of the letter with the **Favorite_Bread** merge field, and adjust the spacing as necessary. See Figure 6-16.

| Figure 6-16 | Main document after inserting merge fields |

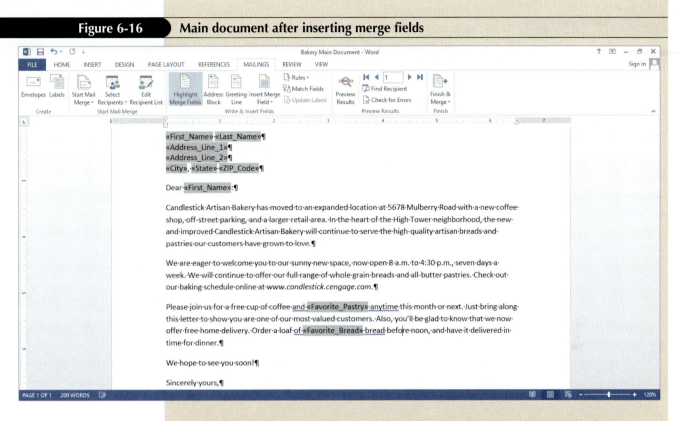

Trouble? The text before and after the inserted merge fields might be marked with a wavy blue underline because Word mistakenly identifies the text as a grammatical error. You can ignore the wavy underlines.

6. Save the document.

The main document now contains all the necessary merge fields.

Previewing the Merged Document

Your next step is to preview the merged document to see how the letter will look after Word inserts the information for each customer. When you preview the merged document, you can check one last time for any missing spaces between the merge fields and the surrounding text. You can also look for any other formatting problems, and, if necessary, make final changes to the data source.

To preview the merged document:

1. In the Preview Results group, click the **Preview Results** button. The data for the first record (Monica Piedmont) replaces the merge fields in the form letter. On the ribbon, the Go to Record box in the Preview Results group shows which record is currently displayed in the document. See Figure 6-17.

Figure 6-17 Letter with merged data for first record

Note that the inside address, which includes information from the Address Line 2 field, contains a total of four lines.

2. Carefully check the Monica Piedmont letter to make sure the text and formatting are correct, and make any necessary corrections. In particular, make sure that the spacing before and after the merged data is correct; it is easy to accidentally omit spaces or add extra spaces around merge fields.

3. In the Preview Results group, click the **Next Record** button . The data for Peter Ahrens is displayed in the letter. As with the preceding record, the inside address for this record includes four lines of information.

4. Click the **Next Record** button again to display the data for Edward Chavezi in the letter. In this case, the inside address includes only three lines of information. See Figure 6-18.

Figure 6-18 Address for third record

5. In the Preview Results group, click the **First Record** button to redisplay the first record in the letter (with data for Monica Piedmont).

The main document of the mail merge is complete. Now that you have previewed the merged documents, you can finish the merge.

Merging the Main Document and the Data Source

When you finish a merge, you can choose to merge directly to the printer. In other words, you can choose to have Word print the merged document immediately without saving it as a separate file. Alternatively, you can merge to a new document, which you can save using a new filename. If your data source includes an E-mail Address field, you can also create a mail merge in email format, generating one email for every email address in the data source.

Maiya wants to save an electronic copy of the merged document for her records, so you'll merge the data source and main document into a new document.

To complete the mail merge:

▶ **1.** In the Finish group, click the **Finish & Merge** button. The Finish & Merge menu displays the three merge options. See Figure 6-19.

Figure 6-19	Finishing the merge

▶ **2.** In the Finish & Merge menu, click **Edit Individual Documents**. The Merge to New Document dialog box opens. Here, you need to specify which records to include in the merge. You want to include all three records from the data source.

▶ **3.** Verify that the **All** option button is selected, and then click the **OK** button. Word creates a new document named Letters1, which contains three pages— one for each record in the data source. See Figure 6-20.

Figure 6-20 Merged document

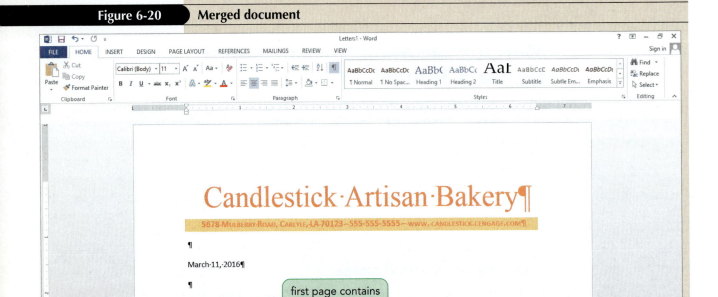

In this new document, the merge fields have been replaced by the specific names, addresses, and so on from the data source.

4. Scroll down and review the contents of the document. Note that each letter is addressed to a different customer, and that the favorite bread and pastry vary from one letter to the next.

5. Scroll back to the first page of the document, and as you scroll, notice that the letters are separated by Next Page section breaks.

6. Save the merged document in the location specified by your instructor, using the filename **Bakery Merged Letters 1**.

7. Close the **Bakery Merged Letters 1** document. The document named "Bakery Main Document" is now the active document.

 After completing a merge, you need to save the main document. That ensures that any changes you might have made to the data source during the course of the mail merge are saved along with the main document.

8. Save and close the **Bakery Main Document** file.

Note that if you need to take a break while working on a mail merge, you can save the main document and close it. The data source and field information are saved along with the document. When you're ready to work on the merge again, you can open the main document and update the connection to the data source. You'll see how this works at the beginning of the next session, when you will learn how to use additional mail merge features.

REVIEW

Session 6.1 Quick Check

1. Define the following:
 a. data source
 b. record
 c. date field
2. What is the first step in performing a mail merge?
3. List at least three types of files that you can use as data sources in a mail merge.
4. Explain how to use the options on the MAILINGS tab to insert a merge field into a main document.
5. What are the two ways to start a new record in the New Address List dialog box?
6. List the three different ways to complete a merge.

Session 6.2 Visual Overview:

The Edit Recipient List button opens the Mail Merge Recipients dialog box.

In the Mail Merge Recipients dialog box, you can make changes that affect individual records or the structure and organization of the data source itself.

To sort a data source according to the contents of a particular field, click that field's column header. To sort in ascending order, click the field header once. To sort in descending order, click it twice.

A checkmark indicates that a record will be included in the merge. By default, all records are checked. To omit a record from the merge, click its check box to delete the checkmark.

To make changes to the contents of individual records, select the data source in the Data Source box, and then click the Edit button to open the Edit Data Source dialog box.

To sort by more than one field, click the Sort command.

You can click the Filter command to further customize a data source. When you **filter** data, you temporarily display only records that contain a particular value in a particular field.

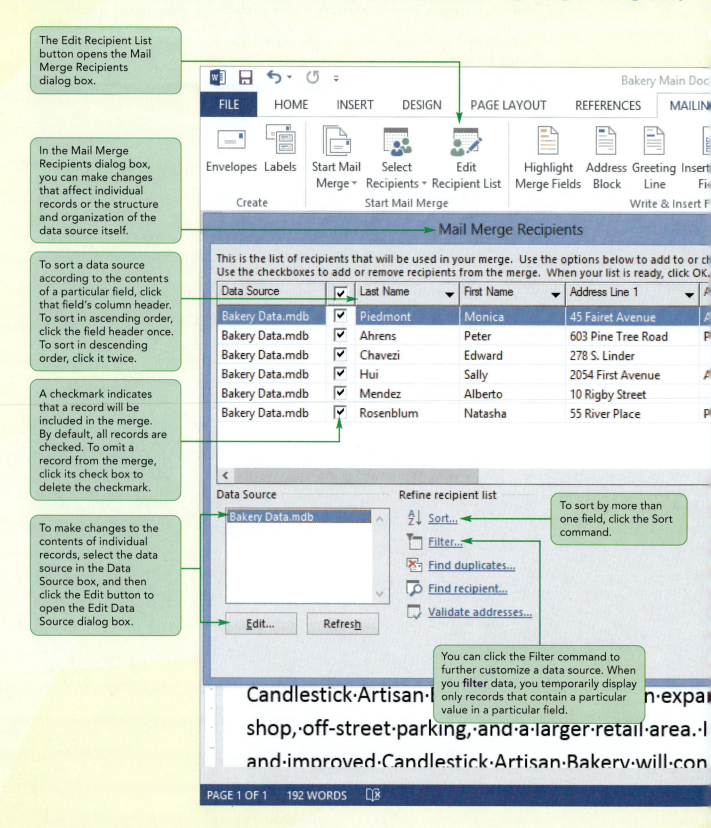

Editing a Data Source

To edit a record in the Edit Data Source dialog box, click in the field you want to change, delete the current contents, and then type something new.

Click the New Entry button to add new records to the data source.

To delete a record from the data source, click any field in the record, and then click the Delete Entry button.

Reopening a Main Document

Performing a mail merge creates a connection between the main document file and the data source file. This connection persists even after you close the main document and exit Word. The connection is maintained as long as you keep both files in their original locations. The two files don't have to be in the same folder; each file just has to remain in the folder it was in when you first performed the mail merge.

When you reopen a main document, you see a warning dialog box explaining that data from a database (that is, the data source) will be placed in the document you are about to open. You can click Yes to open the document with its connection to the data source intact.

PROSKILLS

Teamwork: Sharing Main Documents and Data Sources

In professional settings, a mail merge project often involves files originating from multiple people. The best way to manage these files depends on your particular situation. For instance, at a small office supply company, the marketing manager might supply the text of a main document introducing monthly sales on printer supplies, while the sales manager might supply an updated list of names and addresses of potential customers every month. Suppose that you are the person responsible for performing the mail merge on the first of every month. You'll be able to work more efficiently if you, the marketing manager, and the sales manager agree ahead of time on one storage location for the project. For example, you might set up a special folder on the company network for storing these files.

In large companies that maintain massive databases of customer information, a data source is typically stored at a fixed network location. In those situations, you'll probably need to work with the technical staff who manage the databases to gain access to the data sources you need for your mail merge projects. Maintaining the security of such data sources is extremely important, and you usually can't access them without a password and the appropriate encryption software.

Maiya has new customer information she wants you to add to the data source that you used in the previous mail merge, and she wants to perform another merge with the new data. To add the new customer information, you will start by opening the Bakery Main Document, which is linked to the data source.

To reopen the main document with its connection to the data source intact:

1. Open the document **Bakery Main Document** from the location in which you stored it in Session 6.1.

 Word displays a warning message indicating that opening the document will run a SQL command. SQL (usually pronounced *sequel*) is the database programming language that controls the connection between the main document and the data source.

2. Click the **Yes** button to open the main document with its link to the data source intact.

3. On the ribbon, click the **MAILINGS** tab.

 The main document displays the data for the last record you examined when you previewed the merged document (Monica Piedmont). You can alternate between displaying the merge fields and the customer data by toggling the Preview Results button on the MAILINGS tab.

Trouble? If you see the merge fields instead of the data for one of the bakery customers, skip to Step 5.

4. In the Preview Results group, click the **Preview Results** button to deselect it. The merge fields are displayed in the main document. At the beginning of the letter, the date field, which is not a merge field, continues to display the current date.

5. If necessary, highlight the merge fields by clicking the **Highlight Merge Fields** button in the Write & Insert Fields group.

Maintaining, Breaking, and Reestablishing the Connection to a Data Source

As you have seen, when you reopen a main document, Word displays a warning dialog box, where you can click Yes to open the document with its connection to the data source intact. But what if you want to break the connection between the main document and the data source? One option is to click No in the warning dialog box. In that case, the main document opens with no connection to the data source. If the main document is currently open and already connected to the data source, you can break the connection by clicking Normal Word Document on the Start Mail Merge menu. You can reestablish the connection at any time by starting the mail merge over again and using the Select Recipients button to select the data source.

Keep in mind that you could also break the connection between a main document and its data source if you move one or both of the files to a different folder. Exactly what happens in this case depends on how your computer is set up and where you move the files. In the case of a broken connection, when you open the main document, you'll see a series of message boxes informing you that the connection to the data source has been broken. Eventually, you will see a Microsoft Word dialog box with a button labeled Find Data Source, which you can click, and then use the Select Data Source dialog box to locate and select your data source.

If you are creating mail merges for personal use, it's a good idea to either store the data source in the default My Data Sources folder and keep it there, or store the data source and the main document in the same folder (a folder other than the My Data Sources folder). The latter option is best if you think you might need to move the files to a different computer. That way, if you do need to move them, you can move the entire folder.

Editing a Data Source

After you complete a mail merge, you might need to make some changes to the data source and redo the merge. You can edit a data source in two ways—from within the program used to create the data source, or via the Mail Merge Recipients dialog box in Word. If you are familiar with the program used to create the data source, the simplest approach is to edit the file from within that program. For example, if you were using an Excel worksheet as your data source, you could open the file in Excel, edit it (perhaps by adding new records), save it, and then reselect the file as your data source. To edit the Microsoft Office Address Lists file that you created as a data source for this project, you can use the Mail Merge Recipients dialog box.

REFERENCE

Editing a Microsoft Office Address Lists Data Source in Word

- Open the main document for the data source you want to edit.
- On the ribbon, click the MAILINGS tab.
- In the Start Mail Merge group, click the Edit Recipient List button.
- In the Data Source box in the Mail Merge Recipients dialog box, select the data source you want to edit, and then click the Edit button.
- To add a record, click the New Entry button, and then enter the data for the new record.
- To delete a record, click any field in the record, and then click the Delete Entry button.
- To add or remove fields from the data source, click the Customize Columns button, click Yes in the warning dialog box, make any changes, and then click the OK button. Remember that if you remove a field, you will delete any data entered into that field for all records in the data source.
- Click the OK button in the Edit Data Source dialog box, click the Yes button in the Microsoft Office Word dialog box, and then click the OK button in the Mail Merge Recipients dialog box.

Maiya would like you to add information for three new customers to the data source.

To edit the data source by adding records:

1. In the Start Mail Merge group, click the **Edit Recipient List** button. The Mail Merge Recipients dialog box opens, displaying the contents of the data source that is currently connected to the main document—the Bakery Data file.

 This dialog box is designed to let you edit any data source, not just the one currently connected to the main document. To edit the Bakery Data file, you first need to select it in the Data Source box in the lower-left corner. If you had multiple data sources stored in the same folder as the Bakery Data file, you would see them all in this list box.

2. In the Data Source box, click **Bakery Data.mdb**. The filename is selected.

 Note that the file has the extension .mdb, which is the file extension for an Access database file—the default format for a data source created in Word. See Figure 6-21.

Figure 6-21 **Bakery Data.mdb file selected in the Mail Merge Recipients dialog box**

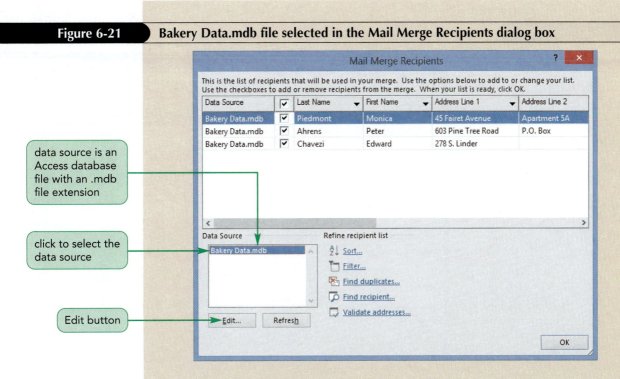

3. Click the **Edit** button. The Edit Data Source dialog box opens.

4. Click the **New Entry** button, and then enter the information for the three new records shown in Figure 6-22.

Figure 6-22 **New customer data**

First Name	Last Name	Address Line 1	Address Line 2	City	State	Zip Code	E-Mail Address	Phone	Favorite Bread	Favorite Pastry
Sally	Hui	2054 First Avenue	Apartment 2B	Carlyle	LA	70129	hui@sample.cengage.com	555-555-5555	sourdough	cinnamon roll
Alberto	Mendez	10 Rigby Street		Baptiste	LA	70128	mendez@sample.cengage.com	555-555-5555	sourdough	profiterole
Natasha	Rosenblum	55 River Place	P.O. Box 795	Carlyle	LA	70123	rosenblum@sample.cengage.com	555-555-5555	raisin	cinnamon roll

© 2014 Cengage Learning

When you are finished, you will have a total of six records in the data source. Notice that the record for Alberto Mendez contains no data in the Address Line 2 field.

5. Click the **OK** button, and then click the **Yes** button in the message box that asks if you want to update the Bakery Data.mdb file. You return to the Mail Merge Recipients dialog box, as shown in Figure 6-23.

Figure 6-23 New records added to data source

Trouble? If your records look different from those in Figure 6-23, select the data source, click the Edit button, edit the data source, and then click the OK button.

You'll leave the Mail Merge Recipients dialog box open so you can use it to make other changes to the data source.

Sorting Records

You can sort, or rearrange, information in a data source table just as you can sort information in any other table. To quickly sort information in ascending order (A to Z, lowest to highest, or earliest to latest) or in descending order (Z to A, highest to lowest, or latest to earliest), click a field's heading in the Mail Merge Recipients dialog box. The first time you click the heading, the records are sorted in ascending order. If you click it a second time, the records are sorted in descending order.

To perform a more complicated sort, you can click the Sort command in the Mail Merge Recipients dialog box to open the Filter and Sort dialog box, where you can choose to sort by more than one field. For example, you could sort records in ascending order by last name, and then in ascending order by first name. In that case, the records would be organized alphabetically by last name, and then, in cases where multiple records contained the same last name, those records would be sorted by first name.

REFERENCE

Sorting a Data Source by Multiple Fields

- On the ribbon, click the MAILINGS tab.
- In the Start Mail Merge group, click the Edit Recipient List button to open the Mail Merge Recipients dialog box.
- Click Sort to open the Sort Records tab in the Filter and Sort dialog box.
- Click the Sort by arrow, select the first field you want to sort by, and then select either the Ascending option button or the Descending option button.
- Click the Then by arrow, select the second field you want to sort by, and then select either the Ascending option button or the Descending option button.
- If necessary, click the Then by arrow, select the third field you want to sort by, and then select either the Ascending option button or the Descending option button.
- Click the OK button to close the Filter and Sort dialog box.
- Click the OK button to close the Mail Merge Recipients dialog box.

As Maiya looks through the letters to her customers in the merged document, she notices one problem—the letters are not grouped by zip codes. Currently, the letters are in the order in which customers were added to the data source file. Maiya plans to use business mail (also known as bulk mail) to send her letters, and the U.S. Postal Service offers lower rates for mailings that are separated into groups according to zip code. She asks you to sort the data file by zip code and then by last name, and then merge the main document with the sorted data source.

To sort the data source by zip code:

1. In the Mail Merge Recipients dialog box, click **Sort**. The Filter and Sort dialog box opens, with the Sort Records tab displayed.

2. Click the **Sort by** arrow to display a menu, scroll down in the menu, and then click **ZIP Code**. The Ascending button is selected by default, which is what you want.

3. In the Then by box, directly below the Sort by box, click the **Then by** arrow, and then click **Last Name**. See Figure 6-24.

Figure 6-24 **Sorting by zip code and by last name**

click to select the Last Name field

click to select the ZIP Code field

Filter and Sort

Filter Records	Sort Records			
Sort by:	ZIP Code		● Ascending	○ Descending
Then by:	Last Name		● Ascending	○ Descending
Then by:			● Ascending	○ Descending

Clear All OK Cancel

▶ **4.** Click the **OK** button. Word sorts the records from lowest zip code number to highest; and then, within each zip code, it sorts the records by last name.

In the Mail Merge Recipients dialog box, the record for Edward Chavezi, with zip code 70123, is now at the top of the data source list. The record for Natasha Rosenblum, which also has a zip code of 70123, comes second. The remaining records are sorted similarly, with the record for Monica Piedmont the last in the list. When you merge the data source with the form letter, the letters will appear in the merged document in this order.

▶ **5.** Click the **OK** button. The Mail Merge Recipients dialog box closes.

▶ **6.** On the MAILINGS tab, in the Preview Results group, click the **Preview Results** button. The data for Edward Chavezi is displayed in the main document.

▶ **7.** In the Finish group, click the **Finish & Merge** button, and then click **Edit Individual Documents**.

▶ **8.** In the Merge to New Document dialog box, verify that the **All** option button is selected, and then click the **OK** button. Word generates the new merged document with six letters—one letter per page as before, but this time the first letter is addressed to Edward Chavezi.

▶ **9.** Scroll down and verify that the letters in the newly merged document are arranged in ascending order by zip code and then in ascending order by last name.

▶ **10.** Save the new merged document in the location specified by your instructor, using the filename **Bakery Merged Letters 2**, and then close it. You return to the Bakery Main Document.

▶ **11.** Save the **Bakery Main Document** file and keep it open for the next set of steps.

Next, Maiya would like you to create a set of letters to send to customers who listed "cinnamon roll" as their favorite pastry.

Filtering Records

TIP

To omit an individual record from a merge, you can deselect the corresponding check box in the Mail Merge Recipients dialog box rather than using a filter.

Maiya wants to inform customers that cinnamon rolls are now available with or without pecans. She asks you to modify the form letter and then merge it with the records of customers who have indicated that cinnamon rolls are their favorite pastry. To select specific records in a data source, you filter the data source to temporarily display only the records containing a particular value in a particular field.

To filter the data source to select specific records for the merge:

▶ **1.** In the Preview Results group, click the **Preview Results** button to deselect it and display the merge fields in the Bakery Main Document file instead of the data from the data source.

▶ **2.** Save the Bakery Main Document with the new name **Cinnamon Main Document** in the location specified by your instructor.

▶ **3.** In the document, scroll down to the third paragraph in the body of the letter, and then click to the right of the Favorite_Pastry merge field.

4. Insert a space, type **(now available with or without pecans)** and then verify that the sentence reads "Please join us for a free cup of coffee and <<Favorite_Pastry>> (now available with or without pecans) anytime this month or next."

5. In the Start Mail Merge group, click the **Edit Recipient List** button to open the Mail Merge Recipients dialog box, and then scroll to the right so you can see the Favorite Pastry field.

6. In the header row, click the **Favorite Pastry** arrow. A menu opens, listing all the entries in the Favorite Pastry field as well as a few other options. See Figure 6-25.

Figure 6-25	Filtering records in a data source

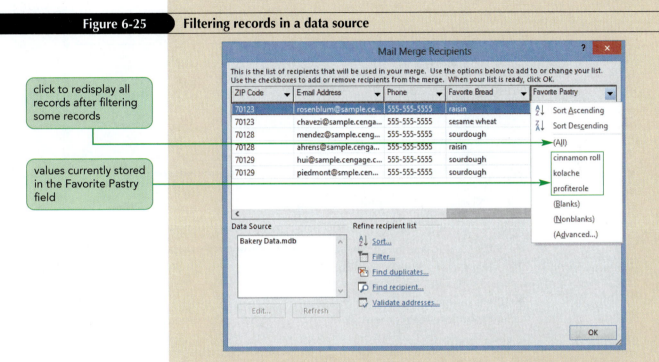

click to redisplay all records after filtering some records

values currently stored in the Favorite Pastry field

Trouble? If the records sort by Favorite Pastry, with all the records for cinnamon rolls at the top, you clicked the Favorite Pastry column header instead of the arrow. That's not a problem; you don't need to undo the sort. Repeat Step 6, taking care to click the arrow.

You can use the "(All)" option to redisplay all records after previously filtering a data source. The "(Advanced)" option takes you to the Filter Records tab in the Filter and Sort dialog box, where you can perform complex filter operations that involve comparing the contents of one or more fields to a particular value to determine if a record should be displayed or not. In this case, however, you can use an option in this menu.

7. Click **cinnamon roll**. Word temporarily hides all the records in the data source except those that contain "cinnamon roll" in the Favorite Pastry field. See Figure 6-26.

Figure 6-26 Filtered data source

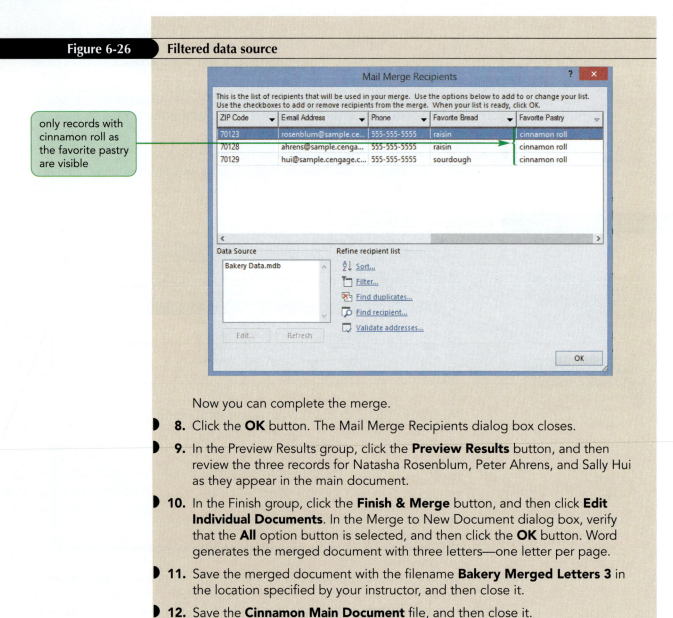

only records with cinnamon roll as the favorite pastry are visible

Now you can complete the merge.

▶ 8. Click the **OK** button. The Mail Merge Recipients dialog box closes.

▶ 9. In the Preview Results group, click the **Preview Results** button, and then review the three records for Natasha Rosenblum, Peter Ahrens, and Sally Hui as they appear in the main document.

▶ 10. In the Finish group, click the **Finish & Merge** button, and then click **Edit Individual Documents**. In the Merge to New Document dialog box, verify that the **All** option button is selected, and then click the **OK** button. Word generates the merged document with three letters—one letter per page.

▶ 11. Save the merged document with the filename **Bakery Merged Letters 3** in the location specified by your instructor, and then close it.

▶ 12. Save the **Cinnamon Main Document** file, and then close it.

Next, you'll create and print mailing labels for the form letters.

Creating Mailing Labels

Maiya could print the names and addresses for the letters directly on envelopes, or she could perform a mail merge to create mailing labels. The latter method is easier because she can print 14 labels at once rather than printing one envelope at a time.

Maiya has purchased Avery® Laser Printer labels, which are available in most office-supply stores. Word supports most of the Avery label formats, allowing you to choose the layout that works best for you. Maiya purchased labels in 8 1/2 × 11-inch sheets that are designed to feed through a printer. Each label measures 4 × 1.33 inches. Each sheet contains seven rows of labels, with two labels in each row, for a total of 14 labels. See Figure 6-27.

TIP

It is a good idea to print one page of a label document on regular paper so you can check your work before printing on the more expensive sheets of adhesive labels.

Figure 6-27 Layout of a sheet of Avery® labels

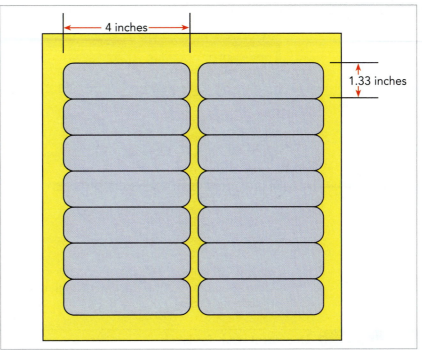

© 2014 Cengage Learning

Performing a mail merge to create mailing labels is similar to performing a mail merge to create a form letter. You begin by selecting Labels as the type of main document, and then you specify the brand and product number for the labels you are using. You will also need to specify a data source file. In this case, you'll use the Microsoft Office Address Lists data source file, Bakery Data.mdb, which you created and used in the form letter mail merges.

To specify the main document for creating mailing labels:

1. Open a new, blank document, and then save the document as **Bakery Labels Main Document** in the location specified by your instructor.

2. Make sure nonprinting characters are displayed, and zoom out so you can see the whole page.

3. On the ribbon, click the **MAILINGS** tab.

4. In the Start Mail Merge group, click the **Start Mail Merge** button.

 At this point, if you wanted to merge to envelopes instead of labels, you could click Envelopes to open the Envelope Option dialog box, where you could select the envelope size you wanted to use. In this case, however, you want to merge to labels.

5. Click **Labels**. The Label Options dialog box opens.

6. Click the **Label vendors** arrow to display a list of vendors, scroll down, and then click **Avery US Letter**.

7. Scroll down the Product number box, and then click **5162 Easy Peel Address Labels**. See Figure 6-28.

Figure 6-28 **Label Options dialog box**

select this brand of label

select this product

8. Click the **OK** button. The Label Options dialog box closes, and Word inserts a table structure into the document, with one cell for each of the 14 labels on the page, as shown in Figure 6-29.

Figure 6-29 **Document ready for labels**

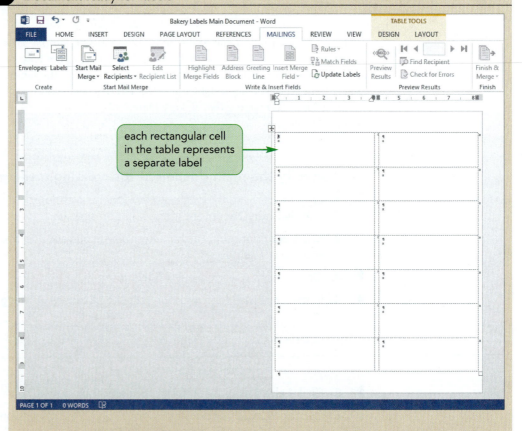

each rectangular cell in the table represents a separate label

As with all table gridlines, these gridlines are visible only on the screen; they will not be visible on the printed labels.

Trouble? If you don't see the table gridlines, click the TABLE TOOLS LAYOUT tab, and then, in the Table group, click the View Gridlines button to select it.

You have finished setting up the document. Next, you need to select the data source you created earlier. Note that the changes you made to the data source as a whole earlier in this session (sorting the records and selecting only some records) have no effect on the data source in this new mail merge. However, the changes you made to individual records (such as editing individual records or adding new records) are retained.

To continue the mail merge for the labels:

1. In the Start Mail Merge group, click the **Select Recipients** button, and then click **Use an Existing List**. The Select Data Source dialog box opens.

2. Navigate to the location where you stored the Bakery Data file, select the **Bakery Data** file, and then click the **Open** button. The Select Data Source dialog box closes and you return to the main document.

3. Change the Zoom level to **120%** so you can read the document.

 In each label except the first one, the code <<Next Record>> is displayed. This code tells Word to retrieve the next record from the data source for each label.

4. Verify that the insertion point is located in the upper-left label, and make sure the MAILINGS tab is still selected on the ribbon.

TIP

You can only use the AddressBlock merge field if you include a State field in your data source.

5. In the Write & Insert Fields group, click the **Address Block** button. The Insert Address Block dialog box opens. The left pane displays possible formats for the name in the address block. The default format, "Joshua Randall Jr.," simply inserts the first and last name, which is what Maiya wants. The Preview pane on the right currently shows the first address in the data source, which is the address for Monica Piedmont.

6. In the Preview section of the Insert Address Field dialog box, click the **Next** button ▷. The record for Peter Ahrens is displayed in the Preview pane, as shown in Figure 6-30.

Figure 6-30 Previewing addresses in the Insert Address Block dialog box

7. Click the **OK** button. The Insert Address Block dialog box closes, and an AddressBlock merge field is displayed in the upper-left label on the page. Next, you need to update the remaining labels to match the one containing the AddressBlock merge field.

8. In the Write & Insert Fields group, click the **Update Labels** button. The AddressBlock merge field is inserted into all the labels in the document, as shown in Figure 6-31.

Figure 6-31 **Field codes inserted into document**

In all except the upper-left label, the Next Record code is displayed to the left of the AddressBlock merge field.

You are ready to preview the labels and complete the merge. To ensure that you see all the labels in the preview, make sure the Go to Record box in the Preview Results group displays the number "1".

To preview the labels and complete the merge:

1. If necessary, click the **First Record** button ⏮ in the Preview Results group to display "1" in the Go to Record box.

2. In the Preview Results group, click the **Preview Results** button. The addresses for Maiya's six customers are displayed in the main document. See Figure 6-32.

Figure 6-32 Previewing addresses in labels

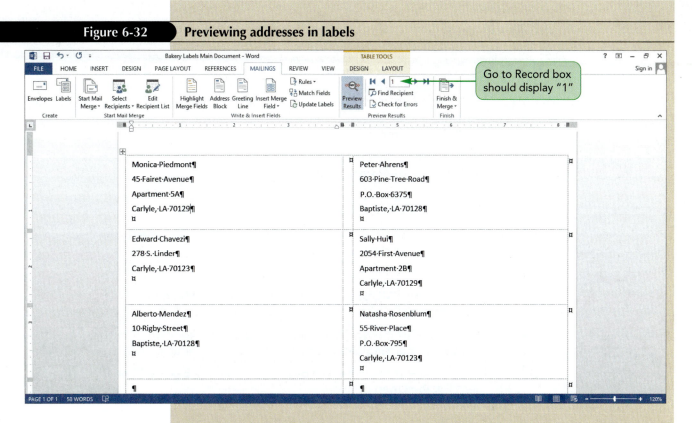

3. In the Finish group, click the **Finish & Merge** button, and then click **Edit Individual Documents**.

4. In the Merge to New Document dialog box, verify that the **All** option button is selected, and then click the **OK** button. The finished labels are inserted into a new document named Labels1.

5. Scroll through the document. The document contains space for 14 labels; but because the data source contains only six records, the new document only contains addresses for six labels.

6. In the upper-left label, change "Monica Piedmont" to your first and last names, and then save the merged document as **Bakery Merged Labels** in the location specified by your instructor.

7. Close the **Bakery Merged Labels** document, then save and close the **Bakery Labels Main Document** file.

Creating a Telephone Directory

Next, Maiya wants you to create a telephone directory for all bakery employees. Maiya has already created a Word document containing the phone numbers; you will use that document as the data source for the merge. You'll set up a mail merge as before, except this time you will select Directory as the main document type. You'll start by examining the Word document that Maiya wants you to use as the data source, and then you'll create the main document.

To review the data source and create the main document for the directory:

1. Open the document **Phone** from the Word6 ▸ Tutorial folder, and then save it as **Bakery Phone Data** in the location specified by your instructor. The information in this document is arranged in a table with three column headings—"First Name," "Last Name," and "Phone." The information in the table has already been sorted in alphabetical order by last name.

2. Replace "Maiya Kandel" with your first and last names, and then save and close the **Bakery Phone Data** document.

3. Open a new, blank document, display nonprinting characters and the rulers, if necessary, and then change the Zoom level to **120%**.

4. Save the main document as **Bakery Directory Main Document** in the location in which you saved the Bakery Phone Data document.

5. On the ribbon, click the **MAILINGS** tab.

6. In the Start Mail Merge group, click the **Start Mail Merge** button, and then click **Directory**.

7. In the Start Mail Merge group, click the **Select Recipients** button, and then click **Use an Existing List** to open the Select Data Source dialog box.

8. Navigate to and select the Word document named **Bakery Phone Data**, and then click the **Open** button.

You're ready to insert the fields in the main document. Maiya wants the directory to include the names at the left margin of the page and the phone numbers at the right margin, with a dot leader in between. Recall that a dot leader is a dotted line that extends from the last letter of text on the left margin to the beginning of the nearest text aligned at a tab stop.

To set up the directory main document with dot leaders:

1. With the insertion point in the first line of the document, insert the **First_Name** merge field, insert a space, and then insert the **Last_Name** merge field.

2. In the Write & Insert Fields group, click the **Highlight Merge Fields** button. The First_Name and Last_Name merge fields are displayed on a gray background. Now you'll set a tab stop at the right margin (at the 6-inch mark on the horizontal ruler) with a dot leader.

3. On the ribbon, click the **HOME** tab.

TIP
You can click the Clear All button in the Tabs dialog box to delete all the tab stops in the document.

4. In the Paragraph group, click the **Dialog Box Launcher** to open the Paragraph dialog box, and then in the lower-left corner of the Indents and Spacing tab, click the **Tabs** button. The Tabs dialog box opens.

5. In the Tab stop position box, type **6**, and then click the **Right** option button in the Alignment section.

6. Click the **2** option button in the Leader section. See Figure 6-33.

Figure 6-33 **Creating a tab with a dot leader**

7. Click the **OK** button. Word clears the current tab stops and inserts a right-aligned tab stop at the 6-inch mark on the horizontal ruler.

8. Press the **Tab** key to move the insertion point to the new tab stop. A dotted line stretches across the page, from the Last_Name merge field to the right margin.

9. On the ribbon, click the **MAILINGS** tab.

10. Insert the **Phone** merge field at the insertion point. The dot leader shortens to accommodate the inserted merge fields.

11. Press the **Enter** key. The completed main document should look like the one shown in Figure 6-34.

> Be sure to press the Enter key here to ensure that each name and telephone number is displayed on a separate line.

Figure 6-34 **Completed main document for the telephone directory**

You are now ready to merge this file with the data source.

To finish the merge for the telephone directory:

1. In the Preview Results group, click the **Preview Results** button, and then review the data for the first record in the document.

2. In the Finish group, click the **Finish & Merge** button, and then click **Edit Individual Documents**. In the Merge to New Document dialog box, verify that the **All** option button is selected, and then click the **OK** button. Word creates a new document named Directory1 that contains the completed telephone list.

3. Press the **Enter** key to insert a new paragraph at the beginning of the document.

4. Click in the new paragraph, type **Candlestick Artisan Bakery Employee Directory** and then format the new text in 22-point, Times New Roman, with the Orange, Accent 2 font color. See Figure 6-35.

Figure 6-35 **Completed telephone directory**

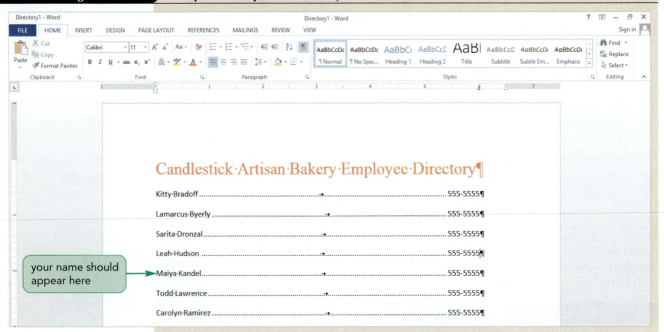

5. Save the document as **Bakery Merged Directory** in the location in which you saved the main document, and then close it.

6. Save and close the **Bakery Directory Main Document** file.

Maiya needs your help with one other task related to managing information about the bakery's customers and employees.

Converting Text to a Table

TIP

To convert a table to text, click in the table, click the TABLE TOOLS LAYOUT tab, click Convert to Text in the Data group, click the separator you prefer, and then click OK.

To be completely proficient in mail merges, you should be able to take information from a variety of sources and set it up for use as a data source. In particular, it's helpful to be able to convert text to a table. For example, address information exported from email and contact management programs often takes the form of a **CSV (comma-separated value) file**, a text file in which each paragraph contains one record, with the fields separated by commas. CSV files can have a .txt or .csv file extension. The commas in a CSV file are known as **separator characters**, or sometimes **delimiters**.

You can use the Convert Text to Table command on the Table menu to transform text from a Word document or a CSV file into a table. But first you need to make sure the text is set up correctly; that is, you need to make sure that separator characters are used

consistently to divide the text into individual fields. In a CSV file, commas are used as separator characters, but you might encounter a Word document that uses tab characters, or other characters, as separator characters. After you verify that separator characters are used consistently within a document, you need to make sure each paragraph in the document contains the same number of fields.

Upon conversion, each field is formatted as a separate cell in a column, and each paragraph mark starts a new row, or record. Sometimes a conversion might not turn out the way you expect. In that case, undo it and then review the text to make sure each paragraph contains the same number of data items, with the items divided by the same separator character.

Maiya's assistant, who isn't familiar with Word tables, typed some information about new customers as text in a Word document. She forgot to include an email address and phone number for each customer. Maiya wants to convert the text to a table, and then add columns for the missing information. The next time the customers visit the bakery, she can ask them for the missing information and then add it to the table.

To convert text into a table:

1. Open the document named **Customer** from the Word6 ▸ Tutorial folder, and then save it as **Customer Table** in the location specified by your instructor.

2. Display nonprinting characters, if necessary, and then change the Zoom level to **120%**. See Figure 6-36.

Figure 6-36 **Text with inconsistent separator characters**

The document consists of three paragraphs, each of which contains a customer's name, address, city, state, zip code, favorite bread, and favorite pastry. Some of the fields are separated by commas and spaces (for example, the address and the city), but some are only separated by spaces, with no punctuation character (for example, the first and last names). Also, the favorite bread and favorite pastry are enclosed in parentheses. You need to edit this information so that fields are separated by commas, with no parentheses enclosing the last two items.

3. Edit the document to insert a comma after each first name, city, and zip code, and then delete the parentheses in each paragraph.

Before you can convert the text into a table, you also need to make sure each paragraph includes the same fields. Currently, the first paragraph includes two pieces of address information—a street address and an apartment number, which is equivalent to an Address Line 1 field and an Address Line 2 field. However, the other paragraphs only include an Address Line 1 field.

4. In the second paragraph, click to the right of the comma after "Road," press the **spacebar**, and then type **,** (a comma).

5. In the third paragraph, click to the right of the comma after "Avenue," press the **spacebar**, and then type **,** (a comma). Now the second and third paragraphs each contain a blank field. See Figure 6-37.

Figure 6-37 Text set up for conversion to a table

- each paragraph now has a comma after the first name, city, and zip code
- parentheses around the last two items in each paragraph have been deleted

Kasey, Navona, 2343 Lombard Street, Apartment 3D, Carlyle, LA, 70129, sesame wheat, kolache¶

Kyle, Lamphier, 90 South Post Road, , Baptiste, LA, 70128, raisin, cinnamon roll¶

- blank fields

Melody, Banks, 1222 Mayfield Avenue, , Carlyle, LA, 70123, sourdough, profiterole¶

6. Press the **Ctrl+A** keys to select the entire document.

7. On the ribbon, click the **INSERT** tab.

8. In the Tables group, click the **Table** button, and then click **Convert Text to Table**. The Convert Text to Table dialog box opens. See Figure 6-38.

Figure 6-38 Converting text to a table

- corresponds to nine pieces of information in each of the three paragraphs
- this option button is selected by default

Note that the Number of columns setting is 9, and the Number of rows setting is 3. This corresponds to the nine fields in each of the three paragraphs.

In the Separate text at section of the dialog box, you can choose from three possible separator characters—paragraphs, commas, and tabs. If the text in your document was separated by a character other than paragraphs, commas, or tabs, you could type the character in the box to the right of the Other button. In this case, though, the default option, Commas, is the correct choice because the information in each paragraph is separated by commas.

▶ **9.** Click the **OK** button. The Convert Text to Table dialog box closes, and the text in the document is converted into a table consisting of nine columns and three rows.

▶ **10.** Save the document.

Now that you have converted the text to a table, you need to finish the table by adding the columns for the phone numbers and email addresses, and adding a header row to identify the field names.

To finish the table by adding columns and a header row:

▶ **1.** Switch to **Landscape** orientation, and then select the column containing the zip codes.

▶ **2.** On the ribbon, click the **TABLE TOOLS LAYOUT** tab.

▶ **3.** In the Rows & Columns group, click the **Insert Right** button twice to add two blank columns to the right of the column containing zip codes.

▶ **4.** Select the table's top row, and then in the Rows & Columns group, click the **Insert Above** button.

▶ **5.** Enter the column headings shown in Figure 6-39 and format them in bold.

Figure 6-39 Table with new columns and column headings

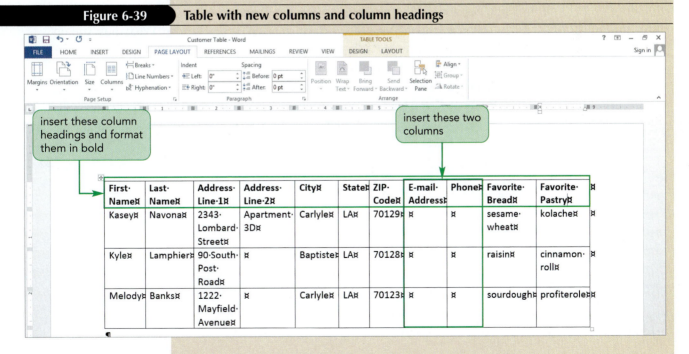

insert these column headings and format them in bold

insert these two columns

First Name	Last Name	Address Line 1	Address Line 2	City	State	ZIP Code	E-mail Address	Phone	Favorite Bread	Favorite Pastry
Kasey	Navona	2343 Lombard Street	Apartment 3D	Carlyle	LA	70129			sesame wheat	kolache
Kyle	Lamphier	90 South Post Road		Baptiste	LA	70128			raisin	cinnamon roll
Melody	Banks	1222 Mayfield Avenue		Carlyle	LA	70123			sourdough	profiterole

▶ **6.** Save the **Customer Table** document, and then close it.

You have finished converting text into a table. Maiya can use the table later as the data source for another mail merge. As her business expands, she plans to continue to use Word's mail merge feature to inform her customers about new products and specials.

Combining Data with a Microsoft Office Address Lists File

If you have data in a Word file that you want to combine with data in a Microsoft Office Address Lists file, or any other Microsoft Access file, start by setting up the Word document as a table. That way, you can be sure that each record includes the same fields. You can also review the table quickly to confirm that you have entered data in the various fields in a consistent format. Once you are confident that you have set up the table correctly, you can begin the process of combining it with the Microsoft Office Address Lists file.

First, delete the heading row, and then convert the table back to text, separating the fields with commas. Next, save the Word file as a Plain Text file with the .txt file extension. Finally, open the Microsoft Office Address Lists file in Access, click the EXTERNAL DATA tab, and then click the Text File button in the Import & Link group to begin importing the text file into the Microsoft Office Address Lists file. In the Get External Data - Text File dialog box, click the Append a copy of the records to the table button, and then click the Browse button to select the plain text file.

Session 6.2 Quick Check

1. What must you do to maintain the connection between a main document and its data source after you close the main document?
2. Assuming Word is running but no documents are open, what's the first step in editing a Microsoft Office Address Lists data source that you created in Word?
3. Suppose you want to edit a Microsoft Office Address Lists data source named Phone, and the Mail Merge Recipients dialog box is open. What must you do to begin editing the data source?
4. What's the quickest way to sort a data source by one field?
5. Explain how to filter a data source.
6. Suppose you have a blank document open with the MAILINGS tab selected. What's the next step in using mail merge to create mailing labels?

SAM Projects

Put your skills into practice with SAM Projects! SAM Projects for this tutorial can be found online. If you have a SAM account, go to www.cengage.com/sam2013 to download the most recent Project Instructions and Start Files.

Review Assignments

Data Files needed for the Review Assignments: Additional.docx, Business.docx, Free.docx

The new and improved Candlestick Artisan Bakery is a big hit. Maiya has greatly expanded her customer base, and she now has a thriving home delivery business. Customers sign up for weekly deliveries with the promise of a free dessert every six months. On the home delivery sign-up form, customers can choose between a free apple tart or chocolate cake. Now she wants to send a letter inviting weekly home delivery customers to reserve their free dessert three days before they want it delivered. She also needs to create a directory of other businesses she deals with frequently. Finally, she needs to convert some additional customer information into a table that she can use as a data source. Complete the following steps:

1. Open the document **Free** from the Word6 ▶ Review folder included with your Data Files, and then save the document as **Free Dessert Main Document** in the location specified by your instructor.
2. In the letter's closing, replace Maiya's first and last names with your own.
3. In the first paragraph, replace the placeholder text "[INSERT DATE FIELD]" with a date field that displays the current month, day, and year—in the format March 11, 2016.
4. Begin the mail merge by selecting Letters as the type of main document.
5. Create a data source with the following fields in the following order: First Name, Last Name, Address Line 1, Address Line 2, City, State, ZIP Code, E-mail Address, Phone, and Free Dessert. Remove any extra fields, and rename fields as necessary.
6. Create four records using the information shown in Figure 6-40.

Figure 6-40 Information for new data source

First Name	Last Name	Address Line 1	Address Line 2	City	State	ZIP Code	E-mail Address	Phone	Free Dessert
Jeane	Cutler	299 Allen Boulevard	Apartment 8D	Carlyle	LA	70129	cutler@sample.cengage.com	555-555-5555	apple tart
Kent	Hesse	933 Chilton Avenue		Beatty	LA	70120	hesse@sample.cengage.com	555-555-5555	chocolate cake
Tyrell	Greely	52 Eton Place	P.O. Box 9080	Carlyle	LA	70128	greely@sample.cengage.com	555-555-5555	apple tart
Katya	Pushkin	821 Ruby Road		Carlyle	LA	70129	pushkin@sample.cengage.com	555-555-5555	chocolate cake

© 2014 Cengage Learning

7. Save the data source as **Dessert Data** in the location in which you saved the main document.
8. Edit the data source to replace "Kent Hesse" with your first and last names.
9. Sort the data source in ascending order by zip code and then by last name.
10. Replace the placeholder text "[INSERT INSIDE ADDRESS]" with an inside address consisting of the necessary separate merge fields. Adjust the paragraph spacing in the inside address as necessary.

11. In the salutation, replace the placeholder text "[INSERT FIRST NAME]" with the First_Name merge field.

12. In the body of the letter, replace the placeholder text "[INSERT FREE DESSERT]" with the Free_Dessert merge field.

13. Save your changes to the main document, and then preview the merged document. Correct any formatting or spacing problems.

14. Merge to a new document, save the merged document as **Merged Free Dessert Letters** in the location in which you saved the main document, and then close the file.

15. Filter the data source to display only records for customers who requested a free apple tart, and then complete a second merge. Save the new merged document as **Merged Apple Tart Letters** in the location in which you saved the main document. Close all documents, saving all changes.

16. Open a new, blank document, and create a set of mailing labels using the vendor Avery US Letters and product number 5162. Save the main document as **Dessert Labels Main Document** in the location in which you saved the Dessert Data file.

17. Select the Dessert Data file you created earlier in this assignment as the data source.

18. Insert an AddressBlock merge field in the "Joshua Randall Jr." format, and then update the labels.

19. Preview the merged labels, merge to a new document, and then save the new document as **Merged Dessert Labels** in the location in which you saved the main document. Save and close all open documents.

20. Open the document **Business** from the Word6 ▸ Review folder, and then save it as **Business Data** in the location specified by your instructor.

21. Open a new, blank document, and then save it as **Business Directory Main Document** in the location in which you saved the Business Data file. Create a directory main document. Select the Business Data file as the data source.

22. Set a right tab at 6 inches with a dot leader and insert the necessary merge fields. At the top of the merged document, insert the heading **Candlestick Artisan Bakery Business Contacts** and format the heading in 22-point, Times New Roman, with the Orange, Accent 2 font color. Save the merged document as **Merged Business Directory** in the location in which you saved the main document. Save and close all open documents.

23. Open the document **Additional** from the Word6 ▸ Review folder, and then save it as **Additional Data** in the location specified by your instructor. Convert the data in the document to a table with eight columns. Insert a header row with the following column headers formatted in bold—**First Name**, **Last Name**, **Address Line 1**, **Address Line 2**, **City**, **State**, **ZIP Code**, and **Free Dessert**. Replace "David Essenberg" with your first and last names. Save and close the document.

APPLY

Case Problem 1

Data File needed for this Case Problem: Fund.docx

New Morning Children's Theater Nancy Ortega is the business manager for New Morning Children's Theater in Morning View, Colorado. As part of a new fund-raising campaign for the theater, Nancy plans to send out customized letters to last year's donors, asking them to consider donating the same amount or more this year. She asks you to help her create the letters and the envelopes for the campaign. Complete the following steps:

1. Open the document **Fund** from the Word6 ▸ Case1 folder, and then save it as **Fund-Raising Main Document** in the location specified by your instructor. In the closing, replace "Nancy Ortega" with your first and last names.

2. In the first paragraph, replace the placeholder text "[INSERT DATE FIELD]" with a date field that displays the current month, day, and year—in the format March 11, 2016.

3. Begin the mail merge by selecting Letters as the type of main document.

4. Create a data source with the following field names, in the following order—Title, First Name, Last Name, Address Line 1, Address Line 2, City, State, ZIP Code, E-mail Address, and Donation Amount.

5. Enter the four records shown in Figure 6-41.

Figure 6-41 Four records for new data source

Title	First Name	Last Name	Address Line 1	Address Line 2	City	State	ZIP Code	E-mail Address	Donation Amount
Mr.	Bennie	Fuhrman	1577 Shanley Boulevard	Unit 2A	Denver	CO	80332	fuhrman@ sample. cengage.com	$500
Mr.	Arwen	Saiz	633 Kennelworth		Denver	CO	80332	saiz@sample. cengage.com	$125
Ms.	Kathy	Royal	4424 Gatehouse Lane		Morning View	CO	80015	royal@sample. cengage.com	$250
Ms.	Laxmi	Sung	844 Winter Way	Apartment 6	Morning View	CO	80311	sung@sample. cengage.com	$1,000

© 2014 Cengage Learning

6. Save the data source as **Fund-Raising Data** in the location in which you saved the main document.

7. Edit the data source to replace "Laxmi Sung" with your first and last names. Change the title to **Mr.** if necessary.

8. Sort the data source alphabetically by last name.

9. Build an inside address using separate merge fields. Include the Title field before the First_Name field.

10. Add a salutation using the Title and Last_Name merge fields, as indicated in the document. Adjust paragraph spacing as necessary, and take care to delete all placeholder text.

11. In the paragraph that begins "In order to produce…," insert the Donation_Amount merge field where indicated. Delete the placeholder text.

12. Save your changes to the Fund-Raising Main Document file. Preview the merged document, and then merge to a new document.

13. Save the merged letters document as **Merged Fund-Raising Letters** in the location in which you saved the main document, and then close it.

14. Save the Fund-Raising Main Document file, and then close it.

15. Open a new, blank document, and then save it as **Fund-Raising Envelopes Main Document** in the location in which you saved the Fund-Raising Data file. The theater has envelopes with a pre-printed return address, so you don't need to type a return address. Select Envelopes as the type of main document, and then select Size 10 (4 1/8 × 9 1/2 in) as the envelope size in the Envelope Options dialog box.

16. Use the Fund-Raising Data file you created earlier as the data source. In the recipient address area of the envelope, insert an AddressBlock merge field in the format "Mr. Joshua Randall Jr.".

17. Filter the records in the Fund-Raising Data file so that only records with Morning View addresses are included in the merge.

18. Merge to a new document.

19. Save the merged document as **Merged Fund-Raising Envelopes** in the location in which you saved the main document, and then close it. Save the main document and close it.

TROUBLESHOOT

Case Problem 2

Data Files needed for this Case Problem: Client.xlsx, Directory.docx, Labels.docx, New.docx

Golden Day Wealth Management As an account manager at Golden Day Wealth Management, you need to send letters to potential clients asking them to consider meeting with an investment adviser. Your data for the mail merge is saved as an Excel file. The data file includes names and addresses, as well as information about each potential client's preferred type of investment and the name of the adviser you think would be the best match for each client. To ensure that you can maintain the connection between the data source and the main document files, you will first start Excel, and then save the data source file to the location specified by your instructor. Complete the following steps:

1. Start Excel. In the Recent screen, click Open Other Workbooks. Navigate to the Word6 ▸ Case2 folder included with your Data Files, and then open the Excel workbook **Client**.
2. Click the FILE tab, click Save As, save the Excel workbook as **Client Data** in the location specified by your instructor, and then close Excel.
3. Open the document **New** from the Word6 ▸ Case2 folder included with your data files.
4. Save the Word document as **New Client Main Document** in the location in which you saved the Client Data file.
5. In the letter's closing, replace "Student Name" with your first and last names.
6. Replace the field that displays the date and time with a date field that displays the current month, day, and year—in the format March 11, 2016.
7. Begin the mail merge by selecting Letters as the type of main document.
8. For the data source, select the Excel workbook Client Data that you just saved. Click the OK button in the Select Table dialog box.
9. From within Word, edit the data source to replace "StudentFirstName" and "StudentLastName" with your first and last names.
10. Delete the placeholder text for the inside address, and then insert an Address Block merge field for the inside address in the format "Joshua Randall Jr.".
11. In the salutation, insert the First_Name merge field where indicated.
12. In the body of the letter, replace the placeholders "[INSERT INVESTMENT TYPE]" and "[INSERT ADVISER NAME]" with the appropriate merge fields.
13. Sort the records in the data source in ascending order by Investment Type.
⚙ **Troubleshoot** 14. Preview the merged document, and note that the lines of the inside address (inserted by the AddressBlock merge field) are spaced too far apart. Make any changes necessary so the inside address and the salutation include the appropriate amount of paragraph and line spacing.
15. Preview all the records in the document.
16. Merge to a new document. Save the merged document as **Merged New Client Letters** in the location in which you saved the main document.
17. Close all open documents, saving all changes.
⚙ **Troubleshoot** 18. Open the document **Labels** from the Word6 ▸ Case2 folder included with your Data Files, and save it as **Problem Labels** in the location specified by your instructor. Attach a comment to the Zip code in the first label that explains what error in the main document would result in a set of labels that includes information for only one record. Save and close the document.
19. Create a main document for generating mailing labels on sheets of Avery US Letter Address labels, product number 5162, using the Client Data file as your data source. Use the AddressBlock merge field in the format "Joshua Randall Jr.". Save the main document as **New Client Labels Main Document** in the location in which you saved the Client Data file.
20. Preview the merged document, merge to a new document, and then save the merged document as **Merged New Client Labels** in the location in which you saved the main document. Close all open documents, saving any changes.

21. Re-open the **New Client Main Document**, maintaining the connection to its data source, and then save it as **New Client Main Document, Filtered** in the same folder. Filter out all records in the data source except records for clients interested in municipal bonds and then, if necessary, sort the filtered records so the one containing your name is displayed first.

⚙ **Troubleshoot** 22. Preview the merged document, fix any problems with line and paragraph spacing in the inside address and salutation, and then complete the merge to a new document. Save the merged document as **Merged Municipal Bonds** in the location in which you saved the main document.

23. Close all open documents, saving any changes.

⚙ **Troubleshoot** 24. Open the document **Directory** from the Word6 ▸ Case2 folder included with your Data Files and save it as **Problem Directory** in the location specified by your instructor. This directory is supposed to list each client, along with his or her preferred investment type. Attach a comment to the first name in the directory that explains what error in the main document would result in a directory formatted like the one in the Problem Directory file.

25. Save and close the document.

Case Problem 3

CHALLENGE

Data Files needed for this Case Problem: Oxford.docx, Springwell.txt

Oxford Fitness and Health Club Christina Oates is the membership manager for Oxford Fitness and Health, a chain of 24-hour health clubs in Columbus, California. Oxford has just bought out a competitor, Springwell Health Club. Christina needs to send a letter to Springwell members explaining that their memberships will be transferred to Oxford. In the letter, she also wants to remind Springwell members when their current memberships will expire. The customer data has been saved in a text file, with the data fields separated by commas. Christina needs your help to convert the text file to a Word table, which she can then use as the data source for a mail merge. Complete the following steps:

1. In Word, open the text file **Springwell.txt** from the Word6 ▸ Case3 folder included with your Data Files. (*Hint*: If the file is not listed in the Open dialog box, make sure All Files is selected in the box to the right of the File name box.)

2. Save the Springwell.txt file as a Word document named **Springwell Data** in the location specified by your instructor. (*Hint*: In the Save As dialog box, remember to select Word Document as the file type.)

3. Format the document text using the Normal style, and then switch to Landscape orientation.

4. Convert the text to a table with eight columns. Insert a header row with the following column headers formatted in bold—**First Name**, **Last Name**, **Address Line 1**, **Address Line 2**, **City**, **State**, **ZIP Code**, and **Expiration**.

5. Replace "Tom Dylan" with your first and last names, save the document, and then close it.

6. Open the document **Oxford** from the Word6 ▸ Case3 folder, and then save it as **Oxford Main Document** in the location in which you saved the Springwell Data file.

7. In the letter's closing, replace "Christina Oates" with your first and last names.

8. In the first paragraph, replace the placeholder text "[INSERT DATE FIELD]" with a date field that displays the current month, day, and year—in the format 3/11/16.

9. Select Letters as the type of main document.

10. Select the Springwell Data document as the data source.

11. Replace the placeholder text "[INSERT INSIDE ADDRESS]" with an AddressBlock merge field in the format "Joshua Randall Jr.". Format the paragraph containing the AddressBlock merge field using the No Spacing style.

⊕ **Explore** 12. Delete the placeholder text "[INSERT SALUTATION]." Insert a salutation using the Greeting Line button in the Write & Insert Fields group on the MAILINGS tab. In the Insert Greeting Line dialog box, create a salutation that includes "Dear" and the customer's first name followed by a colon. For invalid recipient names (that is, recipients for which the First Name field in the data source is blank), select the "(none)" option. Add 12 points of paragraph spacing before the salutation paragraph.

13. In the body of the letter, replace the placeholder text "[INSERT EXPIRATION]" with the Expiration merge field.

⊕ **Explore** 14. Use the Rules button in the Write & Insert Fields group on the MAILINGS tab to replace the placeholder text "[SEE YOU SOON]" with a merge field that displays the message **We hope to see you soon at our new downtown location, opening early next year!** if the value in the ZIP Code field is equal to 90849; otherwise, the field should display **We hope to see you soon!** (*Hint*: In the Rules menu, click If…Then…Else…, select ZIP_Code as the Field name, select Equal to as the Comparison, and type **90849** in the Compare to box. Insert the appropriate text in the Insert this text box and in the Otherwise insert this text box.)

⊕ **Explore** 15. In the Mail Merge Recipients dialog box, use the Filter command to display only the records that include either April 1 or May 1 in the Expiration field. (*Hint*: On the Filter Records tab of the Query Options dialog box, you need to fill in two rows. Select Expiration in the Field box in both rows; select Equal to in the Comparison box for both rows; type the correct dates in the Compare to boxes; and in the first list box on the far left, select Or instead of And.)

16. In the Mail Merge Recipients dialog box, sort the displayed records alphabetically by last name.

17. Preview the merged documents, adjust spacing around the merge fields as necessary, and then merge to a new document. Save the merged document as **Merged Oxford Letters** in the location in which you saved the main document.

18. Close all open documents, saving any changes.

Case Problem 4

RESEARCH

There are no data files needed for this Case Problem.

Bureau of Labor Statistics Tracy Sheehan is a professor of economics at a large university. She is beginning research for an article on the country's fastest growing occupations, as listed in a report issued by the United States Department of Labor's Bureau of Labor Statistics. Before she can get started, Professor Sheehan needs to organize a great deal of printed information into file folders. As her student intern, it's your job to create labels for the file folders, with one label for each of the occupations. You will retrieve the list of occupations from the Bureau of Labor Statistics website, and then use it as the data source for a mail merge. Complete the following steps:

1. Open a new, blank document, and then save it as **Occupations Data from the US BLS** in the location specified by your instructor.

2. Open a browser and go to the Bureau of Labor Statistics website at www.bls.gov.

3. Use the Search BLS.gov box to search for **Table 1.3: Fastest growing occupations, 2010 and projected 2020**.

4. In the search results, click the Fastest growing occupations link, and then verify that the table named "Table 1.3: Fastest growing occupations, 2010 and projected 2020" is displayed in your browser.

5. Click and drag the mouse to select the entire table, and then use the appropriate keyboard shortcut to copy the table. Do not include the Source row at the bottom of the table.

6. Switch to the **Occupations Data from the US BLS** document in Word, and then paste the table in the Word document.

7. Click and drag the mouse to select the gray-shaded header row and the "Total, All Occupations" row, and then delete the selected rows.

8. Delete the first column on the left, which contains the numeric codes.

9. On the right side of the table, delete all the columns of numbers except for the last one, which contains the median annual wage. When you are finished, the table should contain two columns. In the top row, you should see "Personal Care Aides" in the left column and "19,640" in the right column.

10. Insert a header row in the table with the boldface column headers **Occupation** and **Median Annual Wage**.

11. Save and close the Occupations Data from the US BLS file.

12. Open a new, blank document, and then save it as **File Labels Main Document** in the location in which you saved the Occupations Data from the US BLS file.

13. Select Labels as the type of main document, using the Avery product 5966 Filing Labels.

14. Select the Occupations Data from the US BLS file as your data source.

15. In the first label, insert the Occupation merge field, type **,** (a comma), insert a space, type **$** (a dollar sign), and then insert the Median_Annual_Wage merge field.

16. Format the Occupation merge field in bold.

17. Update the labels and preview the merge results. The first label should read "Personal Care Aides, $19,640". "Personal Care Aides" should be formatted in bold.

18. In the "Veterinarians" label at the end of the document, type **,** (a comma) after the median annual wage, and then type your first and last names.

19. Merge to a new document, and then save the new document as **Merged File Labels** in the location in which you saved the main document.

20. Close the Merged File Labels document and any other open documents, saving any changes.

TUTORIAL 7

OBJECTIVES

Session 7.1
- Track changes in a document
- Compare and combine documents
- Accept and reject tracked changes
- Embed an Excel worksheet
- Modify an embedded Excel worksheet

Session 7.2
- Link an Excel chart
- Modify and update a linked Excel chart
- Create bookmarks
- Insert and edit hyperlinks
- Save a Word document as a webpage
- Format a web document
- View a web document in a web browser
- Create and publish a blog post

Collaborating with Others and Integrating Data

Preparing an Information Sheet and a Webpage

Case | *Rain Gardens for Carrel Springs*

Anya Pathak is the community outreach coordinator for the Carrel Springs Watershed Foundation, an environmental organization based in Carrel Springs, Kansas, devoted to improving water quality throughout the Carrel Springs area. Anya is currently working on an information sheet about rain gardens, a special type of garden designed to retain and absorb polluted rain runoff. She has asked Oliver Miller, the foundation's publicity director, to review a draft of her document. While Oliver is revising the document, Anya has asked you to work on another copy, making additional changes. When you are finished with your review, Anya wants you to merge Oliver's edited version of the document with your most recent draft.

After you create a new version of the document for Anya, she wants you to add some budget figures from an Excel workbook. She also needs you to add a pie chart Oliver created. To make the document available to the organization's members, Anya asks you to help distribute it in electronic form and publish it on the organization's website. Finally, Anya wants you to help her create a blog post in Word discussing potential sites for rain gardens.

STARTING DATA FILES

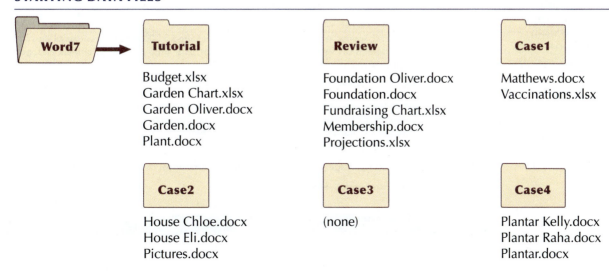

Word7 →

Tutorial
Budget.xlsx
Garden Chart.xlsx
Garden Oliver.docx
Garden.docx
Plant.docx

Review
Foundation Oliver.docx
Foundation.docx
Fundraising Chart.xlsx
Membership.docx
Projections.xlsx

Case1
Matthews.docx
Vaccinations.xlsx

Case2
House Chloe.docx
House Eli.docx
Pictures.docx

Case3
(none)

Case4
Plantar Kelly.docx
Plantar Raha.docx
Plantar.docx

Session 7.1 Visual Overview:

When you point to a tracked change in the document, a ScreenTip displays the name of the reviewer who made the change, when the change was made, and what the change was.

When you click this button to turn on Track Changes, Word marks the changes you make to the document with revision marks, or **tracked changes**.

Garden Combined - Wo

| FILE | HOME | INSERT | DESIGN | PAGE LAYOUT | REFERENCES | MAILINGS | R |

ABC ✓ Spelling & Grammar Translate Language New Comment Delete ▢ Previous ▢ Next ▤ Show Comments Track Changes ▾ All Mar Show M Reviewi

Proofing Language Comments Tracking

Anya Pathak, 4/14/2016 2:35:00 PM
inserted:
perennials

A vertical line appears in the left margin next to text that has been changed in any way.

Inserted text appears with an underline and a contrasting color, with a different color for each person, or reviewer, who edits the document. Here, text inserted by Anya is red, and text inserted by Oliver is orange.

Text with a comment attached is highlighted in color so you can easily see the reference point for the comment.

Rain Gar~~~~~~~~~rings¶

Planted with colorful perennials, a rain garden is beautiful, low-maintenance, relatively inexpensive, a
what is a rain garden, exactly? It's a garden in a shallow, bowl-shaped depression that allows it to ho
runoff from buildings, driveways, roads, and lawns. The rain is then absorbed into the garden, preven
pollutant-laden runoff from flowing into storm sewers, and from there into lakes, rivers, and streams.¶

A rain garden transforms the water it absorbs, replenishing the aquifer with fresh, pollutant-free wate
estimate that a well-designed rain garden can remove up to 95% of fertilizers an
chemicals from rainwater runoff, and up to 85% of sediment. Preventing
contaminants from reaching the Carrel Springs watershed is essenti
the area's plants and wildlife healthy and vibrant. For example,
nutrient-rich fertilizer from flowing into the watershed reduces th
algal bloom, in which algae spreads throughout lakes and strea
available oxygen and, eventually, killing native fish.¶

Over the past five years, the Carrel Springs Watershed Founda
with the Carrel Springs Department of Streets and Maintenance
scale rain gardens on public lands that link directly to major stor
Homeowners can do their part by installing their own rain garde
terraces between sidewalks and city streets.¶

3,000 Rain Gardens¶

The Carrel Springs Watershed Foundation has identified 3,000 potential residential sites for rain gar
Carrel Springs city limits. As illustrated in this chart, on a large percentage of these sites, gardens have
installed or will be soon.¶

[Insert Excel chart]¶

Except for an annual fall cleanup, a rain garden requires no ongoing maintenance, making it an attra
homeowners who want to minimize outdoor upkeep. Residents can apply for grants to pay for excava
drainage installation. Volunteer gardeners from the Prairie Friends Native Plant Society are available
free design and planting assistance.¶

The following budget, created by Anya Pathak, summarizes the costs for a typical 200-square-foot g

[Insert Excel worksheet]¶

PAGE 1 OF 1 406 WORDS

Tracking Changes

The REVIEW tab contains all the options you need for editing a document using tracked changes and comments.

The All Markup setting in the Display for Review box displays tracked changes. To hide all track changes marks except for the vertical line in the left margin, select Simple Markup instead. In Simple Markup view, comments are displayed as icons in the margin.

Explanations of tracked changes, known as **balloons**, are listed to the right of the document, with a line connecting each explanation to the corresponding text in the document. Track change balloons are only visible in All Markup view.

Green font and a green double underline indicate that this text was moved from one location in the document and inserted in this new location.

The names associated with a tracked change or comment correspond to the user's name and initials as specified on the General tab of the Word Options dialog box. The user whose name is associated with a tracked change is known as a **reviewer**.

Comments are often used along with Track Changes.

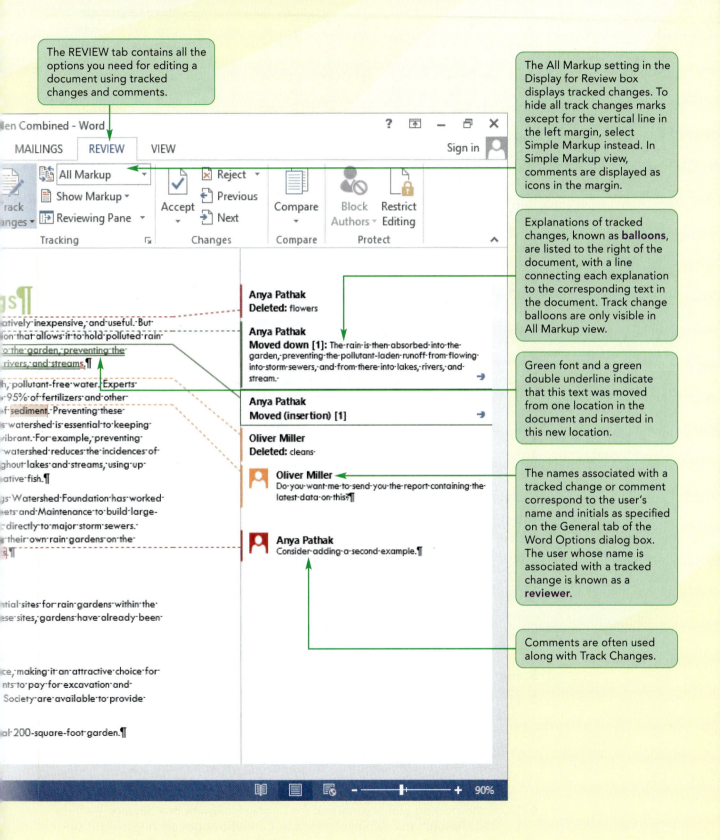

Editing a Document with Tracked Changes

The Track Changes feature in Word simulates the process of marking up a hard copy of a document with a colored pen, but offers many more advantages. Word keeps track of who makes each change, assigning a different color to each reviewer and providing ScreenTips indicating details of the change, such as the reviewer's name and the date and time the change was made. Using the buttons on the REVIEW tab, you can move through the document quickly, accepting or rejecting changes with a click of the mouse.

Anya is ready to revise her first draft of the document. She asks you to turn on Track Changes before you make the edits for her. To ensure that her name is displayed for each tracked change, and that your screens match the figures in this tutorial, you will temporarily change the username on the General tab of the Word Options dialog box to "Anya Pathak." You'll also change the user initials to "AP."

To change the username and turn on Track Changes:

1. Open the document **Garden** located in the Word7 ▸ Tutorial folder included with your Data Files, and then save it as **Garden Anya** in the location specified by your instructor.

2. Switch to Print Layout view if necessary, display the rulers and nonprinting characters, and change the document Zoom level to **110%**. You'll use this zoom setting for the first part of this tutorial to ensure that you can see all the tracked changes in the document.

3. On the ribbon, click the **REVIEW** tab.

4. In the Tracking group, click the **Dialog Box Launcher** to open the Track Changes Options dialog box, and then click **Change User Name**. The Word Options dialog box opens, with the General tab displayed.

5. On a piece of paper, write down the current username and initials, if they are not your own, so you can refer to it when you need to restore the original username and initials later in this tutorial. Although the user initials do not appear on the Word screen, in a printed document, the username is replaced with the user initials to save space. Therefore, you should always change the user initials whenever you change the username.

6. Click in the **User name** box, delete the current username, and then type **Anya Pathak**.

7. Click in the **Initials** box, delete the current initials, and then type **AP**.

8. Click the **Always use these values regardless of sign in to Office** checkbox to insert a check, if necessary.

9. Click the **OK** button. The Word Options dialog box closes, and you return to the Track Changes Options dialog box.

10. Click the **OK** button to close the Track Changes Options dialog box.

11. In the Tracking group, click the **Track Changes** button. Blue highlighting on the Track Changes button tells you that it is selected, indicating that the Track Changes feature is turned on.

 Trouble? If you see a menu, you clicked the Track Changes button arrow rather than the button itself. Press the Esc key to close the menu, and then click the Track Changes button to turn on Track Changes.

12. In the Tracking group, verify that the Display for Review box displays "All Markup." This setting ensures that tracked changes are displayed in the document as you edit it.

Trouble? If the Display for Review box does not display "All Markup," click the Display for Review arrow, and then click All Markup.

▶ **13.** In the Tracking group, click the **Show Markup** button, and then point to **Balloons**. See Figure 7-1.

Figure 7-1	Track Changes turned on

▶ **14.** If you do not see a checkmark next to Show Revisions in Balloons, click **Show Revisions in Balloons** now to select it and close the menu. Otherwise, click anywhere in the document to close the menu.

Now that Track Changes is turned on, you can begin editing Anya's document. First, Anya needs to change the word "flowers" in the first sentence to "perennials."

To edit Anya's document and view the tracked changes:

▶ **1.** In the line below the "Rain Gardens in Carrel Springs" heading, select the word **flowers** and then type **perennials**. The new word, "perennials," is displayed in color, with an underline. A vertical line is displayed in the left margin, drawing attention to the change. To the right of the document, the username associated with the change (Anya Pathak) is displayed, along with an explanation of the change. See Figure 7-2.

Figure 7-2	Edit marked as tracked change

2. Move the mouse pointer over the newly inserted word "perennials." A ScreenTip displays information about the edit, along with the date and time the edit was made.

3. Move the mouse pointer over the explanation of the change to the right of the document. The explanation is highlighted, and the dotted line connecting the change in the document to the explanation turns solid. In a document with many tracked changes, this makes it easier to see which explanation is associated with which tracked change.

 Next, Anya wants you to move the second-to-last sentence in this paragraph to the end of the paragraph.

4. Press the **Ctrl** key, and then click in the sentence that begins "The rain is then absorbed into the garden…." The entire sentence is selected.

5. Drag the sentence to insert it at the end of the paragraph, and then click anywhere in the document to deselect it. See Figure 7-3.

Figure 7-3 **Tracked changes showing text moved to a new location**

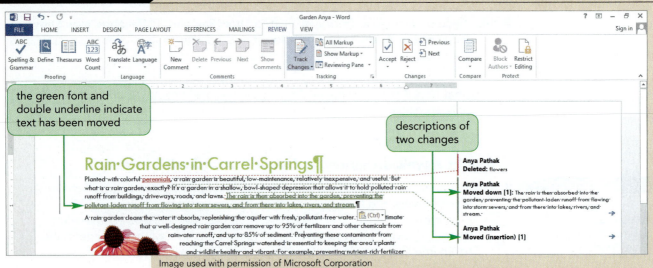

Image used with permission of Microsoft Corporation

The sentence is inserted with a double underline in green, which is the color Word uses to denote moved text. Word also inserts a space before the inserted sentence, and marks the nonprinting space character as a tracked change. A vertical bar in the left margin draws attention to the moved text.

To the right of the document, descriptions of two new changes are displayed. The "Moved down [1]" change shows the text of the sentence that was moved. The "Moved (insertion) [1]" change draws attention to the sentence in its new location at the end of the paragraph.

A blue, right-facing arrow next to a tracked change explanation indicates that the change is related to another change. You can click the arrow to select the related change.

6. Next to the "Moved (insertion) [1]" change, click the blue, right-facing arrow to select the moved sentence in the "Moved down [1]" balloon. See Figure 7-4.

Figure 7-4	Selecting a related change

clicking this arrow selects the related change

related change

Image used with permission of Microsoft Corporation

After reviewing the sentence in its new location at the end of the paragraph, Anya notices that she needs to add an "s" to the end of the word "stream."

7. In the sentence you moved in Step 5, click to the right of the "m" in "stream," and then type the letter **s**. The newly inserted letter is displayed in the same color as the word "perennials" at the beginning of the paragraph.

Finally, Anya asks you to insert a comment reminding her to consider adding a second example of the damage caused by rain runoff. Comments are commonly used with tracked changes. In All Markup view, they are displayed, along with other edits, to the right of the document.

8. In the line of text above the "3,000 Rain Gardens" heading, double-click the word **streets**.

9. In the Comments group, click the **New Comment** button. The word "streets" is highlighted in the same color used for the word "perennials," and the insertion point moves to the right of the document, ready for you to type the comment text.

10. Type **Consider adding a second example.** See Figure 7-5.

Figure 7-5	Comment added to document

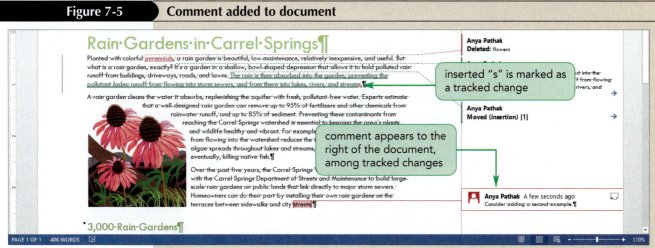

inserted "s" is marked as a tracked change

comment appears to the right of the document, among tracked changes

Image used with permission of Microsoft Corporation

11. Save your document.

Adjusting Track Changes Options

The default settings for Track Changes worked well as you edited Anya's document. However, you can change these settings if you prefer. For instance, you could choose not to display formatting changes as tracked changes, or you could select a different color for inserted text. To get a more streamlined view of the document, you can switch from All Markup view to Simple Markup view.

To view Track Changes options:

1. In the Tracking group, click the **Dialog Box Launcher**. The Track Changes Options dialog box opens. See Figure 7-6.

| Figure 7-6 | Track Changes Options dialog box |

if you deselect a check box, that type of change is no longer marked as a tracked change

you could select Nothing here to hide balloons

The check boxes in the Show section control which types of edits are marked as tracked changes. For example, the Formatting check box is currently selected. If you didn't want formatting changes to be marked as tracked changes, you could deselect the Formatting check box. Note that Revisions is currently selected in the "Balloons in All Markup view show" box. To turn off the balloon feature, so that no track changes or comment balloons are displayed to the right of the document in All Markup view, you could select Nothing instead.

2. Click **Advanced Options**. The Advanced Track Changes Options dialog box opens.

The options in this dialog box allow you to select the colors you want to use for various types of edits. For example, you can use the Color box next to the Insertions box to select a color to use for inserted text. Note that the default setting for Insertions, Deletions, Comments, and Formatting is By author. This means that Word assigns one color to each person who edits the document. When you are working with multiple reviewers, you should always retain the By author settings to ensure that you can easily distinguish the edits made by each reviewer.

3. Click the **Cancel** button to close the Advanced Track Changes Options dialog box, and then click the **Cancel** button to close the Track Changes Options dialog box.

After reviewing the tracked changes with you, Anya decides the number of details shown in All Markup view makes the document too difficult to read. She wants you to switch to Simple Markup view instead.

To switch to Simple Markup view:

▶ 1. In the Tracking group, click the **Display for Review** arrow, and then click **Simple Markup**. See Figure 7-7.

Figure 7-7 Simple Markup view

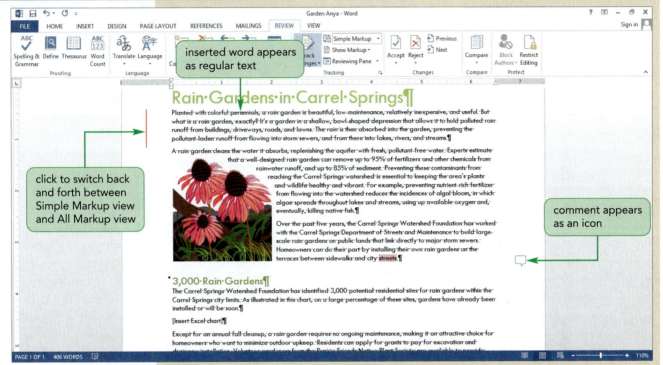

Image used with permission of Microsoft Corporation

Trouble? If the comment balloon is still visible on your screen, click the Show Comments button in the Comments group on the REVIEW tab to deselect it.

All of the tracked changes in the document are now hidden, and the comment balloon is replaced with an icon in the right margin. The inserted word "perennial" is in black font, like the surrounding text, as is the sentence you moved to the end of the paragraph. The only signs that the document contains tracked changes is the red vertical bar in the left margin. You can click a vertical bar to switch back and forth between Simple Markup view and All Markup view.

▶ 2. Click the red vertical bar to the left of the paragraph below the "Rain Gardens in Carrel Springs" heading. The document switches to All Markup view, with all the tracked changes and the comment visible. The vertical bar in the left margin changes from red to gray.

▶ 3. Click the gray vertical bar to the left of the paragraph below the "Rain Gardens in Carrel Springs" heading. The document switches back to Simple Markup view.

Anya has received Oliver's edited copy of the first draft via email, and now she'd like your help in combining her edited copy of the Garden Anya document with Oliver's copy.

Comparing and Combining Documents

When you work in a collaborative environment with multiple people contributing to the same document, Word's Compare and Combine features are essential tools. They allow you to see the difference between multiple versions of a document, with tracked changes highlighting the differences. The Compare and Combine features are similar, but they have different purposes.

The **Compare** feature, which is designed to help you quickly spot the differences between two copies of a document, is intended for documents that do not contain tracked changes. In a compared document, differences between the revised document and the original document are marked with tracked changes, with all the tracked changes assigned to the username associated with the revised document.

The **Combine** feature, which is designed for documents that do contain tracked changes, allows you to see which reviewers made which changes. In a combined document, each reviewer's tracked changes are displayed, with each tracked change assigned to the reviewer who made that change. The Combine feature works well when you want to combine, or **merge**, two documents to create a third, combined document, with which you can then combine additional documents, until you have incorporated all the tracked changes from all your reviewers. Because the Combine feature allows you to incorporate more than two documents into one, it's the option you'll use most when collaborating with a group.

When you compare or combine documents, you select one document as the original and one as the revised document. Together, these two documents are known as the **source documents**. By default, Word then creates a new, third document, which consists of the original document's text edited with tracked changes to show how the revised document differs. The source documents themselves are left unchanged. If Word detects a formatting conflict—that is, if identical text is formatted differently in the source documents—Word displays a dialog box allowing you to choose which formatting you want to keep. You can choose to keep the formatting of the original document or the revised document, but not both. Occasionally, Word will display this formatting conflict dialog box even if both source documents are formatted exactly the same. If so, keep the formatting for the original document, and continue with the process of combining the documents.

REFERENCE

Comparing and Combining Documents

- On the ribbon, click the REVIEW tab.
- In the Compare group, click the Compare button.
- Click Compare to open the Compare Documents dialog box, or click Combine to open the Combine Documents dialog box.
- Next to the Original document box, click the Browse button, navigate to the location of the document, select the document, and then click the Open button.
- Next to the Revised document box, click the Browse button, navigate to the location of the document, select the document, and then click the Open button.
- Click the More button, if necessary, to display options that allow you to select which items you want marked with tracked changes, and then make any necessary changes.
- Click the OK button.

When you start combining or comparing documents, it's not necessary to have either the original document or the revised document open. In this case, however, the Garden Anya document, which you will use as the original document, is open. You'll combine this document with Oliver's edited copy.

To combine Anya's document with Oliver's document:

1. Make sure you have saved your changes to the **Garden Anya** document.

2. In the Compare group, click the **Compare** button. A menu opens with options for comparing or combining two versions of a document.

3. Click **Combine**. The Combine Documents dialog box opens.

4. Click the **More** button. The dialog box expands to display check boxes, which you can use to specify the items you want marked with tracked changes.

 Trouble? If the dialog box has a Less button instead of a More button, the dialog box is already expanded to show the check boxes for selecting additional options. In this case, skip Step 4.

 In the Show changes section at the bottom of the dialog box, the New document option button is selected by default, indicating that Word will create a new, combined document rather than importing the tracked changes from the original document into the revised document, or vice versa.

 Now you need to specify the Garden Anya document as the original document. Even though this document is currently open, you still need to select it.

5. Next to the Original document box, click the **Browse** button 🗀 to open the Open dialog box.

6. If necessary, navigate to the location where you saved the Garden Anya document, click **Garden Anya** in the file list, and then click the **Open** button. You return to the Combine Documents dialog box, where the filename "Garden Anya" is displayed in the Original document box.

 Next, you need to select the document you want to use as the revised document.

7. Next to the Revised document box, click the **Browse** button 🗀, navigate to the Word7 ▸ Tutorial folder included with your Data Files, select the document **Garden Oliver**, and then click the **Open** button. The filename "Garden Oliver" is displayed in the Revised document box. See Figure 7-8.

Figure 7-8	Selecting the original and revised documents

checked options are marked by tracked changes

default option creates a new, combined document

▶ **8.** Click the **OK** button. The Combine Documents dialog box closes.

Trouble? If you see a dialog box alerting you to a formatting conflict, click the "Your document (Garden Anya)" button is selected, if necessary, and then click the continue with Merge button.

A new document opens. It contains the tracked changes from both the original document and the revised document.

At this point, depending on the previous settings on your computer, you might see only the new, combined document, or you might also see the original and revised documents open in separate windows. You might also see the Reviewing pane, which includes a summary of the number of revisions in the combined document along with a list of all the changes, as shown in Figure 7-9.

Figure 7-9	Two documents combined

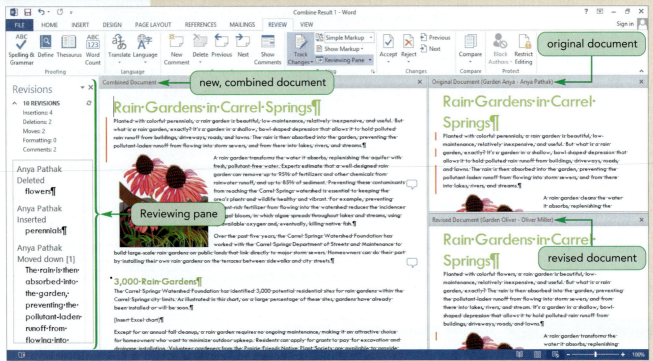

Image used with permission of Microsoft Corporation

Note that your combined document might have a different name than shown in Figure 7-9. For instance, it might be named "Document 1," instead of "Combine Result 1."

▶ **9.** In the Compare group, click the **Compare** button, and then point to **Show Source Documents**.

▶ **10.** If a checkmark appears next to Show Both, press the **Esc** key twice to close both menus; otherwise, click **Show Both**. Your screen should now match Figure 7-9.

Trouble? If the Reviewing pane is still not displayed, click the Reviewing Pane button in the Tracking group to display the Reviewing pane.

Trouble? If your Reviewing pane is displayed horizontally rather than vertically, as shown in Figure 7-9, click the Reviewing Pane button arrow in the Tracking group, and then click Reviewing Pane Vertical.

Note that the combined document and the two source documents are all displayed in Simple Markup view. Instead of Print Layout view, which you typically use when working on documents, the three documents are displayed in Web Layout view. You'll learn more about Web Layout view later in this tutorial. For now, all you need to know is that in Web Layout view, the line breaks change to suit the size of the document window, making it easier to read text in the small windows.

It's helpful to have the source documents displayed when you want to quickly compare the two documents. For example, right now Anya wants to scroll down the documents to see how they differ. When you scroll up or down in the Revised Document pane, the other documents scroll as well.

To scroll the document panes simultaneously:

1. Click in the Revised Document (Garden Oliver - Oliver Miller) pane to display its scroll bar, and then drag the scroll bar down to display the text "3,000 Rain Gardens." The text in the Combined Document pane and in the Original Document (Garden Anya - Anya Pathak) pane scrolls down to match the text in the Revised Document (Garden Oliver - Oliver Miller) pane. See Figure 7-10.

Figure 7-10	Document panes scrolled to compare versions

Image used with permission of Microsoft Corporation

Now that you've reviewed both documents, you can hide the source documents to make the combined document easier to read. After you hide the source documents, you can review the edits in the Reviewing pane.

To hide the source documents and review the edits in the Reviewing pane:

1. In the Compare group, click the **Compare** button, point to the **Show Source Documents** button, and then click **Hide Source Documents**. The panes displaying the original and revised documents close, and the combined document window switches to Print Layout view.

TIP

To hide a reviewer's edits, click the Show Markup button in the Tracking group, point to Specific People, and then click the person's name.

Trouble? If the combined window does not switch to Print Layout view, click the Print Layout view button ▤ on the status bar.

2. Move the mouse over the list of edits in the Reviewing pane to display the vertical scroll bar, and then scroll down and review the list of edits. Notice that the document contains the edits you made earlier (under Anya's name) as well as edits made by Oliver Miller.

Anya prefers to review changes using All Markup view instead of the Reviewing pane.

3. In the Tracking group, click the **Reviewing Pane** button to deselect it. The Reviewing pane closes.

4. In the Tracking group, click the **Display for Review** arrow, and then click **All Markup**.

5. In the Tracking group, click the **Show Markup** arrow, point to Balloons, and then make sure **Show Revisions in Balloons** is selected.

6. Save the document as **Garden Combined** in the location specified by your instructor.

7. In the Tracking group, click the **Track Changes** button to turn off Track Changes. This ensures that you won't accidentally add any additional edit marks as you review the document.

8. Change the Zoom level to **120%**.

Next, you will review the edits in the Garden Combined document to accept and reject the changes as appropriate.

Accepting and Rejecting Changes

The document you just created contains all the edits from two different reviewers—Anya's changes made in the original document, and Oliver's changes as they appeared in the revised document. In the combined document, each reviewer's edits are displayed in a different color, making it easy to see which reviewer made each change.

When you review tracked changes in a document, the best approach is to move the insertion point to the beginning of the document, and then navigate through the document one change at a time using the Next and Previous buttons in the Changes group on the REVIEW tab. This ensures you won't miss any edits. As you review a tracked change, you can either accept the change or reject it.

REFERENCE

Accepting and Rejecting Changes

- Move the insertion point to the beginning of the document.
- On the ribbon, click the REVIEW tab.
- In the Changes group, click the Next button to select the first edit or comment in the document.
- To accept a selected change, click the Accept button in the Changes group.
- To reject a selected change, click the Reject button in the Changes group.
- To accept all the changes in the document, click the Accept button arrow, and then click Accept All Changes.
- To reject all the changes in the document, click the Reject button arrow, and then click Reject All Changes.

To accept and reject changes in the Garden Combined document:

▸ **1.** Press the **Ctrl+Home** keys to move the insertion point to the beginning of the document.

▸ **2.** In the Changes group, click the **Next** button. To the right of the document, in a tracked change balloon, the deleted word "flowers" is selected, as shown in Figure 7-11.

Figure 7-11	First change in document selected

Trouble? If a style-related change is selected instead, click the Accept button in the Changes group, and then continue with Step 3.

Trouble? If the insertion point moves to Oliver's comment, you clicked the Next button in the Comments group instead of the Next button in the Changes group. Repeat Steps 1 and 2.

▸ **3.** In the Changes group, click the **Accept** button. The tracked change balloon is no longer displayed, indicating that the change has been accepted. The inserted word "perennials" is now selected in the document.

Trouble? If you see a menu below the Accept button, you clicked the Accept button arrow by mistake. Press the Esc key to close the menu, and then click the Accept button.

▸ **4.** Click the **Accept** button. To the right of the document, in a tracked change balloon, the sentence that you moved is now selected.

▸ **5.** Click the **Accept** button. The tracked change balloon containing the moved sentence and the related "Moved (insertion) [1]" tracked change balloon are no longer displayed. In the document, the sentence itself is displayed in black, like the surrounding text, indicating that the change has been accepted. Now the space before the moved sentence, which Word automatically inserted when you moved the sentence, is selected.

▸ **6.** Click the **Accept** button to accept the insertion of the space, and then click the **Accept** button again to accept the insertion of the letter "s" at the end of "stream." In a tracked change balloon to the right of the document, Oliver's deletion of the word "cleans" is selected. See Figure 7-12.

Figure 7-12 | **Reviewing Oliver's changes**

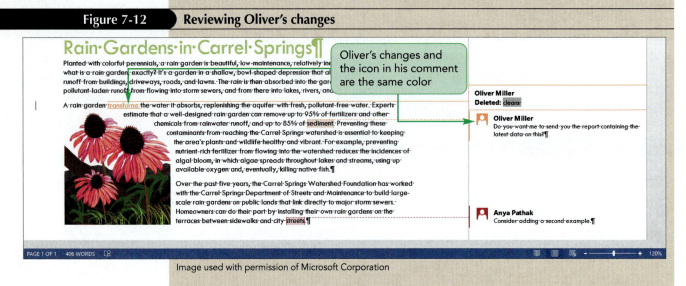

Oliver's changes and the icon in his comment are the same color

Image used with permission of Microsoft Corporation

Oliver deleted the word "cleans" and replaced it with the word "transforms," which is displayed in the document as a tracked change. The inserted word, the tracked change balloon for the deleted word, and the icon in Oliver's comment are all the same color.

Anya prefers to keep the original word, "cleans," so you need to reject Oliver's change.

7. In the Changes group, click the **Reject** button to reject the deletion of the word "cleans." The tracked change balloon is no longer displayed, and the word "cleans" is restored in the document, to the left of the inserted word "transforms," which is now selected. See Figure 7-13.

Figure 7-13 | **Document after rejecting change**

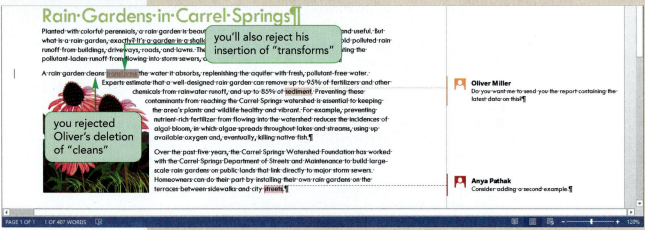

you'll also reject his insertion of "transforms"

 you rejected Oliver's deletion of "cleans"

Image used with permission of Microsoft Corporation

Next, you need to reject the insertion of this word.

8. Click the **Reject** button. The inserted word "transforms" is removed from the document, and the insertion point moves to the beginning of Oliver's comment. Anya has already talked to Oliver about the report mentioned in his comment, so you can delete the comment.

9. In the Comments group, click the **Delete** button to delete the comment.

▶ **10.** In the Changes group, click the **Next** button. (You could also click the Next button in the Comments group since the next item is a comment.) The insertion point moves to Anya's comment. Anya has decided not to add a second example, so you can delete her comment, too.

▶ **11.** In the Comments group, click the **Delete** button.

▶ **12.** In the Changes group, click the **Next** button. A Microsoft Word dialog box opens with a message indicating that there are no more comments or tracked changes in the document.

▶ **13.** Click the **OK** button to close the dialog box.

▶ **14.** In the fourth paragraph from the end of the document, replace "Anya Pathak" with your first and last names, and then save the document.

Now that you have finished editing and reviewing the document with tracked changes, you need to restore the original username and initials settings. Then you can close Anya's original document, which you no longer need.

To restore the original username and initials settings and close Anya's original document:

▶ **1.** In the Tracking group, click the **Dialog Box Launcher** to open the Track Changes Options dialog box.

▶ **2.** Click the **Change User Name** button, and then change the username and initials back to their original settings on the General tab of the Word Options dialog box.

▶ **3.** Click the **OK** button to close the Word Options dialog box, and then click the **OK** button again to close the Track Changes Options dialog box.

▶ **4.** On the taskbar, click the **Word** button [w], and then click the **Garden Anya - Word** thumbnail to display the document.

▶ **5.** Close the Garden Anya document.

▶ **6.** Save the **Garden Combined** document, and then display the rulers.

▶ **7.** On the ribbon, click the **HOME** tab.

INSIGHT

Checking for Tracked Changes

Once a document is finished, you should make sure it does not contain any tracked changes or comments. This is especially important in situations where comments or tracked changes might reveal sensitive information that could jeopardize your privacy, or the privacy of the organization you work for.

You can't always tell if a document contains comments or tracked changes just by looking at it because the comments or changes for some or all of the reviewers might be hidden. Also, the Display for Review box in the Tracking group on the REVIEW tab might be set to No Markup, in which case all tracked changes would be hidden. To determine whether or not a document contains any tracked changes or comments, open the Reviewing pane and verify that the number of revisions for each type is 0. You can also use the Document Inspector to check for a variety of issues including leftover comments and tracked changes. To use the Document Inspector, click the FILE tab, click Info, click Check for Issues, click Inspect Document, and then click the Inspect button.

Now that you have combined Oliver's edits with Anya's, you are ready to add the budget and the pie chart to the document.

Embedding and Linking Objects from Other Programs

The programs in Office 2013 are designed to accomplish specific tasks. As you've seen with Word, you can use a word-processing program to create, edit, and format documents such as letters, reports, newsletters, and proposals. On the other hand, Microsoft Excel, a **spreadsheet program**, allows you to organize, calculate, and analyze numerical data in a grid of rows and columns, and to illustrate data in the form of charts. A spreadsheet created in Microsoft Excel is known as a **worksheet**. Each Excel file—called a **workbook**—can contain multiple worksheets. Throughout this tutorial, a portion of an Excel worksheet is referred to as a **worksheet object**, and a chart is referred to as a **chart object**.

Sometimes it is useful to combine information created in the different Office programs into one file. For her document, Anya wants to use budget data from an Excel worksheet. She also wants to include an Excel chart that shows the percentage of completed rain gardens. You can incorporate the Excel data and chart into Anya's Word document by taking advantage of **object linking and embedding**, or **OLE**, a technology that allows you to share information among the Office programs. This process is commonly referred to as **integration**.

Before you start using OLE, you need to understand some important terms. Recall that in Word, an object is anything that can be selected and modified as a whole, such as a table, picture, or block of text. Another important term, **source program**, refers to the program used to create the original version of an object. The program into which the object is integrated is called the **destination program**. Similarly, the original file that contains the object you are integrating is called the **source file**, and the file into which you integrate the object is called the **destination file**.

You can integrate objects by either embedding or linking. **Embedding** is a technique that allows you to insert a copy of an object into a destination document. You can double-click an embedded object in the destination document to access the tools of the source program, allowing you to edit the object within the destination document using the source program's tools. Because the embedded object is a copy, any changes you make to it are not reflected in the original source file, and vice versa. For instance, you could embed data from a worksheet named Itemized Expenses into a Word document named Travel Report. Later, if you change the Itemized Expenses file, those revisions would not be reflected in the Travel Report document. The opposite is also true; if you edit the embedded object from within the Travel Report file, those changes will not be reflected in the source file Itemized Expenses. The embedded object retains no connection to the source file.

Figure 7-14 illustrates the relationship between an embedded Excel worksheet object in Anya's Word document and the source file.

Figure 7-14 Embedding an Excel worksheet object in a Word document

source file is an Excel workbook named Budget; changes made to this file will *not* be reflected in the destination file

source program is Excel

destination file is the Garden Combined Word document; changes made to this file will *not* be reflected in the source file

destination program is Word

embedded worksheet object

© 2014 Cengage Learning; Image used with permission of Microsoft Corporation

Linking is similar to embedding, except that the object inserted into the destination file maintains a connection to the source file. Just as with an embedded object, you can double-click a linked object to access the tools of the source program. However, unlike with an embedded object, changes to a linked object show up in both the destination file and the source file. The linked object in the destination document is not a copy; it is a shortcut to the original object in the source file.

Figure 7-15 illustrates the relationship between the data in Oliver's Excel chart and the linked object in Anya's Word document.

Figure 7-15	Linking an Excel chart object to a Word document

source file is an Excel workbook named Rain Garden Chart; changes made to this file will be reflected in the destination file

source program is Excel

destination file is the Garden Combined Word document; changes made to this file will be reflected in the source file

destination program is Word

linked chart object

© 2014 Cengage Learning

Decision Making: Choosing Between Embedding and Linking

Embedding and linking are both useful when you know you'll want to edit an object after inserting it into Word. But how do you decide whether to embed or link the object? Create an embedded object if you won't have access to the original source file in the future, or if you don't need (or want) to maintain the connection between the source file and the document containing the linked object. Two advantages of embedding are that the source file is unaffected by any editing in the destination document, and the two files can be stored separately. You could even delete the source file from your disk without affecting the copy embedded in your Word document. A disadvantage is that the file size of a Word document containing an embedded object will be larger than the file size of a document containing a linked object.

Create a linked object whenever you have data that is likely to change over time, and when you want to keep the object in your document up to date. In addition to the advantage of a smaller destination file size, both the source file and the destination file can reflect recent revisions when the files are linked. A disadvantage to linking is that you have to keep track of two files (the source file and the destination file) rather than just one.

Embedding an Excel Worksheet Object

To embed an object from an Excel worksheet into a Word document, you start by opening the Excel worksheet (the source file) and copying the Excel object to the Office Clipboard. Then, in the Word document (the destination file), you open the Paste Special dialog box. In this dialog box, you can choose to paste the copied Excel object in a number of different forms. To embed it, you select Microsoft Office Excel Worksheet Object.

Anya wants to include the budget for a typical rain garden in her document. If she needs to adjust numbers in the budget later, she will need access to the Excel tools for recalculating the data. Therefore, you'll embed the Excel object in the Word document. Then you can use Excel commands to modify the embedded object from within Word.

To embed the Excel data in the Word document:

▶ **1.** Scroll down to the paragraph above the "Picking Your Plants" heading, and then delete the placeholder text **[Insert Excel worksheet]**, taking care not to delete the paragraph mark after it. The insertion point should now be located in a blank paragraph above the "Picking Your Plants" heading.

Now you need to open Oliver's Excel file and copy the budget.

▶ **2.** Start Microsoft Excel 2013, open the file **Budget** located in the Word7 ▶ Tutorial folder included with your Data Files, and then maximize the Excel program window if necessary. See Figure 7-16.

Figure 7-16 Budget file open in Excel

An Excel worksheet is arranged in rows and columns, just like a Word table. The intersection between a row and a column is called a **cell**; an individual cell takes its name from its column letter and row number. For example, the intersection of column A and row 1 in the upper-left corner of the worksheet is referred to as cell A1. Currently, cell A1 is selected, as indicated by its dark outline.

To copy the budget data to the Office Clipboard, you need to select the entire block of cells containing the budget.

▶ **3.** Click cell **A1** (the cell containing the text "Typical Rain Garden Budget"), press and hold the **Shift** key, and then click cell **B5** (the cell containing "$825"). See Figure 7-17.

Figure 7-17 **Budget data selected in worksheet**

Now that the data is selected, you can copy it to the Office Clipboard.

Be sure to keep Excel open; otherwise you won't have access to the commands for embedding the data in Word.

4. Press the **Ctrl+C** keys. The border around the selected cells is now flashing, indicating that you have copied the data in these cells to the Office Clipboard. Next, you will switch to Word without closing Excel.

5. On the taskbar, click the **Word** button [W] to return to the Garden Combined document. The insertion point is still located in the blank paragraph above the "Picking Your Plants" heading.

6. On the ribbon, click the **HOME** tab.

7. In the Clipboard group, click the **Paste button arrow**, and then click **Paste Special** to open the Paste Special dialog box.

8. In the As list, click **Microsoft Excel Worksheet Object**. See Figure 7-18.

Figure 7-18 **Paste Special dialog box**

Next, you can choose to embed the Excel object or link it, depending on whether you select the Paste button (for embedding) or the Paste link button (for linking). The Paste button is selected by default, which is what you want in this case.

9. Click the **OK** button. The Excel worksheet object is inserted in the Word document, as shown in Figure 7-19.

Figure 7-19	Excel worksheet object embedded in Word document

Trouble? If you don't see the top or bottom horizontal gridline in the embedded Excel object, don't be concerned. It won't affect the rest of the steps.

At this point, the Excel data looks like an ordinary table. But because you embedded it as an Excel worksheet object, you can modify it from within Word, using Excel tools and commands.

Modifying an Embedded Worksheet Object

After you embed an object in Word, you can modify it in two different ways. First, you can click the object to select it, and then move or resize it just as you would a graphic object. Second, you can double-click the object to display the tools of the source program on the Word ribbon, and then edit the contents of the object. After you modify the embedded object using the source program tools, you can click anywhere else in the Word document to deselect the embedded object and redisplay the usual Word tools on the ribbon.

Anya would like to center the Excel object on the page. Also, the value for Plants is incorrect, so she asks you to update the budget with the new data.

To modify the embedded Excel object:

1. Click anywhere in the Excel object. Selection handles and a dotted outline are displayed around the Excel object, indicating that it is selected. With the object selected, you can center it as you would center any other selected item.

2. Make sure the HOME tab is selected on the ribbon.

3. In the Paragraph group, click the **Center** button ▤. The Excel object is centered between the left and right margins of the document.

4. Double-click anywhere inside the Excel object. The object's border changes to resemble the borders of an Excel worksheet, with horizontal and vertical scroll bars, row numbers, and column letters. The Word tabs on the ribbon are replaced with Excel tabs.

Trouble? If you don't see the Excel borders around the worksheet object, click outside the worksheet object to deselect it, and then repeat Step 4. If you still don't see the Excel borders, save the document, close it, reopen it, and then repeat Step 4.

You need to change the value for Plants from $175 to $225. Although you can't see it, a formula automatically calculates and displays the total in cell B5. After you increase the value for Plants, the formula will increase the total in cell B5 by $50.

▶ 5. Click cell **B4**, which contains the value $175, and then type **225**.

▶ 6. Press the **Enter** key. The new value "$225" is displayed in cell B4. The budget total in cell B5 increases from $825 to $875. See Figure 7-20.

Figure 7-20 **Revised data in embedded Excel object**

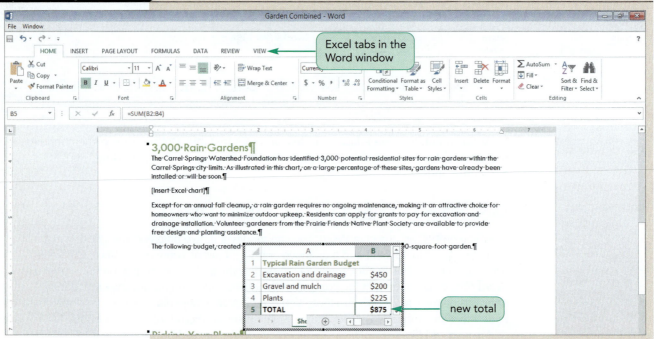

▶ 7. In the document, click outside the borders of the Excel object to deselect it. The Word tabs are now visible on the ribbon again.

▶ 8. On the taskbar, click the **Microsoft Excel** button ☒ to display the Excel window.

Because you embedded the Excel object rather than linking it, the Plant value of $175 and the Total of $825 remain unchanged.

▶ 9. On the ribbon, click the **FILE** tab, and then click **Close** in the navigation bar. The Budget workbook closes, but Excel remains open.

In this session, you worked with tracked changes in a document. You learned how to combine and compare documents, and you accepted and rejected tracked changes in a combined document. You also embedded an Excel Worksheet object in a Word document and modified the embedded worksheet object from within Word. In the next session, you'll learn how to link an object instead of embedding it. You'll also create bookmarks, and insert and edit hyperlinks in a document. You'll save a Word document as a webpage, format the webpage, and then view it in a web browser. Finally, you'll learn how to create and publish a blog post.

REVIEW

Session 7.1 Quick Check

1. Explain how to turn on Track Changes.
2. How do you open the Track Changes Options dialog box?
3. If you have two documents that contain tracked changes, should you use the Compare feature or the Combine feature?
4. Explain the difference between a linked object and an embedded object.
5. What button do you use in Word to embed an object that you've copied to the Clipboard?
6. How do you start editing an embedded Excel object in Word?

Session 7.2 Visual Overview:

To link an Excel chart object to a Word document, you first need to open the Excel workbook that contains the chart.

The two paste buttons with chain links on them allow you to paste the chart as a linked object. Here, the mouse is pointing to the Use Destination Theme & Link Data button, which pastes the chart using the green theme colors of the Word document, which is the destination file.

The Keep Source Formatting & Link Data button pastes the chart using the blue theme colors of the Excel workbook, which is the source file.

Linking an Excel chart to a Word document is essentially a copy-and-paste operation. You need to click the chart to select it, and then copy it to the Office Clipboard. The border around this chart tells you it is selected. To quickly copy the chart to the Office Clipboard, you can press the Ctrl+C keys.

In the Word document, you need to click where you want to insert the chart, and then click the Paste button arrow to display the Paste Options menu. Remember to keep Excel open when you switch to the Word document; otherwise, the linking options you need won't be visible in this menu.

Word displays a Live Preview of the pasted chart when you place the mouse pointer over a button in the Paste Options menu. In this Live Preview, the green chart matches the theme colors of the Word document because the mouse pointer is currently positioned over the Use Destination Theme & Link Data button.

Linking an Excel Chart Object

You can edit a linked chart object from within the Word document.

After you select the chart in the Word document, you click the Edit Data button on the CHART TOOLS DESIGN tab. This opens a spreadsheet window with the Excel source file displayed.

If the chart in the Word window does not change to reflect changes made to data in the spreadsheet window, you can click the Refresh Data button to update the chart in the Word window.

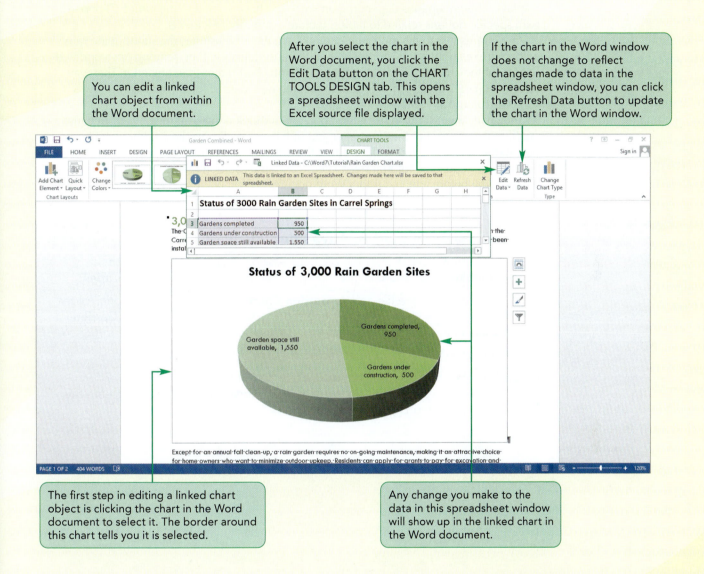

The first step in editing a linked chart object is clicking the chart in the Word document to select it. The border around this chart tells you it is selected.

Any change you make to the data in this spreadsheet window will show up in the linked chart in the Word document.

Linking an Excel Chart Object

When you link an object to a Word document, you start by selecting the object in the source program and copying it to the Office Clipboard. Then you return to Word and select one of the linking options from the Paste Options menu. The Paste Options menu displays different options depending on what you have copied to the Office Clipboard, with specific options related to tables, pictures, and other elements.

Anya wants you to insert Oliver's Excel chart, which illustrates the status of the rain garden project, into her Word document. Because Oliver will be sending Anya updated figures for the chart soon, she decides to link the chart rather than embed it. That way, once the chart is updated in the source file, the new data will be displayed in Anya's Word document as well.

The chart Anya wants to use is stored in a workbook named Garden Chart. Because you'll make changes to the chart after you link it, you will save the workbook with a new name before you link it. This leaves the original workbook file unchanged in case you want to repeat the tutorial steps later. Normally, you don't need to save a file with a new name before you link it to a Word document.

To link the Excel chart to Anya's document:

▶ **1.** If you took a break after the previous session, make sure the **Garden Combined** document is open in Print Layout view, and that Excel is open.

▶ **2.** In Excel, open the file named **Garden Chart** from the Word7 ▶ Tutorial folder included with your Data Files, and then save it with the name **Rain Garden Chart** in the location specified by your instructor.

The worksheet includes data and a pie chart illustrating the data.

▶ **3.** Click the chart border. Do not click any part of the chart itself. A selection border is displayed around the chart. The worksheet data used to create the chart is also highlighted in purple and blue. See Figure 7-21.

| Figure 7-21 | Pie chart selected in worksheet |

Trouble? If you see borders or handles around individual elements of the pie chart, you clicked the chart itself rather than the border. Click in the worksheet outside the chart border, and then repeat Step 3.

4. Press the **Ctrl+C** keys to copy the pie chart to the Office Clipboard.

5. On the taskbar, click the **Microsoft Word** button to display the Word window with the Garden Combined document.

6. On the ribbon, make sure the HOME tab is selected.

7. In the second paragraph after the "3,000 Rain Gardens" heading, delete the placeholder text **[Insert Excel chart]** but not the paragraph symbol after it, and then verify that the insertion point is located in a blank paragraph between two paragraphs of text.

8. In the Clipboard group, click the **Paste button arrow** to display the Paste Options menu.

9. Move the mouse pointer over the icons on the Paste Options menu, and notice the changing appearance of the chart's Live Preview, depending on which Paste Option you are previewing.

For linking, you can choose between the Use Destination Theme & Link Data option, which formats the chart with the font and green colors of the Word document's current theme, and the Keep Source Formatting & Link Data option, which retains the font and blue colors of the Excel workbook. See Figure 7-22.

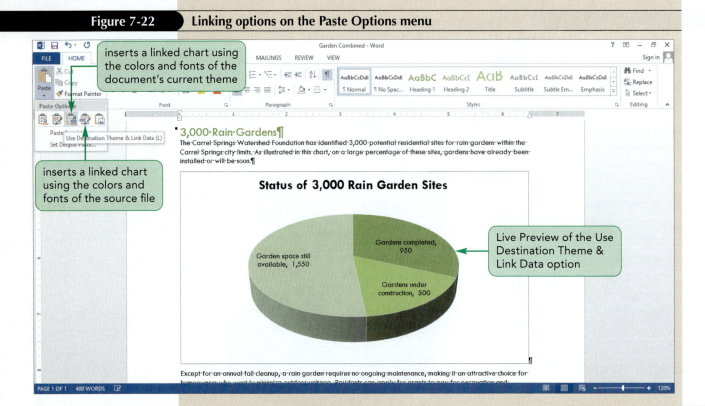

Figure 7-22 Linking options on the Paste Options menu

inserts a linked chart using the colors and fonts of the document's current theme

inserts a linked chart using the colors and fonts of the source file

Live Preview of the Use Destination Theme & Link Data option

Use the button's ScreenTip to verify you are about to click the Use Destination Theme & Link Data button. It's easy to click the wrong button on the Paste Options menu.

10. On the Paste Options menu, click the **Use Destination Theme & Link Data** button. The chart is inserted in the document. It is formatted with the green colors and font of the Circuit theme used in the Word document.

INSIGHT

Storing Linked Files

When linking objects, it is important to keep the source and destination files in their original storage locations. If you move the files or the folders in which they are stored, you will disrupt the connection between the source file and the document containing the linked object because the shortcut in the destination file will no longer have a valid path to the source file.

For example, suppose you insert a linked Excel file into a Word document, and then later a colleague moves the Excel file to a different folder. The next time you open the Word document and try to update the linked object, you will see a dialog box explaining that the linked file is not available. At that point, you can make the link functional again by updating the path to the linked objects. To do so, click the FILE tab on the ribbon, and then click Info in the navigation bar, if necessary. On the Info screen, click Edit Links to Files. In the Links dialog box, click the link whose location has changed, click the Change Source button, and then navigate to the new location of the source file.

Modifying the Linked Chart Object

The advantage of linking compared to embedding is that you can change the data in the source file, and those changes will automatically be reflected in the destination file as well.

Anya has received Oliver's updated rain garden status figures, and she wants the chart in her document to reflect this new information. You will update the data in the source file. You'll start by closing Excel so you can clearly see the advantages of working with a linked object.

To modify the chart in the source file:

▶ **1.** On the taskbar, click the **Microsoft Excel** button ▧ to display the Excel window, and then close Excel.

▶ **2.** On the taskbar, click the **Microsoft Word** button ▧, if necessary, to display the Word window.

▶ **3.** Click anywhere in the white area inside the chart border. The selection border is displayed around the chart, and the two CHART TOOLS contextual tabs are displayed on the ribbon.

▶ **4.** On the ribbon, click the **CHART TOOLS DESIGN** tab. See Figure 7-23.

| Figure 7-23 | Chart selected in Word |

▶ **5.** In the Data group, click the **Edit Data** button. A small spreadsheet that contains the chart data opens on top of the Word document. Your spreadsheet might be larger or smaller than the one shown in Figure 7-24.

TIP

To edit the source file directly in Excel, click the Edit Data button arrow to display a menu, and then click Edit Data in Excel 2013.

Figure 7-24 Spreadsheet window with chart data

The file path at the top of the spreadsheet window shows the location of the linked file you are about to edit.

6. In the Excel window, click cell **B3**, which contains the value "950," and then type **975**.

7. Press the **Enter** key. The new value is entered in cell B3, and the label in the "Gardens completed" section of the pie chart changes from 950 to 975 in the linked chart in the Word document. Although you can't see the pie chart in the Excel spreadsheet window, it has also been updated to display the new value.

Trouble? If the chart in the Word document does not change to show the new value, click anywhere in the white area inside the chart border, and then click the Refresh Data button in the Data group on the CHART TOOLS DESIGN tab in the Word window. Then, click cell B4 in the spreadsheet window.

8. In the Excel window, type **475** in cell B4, and then press the **Enter** key. The new number is entered in cell B4, and the value in the "Gardens under construction" section of the pie charts in both the Excel and Word windows changes to match. See Figure 7-25.

| Figure 7-25 | Modifying the linked chart data |

9. At the top of the spreadsheet window, click the **Save** button 🖫, and then click the **Close** button ❌ to close the spreadsheet window.

10. In the Word document, click anywhere outside the chart to deselect it, and then save the Garden Combined document.

When you edited the data in the spreadsheet window, you were actually editing the Rain Garden Chart workbook. If you wanted, you could start Excel and open the Rain Garden Chart workbook to verify that it contains the new values.

INSIGHT

Editing a Linked Worksheet Object

The steps for editing a linked worksheet object are slightly different from the steps for editing a linked chart object. Instead of editing a linked worksheet object from within Word, you need to start Excel, open the workbook, and then edit the worksheet in Excel. You can quickly open the workbook in Excel by right-clicking the linked worksheet object in Word, pointing to Linked Worksheet Object on the shortcut menu, and then clicking Edit Link. This opens the workbook in Excel, where you can edit the data and save your changes. When you are finished, close the workbook, and then return to the Word document. Finally, to update the data within the Word document, right-click the linked worksheet object in the Word document to open a shortcut menu, and then click Update Link.

Anya is finished with her work on the chart. She does not expect the data in it to change, so she wants to break the link between the Excel workbook and the Word document.

Breaking Links

If you no longer need a link between files, you can break it. When you break a link, the source file and the destination file no longer have any connection to each other, and changes made in one file do not affect the other. However, the object in the Word document still retains its connection to the source program. Double-clicking the object allows you to edit it using the tools of the source program. In other words, it behaves like an embedded object.

Breaking a Link to a Source File

- On the ribbon, click the FILE tab.
- On the Info screen, click Edit Links to Files to open the Links dialog box.
- In the list of links in the document, click the link that you want to break.
- Click the Break Link button.
- Click the Yes button in the dialog box that opens asking you to confirm that you want to break the link.
- Click the OK button to close the Links dialog box.

Now, you will break the link between Anya's document and the Rain Garden Chart workbook.

To break the link between the Word document and the Excel workbook:

1. On the ribbon, click the **FILE** tab. Backstage view opens with the Info screen displayed.

2. On the Info screen, click **Edit Links to Files**. The Links dialog box opens with the only link in the document (the link to the Rain Garden Chart workbook) selected. See Figure 7-26.

Figure 7-26	The Links dialog box

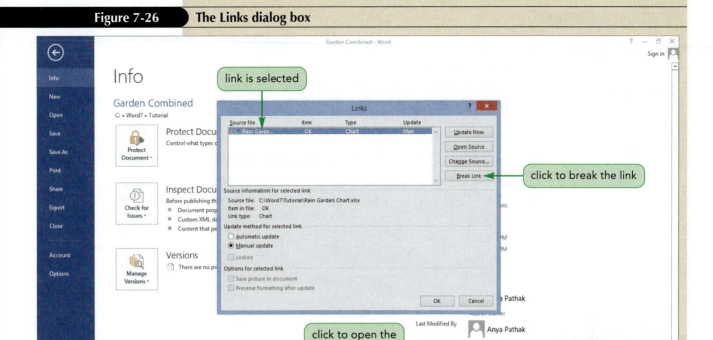

3. In the Links dialog box, click the **Break Link** button, and then click **Yes** in the dialog box that opens asking if you are sure you want to break the link. The list in the Links dialog box now indicates there is no source file for the chart in the document.

4. Click the **OK** button to close the dialog box. You return to the Info screen in Backstage view.

 With the link broken, you can no longer edit the Excel data from within Word. You can verify this by looking at the CHART TOOLS DESIGN tab.

5. At the top of the navigation bar, click the **Back** button ← to close Backstage view and return to the document.

6. Click anywhere inside the chart border to select the chart.

7. On the ribbon, click the **CHART TOOLS DESIGN** tab, if necessary. Notice that the Edit Data button in the Data group is grayed out, indicating this option is no longer available.

8. Click anywhere outside the chart border to deselect it, and then save the document.

Next, Anya asks you to turn your attention to adding hyperlinks to her document. Although hyperlinks are widely used in webpages, you can also use them in ordinary Word documents.

Using Hyperlinks in Word

TIP

Hyperlinks are commonly referred to as "links," but take care not to confuse them with the OLE links you worked with earlier in this tutorial.

A hyperlink is a word, phrase, or graphic that you can click to jump to another part of the same document, to a separate Word document, to a file created in another program, or to a webpage. When used thoughtfully, hyperlinks make it possible to navigate a complicated document or a set of files quickly and easily. And as you know, you can also include email links in documents, which you can click to create email messages.

Anya wants you to add two hyperlinks to the document—one that jumps to a location within the document, and one that opens a different document.

Inserting a Hyperlink to a Bookmark in the Same Document

Creating a hyperlink within a document is actually a two-part process. First, you need to mark the text you want the link to jump to—either by formatting the text with a heading style, or by inserting a bookmark. A **bookmark** is an electronic marker that refers to specific text, a picture, or another object in a document. Second, you need to select the text that you want users to click, format it as a hyperlink, and specify the bookmark or heading as the target of the hyperlink. The **target** is the place in the document to which the link connects. In this case, Anya wants to create a hyperlink at the beginning of the document that targets the budget (which is now an embedded Excel worksheet object) near the end of the document. Figure 7-27 illustrates this process.

Figure 7-27	Hyperlink that targets a bookmark

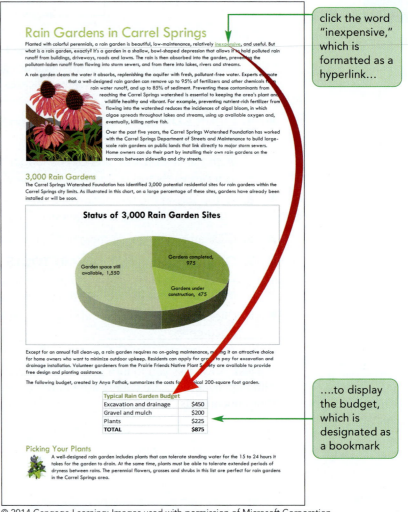

click the word "inexpensive," which is formatted as a hyperlink...

....to display the budget, which is designated as a bookmark

© 2014 Cengage Learning; Images used with permission of Microsoft Corporation

To create a hyperlink in Anya's document, you'll first need to designate the budget as a bookmark.

To insert a bookmark:

1. Scroll down and click the budget worksheet object, at the top of page 2. A dotted outline and handles are displayed around the budget, indicating that it is selected.

2. On the ribbon, click the **INSERT** tab.

3. In the Links group, click the **Bookmark** button. The Bookmark dialog box opens. You can now type the bookmark name, which cannot contain spaces.

4. In the Bookmark name box, type **Budget**. See Figure 7-28.

Figure 7-28 Creating a bookmark

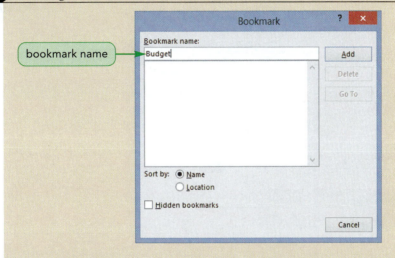

bookmark name

5. Click the **Add** button. The Bookmark dialog box closes. Although you can't see any change in the document, the budget worksheet object has been designated as a bookmark.

The bookmark you just created will be the target of a hyperlink, which you will create next.

REFERENCE

Creating a Hyperlink to a Location in the Same Document

- Select the text, graphic, or other object that you want to format as a hyperlink.
- On the ribbon, click the INSERT tab.
- In the Links group, click the Hyperlink button to open the Insert Hyperlink dialog box.
- In the Link to pane, click Place in This Document.
- In the Select a place in this document list, click the bookmark or heading you want to link to, and then click the OK button.

Anya wants you to format the word "inexpensive" at the beginning of the document as a hyperlink that will target the bookmark you just created.

To create and test a hyperlink to the bookmark:

1. Scroll up to page 1, and then, in the first line under the "Rain Gardens in Carrel Springs" heading, select the word **inexpensive**.

2. In the Links group, click the **Hyperlink** button. The Insert Hyperlink dialog box opens.

3. In the Link to pane, click **Place in This Document** to select it, if necessary. The "Select a place in this document" list shows the headings and bookmarks in the document. Here you can click the bookmark or heading you want as the target for the hyperlink.

4. Under Bookmarks, click **Budget**. See Figure 7-29.

Figure 7-29 | Inserting a hyperlink to a location in the same document

headings in the document

click to create a custom ScreenTip for the hyperlink

select this option

bookmark you created

You can click the ScreenTip button to open the Set Hyperlink ScreenTip dialog box and type custom text for the hyperlink's ScreenTip, which appears when you place the mouse pointer over the hyperlink in the document. In this case, however, Anya prefers to use the default ScreenTip.

TIP

To change a hyperlink's font color, open the Styles pane and modify the Hyperlink style.

5. Click the **OK** button. The word "inexpensive" is now formatted in the hyperlink style for the Circuit theme, which applies a green font color with an underline. The hyperlink targets the Budget bookmark that you created in the last set of steps. You can verify this by clicking the hyperlink.

6. Move the mouse pointer over the hyperlink **inexpensive**. The default ScreenTip displays the name of the bookmark and instructions for following the link. See Figure 7-30.

Figure 7-30 **Displaying the ScreenTip for a hyperlink**

7. Press and hold the **Ctrl** key, and then click the **inexpensive** hyperlink. The insertion point jumps to the budget at the top of page 2.

8. Scroll up to review the "inexpensive" hyperlink. It is now turquoise, which is the color for clicked links in the Circuit theme.

9. Save your document.

Next, you will create a hyperlink that jumps to a different document.

Creating Hyperlinks to Other Documents

When you create a hyperlink to another document, you need to specify the document's filename and storage location as the hyperlink's target. The document can be stored on your computer or on a network; it can even be a webpage stored somewhere on the web. In that case, you need to specify the webpage's URL (web address) as the target. When you click a hyperlink to another document, the document opens on your computer, with the beginning of the document displayed. Keep in mind that if you move the document containing the hyperlink, or if you move the target document, the hyperlink will no longer work. If you create a hyperlink to a webpage on the Internet, the link will continue to work no matter where you store the document containing the hyperlink.

Anya wants to insert a hyperlink that, when clicked, will open a Word document containing a list of plants that grow well in rain gardens. You'll start by opening the document containing the plant list and saving it with a new name.

To create a hyperlink to the Plant List document:

▶ **1.** Open the document **Plant** located in the Word7 ▸ Tutorial folder included with your Data Files, save it as **Plant List** in the location specified by your instructor, and then close it.

▶ **2.** In the Garden Combined document, scroll down to the end of the document, and then select the word **list** in the second-to-last line.

▶ **3.** On the ribbon, click the **INSERT** tab.

▶ **4.** In the Links group, click the **Hyperlink** button. The Insert Hyperlink dialog box opens.

▶ **5.** In the Link to pane, click **Existing File or Web Page**. The dialog box displays options related to selecting a file or a webpage.

▶ **6.** Click the **Look in** arrow, navigate to the location where you stored the Plant List file, if necessary, and then click **Plant List** in the file list. See Figure 7-31.

Figure 7-31 ▶ **Inserting a hyperlink to a different document**

▶ **7.** Click the **OK** button. The new "list" hyperlink is formatted in green with an underline. Now, you will test the hyperlink.

▶ **8.** Press and hold the **Ctrl** key, and then click the **list** hyperlink. The Plant List document opens. See Figure 7-32.

Figure 7-32	Plant List document

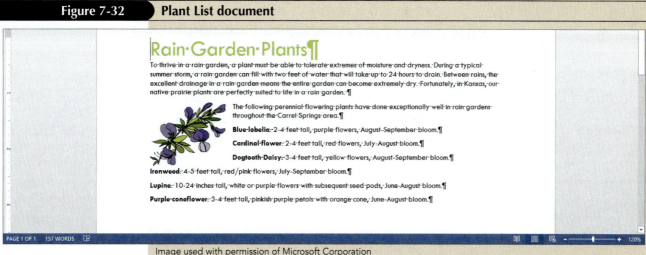

Image used with permission of Microsoft Corporation

9. Close the Plant List document, and then return to the Garden Combined document. The link is now turquoise because you clicked it.

10. Save your document.

Now that you have finalized the document and added the necessary hyperlinks, your next step is to save the document as a webpage.

Saving a Word Document as a Webpage

Webpages are special documents designed to be viewed in a program called a browser. One widely used browser is Internet Explorer. Because webpages include code written in Hypertext Markup Language, or HTML, they are often referred to as HTML documents.

To create sophisticated webpages (or a complete website), you'll probably want to use a dedicated HTML editor, such as Adobe Dreamweaver. However, in Word you can create a simple webpage from an existing document by saving it as a webpage. When you do so, Word inserts HTML codes that tell the browser how to format and display the text and graphics. Fortunately, you don't have to learn Hypertext Markup Language to create webpages with Word. When you save the document as a webpage, Word creates all the necessary HTML codes (called tags); however, you won't actually see the HTML codes in your webpage.

You can choose from three different webpage file types in Word. The main differences among these file types are file size and the way special elements, such as WordArt or embedded or linked objects, are treated when they are displayed in a browser:

• Single File Web Page—Saves the document as an MHTML file, which is similar to an HTML file, with all graphics stored in the file along with the text; a Single File Web Page file also retains the formatting of the original Word document. A document saved as a Single File Web Page can be more than three or four times the size of the original Word document. In the file name for a Single File Web Page file, avoid including spaces and special characters such as exclamation marks or percent signs, because they can prevent the browser from displaying the page correctly.

• Web Page—Saves the document as an HTML file, with a separate folder containing graphics and other elements that control the page's formatting. The HTML file created using the Web Page file type is approximately the same size as the original Word document, but the accompanying files can be two or three times the size of the Word document.

- **Web Page, Filtered**—Saves the document as an HTML file, with graphics stored in a separate folder. This file type retains less information than the other two formats, so some of the document formatting might change or disappear when you use this file type. Before you save a Word document as a filtered webpage, Word displays a dialog box warning you that some Office features (typically formatting) may not be available when you reopen the page. The total file size of a filtered webpage and its accompanying graphics files is smaller than the Word document from which it is created.

The Single File Web Page file type is a good choice when you plan to share your webpage only over a small network and not over the Internet. Having to manage only one file is more convenient than having to keep track of a group of files. But when you want to share your files over the Internet, it's usually better to use the Web Page, Filtered option. This will keep your overall file size as small as possible. A group of smaller files travels across the web faster than one large file, so this division of files makes it easier to share your documents online.

Note that the folder Word creates to store the accompanying files has the same name as your webpage, plus an underscore and the word "files." For instance, a webpage saved as Finance Summary would be accompanied by a folder named Finance Summary_files.

Saving a Word Document as a Webpage

- Open the Save As dialog box and navigate to the location where you want to save the webpage.
- Click the Save as type arrow, and then click Single File Web Page; Web Page; or Web Page, Filtered.
- If desired, type a new filename in the File name box.
- Click the Change Title button to open the Enter Text dialog box.
- In the Page title box, type a title, which will be displayed at the top of the browser window, and then click the OK button.
- In the Save As dialog box, click the Save button. If you saved the document using the Web Page, Filtered option, click Yes in the warning dialog box.

After you save a document as a webpage, Word displays it in **Web Layout view**, which displays the document similarly to the way it would be displayed in a web browser. In Web Layout view, the text spans the width of the screen, with no page breaks, and without any margins or headers and footers. Also, text wrapping around graphics often changes in Web Layout view, as the text expands to fill the wider area of the screen.

To save the Garden Combined document as a webpage:

1. On the ribbon, click the **FILE** tab, and then click **Save As** in the navigation bar.

2. In the Save As dialog box, navigate to the location specified by your instructor.

 Because Anya wants to retain the document formatting, she asks you to use the Single File Web Page type.

3. Click the **Save as type** arrow, and then click **Single File Web Page**.

4. In the File name box, change the filename to **Rain_Garden_Webpage**.

5. At the bottom of the Save As dialog box, click the **Change Title** button to open the Enter Text dialog box, and then type **Rain Gardens in Carrel Springs** in the Page title box. This title will be displayed at the top of the browser window. See Figure 7-33.

Figure 7-33	Webpage title in Enter Text dialog box

this title will appear at the top of the browser window

name of the webpage file

file type

6. In the Enter Text dialog box, click the **OK** button.

7. In the Save As dialog box, click the **Save** button. The document is converted into a webpage and displayed in Web Layout view. The text spans the document window and is no longer constrained by the page margins. The filename Rain_Garden_Webpage is displayed in the Word title bar. The title you specified in Step 5 won't be visible until you open the webpage in a browser, at which point it will be displayed in the browser's title bar.

8. Scroll up to the beginning of the document.

Because the text spans the entire document window, it's often necessary to increase the Zoom level in Web Layout view to make the text easier to read.

9. Change the Zoom level to **200%**. Unlike in Print Layout view, when you zoom in on the document in Web Layout view, the line breaks adjust to ensure that as much text as possible remains visible in the document window.

10. Change the Zoom level to **140%**. The line breaks readjust to accommodate the new Zoom level. See Figure 7-34.

Figure 7-34 New webpage displayed in Web Layout view

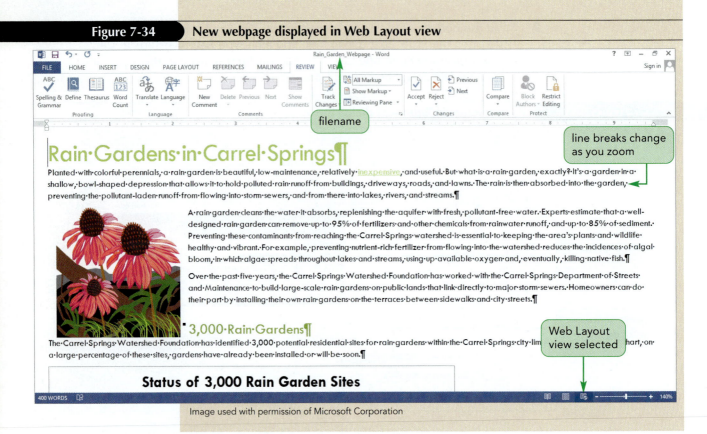

Image used with permission of Microsoft Corporation

Next, Anya asks you to adjust the document's formatting to improve its appearance in Web Layout view.

Formatting a Webpage

You can edit and format text, colors, and graphics in a webpage the same way you edit and format a normal Word document. Anya asks you to start by adjusting the webpage's graphics and text.

Modifying Graphics and Text for Web Layout View

After you convert a Word document into a webpage, you might need to adjust the position, size, and formatting settings for the graphics to make them look better as the user zooms in or out on the page.

To adjust the graphics in the Rain_Garden_Webpage file:

1. Drag the picture of the pink flowers up and to the left slightly to position it directly below the "Rain Gardens in Carrel Springs" heading, with its anchor symbol next to the picture's upper-left corner.

2. Change the picture's height to **1.5** inches. The picture's width adjusts to 1.48 inches automatically.

3. Scroll down in the document, and then click the chart object.

4. Make sure the HOME tab is displayed on the ribbon.

5. In the Paragraph group, click the **Center** button ☰.

6. Scroll down in the document, click the bluebell picture at the bottom of the webpage, and change its height to **1** inch. Its width automatically changes to 0.87 inches.

After you convert a Word document to a webpage, you typically also need to adjust the text's formatting to accommodate the wider text, which spans the width of the viewer's screen. In particular, it's often helpful to use a larger font size for headings. Anya asks you to increase the font size for the title and headings.

To increase the font size for the title and headings:

1. Select the title **Rain Gardens in Carrel Springs** at the top of the webpage.

2. In the Font group, click the **Increase Font Size** button A͡ twice to increase the font size from 28 points to 48 points.

3. Change the font size for the "3,000 Rain Gardens" heading and the "Pick Your Plants" heading to 28 points, and then deselect any selected text.

4. Save your work.

Next, you'll make more changes to the Rain_Garden_Webpage file to improve its online appearance.

Applying a Background Fill Effect

When formatting a webpage, you can focus on how the page will look on the screen, without having to consider how it will look when printed. This means you can take advantage of some formatting options that are only visible on the screen, such as a background page color or a background fill effect. A **fill effect** is a repeating graphic element, such as a texture, a photo, or a color gradient. It's essential to use fill effects judiciously. In the hands of a trained graphic designer, they can be striking; if used carelessly, they can be garish and distracting. As a general rule, you should avoid using photos and textures, and instead stick with simple colors or color gradients.

Anya decides to use a gradient background in shades of green.

To apply a background fill effect to the document:

1. On the ribbon, click the **DESIGN** tab.

2. In the Page Background group, click the **Page Color** button. The Page Color gallery opens, with a menu at the bottom. You could click a color in the gallery to select it as a background color for the page. To select another type of background effect, you need to click Fill Effects.

3. Click **Fill Effects** to open the Fill Effects dialog box, and then click the **Gradient** tab, if necessary. Note that you could use other tabs in this dialog box to add a textured, patterned, or picture background.

4. In the Colors section, click the **Two colors** button. The Color 1 and Color 2 boxes and arrows are displayed.

5. Click the **Color 1** arrow, and then click **Lime, Accent 1, Lighter 80%**, the fifth color from the left in the second row of the Theme Colors section.

6. Click the **Color 2** arrow, and then click **Sky Blue, Background 2, Lighter 60%**, the third color from the left in the third row of the Theme Colors section.

7. In the Shading styles section, click the **Vertical** option button to change the gradient pattern so it stretches vertically up and down the page. Compare your dialog box to Figure 7-35.

Figure 7-35 ▶ **Selecting a gradient background**

8. Click the **OK** button. The document's background is now a gradient that varies between lime green and sky blue.

9. Scroll down so you can see the budget near the bottom of the webpage.

The gradient background is light enough to make the document text easy to read. However, it's now hard to see the gridlines of the budget worksheet object. You can fix that by changing the object's background color.

To change the background for the budget worksheet object:

1. Right-click the budget worksheet object to display a shortcut menu, and then click **Format Object**. The Format Object dialog box opens, with the Picture tab displayed.

2. Click the **Colors and Lines** tab to display settings related to the colors used in the worksheet object. In the Fill section, the Color box currently displays "No Color," indicating that the object's background is the same as the webpage's background.

3. In the Fill section, click the **Color** arrow, and then click **White, Background 1**, the first square in the top row of the Theme Colors section. See Figure 7-36.

Figure 7-36 Format Object dialog box

Format Object ? ×

| Colors and Lines | Size | Layout | Picture | Text Box | Alt Text |

Fill

white fill color selected → Color: [] ▼ Fill Effects...

Transparency: < [] > 0 %

Line

Color: [No Color] ▼ Style: [] ▼

Dashed: [] ▼ Weight: 0.75 pt

Arrows

Begin style: [] ▼ End style: [] ▼

Begin size: [] ▼ End size: [] ▼

OK Cancel

▶ **4.** Click the **OK** button to close the Format Object dialog box. The budget now has a white background, which makes the gridlines easier to see.

▶ **5.** Click outside the budget to deselect it, and then save the document.

Next, you will add horizontal lines to separate the various sections of the webpage.

Inserting Horizontal Lines

Horizontal lines allow you to see at a glance where one part of a webpage ends and another begins. You can also add horizontal lines to regular Word documents.

Anya wants you to add a horizontal line before the "3,000 Rain Gardens" heading and before the "Picking Your Plants" heading.

To insert horizontal lines into the webpage:

▶ **1.** Scroll up and click at the beginning of the "3,000 Rain Gardens" heading.

▶ **2.** On the ribbon, click the **HOME** tab.

▶ **3.** In the Paragraph group, click the **Borders button arrow** [⊞ ▼] to open the Borders gallery, and then click **Horizontal Line** to insert a default gray line.

Anya wants to change the line's color. She also wants to make the line shorter, so it doesn't span the full page.

▶ **4.** Right-click the horizontal line to display a shortcut menu, and then click **Format Horizontal Line**. The Format Horizontal Line dialog box opens, with settings for changing the line's width, height, alignment, and color. The current Width setting is 100%, meaning that the line spans the entire page from left to right. To leave a little space on each side, you need to lower the percentage.

5. Triple-click the **Width** box, and then type **75**. Because the Center alignment option at the bottom of the dialog box is selected by default, the shorter line will be centered on the page, with space to its left and its right.

6. Click the **Color** arrow, and then click **Lime, Accent 1**, the fifth square from the left in the top row of the Theme Colors section. The Color gallery closes, and the Use solid color (no shade) check box is now selected. See Figure 7-37.

Figure 7-37 | **Format Horizontal Line dialog box**

this setting leaves space on both sides of the line

selected by default

7. Click the **OK** button, and then click anywhere in the document to deselect the horizontal line. Your webpage should look similar to Figure 7-38.

Figure 7-38 | **Newly inserted horizontal line**

Now, you can copy the line, and then insert it before the other heading.

TIP

To remove a horizontal line, click the line to select it, and then press the Delete key.

8. Click the horizontal line to select it, and then press the **Ctrl+C** keys to copy it to the Clipboard.

9. Scroll down, click to the left of the "P" in the "Picking Your Plants" heading, and then press the **Ctrl+V** keys to insert the horizontal line before the heading.

10. Save the document.

You've finished formatting the webpage. Next, you'll create a new hyperlink and edit the existing one.

Editing Hyperlinks

Anya's webpage contains two hyperlinks—the "inexpensive" link, which jumps to the budget, and the "list" link, which jumps to a Word document containing a list of plants suitable for rain gardens. You originally created these hyperlinks in Anya's Word document, and they are still functional, even after you saved the document as a webpage. However, before Anya can publish her page on the web, she needs to save the Plant List document as a webpage, format it to match the Rain_Garden_Webpage file, and then edit the hyperlink that connects the two pages.

To save the Plant List document as a webpage:

1. Scroll down, if necessary, to the end of the webpage, press and hold the **Ctrl** key, and then click the **list** hyperlink. The Plant List document opens.

2. Save the document using the Single File Web Page file type, in the location specified by your instructor. Name the webpage **Plant_List_Webpage** and use **Recommended Plants** as the title.

You need to adjust the font size for the headings in this document, and then change the page's background.

3. Select the **Rain Garden Plants** heading, increase its font size to **48** points, and then deselect the heading.

4. On the ribbon, click the **DESIGN** tab.

5. In the Page Background group, click the **Page Color** button, and then click **Fill Effects**.

6. In the Fill Effects dialog box, click the **Two colors** button.

7. Click the **Color 1** arrow, and then click **Lime, Accent 1, Lighter 80%**, the fifth color from the left in the second row of the Theme Colors section.

8. Click the **Color 2** arrow, and then click **Sky Blue, Background 2, Lighter 60%**, the third color from the left in the third row of the Theme Colors section.

9. In the Shading styles section, click the **Vertical** button, and then click the **OK** button.

10. Save the webpage file, and then close it. You return to the Rain_Garden_Webpage file in Word.

Now, you need to edit the hyperlink in the Rain_Garden_Webpage file so it targets the new webpage file named Plant_List_Webpage, instead of the old Word document named Plant List.

To edit the list hyperlink:

▶ **1.** Position the pointer over the **list** hyperlink at the end of the webpage to display a ScreenTip, which indicates that the link will jump to a document named Plant List.docx.

▶ **2.** Right-click the **list** hyperlink to open a shortcut menu, and then click **Edit Hyperlink**. The Edit Hyperlink dialog box opens. It looks just like the Insert Hyperlink dialog box, which you have already used. To edit the hyperlink, you simply select a different target file.

▶ **3.** In the Link to pane, verify that the **Existing File or Web Page** option is selected.

▶ **4.** Navigate to the location where you saved the Plant_List_Webpage file, if necessary, and then click **Plant_List_Webpage** in the file list.

▶ **5.** Click the **OK** button. You return to the Rain_Garden_Webpage file.

▶ **6.** Place the mouse pointer over the **list** hyperlink to display a ScreenTip, which indicates that the link will now jump to a webpage named Plant_List_Webpage.mht.

The edited hyperlink now correctly targets the webpage containing the plant list. After users read the plant list, they most likely will want to return to the main webpage. Therefore, Anya asks you to insert a hyperlink in the Plant_List_Webpage file that will take readers back to the Rain_Garden_Webpage file.

To open the Plant_List_Webpage file, you might be tempted to click the "list" hyperlink in the Rain_Garden_Webpage file. However, if you do, the webpage would open in Internet Explorer. To open a webpage in Word, you need to use the Open command in Backstage view.

To insert a hyperlink in the Plant_List_Webpage file:

▶ **1.** On the ribbon, click the **FILE** tab, and then click **Open** in the navigation bar.

▶ **2.** Navigate to and click the **Plant_List_Webpage** file, and then click the **Open** button. The Plant_List_Webpage file opens.

▶ **3.** Press the **Ctrl+End** keys to move the insertion point to the end of the document, and then press the **Enter** key.

▶ **4.** Type **Return to main page.**

▶ **5.** Select the text **Return to main page.**

▶ **6.** On the ribbon, click the **INSERT** tab.

▶ **7.** In the Links group, click the **Hyperlink** button, and then click **Existing File or Web Page**, if necessary.

▶ **8.** Navigate to the location where you stored the Rain_Garden_Webpage file, if necessary, and then click **Rain_Garden_Webpage** in the file list.

▶ **9.** Click the **OK** button. Word formats the selected text as a hyperlink.

▶ **10.** Save the Plant_List_Webpage file, and then close it. You return to the Rain_Garden_Webpage file.

▶ **11.** Save and close the **Rain_Garden_Webpage** file, but do not exit Word.

Now, after a user reviews the list of plants, he or she can click the hyperlink to return to the main webpage.

Keeping Track of Documents Containing Hyperlinks

When your documents or webpages include hyperlinks to other documents or web-pages, you must keep track of where you store the target files. If you move a target file to a different location, hyperlinks to it will not function properly. In this case, you created a hyperlink in the Rain_Garden_Webpage file that links to the Plant_List_Webpage file, and vice versa. To ensure that these hyperlinks continue to function, you must keep both webpages in the folder they were in when you created the link. If you have to move a target webpage, you must edit the hyperlink to select the target webpage in its new location.

Now, Anya suggests you view both webpages in a browser and test the hyperlinks.

Viewing the Webpage in a Browser

You're now ready to view the finished webpages in Internet Explorer, a web browser. In the browser, you can test the hyperlinks and verify that the formatting looks the way you intended. In a browser, you don't have to press the Ctrl key to use a hyperlink. Instead, you simply click the link.

To view the webpages in a web browser:

1. Start Internet Explorer.

2. On the Internet Explorer title bar, click the **Maximize** button ☐, if necessary, so that the program window fills the entire screen.

3. On the menu bar, click **File**, and then click **Open**. The Open dialog box opens.

 Trouble? If you do not see a menu bar below the title bar in the browser window, right-click the title bar to open the shortcut menu, and then click Menu bar to place a checkmark next to this option.

4. Click the **Browse** button, navigate to the location where you saved the Rain_Garden_Webpage file, click the **Rain_Garden_Webpage** file, and then click the **Open** button. You return to the Open dialog box.

5. Click the **OK** button. The Open dialog box closes, and Anya's webpage is displayed in the browser window. The title "Rain Gardens in Carrel Springs" is displayed in the tab above the Internet Explorer menu bar. See Figure 7-39.

Figure 7-39 **Webpage displayed in a browser window**

Image used with permission of Microsoft Corporation

6. Scroll down and review the webpage. Anya points out that the font size is too small to read easily in the browser window. You can fix this by zooming in.

7. In the menu bar, click **View**, point to **Zoom**, and then click **150%**. The browser window zooms in, making the text easier to read.

8. Scroll back up and click the **inexpensive** hyperlink. The budget is displayed in the browser window. Note that the font in the budget looks different in the browser than it did in Word. Fonts often appear less sharply delineated in a browser than they do in the Word window.

9. In the last paragraph of the document, click the **list** hyperlink. The browser opens the Plant_List_Webpage file.

10. At the bottom of the page, click the **Return to main page.** hyperlink to display the Rain_Garden_Webpage file in your browser.

11. Close Internet Explorer.

PROSKILLS

Teamwork: Emailing Word Documents

Creating and publishing webpages is a powerful way to share documents among colleagues. But sometimes emailing a document as an attachment is the simplest way to share a file. To get started emailing a document, first make sure you have set up Microsoft Outlook as your email program. Then, in Word, open the document you want to email. On the ribbon, click the FILE tab, and then click Share in the navigation bar. On the Share screen, click Email, and then select the email option you want. When you email documents, keep in mind the following:

- Many email services have difficulty handling attachments larger than 4 MB. Consider storing large files in a compressed (or zipped) folder to reduce their size before emailing them.
- Other word-processing programs and early versions of Word might not be able to open files created in Word 2013. To avoid problems with conflicting versions, you have two options. You can save the Word document as a rich text file (using the Rich Text File document type in the Save As dialog box) before emailing it; all versions of Word can open rich text files. Another option is to save the document as a PDF.
- If you plan to email a document that contains links to other files, remember to email all the linked files.
- Attachments, including Word documents, are sometimes used maliciously to spread computer viruses. Remember to include an explanatory note with any email attachment so that the recipient can be certain the attachment is legitimate. Also, it's important to have a reliable virus checker program installed if you plan to receive and open email attachments.

The new webpages are just one way to share information about rain gardens. Anya also wants to write a blog post discussing the potential rain garden sites the foundation has identified. She asks you to help her create a blog post in Word.

Creating and Publishing a Blog Post

Creating a blog post in Word is similar to creating a new Word document except that instead of clicking Blank document in Backstage view, you click Blog post. Note that before you can publish your blog post using Word, you need to register a blog account with an Internet blog provider that is compatible with Microsoft Word 2013.

Anya asks you to help her create a blog post about the new webpages.

To create and publish a blog post:

1. On the ribbon, click the **FILE** tab, and then click **New** in the navigation bar to display the icons for the various document templates.

2. Scroll down if necessary, and then click **Blog post**.

3. In the Blog post window, click the **Create** button. A blank blog post opens. Assuming you have not previously registered for a blog account, you also see the Register a Blog Account dialog box.

To register a blog account, you could click the Register Now button to open the New Blog Account dialog box. From there, you could follow the prompts to register your blog account. Anya will register her blog account later, so you can skip the registration step for now.

▶ **4.** Click the **Register Later** button to close the dialog box.

▶ **5.** At the top of the blog post, click the **[Enter Post Title Here]** placeholder, and then type **Rain Gardens in Carrel Springs**.

▶ **6.** Click in the blank paragraph below the blog title, and then type **The Carrel Springs Watershed Foundation has identified 3,000 potential residential sites for rain gardens within the Carrel Springs city limits.** See Figure 7-40.

Figure 7-40 **Blog post**

you can use the tools on this tab to add graphics, hyperlinks, and other elements

Rain·Gardens·in·Carrel·Springs¶

The·Carrel·Springs·Watershed·Foundation·has·identified·3,000·potential·residential·sites·for·rain·gardens·within·the·Carrel·Springs·city·limits.¶

click to publish the blog post if you already have a blog account, or to set up a blog account

At this point, you could use the tools on the INSERT tab to add hyperlinks, graphics, and other items to your blog post. Anya plans to add more text and some graphics to her blog post later. For now, you can save the post, and then explore options for publishing it.

▶ **7.** Save the blog post as **Rain Garden Blog Post** in the location specified by your instructor. Note that a blog post is a regular Word document file, with a .docx extension.

▶ **8.** On the BLOG POST tab, in the Blog group, click the **Publish** button.

Assuming you have not previously registered for a blog account, you see the Register a Blog Account dialog box again. At this point, you could click the Register an Account button and then follow the on-screen instructions to register a blog account and publish your blog. Because Anya plans to do that later, you can close the blog post for now.

Trouble? If you see a menu below the Publish button, you clicked the Publish button arrow instead of the Publish button. Press the Esc key, and then click the Publish button.

TIP

To add, remove, or change blog accounts, click the Manage Accounts button in the Blog group on the BLOG POST tab.

▶ **9.** Click the **Cancel** button to close the Register a Blog Account dialog box, and then click the **OK** button in the Microsoft Word dialog box.

▶ **10.** Close the blog post.

Anya plans to write weekly blog posts describing the foundation's progress with the rain garden projects. Combined with the new webpages, they will help generate interest in the foundation's work.

Session 7.2 Quick Check

REVIEW

1. Explain how to break a link between a Word file and another file.
2. What is the first step in creating a hyperlink to a location in the same document?
3. Are page backgrounds displayed on a printed page?
4. What is the difference between the way text is displayed in Web Layout view and the way it is displayed in Print Layout view?
5. What file type should you use if you want to share a webpage over the Internet?
6. Explain how to edit a hyperlink.
7. What is the file extension for a blog post file?

ASSESS

SAM Projects

Put your skills into practice with SAM Projects! SAM Projects for this tutorial can be found online. If you have a SAM account, go to www.cengage.com/sam2013 to download the most recent Project Instructions and Start Files.

PRACTICE

Review Assignments

Data Files needed for the Review Assignments: Foundation Oliver.docx, Foundation.docx, Fundraising Chart.xlsx, Membership.docx, Projections.xlsx

Anya is working on a new document about the Carrel Springs Watershed Foundation. She has written a draft of the document and has emailed it to Oliver. While he reviews it, Anya asks you to turn on Track Changes and continue working on the document. Then, she can combine her edited version of the document with Oliver's, accepting or rejecting changes as necessary. She also needs you to insert some data from an Excel worksheet as an embedded object and insert an Excel chart as a linked object. She then wants you to create a version of the document with hyperlinks, format the document for viewing as a webpage, save it as a webpage, and view it in a browser. Complete the following steps:

1. Open the document **Foundation** from the Word7 ► Review folder included with your Data Files. Save the file as **Foundation Anya** in the location specified by your instructor.
2. Change the username to **Anya Pathak** and the user initials to **AP**, and then turn on Track Changes.
3. In the second paragraph, move the sentence that begins "Over the years…" to the end of the paragraph, and then add an **s** to the last word in the sentence.
4. In the third paragraph, in the first sentence, change "Harrison Paulson" to your first and last names, and then change "south" to **west** so the sentence reads "…west of Carrel Springs."
5. In the fourth paragraph, in the first line, attach a comment to the phrase "Since that day" that reads **Consider inserting exact date?**
6. Save your changes to the Foundation Anya document.
7. Combine the Foundation Anya document with Oliver's edited version, which is named **Foundation Oliver**, located in the Word7 ► Review folder included with your Data Files. Use the Foundation Anya document as the original document.
8. Save the combined document as **Foundation Combined** in the location specified by your instructor.
9. Turn off Track Changes, and then reject Oliver's deletion of "five" and his insertion of "seven." Accept all the other changes in the document. Delete all comments.
10. Change the username and initials back to their original settings, and then save the Foundation Combined document. Close the Foundation Anya document, saving changes if you didn't save them earlier.
11. In the Foundation Combined document, replace the placeholder "[Insert Excel worksheet]" with the fundraising projections in the **Projections.xlsx file**, which is located in the Word7 ► Review folder included with your Data Files. Include everything from cell A1 through cell B6. Insert the worksheet as an embedded object, and then close the Projections.xlsx file.
12. Center the embedded object, and then change the "Spring native plant sale" value in the embedded worksheet object from $70,000 to **$80,000**. Don't be concerned if you see pound symbols (#) in some of the cells.
13. Open the workbook **Fundraising Chart.xlsx** in the Word7 ► Review folder included with your Data Files, and then save it as **CSWF Fundraising Chart.xlsx** in the location specified by your instructor. Copy the chart to the Office Clipboard.

14. Return to the Foundation Combined document, and then replace the placeholder "[Insert Excel chart]" with a linked copy of the chart using the destination theme. Save the Foundation Combined document, and then close it.

15. Return to the CSWF Fundraising Chart workbook in Excel. Edit the data in the workbook by changing the percentage for state and federal grants to **35%**, and the percentage for private donations to **45%**. Save the workbook, and then close Excel.

16. Open the **Foundation Combined** document and review the chart. If it doesn't contain the new percentages, click the chart, and use the Refresh Data button to update the chart.

17. Save the Foundation Combined document, and then save the document with the new name **Foundation No Links** in the location specified by your instructor.

18. Break the link to the Excel workbook, and then save the document.

19. Format the Excel worksheet object as a bookmark named **Projections**. In the third line of the second paragraph, format the word "funds" as a hyperlink that targets the "projections" bookmark. Test the hyperlink to make sure it works. Save the document.

20. Open the document **Membership** from the Word7 ▶ Review folder included with your Data Files, and then save the file as **Membership Levels** in the location specified by your instructor. Close the Membership Levels document and return to the Foundation No Links document.

21. Format the last word in the document, "here," as a hyperlink that targets the Membership Levels document. Test the hyperlink to make sure it works, and then close the Membership Levels document. Save the Foundation No Links document.

22. Save the Foundation No Links document as a webpage in the location specified by your instructor using the Single File Web Page file type. Use **Foundation_Webpage** for the filename and **CSWF Main Page** as the page title.

23. Add a two-color gradient page color using Turquoise, Accent 1, Lighter 60% as Color 1 and White, Background 1 as Color 2—with the shading style set to Diagonal up.

24. Change the background color for the worksheet object to white, and center the chart.

25. Insert a horizontal line before the "Fundraising for the Future" heading. Keep the default color, but change the width to 75%. Insert an identical horizontal line before the "Become a Member" heading.

26. At the beginning of the page, change the font size for the "Carrel Springs Watershed Foundation" title to 36 points. Save the webpage.

27. Open the document **Membership Levels**, and then save it as a webpage using the Single File Web Page type. Use **Membership_Levels_Webpage** for the filename and **CSWF Membership Page** as the page title.

28. Format the new webpage to match the Foundation_Webpage file by adding the same white and turquoise gradient page color with the Diagonal up shading style, and by changing the font size for the text "Join the Carrel Springs Watershed Foundation" to 36 points.

29. At the end of the Membership_Levels_Webpage document, insert a new paragraph that is not part of the bulleted list, and then insert the text **Click to return to main page**.

30. Format the new text as a hyperlink that targets the Foundation_Webpage file, save the Membership_Levels_Webpage file, and then close it.

31. In the Foundation_Webpage file, edit the "here" hyperlink at the end of the page to target the Membership_Levels_Webpage. Save the Foundation_Webpage document, close the document, and then close it.

32. Start Internet Explorer, and then open the **Foundation_Webpage** file in the browser window. Review the webpage in the browser, note the differences in the gradient style and fonts, test the hyperlinks, and then, if necessary, open the webpages in Word again, correct any problems with the hyperlinks, and then test them again in Internet Explorer.

33. When you are certain all the links work, close the browser, and then close any open Word documents.

34. Create a new blog post without attempting to register a blog account. Save the blog post as **Foundation Blog Post** in the location specified by your instructor. Insert **Fundraising for the Future** as the post title, and then type the following as the text of the blog post: **The Carrel Springs Watershed Foundation finances water improvement programs throughout the Carrel Springs area**.

35. Save and close the Foundation Blog Post file.

Case Problem 1

Data Files needed for this Case Problem: Matthews.docx, Vaccinations.xlsx

Big Bay Veterinary Clinic You recently started working as a veterinary assistant at Big Bay Veterinary Clinic in Coleton, Alaska. A client just called the clinic and asked you to send a summary of her dog's current vaccinations. The vaccination information is stored in an Excel workbook. You need to respond with a letter that contains the vaccination information embedded as an Excel worksheet object. After you embed the worksheet object, you need to make some edits to the document using Track Changes. Finally, the clinic manager is considering using Word to create posts for the clinic's new blog, so she asks you to create a sample blog post. Complete the following steps:

1. Open the document **Matthews** from the Word7 ► Case1 folder included with your Data Files. Save the file as **Matthews Letter** in the location specified by your instructor.

2. In the signature line, replace "Student Name" with your name.

3. Delete the placeholder "[Insert Excel worksheet]."

4. Start Excel, open the workbook **Vaccinations** from the Word7 ► Case1 folder included with your Data Files, and then save it as **Vaccinations Summary** in the location specified by your instructor.

5. Select the two-column list of vaccination types and dates, from cell A7 through cell B11, and then copy the selection to the Clipboard.

6. Insert the worksheet data into the Word document in the blank paragraph that previously contained the placeholder text. Insert the data as a linked object that uses the destination styles.

7. Save the Word document, and then return to the Vaccinations Summary workbook and close Excel.

8. Starting from within the Word window, edit the linked worksheet object to change the date for the Distemper vaccination to **7/20/2016**. (*Hint*: Remember that the steps for editing a linked worksheet object are different from the steps for editing a linked chart.) Save the workbook, close Excel, and then update the link in Word.

9. Save the Matthews Letter document, and then save it again as **Matthews Letter No Links** in the location specified by your instructor.

10. Break the link in the Matthews Letter No Links document.

11. If necessary, change the username to your first and last names, change the initials to your initials, and then turn on Track Changes.

12. At the beginning of the letter, delete the date, and then type the current date using the format 3/1/16.

13. In the inside address, change "Road" to **Lane**.

14. At the end of the paragraph that reads "Please call if you have any questions." add the sentence **In the future, I can send you summaries by email if you prefer**.

15. Open the Reviewing pane and note the total number of revisions, the number of insertions, and the number of deletions in the document. Attach a comment to the word "Clinic" in the first paragraph that reads **This document contains x insertions and x deletions. It contains a total of x revisions**. Replace the three instances of *x* with the correct numbers. (*Hint*: The total number of revisions will change when you insert the comment. The number that you type in the comment should reflect this updated total.)

16. Close the Reviewing pane, save your changes to the Matthews Letter No Links document, and then save it with the new name **Matthews Letter Changes Accepted** in the location specified by your instructor.

17. Turn off Track Changes, delete the comment, and then reject the replacement of "Lane" for "Road." Accept all the other changes in the document.

18. Return the username and initials to their original settings.

19. Save the Matthews Letter Changes Accepted document, and then close it.

20. Create a new blog post without attempting to register a blog account. Save the blog post as **Clinic Blog Post** in the location specified by your instructor. Insert **News from Big Bay Veterinary Clinic** as the post title, and then type the following as the text of the blog post: **Lyme disease is on the rise in this area, so make sure your pets are fully protected from ticks**.

21. Save and close the blog post.

Case Problem 2

Data Files needed for this Case Problem: House Chloe.docx, House Eli.docx, Pictures.docx

Kensington Financial, Department of Human Resources Chloe Zimmer is an assistant in the Human Resources Department at Kensington Financial, an investment firm with offices in Chicago, New York, and London. When a Kensington employee is transferred to a new city, the Human Resources Department helps with the transition—in some cases, by helping the employee sell his or her home. Right now, Chloe is working at the Chicago office with Eli Ravenna, who has been transferred to London. He is hoping to sell his house himself so he doesn't have to pay a real estate agent fee. It's Chloe's job to help publicize Eli's house by creating a flyer to post around the office, and a webpage for a neighborhood newsletter. She's already edited the house description using Track Changes. Now, she asks for your help in combining her copy of the edited file with Eli's. Then, you'll save and format the documents as webpages so Chloe can post them on the company's network. Complete the following steps:

1. Open the document **House Eli** from the Word7 ▶ Case2 folder included with your Data Files, review its contents, and then close it.

2. Open the document **House Chloe** from the Word7 ▶ Case2 folder included with your Data Files, and then review its contents.

3. Combine the House Chloe and House Eli documents, using the House Chloe file as the original document. If you see a dialog box alerting you to a formatting conflict, use the formatting in the House Chloe file. Save the resulting new document as **House Combined** in the location specified by your instructor. Close the House Chloe document.

4. In the House Combined document, review the tracked changes. Reject Eli's deletion of "Square." Accept the rest of the changes in the document, and then delete the comment.

5. Change the username and initials to yours, and then turn on Track Changes, if necessary.

6. Change the street address in the second paragraph to **2245**, and then add a new sentence at the end of the document that reads **Click here to see pictures of this charming residence**.

7. Save the House Combined document, and then save it again as **House For Sale** in the location specified by your instructor.

8. Accept all changes in the House For Sale document, turn off Track Changes, and then change the username and initials back to their original settings.

9. Open the document **Pictures** from the Word7 ▶ Case2 folder included with your Data Files, and then save it as **House Pictures** in the location specified by your instructor.

⚙ **Troubleshoot** 10. Because the House for Sale and House Pictures documents will be linked when the documents are posted online, the theme and styles of both documents should match. Make any necessary changes to the theme and the style set in the House Pictures document to match the settings in the House For Sale document.

⚙ **Troubleshoot** 11. The House Pictures document contains an erroneous hyperlink that jumps to an unrelated external website. Remove that hyperlink from the document. Check the two remaining hyperlinks to make sure they jump to the appropriate targets—either a spot in the current document, or the House for Sale document. Make any necessary edits to the hyperlink to correct any errors.

12. In the House for Sale document, format the last sentence as a hyperlink that jumps to the House Pictures document. Save both documents.

13. Save the House for Sale document as a Single File Web Page file using **House_for_Sale_Webpage** as the filename and **2245 Cinnamon Trail** as the title. Save the webpage in the location specified by your instructor.

14. Save the House Pictures document as a Single File Web Page file using **House_Pictures_Webpage** as the filename and **Pictures** as the title. Save the webpage in the location specified by your instructor.

15. Edit the hyperlinks so they target the correct files, and then save and close both files.

16. Close Word, open the **House_For_Sale_Webpage** file in a browser, and then test the hyperlinks. If necessary, open the webpages in Word and make corrections to ensure that all the hyperlinks work correctly. Then save your changes and test the hyperlinks in a browser again. When you're finished, close your browser.

Case Problem 3

CREATE

There are no Data Files needed for this Case Problem.

Fabricante Tech You have just started an internship at Fabricante Tech, a company that designs and hosts webpages for businesses of all sizes. Before you begin learning how to use a full-blown web design program, your supervisor asks you to demonstrate your understanding of hyperlinks by creating a set of linked pages using Microsoft Word. The pages should focus on a topic of interest to you, and should include multiple graphics and links to live webpages accessible via the Internet. Your supervisor asks you to use all your formatting skills to create an attractive set of pages. Complete the following steps:

1. Select a topic that interests you, such as your favorite hobby, your school, a sports team, a vacation destination, or a company you'd like to work for some day. Because you are creating sample webpages for your work supervisor, choose a topic that is appropriate for a professional setting.

2. Open a new, blank Word document and save it as a Web Page, Filtered file using **Main Page** as the filename and a title that describes your topic. Save the webpage in the location specified by your instructor.

3. Create two more new, blank webpages, using the Web Page, Filtered file type. Name these files **Linked Page 1** and **Linked Page 2**, with appropriate titles, and save them in the location specified by your instructor.

4. In the Main Page file, add text and at least three pictures that introduce the reader to your topic. Use your own pictures or download some from Office.com. Include at least three headings.

5. In the Linked Page 1 file, add text that provides more detail about one aspect of your topic. The text should mention one external webpage available via the Internet. Include at least one picture and at least one heading at the beginning of the page. Do the same in the Linked Page 2 file.

6. In the Linked Page 1 file, format the text that refers to an external webpage as a hyperlink that jumps to that page. Do the same in the Linked Page 2 file. (*Hint*: Use Internet Explorer to display the external webpage, right-click the URL in the box at the top of the browser window, and then click Copy. In the Insert Hyperlink dialog box, use the appropriate keyboard shortcut to paste the URL into the Address box.)

7. In the Main Page file, add hyperlinks that jump to the Linked Page 1 file and to the Linked Page 2 file.

8. In the Linked Page 1 and Linked Page 2 files, add hyperlinks that jump back to the Main Page file.

9. Format the three pages identically, using a theme, heading styles, and a style set of your choice. Use horizontal lines to separate the different sections on each page, and add a two-color gradient page background to all three files.

10. Close Word, open the **Main Page** file in a browser, and then test the hyperlinks. If necessary, open the webpage files in Word and make corrections to ensure that all the hyperlinks work correctly. Then save your changes and test the hyperlinks in a browser again. When you're finished, close your browser and close any open Word documents.

Case Problem 4

CHALLENGE

Data Files needed for this Case Problem: Plantar Kelly.docx, Plantar Raha.docx, Plantar.docx

Idaho Valley Physical Therapy Clinic Ethan Henderson is a physical therapist at Idaho Valley Physical Therapy, in Taylorville, Idaho. He is creating a series of fact sheets that he can email to clients. The fact sheets will summarize treatments for many common ailments diagnosed by Ethan and his colleagues at the clinic. Each fact sheet will also include a link to an Internet video that clients can view when they need a reminder about how to do their prescribed exercises. Ethan has already emailed a draft of his first fact sheet to his two colleagues, Kelly and Raha, and he now needs to combine their copies with his to create a final draft. However, because Kelly forgot to turn on Track Changes before she edited the document, he'll need to compare her draft with his so that he can see her changes marked as tracked changes.

After he finishes accepting and rejecting changes, Ethan wants you to show him how to add a video to the document. The clinic is preparing a series of videos that he will eventually incorporate into his fact sheets before distributing them; but for now, he asks you to show him how to insert any video from the Internet. Finally, after the fact sheet is finished, Ethan would like you to help him create a chart that illustrates the average distance each client travels to the clinic. Complete the following steps:

1. Open the document **Plantar** from the Word7 ▶ Case4 folder included with your Data Files, save it as **Plantar Ethan** in the location specified by your instructor, review the document to familiarize yourself with its contents, and then close it.

2. Open the document **Plantar Kelly** from the Word7 ▶ Case4 folder, review its contents, and then close it.

⊕ **Explore** 3. Compare the Plantar Ethan document with the Plantar Kelly document, using Plantar Ethan as the original document, and show the changes in a new document.

4. Review the new document to verify that Kelly's changes to Ethan's draft are now displayed as tracked changes, and then save the document as **Plantar Kelly Tracked Changes** in the location specified by your instructor.

5. Combine the Plantar Kelly Tracked Changes document with the Plantar Raha document, using the Plantar Kelly Tracked Changes file as the original document.

6. Save the new document as **Plantar Fasciitis Fact Sheet** in the location specified by your instructor.

7. Accept all changes in the document, and then turn off Track Changes, if necessary.

⊕ **Explore** 8. Use Word Help to learn how to insert an Internet video in a document. In the blank paragraph at the end of the document, insert a video of someone demonstrating Achilles tendon stretches. Take care to choose a video that is appropriate for a professional setting. After you insert the video in the document, click the Play button on the video image to test it. Press the Esc button to close the video window when you are finished watching it.

⊕ **Explore** 9. In the Word document, size the video image just as you would an ordinary picture so that it fits on the first page.

10. Save the Plantar Fasciitis Fact Sheet document and close it.

11. Open a new, blank document, and then save it as **Client Travel Time Chart** in the location specified by your instructor.

⊕ **Explore** 12. Use Word Help to learn how to create a chart using Word's Chart tool. Create a bar chart using the 3-D Stacked Bar type. Include the data shown in Figure 7-41. For the chart title, use **Miles Driven by Clients for Weekly, Monthly, and Annual Appointments**.

| Figure 7-41 | Data for bar chart |

▮▮ 🖫 ↶ ⤳ 🗔		Chart in Microsoft Word								✕
◢	A	B	C	D	E	F	G	H	I	▲
1		Weekly	Monthly	Annually						
2	0-10 miles	14	36	66						
3	11-25 miles	16	40	70						
4	26-50 miles	27	56	69						
5	51-99 miles	38	75	117						
6										
7										▼

⊕ **Explore** 13. Format the chart with the Style 8 chart style.

14. Change the document's theme to Celestial.

15. Save and close all documents.

Teamwork

Collaborating with Others to Create Documents

Collaboration means working together to achieve a specific goal through teamwork.

Organizations establish collaborative teams for completing a wide variety of tasks, with long- or short-term goals. Sometimes team members collaborate on projects by working side by side. However, it's increasingly common for the members of a team to collaborate from different geographical locations, using telecommunications technologies and social networks to complete tasks.

When forming a team, it is important to understand the skills each team member has, and how those skills can best be used as the team collaborates to achieve its goals. An effective team is made up of people with abilities and talents that are complementary and well suited to the tasks at hand. It's also essential that each team member understand his or her responsibilities. On a truly integrated team, team members support each other and agree to share new responsibilities when they arise, rather than waiting around for someone else to pick up the slack.

The Structure of a Team

When structuring a team, it is important to identify team leaders, work coordinators, idea people, and critics. Each member must recognize the significance of his or her individual contributions to the team's overall success in meeting its goals. Some team members will serve specific roles on the team. For example, task specialists spend a lot of time and effort ensuring that the team achieves its goals by presenting ideas, sharing opinions, collecting information, sorting details, and motivating the team to stay on track. When stresses occur due to time constraints or heavy workloads, positive team morale and a sense of shared focus and camaraderie become essential. Some team members hold the role of managing social satisfaction by strengthening the team's social bonds through encouragement, empathy, conflict resolution, compromise, and tension reduction—the latter can be accomplished through humor or organizing social activities outside of the work environment. Often, individual team members will serve more than one role on the team. For example, the task specialist might also be the team leader, and the idea person might also fill the social satisfaction role.

In this exercise, you will work with a team to create documents. As you structure your team to complete these tasks, consider the roles team members must fill. Before beginning, you should discuss the roles each member is comfortable assuming, and determine how complementary your collective abilities are.

To ensure your team works effectively to complete tasks and achieve its goals:

- Recognize that everyone brings something of value to the team.
- Respect and support each other as you work toward the common goal.
- Try to see things from the other person's perspective when conflicts or criticisms arise.
- Encourage or support team members who might need assistance.
- Address negative or unproductive attitudes immediately so they don't damage team energy and morale.
- Seek outside help if the team gets stuck and can't move forward.
- Provide periodic positive encouragement or rewards for contributions.

Using Technology in Teamwork

Team members often work together from separate locations. Also, most of the time, teams need to produce work on accelerated schedules, and therefore need to work efficiently. In these instances, teams depend on technology to accomplish work tasks. Corporate intranets and networks, email and voice mail, texting

and instant messaging, teleconferencing and software collaboration tools, social networks, and cell phones can all support teamwork. Before beginning a team project, identify the technology tools the team will use to communicate and document work activities. Then, determine how the team will organize, combine, and make available the documents and files it produces.

PROSKILLS

Create a Report Template, a Directory, and a Webpage

At this point, you should feel confident that you have the word-processing skills required to create, revise, and distribute useful documents in your professional and personal life. But there's no need to wait to use these new skills. You can create some practical documents right now, starting with a template for a report that you need to create routinely. In the following exercise, work with your team members to create documents using the Word skills and features presented in Tutorials 5 through 7.

Note: Please be sure *not* to include any personal information of a sensitive nature in the documents you create to be submitted to your instructor for this exercise. Later on, you can update the documents with such information for your own personal use.

1. Meet with your team to plan a new document template to use for school reports or another type of report that you might have to create on a regular basis. Work with your group to select an appropriate template installed with Word, delete or edit document controls as necessary, insert placeholder text as necessary, and customize the theme. Select an appropriate style set, and create at least one new style that will be useful in your report. As a group, take the time to plan your template to ensure that it will be useful for a series of similar documents.

2. Use your template as the basis for a new report. Insert a file containing the text of a report you or a team member wrote for one of your classes, or insert appropriate text of your choosing, and then format the text using the template styles. Remember to include a table of contents in the report. At the end of the report, include a hyperlink that jumps to the beginning of the report.

3. If you or a team member are familiar with Excel, open a new workbook, enter some data that supports one of the points in the team's report, and then embed the worksheet data in the report. If you don't know how to enter data in Excel, you can embed the data from the Budget file in the Word7 ▸ Tutorial folder included with your Data Files, and then edit the data as necessary. Note that you can widen a column in Excel by dragging the right border of the column's header (the letter at the top of the column).

4. Email a copy of your report to a team member. Have him or her edit the document with Track Changes turned on, and then send the report back to you.

5. Combine your edited copy of the document with the copy edited by your team member. Accept or reject changes as necessary. Save the new, combined document with a new name.

6. Meet with your team and choose a type of information, such as email addresses or birthdays, that the group would like to organize in a single document. Create a Word table, and then enter fictitious information into the table. You can replace this with real information later for your personal use, after you've handed in your assignments. Sort the information based on one of the columns.

7. Create a main document for a directory that includes a dot leader. Use the group's Word table from Step 6 as the data source. Insert the necessary merge codes into the main document and complete the merge.

8. Format the merged document with a two-color gradient page color and add a title. Format the title appropriately. Save the document as a webpage that consists of only one file.

GLOSSARY/INDEX

TASK REFERENCE

TASK	PAGE #	RECOMMENDED METHOD
All Markup view, switch to	WD 357	Click REVIEW tab, click the Display for Review arrow in the Tracking group, click All Markup
Background fill effect, add	WD 397	Click DESIGN tab, click the Page Color button in the Page Background group, click Fill Effects, click the Gradient tab, click One color or Two colors, select colors and shading style, click OK
Bibliography, insert	WD 109	Create citations in the document, click the desired location for the bibliography, click the Bibliography button in the Citations & Bibliography group on REFERENCES tab, click a bibliography style
Blog post, create	WD 405	Click FILE tab, click New, click Blog post, click the Create button
Bookmark, create	WD 389	Select text, click INSERT tab, click the Bookmark button in the Links group, type bookmark name, click Add
Border, insert around page	WD 226	Click DESIGN tab, click the Page Borders button in the Page Background group, click the Page Border tab, click Box
Border, insert around paragraph	WD 45	Click in a paragraph, click ⊞ ▾ in the Paragraph group on the HOME tab, click a border style
Bullets, add to paragraph	WD 71	Select paragraphs, click ▤ in the Paragraph group on the HOME tab
Character spacing, adjust	WD 258	Select text, click the Dialog Box Launcher in the Font group on the HOME tab, click the Advanced tab, click the Spacing arrow, select a spacing option, type a point measurement in the By box, click the OK button
Citations, create and edit	WD 103	See Reference box: Creating Citations
Clip art, insert	WD 213	Click INSERT tab, click the Online Pictures button in the Illustrations group, type keywords in the Office.com Clip Art search box, press Enter, click an image, click the Insert button
Clipboard task pane, open	WD 76	In Clipboard group on HOME tab, click the Dialog Box Launcher
Column, delete from table	WD 136	Select the column to delete, click the Delete button on the Mini toolbar, click Delete Columns
Column, insert in table	WD 135	Point to the border between two columns, click ⊕
Columns, format section in	WD 181	Click PAGE LAYOUT tab, click Columns button in the Page Setup group, select options, click OK
Comments, display and insert	WD 67	See Reference box: Working with Comments
Compressed folder, extract all files and folders from	FM 27	Click the compressed folder, click the Compressed Folder Tools Extract tab, click the Extract all button
Compressed folder, open	FM 27	Double-click the compressed folder
Cover page, insert	WD 164	Click INSERT tab, click the Cover Page button in the Pages group, click cover page
Cover page, delete	WD 164	Click INSERT tab, click the Cover Page button in the Pages group, click Remove Current Cover Page
Date field, insert	WD 302	Click INSERT tab, click the Date & Time button in the Text group, click a Date format, click OK
Documents, compare or combine	WD 362	See Reference box: Comparing and Combining Documents

TASK	PAGE #	RECOMMENDED METHOD
Document, print	WD 25	Click FILE tab, click Print, click Print button
Document, save as a PDF	WD 227	Click FILE tab, click Export, click the Create PDF/XPS Document button, navigate to the location where you want to save the PDF, click the Publish button
Documents library, open	FM 10	In File Explorer, click ▷ next to Libraries, click ▷ next to Documents
Drop cap, insert	WD 200	Click in paragraph, click the INSERT tab, click the Drop Cap button in the Text group, select options, click OK
Endnotes and footnotes, create	WD 150	*See* Reference box: Inserting a Footnote or an Endnote
Envelope, create and save in current document	WD 28	Click the MAILINGS tab, click the Envelopes button in the Create group, enter return address, if necessary, enter delivery address, click Add to Document
File Explorer, open	FM 10	Click 📁 on the taskbar
File Explorer, return to a previous location	FM 9	Click ⬅
File list, sort	FM 14	Click the column heading button
File, copy	FM 24	Right-click the file, click Copy, right-click destination, click Paste
File, delete	FM 25	Right-click the file, click Delete
File, move	FM 21	Drag the file to the folder
File, open from File Explorer	FM 15	Right-click the file, point to Open with, click an application
File, rename	FM 26	Right-click the file, click Rename, type the new filename, press Enter
File, save with new name in WordPad	FM 18	Click the File tab, click Save as, enter the filename, click Save
Files and folders, compress	FM 27	Select the files to compress, click the Share tab, click the Zip button in the Send group
Files, select multiple	FM 24	Press and hold the Ctrl key and click the files
Files, view in Large Icons view	FM 13	Click the View tab, click 🖼 in the Layout group
Folder, create	FM 19	Click the New folder button in the New group on the Home tab
Footer, add	WD 160	Double-click the bottom margin, type footer text, or select a preformatted footer by clicking the Footer button in the Header & Footer group on the DESIGN tab
Go To, use to find document elements	WD 247	Click HOME tab, click the Find button arrow in the Editing group, click a document element in the Go to what box, click Next or Previous
Graphic object, resize	WD 50	Click graphic object, click the FORMAT tab, change the height and width settings in the Size group
Graphic object, wrap text around	WD 187	Click graphic object, click 🖾 next to the graphic object, click a text wrapping option
Header, add	WD 159	Double-click the top margin, type header text, or select a preformatted header by clicking the Header button in the Header & Footer group on the DESIGN tab

TASK	PAGE #	RECOMMENDED METHOD
Horizontal line, insert	WD 399	Click HOME tab, click ⬛ ▼ in the Paragraph group, click Horizontal Line
Hyperlink to a location in the same document, create	WD 389	*See* Reference box: Creating a Hyperlink to a Location in the Same Document
Hyperlink to another file or webpage, create	WD 391	*See* Reference box: Creating a Hyperlink to Another Document
Hyperlink, edit	WD 402	Right-click the hyperlink, click Edit hyperlink, select a document or webpage as the target file, click OK
Hyperlink, remove	WD 12	Right-click hyperlink, click Remove Hyperlink
Hyphenation, turn on	WD 153	Click PAGE LAYOUT tab, click the Hyphenation button in the Page Setup group, click Automatic
Line spacing, change	WD 18	Select text, click ⬛ ▼ in the Paragraph group on HOME tab, click a spacing option
Link, break	WD 386	*See* Reference box: Breaking a Link to a Source File
Mail merge data source, create	WD 307	*See* Reference box: Creating A Data Source for a Mail Merge
Mail merge data source, edit in Word	WD 326	*See* Reference box: Editing a Microsoft Office Address Lists Data Source in Word
Mail merge data source, filter	WD 330	Click MAILINGS tab, select a main document type, select or create a data source, click the Edit Recipient List button in the Start Mail Merge group, click the column header arrow for the field you want to filter by, click field entry
Mail merge data source, sort	WD 329	*See* Reference box: Sorting a Data Source by Multiple Fields
Mail merge main document, select type of	WD 304	Click MAILINGS tab, click the Start Mail Merge button in the Start Mail Merge group, click a main document type
Mail merge, finish by merging to new document	WD 319	Click MAILINGS tab, click the Finish & Merge button in the Finish group, click Edit Individual Documents, click OK
Mail merge, finish by merging to printer	WD 319	Click MAILINGS tab, click the Finish & Merge button in the Finish group, click Print Documents, click OK
Mail merge, insert merge fields in main document for	WD 313	Click REVIEW tab, click the Insert Merge Field button arrow in the Write & Insert Fields group, click a merge field
Mail merge, preview merged document for	WD 317	Click MAILINGS tab, click the Preview Results button in the Preview Results group
Margins, change	WD 23	Click PAGE LAYOUT tab, click the Margins button in the Page Setup group on HOME tab, click a margins option
My Documents folder, open	FM 10	In File Explorer, click ▷ next to Libraries, click ▷ next to Documents, click My Documents
Numbering, add to paragraphs	WD 72	Select paragraphs, click ⬛ in the Paragraph group on HOME tab
Object, embed in Word document	WD 373	Select and copy the object in the source program, return to Word without closing the source program, click destination location, click the Paste button arrow in the Clipboard group on HOME tab, click Paste Special, in the As list box select option that will paste the object as an Object, click OK

TASK	PAGE #	RECOMMENDED METHOD
Object, link to Word document	WD 380	Select and copy the object in the source program, return to Word without closing the source program, click destination location, click the Paste button arrow in the Clipboard group on HOME tab, click Link & Keep Source Formatting or click Link & Use Destination Styles
Page break, insert	WD 108	Click where you want to insert a page break, click INSERT tab, click the Page Break button in the Pages group
Page number, insert	WD 98	Click INSERT tab, click the Page Number button in the Header & Footer group, select options from menu
Page orientation, change	WD 38	Click PAGE LAYOUT tab, click the Orientation button in the Page Setup group, click an orientation
Paragraph spacing, add or remove default	WD 18	Click paragraph, click ⬛ in the Paragraph group on HOME tab, click options to add or remove space before or after paragraphs
Paragraph spacing, select specific setting	WD 48	Click paragraph, click PAGE LAYOUT tab, adjust settings in the Spacing Before and After boxes in Paragraph group
PDF, open in Word	WD 228	Click the FILE tab, click Open, navigate to the folder containing the PDF, click the PDF, click the Open button, click the OK button
Picture, crop	WD 210	Click a picture, click FORMAT tab, click the Crop button in the Size group, drag picture border to crop, deselect picture
Picture, crop to shape	WD 210	Click picture, click FORMAT tab, click Crop button arrow in Size group, point to Crop to Shape, click shape
Picture, insert	WD 49	Click INSERT tab, click Pictures button in the Illustrations group, select picture file, click Insert button
Picture style, apply	WD 51	Click a picture, click FORMAT tab, click the More button in the Picture Styles group, click a style
Quick Part, delete from Building Blocks template	WD 290	Click INSERT tab, click the Quick Parts button in the Text group, click Building Blocks Organizer, click a Quick Part in the Building blocks list, click Delete
Quick Part, insert	WD 288	*See* Reference box: Creating and Using Quick Parts
Quick Part, save to Building Block template or other template	WD 288	*See* Reference box: Creating and Using Quick Parts
Reveal Formatting pane, open	WD 272	Click ⬛ at the bottom of Styles pane, click ⬛ in Style Inspector
Ribbon, expand in File Explorer	FM 13	Click ⬛
Row, delete from table	WD 136	Select the row to delete, click the Delete button on the Mini toolbar, click Delete Rows
Row, insert in table	WD 135	Click a row, click the LAYOUT tab, click the Insert Above or Insert Below button in Rows & Columns group
Section break, insert in document	WD 153	Click where you want to insert a section break, click PAGE LAYOUT tab, click Breaks button in the Page Setup group, click a section break type
Shading, apply to paragraph	WD 45	Click in paragraph, click ⬛ in Paragraph group on HOME tab, click color
Simple Markup view, switch to	WD 361	Click REVIEW tab, click the Display for Review arrow in the Tracking group, click Simple Markup

TASK	PAGE #	RECOMMENDED METHOD
SmartArt, create	WD 156	Click INSERT tab, click the SmartArt button in the Illustrations group, in the left pane of the Choose a SmartArt Graphic dialog box click a category, in the middle pane click a SmartArt style, click OK, replace placeholder text with new text
Spelling and grammar, correct for entire document	WD 36	Click the REVIEW tab, click the Spelling & Grammar button in the Proofing group
Style Inspector, open	WD 270	Click ⁴⁄ᵦ at the bottom of the Styles pane
Style, apply	WD 85	Select text, click a style in the Styles group on HOME tab or click ▼ in the Styles group on HOME tab and click a style
Style, create a new	WD 266	*See* Reference box: Creating a New Style
Style, update	WD 262	*See* Reference box: Updating a Style
Styles pane, change way styles are displayed in	WD 269	Click Options in the bottom-right corner of the Styles pane, select style pane options, click OK
Styles pane, open	WD 261	Click HOME tab, click the Dialog Box Launcher in the Styles group
Style Set, select	WD 256	Click DESIGN tab, click the More button in the Document Formatting group, click a style set
Synonym, replace selected word or text with	WD 249	Right-click a word or selected text, point to Synonyms, click synonym
Table of Contents, add text to	WD 280	Select text, click REFERENCES tab, click the Add Text button in the Table of Contents group, click a level
Table of Contents, create and update	WD 276	*See* Reference box: Generating a Table of Contents
Table, convert to text	WD 340	Click in the table, click the TABLE TOOLS LAYOUT tab, click Convert to Text in the Data group, select a separator character, click OK
Table, insert	WD 128	Click INSERT tab, click the Table button in the Tables group, move the pointer across the grid to select columns and rows
Table, sort	WD 133	*See* Reference box: Sorting the Rows of a Table
Tab stop, set	WD 147	*See* Reference box: Setting, Moving, and Clearing Tab Stops
Tabs, clear all from document	WD 338	Click HOME tab, click the Dialog Box Launcher in the Paragraph group, click Tabs, click Clear All, click OK
Template from Office.com, create a new document from	WD 244	Click FILE tab, click New, click in the Search for online templates box, type a keyword, click a template, click the Create button
Template saved to Templates folder, create new document from	WD 286	Click FILE tab, click New, click PERSONAL, click template
Template, saving a document as	WD 282	*See* Reference box: Saving a Document as a Template
Text box, insert	WD 188	*See* Reference box: Inserting a Text Box
Text Effects, apply	WD 41	Select text, click 🅰 ▾ in the Font group on HOME tab, click a text effect
Text, convert to table	WD 341	Set up text with consistent separator characters and the same number of fields per paragraph, select text, click INSERT tab, click the Table button in the Tables group, click Convert Text to Table, click the appropriate option under "Separate text at," click OK

TASK	PAGE #	RECOMMENDED METHOD
Theme colors, customize	WD 254	Click DESIGN tab, click the Colors button in the Document Formatting group, click Customize Colors, select theme colors, type a name for the new set of colors in the Name box, click Save
Theme colors, select	WD 252	Click DESIGN tab, click the Colors button in the Document Formatting group, click a set of theme colors
Theme fonts, customize	WD 254	Click DESIGN tab, click the Fonts button in the Document Formatting group, click Customize Fonts, select a heading font and a body font, type a name for the new pair of theme fonts in the Name box, click Save
Theme fonts, select	WD 253	Click DESIGN tab, click the Fonts button in the Document Formatting group, click a set of theme fonts
Theme, create a custom	WD 254	Click DESIGN tab, click the Themes button in the Document Formatting group, click Save Current Theme, navigate to a new location if necessary, type a theme name in the File name box, click the Save button
Theme, select new	WD 89	Click DESIGN tab, click Themes button in the Document Formatting group, click a theme
Touch mode, turn on	WD 5	Click ⏷ on the Quick Access toolbar, click Touch/Mouse Mode, click Touch
Track Changes, accept and reject	WD 366	*See* Reference box: Accepting and Rejecting Changes
Track Changes, turn on or off	WD 356	Click REVIEW tab, click the Track Changes button in the Tracking group
Username and initials, change	WD 356	Click REVIEW tab, click the Dialog Box Launcher in the Tracking group, click Change User Name, type new username and initials, click the "Always use these values regardless of sign in to Office" checkbox to insert a check, click OK and then click OK again
View, change in File Explorer	FM 12	*See* Reference box: Changing the View in File Explorer
Webpage, open in Internet Explorer	WD 403	Start Internet Explorer, click File on the menu bar, click Open, select a webpage, click OK
Webpage, save document as	WD 394	*See* Reference box: Saving a Word Document as a Webpage
WordArt, convert text to	WD 204	Select text, click 🖌, click INSERT tab, click the WordArt button in the Text group, click WordArt style